Nigel
21.03.03

CHARMING SMALL HOTEL GUIDES

FRANCE

CHARMING SMALL HOTEL GUIDES

FRANCE

EDITED BY

Fiona Duncan & Leonie Glass

NEW TO THIS EDITION,
THE CHARMING SMALL HOTELS
TRAVEL SERVICE. SEE PAGE 7.

DUNCAN PETERSEN

This new expanded and redesigned 2002 edition
conceived, designed and produced by
Duncan Petersen Publishing Ltd,
31 Ceylon Road, London W14 0PY

11th edition

To the memory of Mel Petersen, 1946-2001
Art Director and founder of Duncan Petersen Publishing

Editorial Director Andrew Duncan
Editors Fiona Duncan & Leonie Glass
Contributing editors Jan Dodd, Luke Glass, Peter Henson, Jenny Rees &
Nicola Swallow
Production Editor Nicola Davies
Art Director Mel Petersen
Designer Don Macpherson

This edition published 2002 by
Duncan Petersen Publishing Ltd,
31 Ceylon Road, London W14 0PY
E-mail: do@appleonline.net
Website: http//www.charmingsmallhotels.co.uk

Sales representation and distribution in the U.K. and Ireland by
Portfolio Books Limited
Unit 5, Perivale Industrial Park
Horsenden Lane South
Greenford, UB6 7RL
Tel: 0208 997 9000 Fax: 0208 997 9097
E-mail: sales@portfoliobooks.com

A CIP catalogue record for this book is available
from the British Library

ISBN 1-903301-19-X

DTP by Duncan Petersen Publishing Ltd
Printed by G. Canale & C., Italy

Contents

SO WHAT EXACTLY DO WE LOOK FOR?
OUR SELECTION CRITERIA

• A peaceful, attractive setting. Obviously, if the entry is in an urban area, we make allowances, but even there we seek out the quiet places.

• A building that is handsome, interesting or historic; or at least with real character.

• Adequate space, but on a human scale. We don't go for places that rely too much on grandeur, or with pretensions that could be intimidating.

• Good taste and imagination in the interior decoration. We reject standardized, chain hotel fixtures, fittings and decorations.

• Bedrooms that look like real bedrooms, not hotel rooms, individually decorated.

• Furnishings and other facilities that are comfortable and well maintained. We like to see interesting antique furniture that is there to be used, not simply revered.

• Proprietors and staff who are dedicated and thoughtful, offering a personal welcome, but who aren't intrusive or overly effusive. *The guest needs to feel like an individual.*

• Interesting food. In France, it's still the norm for food to be above average, although this isn't always the case these days. There are, however, very few, if no, entries in this guide where the food is not of a high standard.

• A sympathetic atmosphere; an absence of loud people showing off their money; or the 'corporate' feel.

A FATTER GUIDE, BUT JUST AS SELECTIVE

In order to accommodate every entry with a whole-page description and colour photograph, we've had to print more pages. *But we have maintained our integrity by keeping the selection to around 330 entries.*

Over the years, the number of charming small hotels in France has increased steadily – not dramatically. We don't believe that there are presently many more than about 350 truly charming small hotels in France, and that, if we included more, we would undermine what we're trying to do: produce a guide which is all about places that are more than just a bed for the night. Every time we consider a new hotel, we ask ourselves whether it has that extra special something, regardless of category and facilities, that makes it worth seeking out.

TYPES OF ACCOMMODATION IN THIS GUIDE

Despite its title, the guide does not confine itself to places called hotels or places that behave like hotels. On the contrary, we actively look for places that offer a home-from-home (see page 10). We include small- and medium-sized hotels; plenty of traditional guesthouses (pensions) and village *auberges*, some offering just bed and breakfast, some offering food at other times of the day, too; restaurants-with-rooms, and some private houses with accommodation provided they offer something special. You will find extremely luxurious places to stay in this book, as well as very basic ones. The majority, however, fall into our second price category (see page 11), at between 90 and 140 Euros for a double room with breakfast, but there are many places which cost considerably less, and some which cost a great deal more.

NO FEAR OR FAVOUR

To us, taking a payment for appearing in a guide seems to defeat the object of producing a guide. If money has changed hands, you can't write the whole truth about a hotel, and the selection cannot be nearly so interesting. The self-evident truth seems to us to be proved at least in part by the fact that pay guides are so keen to present the illusion of independence: few admit on the cover that they take payments for an entry, only doing so in small print on the inside.

Not many people realize that on the shelves of British bookshops there are many more hotel guides that accept payments for entries than there are independent guides. This guide is one of the few that do not accept any money for an entry.

**HOW TO READ
AN ENTRY**

Name of hotel

Type of establishment

Description – never
vetted by the hotel

Places of interest within
reach of the hotel

This sets the hotel
in its geographical
context and
should not be
taken as precise
instructions as to
how to get there;
always ask the
hotel for
directions.

Rooms described as
having a bath usually
also have a shower;
rooms described as
having a shower only
have a shower.

This information is
only an indication for
wheelchair users and
the infirm. Always
check on suitability
with the hotel.

SOUTHERN FRANCE

THE SOUTH-WEST

AGNAC

CH.PECHALBET
~ COUNTRY HOTEL ~

47800 Agnac (Lot-et-Garonne)
TEL and FAX 05 53 83 04 70
E-MAIL pechalbet@caramail.com **WEBSITE** www.eymet-en-perigord.com

WHEN HENRI PEYRE and his wife, Françoise, fled from the crowded shores of the Riviera in 1995 in search of somewhere quiet in the country, their initial idea was to provide *chambres d'hôte* with breakfast only. But they found that guests were most reluctant to tear themselves away from the huge rooms and peace of this beautiful 17thC château to go out to eat in restaurants at the end of the day and last year Mme Peyre gave in to pressure and now cooks dinner. 'It's very pleasant,' says her husband. 'We all gather on the terrace to watch the sunsets, then eat by candlelight and talk and talk. It's sometimes very difficult to get our guests to bed.' Prices are kept deliberately low to encourage people to come for several days, or even weeks, at a time. There is a huge amount of space – rooms, furnished with charming antiques, are enormous and all open on to the terrace. Sheep graze in the park, when autumn comes around logs crackle in the massive stone fireplace and there is mushrooming in the woods. For guests M. Peyre has his own list of what he claims are entirely secret places that he has discovered himself to be visited nearby. Reports please.

~

NEARBY Eymet (4 km); Bergerac (25 km).
LOCATION on 40-hectare country estate; signposted S of Eymet on D933 to Miramont; ample car and garage parking
PRICE ©
FOOD breakfast
ROOMS 5 double and twin, all with bath or shower
FACILITIES 2 sitting rooms, billiard room, bar, dining room, terrace, gardens, swimming pool
CREDIT CARDS AE, SC
DISABLED no special facilities **CHILDREN** welcome
PETS accepted
CLOSED Dec
PROPRIETOR Henri Peyre

Essential booking information.

Some or all the public rooms and bedrooms in an increasing number of hotels are now non-smoking. Smokers should check the hotel's policy when booking.

Closed: when given in months e.g. Nov-Apr, this means from the beginning of the first month to the beginning of the second month. The closing days and months of restaurants are also given.

City, town or village, and region, in which the hotel is located.

Telephoning France from abroad
To call France from the U.K. dial 00, then the international dialling code 33, then dial the number, excluding the initial 0. From the U.S., dial 001 33.

Postal address and telephone, fax, e-mail and website address, if available.

The price, or rather price band, quoted includes the cost of breakfast for two people. We have not quoted prices for lunch and dinner, but we have indicated where half-board is obligatory. Other meals, such as afternoon tea, may also be available, and sometimes included in the price of a room. 'Room service' refers to food and drink, usually full meals, which can be served in the room.

Some or all the public rooms and bedrooms in an increasing number of hotels are now non-smoking. Smokers should check the hotel's policy when booking.

Children are almost always accepted, usually welcomed, in French hotels. There are often special facilities, such as cots, high chairs, baby listening and early supper. Check first if they may join parents in the dining room. We use the word 'accepted' to indicate that children are allowed in a hotel, and 'welcome' where we perceived a positive bias towards them.

We list the following credit cards:
AE   American Express
DC   Diners Club
MC   Mastercard
V   Visa

Always let the hotel know in advance if you want to bring a pet. Even where pets are accepted, certain restrictions may apply, and a small charge may be levied.

In this guide, we have used price bands rather than quoting actual prices. They refer to a standard double room (high season rates, if applicable) with breakfast for two people. Other rates – for other room categories, times of the year, weekend breaks, long stays and so on – may well be available. In some hotels, usually out-of-the-way places or restaurants-with-rooms – half-board is obligatory. Always check when booking. The price bands are as follows:

€   under 90 Euros
€€   90-140 Euros
€€€   140-185 Euros
€€€€   185-275 Euros
€€€€€   over 275 Euros

Tipping
In larger hotels, 1.50 Euros for a piece of luggage taken to your room by an employee is normal, as well as a small tip for the chambermaid. In restaurants, the words *service compris* on the bill indicate that tax and 15% service charge have been included. If pleased with the food and service, however, it is customary to leave an extra tip.

REPORTING TO THE GUIDE

Please write and tell us about your experiences of small
hotels, guesthouses and inns, whether good or bad, whether
listed in this edition or not. As well as hotels in France, we
are interested in hotels in Italy, Spain, Austria, Germany,
Switzerland, Greece and the U.S.A. We assume that reporters
have no objections to our publishing their views unpaid.

Readers whose reports prove particularly helpful may be
invited to join our Travellers' Panel. Members give us notice
of their own travel plans; we suggest hotels that they might
inspect, and help with the cost of accommodation.

The address to write to us is:

Editor, *Charming Small Hotel Guides*,
Duncan Petersen Publishing Limited,
31 Ceylon Road,
London W14 0PY.

Checklist
Please use a separate sheet of paper for each report; include
your name, address and telephone number on each report.

Your reports will be received with particular pleasure if
they are typed, and if they are organized under the following
headings:

Name of establishment
Town or village it is in, or nearest
Full address, including postcode
Telephone number
Time and duration of visit
The building and setting
The public rooms
The bedrooms and bathrooms
Physical comfort (chairs, beds, heat, light, hot water)
Standards of maintenance and housekeeping
Atmosphere, welcome and service
Food
Value for money

We assume that in writing you have no objections to your
views being published unpaid, either verbatim or in an
edited version. Names of major outside contributors are
acknowledged, at the editor's discretion, in the guide.

HOTEL LOCATION MAPS

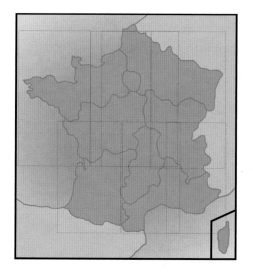

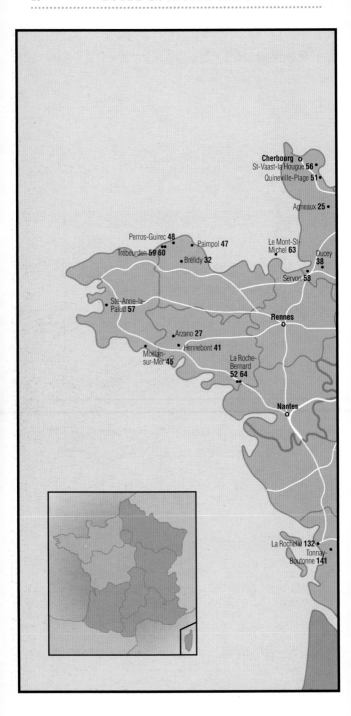

Cherbourg ○
St-Vaast-la-Hougue **56** ●
Quineville-Plage **51** ●

Agneaux **25** ●

Perros-Guirec **48** ●
Paimpol **47** ●
Trébeurden **59 60** ●●
Le Mont-St-Michel **63** ●
Ducey **38** ●
Brélidy **32** ●
Servon **58** ●

Ste-Anne-la-Palud **57** ●

Rennes ○

Arzano **27** ●
Hennebont **41** ●
Moëlan-sur-Mer **45** ●
La Roche-Bernard **52 64** ●

Nantes ○

La Rochelle **132** ●
Tonnay-Boutonne **141** ●

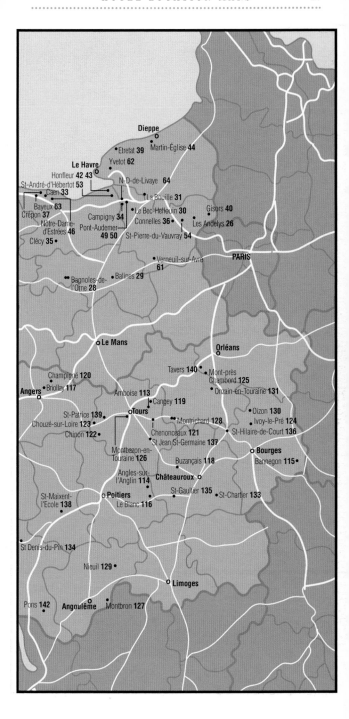

Dieppe
Etretat **39** Martin-Église **44**
Le Havre Yvetot **62**
Honfleur **42 43**
St-André-d'Hébertot **53** N-D-de-Livaye **64**
Caen **33**
Bayeux **63** La Bouille **31**
Crépon **37** Le Bec-Hellouin **30** Gisors **40**
Campigny **34** Connelles **36** Les Andelys **26**
Notre-Dame- Pont-Audemer St-Pierre-du-Vauvray **54**
d'Estrées **46** **49 50**
Clécy **35** **PARIS**
Verneuil-sur-Avre **61**
Bagnoles-de- Balines **29**
l'Orne **28**

Le Mans Orléans

Champigné **120** Tavers **140** Mont-près-
Chambord **125**
Angers Briollay **117** Amboise **113** Onzain-en-Touraine **131**
Cangey **119**
St-Patrice **139** Tours Oizon **130**
Chouzé-sur-Loire **123** Montrichard **128** Ivoy-le-Pré **124**
Chinon **122** Chenonceaux **121** St-Hilaire-de-Court **136**
St Jean St-Germaine **137**
Montbazon-en- Bourges
Touraine **126** Buzançais **118** Bannegon **115**
Angles-sur- Châteauroux
l'Anglin **114**
St-Maixent- Poitiers St-Gaultier **135** St-Chartier **133**
l'Ecole **138** Le Blanc **116**

St Denis-du-Pin **134**
Nieuil **129**
Limoges
Pons **142** Angoulême Montbron **127**

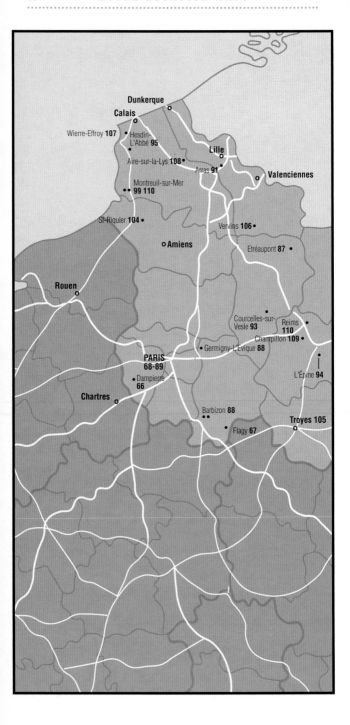

Dunkerque

Calais

Wierre-Effroy **107** • Hesdin-
L'Abbé **95**

Aire-sur-la-Lys **108** •

Lille

Arras **91** •

Valenciennes

Montreuil-sur-Mer
99 110

St-Riquier **104** •

Vervins **106** •

o **Amiens**

Etréaupont **87** •

Rouen

Courcelles-sur-
Vesle **93**

**Reims
110**

Champillon **109** •

**PARIS
68-89**

Germigny-L'Evique **88**

L'Épine **94**

Dampierre
66

Chartres o

Barbizon **88**
••

Troyes 105

Flagy **67**

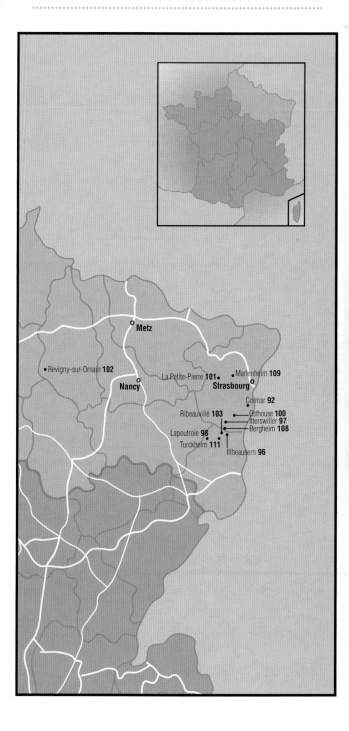

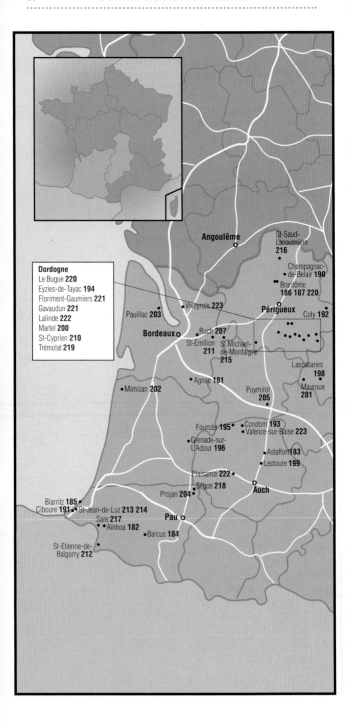

Dordogne
Le Bugue **220**
Eyzies-de-Tayac **194**
Floriment-Gaumiers **221**
Gavaudun **221**
Lalinde **222**
Martel **200**
St-Cyprien **210**
Trémolat **219**

Angoulême

St-Saud-Lacoussière **216**

Champagnac-de-Belair **190**

Brantôme **186 187 220**

Viveyrols **223**

Périgueux

Coly **192**

Pauillac **203**

Bordeaux

Ruch **207**

St-Emilion **211**

St Michael-de-Montaigne **215**

Lascabanes **198**

Mauroux **201**

Agnac **181**

Mimizan **202**

Puymirol **205**

Fourcès **195**

Condom **193**

Valence-sur-Baïse **223**

Grenade-sur-L'Adour **196**

Astaffort **183**

Lectoure **199**

Plaisance **222**

Ségos **218**

Auch

Biarritz **185**

Ciboure **191**

St-Jean-de-Luz **213 214**

Sare **217**

Projan **204**

Pau

Ainhoa **182**

Barcus **184**

St-Etienne-de-Baïgorry **212**

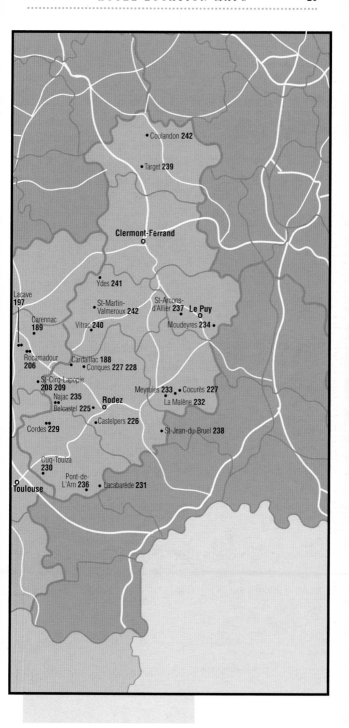

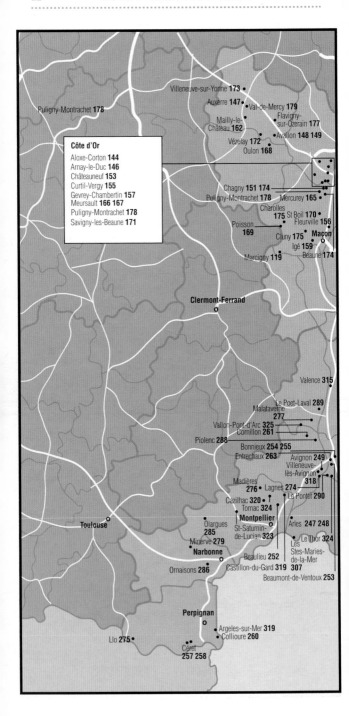

Villeneuve-sur-Yonne **173**
Auxerre **147**
Val-de-Mercy **179**
Flavigny-
sur-Ozerain **177**
Mailly-le-
Château **162**
Avallon **148 149**
Vézelay **172**
Oulon **168**

Puligny-Montrachet **178**

Côte d'Or
Aloxe-Corton **144**
Arnay-le-Duc **146**
Châteauneuf **153**
Curtil-Vergy **155**
Gevrey-Chambertin **157**
Meursault **166 167**
Puligny-Montrachet **178**
Savigny-les-Beaune **171**

Chagny **151 174**
Puligny-Montrachet **178**   Mercurey **165**
Charolles
175 St Boil **170**
Fleurville **156**
Poisson
169
Cluny **175**   **Mâcon**
Igé **159**
Beaune **174**
Marcigny **119**

Clermont-Ferrand

Valence **315**

Le Poet-Laval **289**
Malataverne
277
Vallon-Pont-d'Arc **325**
Cornillon **261**
Piolenc **288**
Bonnieux **254 255**
Entrechaux **263**
Avignon **249**
Villeneuve-
lès-Avignon
318
Madières
276 Lagnes **274**
Cazilhac **320**
Tornac **324**
Le Pontet **290**
Montpellier
Arles **247 248**
Olargues
285
St-Saturnin-
de-Lucian **323**
Le Thor **324**
Minerve **279**
Les
Stes-Maries-
de-la-Mer
307
Narbonne
Beaulieu **252**
Toulouse
Ornaisons **286**
Castillon-du-Gard **319**
Beaumont-de-Ventoux **253**

Perpignan

Argeles-sur-Mer **319**
Collioure **260**
Llo **275**
Céret
257 258

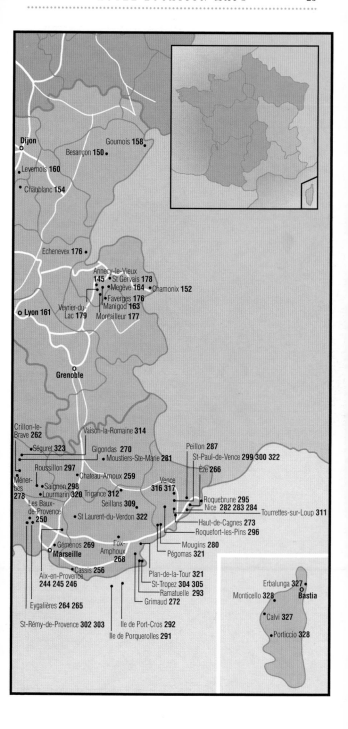

Dijon
Goumois **158**
Besançon **150**
Levernois **160**
Chaublanc **154**

Echenevex **176**

Annecy-le-Vieux **145**
St Gervais **178**
Megève **164**   Chamonix **152**
Veyrier-du- Favergés **176**
Lac **179** Manigod **163**
Montailleur **177**

Lyon **161**

Grenoble

Crillon-le-
Brave **262**   Vaison-la-Romaine **314**
Séguret **323**   Gigondas **270**   Peillon **287**
Roussillon **297**   Moustiers-Ste-Marie **281**   St-Paul-de-Vence **299 300 322**
Méner-   Château-Arnoux **259**   Èze **266**
bes   Saignon **298**   Vence
278   Lourmarin **320**   Trigance **312**   **316 317**
Les Baux-   Seillans **309**   Roquebrune **295**
de-Provence   St Laurent-du-Verdon **322**   Nice **282 283 284**   Tourrettes-sur-Loup **311**
250   Haut-de-Cagnes **273**
Roquefort-les-Pins **296**
Gémenos **269**   Fox-   Mougins **280**
Marseille   Amphoux   Pégomas **321**
Aix-en-Provence   **268**
244 245 246   Cassis **256**   Plan-de-la-Tour **321**
St-Tropez **304 305**   Erbalunga **327**
Ramatuelle **293**   Monticello **328**   Bastia
Eygalières **264 265**   Grimaud **272**
St-Rémy-de-Provence **302 303**   Calvi **327**
Ile de Port-Cros **292**
Ile de Porquerolles **291**   Porticcio **328**

THE NORTH-WEST

HOTELS IN THE NORTH-WEST

THE NORTH-WEST IS familiar territory to many British visitors. Lush Normandy, full of apple orchards and contented cows, is close enough to be convenient for a weekend break, and many people who live in the west of Britain prefer to use the Normandy ports when aiming further south. Particularly well placed for the ports – and beaches – are the traditional Auberge du Clos Normand at Martin-Eglise near Dieppe (page 44), the more sophisticated La Chaumière and Le Manoir du Butin, both at Honfleur near Le Havre (pages 42 and 43), Le Dauphin in the centre of Caen (page 33), and, within striking distance of Cherbourg at St-Vaast-la-Hougue on the Cotentin peninsula, the Hôtel de France et des Fuchsias (page 56), an old favourite of the guide. Our recommendations for this new edition cover the breadth of the region, from the Côte d'Albâtre's chalk cliffs (Le Donjon at Etretat, page 39) and the beautiful banks of the Seine (La Chaîne d'Or at Les Andelys, page 26, and Le Moulin de Connelles, page 36) to the lush landscape of Calvados country (Ferme de la Rançonnière at Crépon, page 37, and the quirky Au Repos des Chineurs at Notre-Dame-d'Estrées, page 46, both new finds) and of the region known as *Suisse Normande* around the Orne valley (Manoir du Lys at Bagnoles-de-l'Orne, page 28).

Although we don't feature a hotel in the Norman capital Rouen, Le St-Pierre, a restaurant-with-rooms is nearby at La Bouille (page 31), and two useful hotels in the centre are Hôtel de la Cathédrale (tel 02 35 71 57 95 fax 02 35 70 15 54) and Le Vieux Carré (tel 02 35 71 67 70 fax 02 35 71 19 17). Both have pretty courtyard gardens.

On the border with Brittany is the most popular tourist sight in France: Mont-St-Michel. One of our hotels, Auberge St-Pierre is on the Mont itself (page 63), but a couple of others (Le Gué du Holme at St-Quentin-sur-le-Homme, page 55, and Auberge du Terroir at Servon, page 58) provide accommodation within reach, but away from the crowds.

To the west, Brittany is bucket-and-spade country, and has much in common with Cornwall – a dramatic coastline, and a vigorous climate. On its rugged north coast, between scores of oyster beds and sandy beaches, in the old fishing port of Paimpol, we have the down-to-earth Repaire de Kerroc'h (page 47) and, in the resort of Perros-Guirec, the upmarket Manoir du Sphinx (page 48). There are two more hotels around the headland in Trébeurden (pages 59 and 60) and a new discovery inland at Brélidy (page 32). Hôtel de la Plage is a popular, if now rather pricey, family hotel at Ste-Anne-la-Palud (page 57) on the windswept west coast. The scenery is tamer and the climate milder on the south coast, and here our recommendations include a château (Château de Locguénolé at Hennebont, page 41), a mill (Les Moulins du Duc at Moëlan-sur-Mer, page 45) and one of the finest restaurants in the region (Auberge Bretonne in La Roche-Bernard, page 52).

THE NORTH-WEST

AGNEAUX

✳ CHATEAU D'AGNEAUX ✳
～ CHATEAU HOTEL ～

avenue Ste-Marie, 50180 Agneaux (Manche)
TEL 02 33 57 65 88 **FAX** 02 33 56 59 21
E-MAIL chateau.agneaux@wanadoo.fr ✳ *or use our travel service*

A S YOU TURN DOWN a rather suburban road, albeit tree-lined, on the out-skirts of St-Lô, you might ask yourself if you've really done the right thing. Don't worry: a delight awaits you. The Château d'Agneaux turns out to be small, perfectly formed (since the tail-end of the 13th century) and to occupy a fairy-tale position high on an almost sheer wooded bluff over-looking a narrow, pastoral section of the Vire valley. The previous owner knocked down the new 16thC wing when he made his home here. The only 21stC intrusion is the occasional sight (but no sound) of a busy little two-car diesel train on the far side of the valley. "TGV Normande!" quips M. Groult, the Château's present, lucky owner whose own sanctuary boasts a fireplace big enough to seat a brass band.

The bedrooms, some in a separate keep, are baronial enough for four-posters to be the rule rather than the exception. The standard of decora-tion, the quality of the furniture and the finely finished bathrooms should suit the fussiest of château-hoppers. If your budget will stretch to it, and you can cope with heights, go for No. 4 – the biggest of them all and with glorious views across and up the valley. The beamed and flagged dining room offers fine regional cuisine and a better than adequate wine list.

～

NEARBY Bayeux (38 km); Normandy beaches; golf.
LOCATION 1.5 km W of St-Lô, turn right in Agneaux signed to Château; car parking
FOOD breakfast, dinner
PRICE €€€-€€€€ **ROOMS** 12; 4 double, 4 twin, 2 suites, all with bath; all rooms have phone, TV, minibar **FACILITIES** sitting room, dining room, meeting room, terrace, garden, tennis **CREDIT CARDS** AE, DC, MC, V **CHILDREN** accepted **DISABLED** 1 ground-floor room **PETS** accepted **CLOSED** never **PROPRIETORS** M. and Mme Groult

THE NORTH-WEST

LES ANDELYS

LA CHAINE D'OR
～ RIVERSIDE HOTEL ～

25-27 rue Grande, Le Petit Andely, 27700 Les Andelys (Eure)
TEL 02 32 54 00 31 **FAX** 02 32 54 05 68
E-MAIL chaineor@wanadoo.fr **WEBSITE** www.planete-b.fr/la-chaine-d-or

UNDER AN HOUR from Paris, on a lazy curve in the Seine and overlooked by the pale remains of Richard the Lionheart's 12thC Château Gaillard, the cares of the world start to recede as soon as you pull into the peaceful gravelled courtyard of this 18thC inn. Owned by Mme Foucault for the last 15 years, it has a young, enthusiastic and professional staff, and despite being only a stone's throw from the centre of this little town, could not be closer to the Seine without falling in. Six of the ten attractively decorated bedrooms look out over the river, one into the courtyard and the remainder towards the town church. Though not an antiques gallery, the furniture is real enough to have collected a few scars over the last hundred years or so, and the bathrooms are a good deal newer.

The restaurant looks out over the river – raw beams, warm yellow rough-plastered walls, fresh flowers and a massive stone fireplace surround the tables that stand on the black-and-white tiled floor. Excellent food, with the quality lasting through the salad and into the cheese and puddings, and a full, but by no means ruinous, wine list should satisfy the pickiest of diners. If you are in the neighbourhood, look no further.

～

NEARBY Giverny (45 km); Lyons-la-Forêt (21 km); Rouen (38 km).
LOCATION in Le Petit Andely on river Seine; car parking
FOOD breakfast, lunch, dinner
PRICE €€€
ROOMS 10; 7 double, 3 twin, all with bath or shower; all rooms have phone, TV; 5 have hairdrier
FACILITIES sitting room, breakfast room, restaurant, meeting room, terrace, courtyard garden
CREDIT CARDS AE, MC, V
CHILDREN accepted **DISABLED** access difficult
PETS accepted
CLOSED late Dec to late Jan; restaurant Sun dinner, Mon and Tues lunch in low season
PROPRIETORS Monique and Carole Foucault

THE NORTH-WEST

ARZANO

CHATEAU DE KERLAREC
~ CHATEAU HOTEL ~

29300 Arzano (Finistère)
TEL 02 98 71 75 06 **FAX** 02 98 71 74 55

COMPLETED IN 1830 by the Dandilo family (descended from a long line of Venetian doges), Château de Kerlarec, already decrepit, was left empty in 1989. Six years later Monique and Michel Bellin arrived looking, I suspect, for somewhere to house her fascinating collection of silver, porcelain, glass, furniture, pictures and *objets*. It must have been touch and go for a while, but eventually they managed to get it all in. The result is rather like the interior of Ali Baba's cave, except her arrangements are artistic rather than haphazard and betray a deep sense of humour and even deeper sense of history. As well as being unmolested architecturally, much of the château's original interior decoration has survived – even the original wallpaper in the *salon* is more or less intact.

The Bellins have the resuscitation of the building well in hand, and have already created a cool white gallery and meeting space beneath the old *porte-cochère*. There are four wonderfully theatrical bedrooms on the second floor: each has an antechamber which doubles as a sitting room, and then a gentle limbo takes you past rafters into a tower bedroom. All are different, with one resembling the set for *The 1001 Nights* and another a confection in white and gold. Given notice, Mme Bellin will lay on crêpes or a vast seafood platter for dinner.

~

NEARBY Lorient (40 km); Quimper (55 km); Iles de Glénan.
LOCATION 6 km E of Quimperlé on the D22; car parking
FOOD breakfast, supper by arrangement
PRICE €
ROOMS 6; 1 double, 5 suites, all with bath or shower; all rooms have phone, TV
FACILITIES sitting room, dining room, meeting room, terrace, garden, swimming pool, tennis
CREDIT CARDS not accepted **CHILDREN** accepted
DISABLED access difficult **PETS** accepted
CLOSED never
PROPRIETORS Monique and Michel Bellin

THE NORTH-WEST

BAGNOLES-DE-L'ORNE

✳ MANOIR DU LYS ✳
∼ COUNTRY HOTEL ∼

La Croix Gauthier, route de Juvigny, 61140 Bagnoles-de-l'Orne (Orne)
TEL 02 33 37 80 69 **FAX** 02 33 30 05 80
E-MAIL manoirdulys@lemel.fr **WEBSITE** www.manoir-du-lys.fr

THIS DELIGHTFUL, typically Norman half-timbered hunting lodge, with geraniums at its foot and dripping from its balconies, has, among its many advantages, not one but two swimming pools, one indoors, the other outside. It was reopened as a hotel by the Quintons in 1985 after a long period of disuse, and many improvements have been introduced in recent years. The new building is harmonious, and bedrooms, including four brand-new suites, are very attractive – all spacious and well equipped, with stylish furnishings far removed from the French norm. The de luxe rooms tend to be long and narrow with balconies overlooking the gardens.

Marie-France oversees the smart dining rooms (also overlooking the gardens, through floor-to-ceiling windows) where you can enjoy her son Franck's delicious Michelin-starred cooking, which is rooted in local tradition but respects contemporary trends. In fine weather you can dine outside. There is also a polished little bar/sitting room with a huge open fire and a grand piano (played on Friday nights). The Quintons are warm hosts and organize popular educational 'mushroom' weekends, during which up to 120 varieties may be picked in the surrounding woods; English-language tuition can be laid on.

∼

NEARBY Alençon (47 km); Suisse Normande; golf.
LOCATION in middle of countryside in forest of Andaines; car parking
FOOD breakfast, lunch, dinner
PRICE €€ **ROOMS** 32; 25 double, 23 with bath, 2 with shower; 7 suites with bath; all have phone, TV, minibar **FACILITIES** bar/sitting room, dining rooms, billiards, garden, indoor and outdoor swimming pools, tennis **CREDIT CARDS** AE, DC, MC, V
CHILDREN welcome **DISABLED** 1 specially adapted bedroom **PETS** accepted
CLOSED early Jan to mid-Feb; restaurant Sun dinner and Mon, Nov to Easter
PROPRIETORS Marie-France and Paul Quinton

THE NORTH-WEST

BALINES

RELAIS MOULIN DE BALISNE
~ CONVERTED MILL ~

Balines, 27130 Verneuil-sur-Avre (Eure)
TEL 02 32 32 03 48 **FAX** 02 32 60 11 22
WEBSITE www.moulin-de-balisne

IN 1965 M. GASTALDI started with just the roof and walls of this old water mill and an almost insurmountable problem: he is a self-confessed perfectionist who wanted an old inn. That meant finding the stone, beams, bricks, slates, doors, windows and floorboards from other buildings of the right vintage and then merging them at the mill. But find them he did, and the result is a gem of a place set in 13 studiously untended hectares which include two lakes and two streams (all with fishing rights), woods and walks beyond over open farmland.

Inside you walk on brick, tile or wooden floors if you can find space between the oriental rugs as you thread your way past a lifetime's collection of antique furniture – all of it used and giving the place a wonderfully warm atmosphere. There is a cosy *salon* and a bigger drawing room where many of the flat surfaces are used to display M. Gastaldi's collection of old decanters. The dining room is indoors during the winter, but in summer the tables follow the sun round the house. The menus are short, varied and interesting and the kitchen happily caters for vegetarians.

The large bedrooms are meticulously decorated and blessed with more beams, rugs and antiques. Excellent value.

~

NEARBY Château de Beaumesnil; Senonches forest; golf.
LOCATION off D54 just S of Balines beside river Avre; car parking
FOOD breakfast, dinner
PRICE ⓔ
ROOMS 10; 8 double, 2 suites, all with bath; all rooms have phone, TV, minibar
FACILITIES 2 sitting rooms, 2 dining rooms, terraces, garden, fishing
CREDIT CARDS AE, DC, MC, V
CHILDREN accepted
DISABLED access difficult
PETS accepted
CLOSED never
PROPRIETOR M. Gastaldi

THE NORTH-WEST

LE BEC-HELLOUIN

AUBERGE DE L'ABBAYE
~ VILLAGE INN ~

27800 Le Bec-Hellouin (Eure)
TEL 02 32 44 86 02 **FAX** 02 32 46 32 23

THIS GERANIUM-DECKED 18thC inn, squarely in the centre of a row of half-timbered houses, looks across the village green to the entrance of the abbey of Notre-Dame du Bec, from which it takes its name. Open to the public, the abbey's well-tended gardens are well worth the short walk needed to get to them. The Sergent family have been here for 40 years and the present relaxed and welcoming team is mother and son.

Everything about the place is in apple-pie order: the tiled floors are polished, the furniture gleams and, despite the complexity of the new French regulations on working hours for catering staff, the kitchens can still turn out meals for residents seven days a week. Snails, lobster and game in season feature strongly on the menu and their *tarte aux pommes* has an almost international reputation. The beamed dining room has immaculate stone walls and the traditional red-and-white checked tablecloths; in summer tables are set under parasols in the central courtyard. Tables and benches for informal meals are ranged along the raised terrace at the front of the inn. The five low-ceilinged bedrooms, up quite a steep flight of stairs, are freshly decorated in cottage style, squeaky clean and all dressed with fresh flowers.

NEARBY Rouen (30 km); Château du Champ-de-Bataille; golf.
LOCATION in village 6 km N of Brionne; car parking
FOOD breakfast, lunch, dinner
PRICE €
ROOMS 10; 5 double, 5 twin, all with bath; all rooms have phone, TV
FACILITIES sitting area, bar/dining room, terrace, courtyard garden
CREDIT CARDS MC, V
CHILDREN accepted
DISABLED access difficult
PETS accepted
CLOSED 2 weeks Jan, last 2 weeks Nov
PROPRIETORS Françoise and Frédéric Sergent

THE NORTH-WEST

LA BOUILLE

✳ LE SAINT PIERRE ✳
∼ RIVERSIDE RESTAURANT-WITH-ROOMS ∼

4 place du Bateau, 76530 La Bouille (Seine-Maritime)
TEL 02 35 18 01 01 **FAX** 02 35 18 12 76

A N HOUR FROM PARIS, and a few minutes less from Le Havre, Le St Pierre is at the centre of a picture-postcard village squeezed between the Seine and the high bluffs to the south. Beyond the river wall a small car ferry plies back and forth, dodging the other river traffic, to save people the long drive in either direction for a bridge. Mme Huet explained in her excellent English (six years' living in Chelsea must tell eventually) why the outside of Le St Pierre was slightly smoke-stained when we saw it: the building next door had just burned down.

Inside, the deep-pile carpet and the muted greens, sponged yellows and attractive watercolours on the walls complement the broad views over the river. Crisp white linen and upholstered chairs in the dining room, and cane chairs and parasols on the broad terrace are the winter and summer settings for a stream of original and popular combinations of flavours and textures from Arnaud Lindivat's kitchen. If you can't make up your mind what to choose, there is always the *menu dégustation* to fall back on.

There are six stylishly modern and comfortable bedrooms on the second floor, three of which look out over the river.

∼

NEARBY Rouen (22 km); Honfleur (45 km); Normandy beaches.
LOCATION in village facing river; car parking
FOOD breakfast, lunch, dinner
PRICE €
ROOMS 6 double, 4 with bath, 2 with shower; all rooms have phone, TV
FACILITIES restaurant, terrace

CREDIT CARDS AE, DC, MC, V
CHILDREN accepted
DISABLED access difficult
PETS accepted
CLOSED Sun dinner, Mon
PROPRIETOR Mme Gisèle Huet

THE NORTH-WEST

BRELIDY

CHATEAU HOTEL DE BRELIDY
~ CHATEAU HOTEL ~

Brélidy, 22140 Bégard (Côtes d'Armor)
TEL 02 96 95 69 38 **FAX** 02 96 95 18 03
E-MAIL chateau.brelidy@wordonline.fr **WEBSITE** www.chateau-brelidy.com

We have had an enthusiastic report of this fine 16thC Breton château, run efficiently yet informally by the friendly Yoncourt-Pemezec family. Behind the austere granite exterior typical of the area's architecture, our reporter discovered a series of comfortable, homely rooms filled with antiques, most of which have been in the family for years. Over three decades, Pierre and Eliane have painstakingly and sympathetically restored their château, retaining the enormous fireplaces, original stone staircase and beamed ceilings. The result is refreshingly natural. Nothing has been dressed up and there's not a trace of pretension. Even dinner feels like a family meal.

Beyond the peaceful 35-hectare garden of lawns and hydrangeas is some of the most glorious countryside you'll see in the region: gentle hills reach to the horizon, punctuated by copses and threaded by hedgerows dotted with wild flowers. Some of the best views are from the vast windows of one of the suites (these alone seem to justify the 300F premium over the cost of a superior double room). Appropriately the bedrooms are named after flowers, and four have their own terraces.

Keen fishermen have a choice of rivers and lakes in the grounds.

~

NEARBY Guingamp (15 km); Lannion (30 km).
LOCATION in countryside outside village, follow signs from the D15; car parking
FOOD breakfast, dinner
PRICE ©©
ROOMS 14; 12 double and twin, 2 suites, all with bath or shower; all rooms have phone, TV, hairdrier
FACILITIES sitting room, dining room, billiards room, Jacuzzi, terrace, garden, fishing **CREDIT CARDS** AE, MC, V
CHILDREN accepted
DISABLED access possible **PETS** accepted
CLOSED early Nov to mid-Apr
PROPRIETORS Pierre and Eliane Yoncourt-Pemezec

THE NORTH-WEST

CAEN

✳ LE DAUPHIN ✳
~ TOWN RESTAURANT-WITH-ROOMS ~

29 rue Gémare, 14000 Caen (Calvados)
TEL 02 31 86 22 26 **FAX** 02 31 86 35 14
E-MAIL dauphin.caen@wanadoo.fr **WEBSITE** www.bestwestern.fr

ANY HOTEL THAT HAS private parking in the centre of Caen is a pearl almost beyond price, and parking is not the only quality that Le Dauphin possesses. A scant three minutes' walk from William the Conqueror's castle, this former priory doesn't really reveal its age until you get inside. Exposed stone walls, beams and the stone staircase all show the kind of restoration that is more preoccupied with quality than with cost: the building is probably in better shape now than it was 200 years ago.

Sylvie and Stéphane Pugnat (he is the chef) make a lively team and give the place a very welcoming atmosphere. The excellent cuisine is Norman, and Stéphane scores extra points by leaving space in his menus for any fish that appealed to him at the market. Crisp white linen, high-backed red velvet chairs, fresh flowers and a thoughtful wine list will keep you company in the restaurant while you wait for your food. The Pugnats have bought the building next door and are starting the work that will add more bedrooms to the 22 they now have, divided between the main building and an annexe. Most of the rooms and bathrooms in the existing annexe are larger than those in the main building, and priced accordingly. Without being an antique roadshow, all the rooms are well decorated, well furnished and thoroughly comfortable.

NEARBY quartier des Quatrans; château; church of St-Pierre. **LOCATION** in town centre, 2 streets W of the château; car parking **FOOD** breakfast, lunch, dinner; room service during day **PRICE** €-€€€ **ROOMS** 22; 20 double and twin, 2 suites, all with bath; all rooms have phone, TV, minibar, hairdrier **FACILITIES** sitting room/bar, restaurant **CREDIT CARDS** AE, DC, MC, V **CHILDREN** accepted **DISABLED** access difficult **PETS** accepted **CLOSED** 2 weeks in Feb, mid-July to early Aug; restaurant Sat lunch, Sun **PROPRIETORS** Sylvie and Stéphane Pugnat

THE NORTH-WEST

CAMPIGNY

LE PETIT COQ AUX CHAMPS
∽ COUNTRY HOTEL ∽

La Pommeraie-Sud, Campigny, 27500 Pont-Audemer (Eure)
TEL 02 32 41 04 19 **FAX** 02 32 56 06 25
E-MAIL le.petit.coq.aux.champs@wanadoo.fr **WEBSITE** www.lepetitcoqauxchamps.fr

A THATCHED HOUSE WITH its own heliport – it sounds unlikely, but convention counts for little at this smart, secluded retreat, in rolling meadows and sweeping forests in the Risle valley. Le Petit Coq offers an intriguing mix of the rustic, the sophisticated and the downright idiosyncratic – a cocktail that may be too heady for some, to judge by our empty postbag.

The building, mostly 19th century, has two main wings with a spacious, airy, modern extension in between. The style varies considerably – modern cane furniture in the large sitting room, while antiques predominate in the restaurant, which has a huge open fireplace at one end. An intimate piano bar has been squeezed into the new building. The bedrooms are all furnished and arranged in different ways, some brightly coloured, others more restrained; none is particularly large.

Jean-Marie Huard, who returned to his Norman roots after some years in highly reputed restaurants in Paris, pays serious attention to detail, presentation and local tradition in his cooking – with impressive results.

∽

NEARBY Pont-Audemer (6 km); Honfleur (30 km); golf.
LOCATION in countryside, 6 km S of Pont-Audemer; car parking
FOOD breakfast, lunch, dinner
PRICE €€€
ROOMS 12; 6 double, 4 twin, 1 family, 1 suite, all with bath; all rooms have, phone, TV, hairdrier
FACILITIES sitting room, 4 dining rooms, bar, garden, swimming pool, heliport
CREDIT CARDS AE, DC, MC, V
CHILDREN welcome
DISABLED ground-floor rooms available
PETS welcome
CLOSED Jan
PROPRIETORS Fabienne Desmonts and Jean-Marie Huard

THE NORTH-WEST

CLÉCY

HOSTELLERIE DU MOULIN DU VEY
~ CONVERTED MILL ~

Le Vey 14570, Clécy (Calvados)
TEL 02 31 69 71 08 **FAX** 02 31 69 14 14
E-MAIL reservations@moulinduvey.com **WEBSITE** www.moulinduvey.com

JUST WHEN WE BEGAN to wonder about this old, creeper-clad water-mill, readers' reports arrived to reassure us about its continuing appeal. 'Bright, tastefully decorated rooms, excellent restaurant, friendly service.' 'Accommodating and relaxing'. 'Good for an overnight stop or short break.'

The Moulin is at the heart of some of the best scenery in the region, where the River Orne has carved a majestic valley between green, rolling hills. It is within easy driving distance of the ferry at Caen, and for British visitors makes an attractive first- or last-night stop.

Both the buildings and the gardens are beautifully kept, and there is a pleasant waterside terrace for eating and drinking, with a garden beyond. Food in the half-timbered, rather barn-like restaurant, just across the courtyard from the main building, is carefully prepared and served, and the less expensive menus are sound value. Bedrooms are comfortable if a little dated, and the ones near the weir can be noisy. They are furnished simply but with touches of style, and are reasonably priced. Some rooms are in annexes: the Manoir de Placy, 400 metres away, and the Relais de Surosne, 3 km away on the other side of the village – a peaceful, small Gothic-style house with a lush garden.

~

NEARBY Thury-Harcourt (10 km); Falaise (30 km).
LOCATION 2 km E of Clécy; car parking
FOOD breakfast, lunch, dinner
PRICE €
ROOMS 25 double and twin and family, all with bath, 1 with shower; all rooms have phone, TV
FACILITIES sitting room, dining room, banqueting room, conference room, terrace, garden **CREDIT CARDS** AE, DC, MC, V
CHILDREN accepted
DISABLED access difficult **PETS** accepted
CLOSED Dec to Feb; restaurant Sun dinner in low season
PROPRIETOR Denise Leduc

THE NORTH-WEST

LE MOULIN DE CONNELLES
~ RIVERSIDE HOTEL ~

route d'Amfreville-sous-les-Monts, 27430 Connelles (Eure)
TEL 02 32 59 53 33 **FAX** 02 32 59 21 83 **E-MAIL** moulindeconnelles@
moulindeconnelles.com **WEBSITE** www.moulindeconnelles.com

SCARCELY A QUARTER OF AN HOUR from Monet's garden at Giverny, Le Moulin de Connelles is a fairy-tale sort of a place, with turrets and gables, beams and arches. It even has its own private 2-hectare island with – if you can find them hidden in its gardens – a heated swimming pool, and tennis courts. Unless you really mean it, be wary of wishing out loud for a boat because in the twinkling of an eye you will be issued with a punt to go exploring in. And, as if the location wasn't enough, the Petiteaus have also made a deeply comfortable, beautifully presented hotel.

Spanning the mill-stream as it does, the (excellent) restaurant seems to be hovering over the water. Steamed salmon parcels, baked sea bass, kidneys cooked in three kinds of mustard are sometimes part of the offering from a highly-regarded kitchen. Sitting under the terrace awning, looking down at the mill's reflection and the lily pads floating in the quiet water, it is difficult to imagine wanting to be anywhere else on a summer evening.

The bedrooms are quietly and impeccably furnished and have the kind of bathrooms that you want to wrap up and take home with you. If you're feeling rich, the view from the corner suite (No. 7) is difficult to beat.

~

NEARBY Rouen (39 km); Evreux (30 km); golf; water sports.
LOCATION off D19 just N of Connelles beside river Seine; car parking
FOOD breakfast, lunch, dinner
PRICE €€
ROOMS 13; 4 double, 4 twin, 5 suites, all with bath; all rooms have phone, TV, minibar, hairdrier, safe
FACILITIES sitting room, meeting room, bar, restaurant, terrace, garden, swimming pool, tennis, fishing
CREDIT CARDS AE, DC, MC, V
CHILDREN accepted **DISABLED** access difficult
PETS accepted
CLOSED hotel and restaurant early Jan to early Feb, Oct-Apr Sun dinner and Mon; restaurant May-Sep lunch on Sun, Mon and Tues
PROPRIETORS Hubert and Luce Petiteau

THE NORTH-WEST

CREPON

✳ FERME DE LA RANCONNIERE ✳
∼ COUNTRY HOTEL ∼

route d'Arromanches, 14480 Crépon (Calvados)
TEL 02 31 22 21 73 **FAX** 02 31 22 98 39
E-MAIL hotel@ranconniere.com **WEBSITE** www.ranconniere.com

THIS FORTIFIED FARM, well placed for visiting the D-Day beaches, is no smallholding. The oldest building is 13th century and the final touches were added sometime in the 15th century. The buildings form three sides of an enormous courtyard, and the fourth side, on the road, is guarded by a crenellated wall – obviously a safe haven for the farmers and their stock in more troubled times. Even out of season when we visited, both restaurants (one beamed and one barrel-vaulted) were bursting with French families who had driven out into the country for Sunday lunch and to celebrate the results of recent mayoral elections. A straw poll of several families revealed that they were there because the food was (a) good, (b) plentiful and (c) good value.

The bedrooms, some in each of the three buildings, are mostly baronial in size and much of their furniture is appropriately massive. Rugs on the tiled floors and tapestries on many of the walls also help to keep the 21st century firmly at bay. Despite their thickness, the walls might not shield you entirely from the popularity of the dining rooms: there is now an annexe in a separate farmhouse which might suit those for whom peace is an absolute priority. Breakfast, highly recommended, is a buffet.

∼

NEARBY Arromanches (7 km); Bayeux (12 km); Caen (25 km); Normandy beaches.
LOCATION on the D65 on the edge of the village; car parking
FOOD breakfast, lunch, dinner
PRICE €€€
ROOMS 48 double, twin and triple, all with bath or shower; all rooms have phone, TV, hairdrier **FACILITIES** sitting room, 2 restaurants, meeting room, lift, garden
CREDIT CARDS AE, DC, MC, V **CHILDREN** accepted

DISABLED 1 specially adapted room **PETS** accepted
CLOSED never
PROPRIETORS Mme Vereecke and Mme Sileghem

THE NORTH-WEST

AUBERGE DE LA SELUNE
~ VILLAGE HOTEL ~

2 rue St-Germain, 50220 Ducey (Manche)
TEL 02 33 48 53 62 **FAX** 02 33 48 90 30
E-MAIL info@selune.com **WEBSITE** www.selune.com

WHEN WE LAST VISITED, we found that extensive renovations have changed the character of this redoubtable small hotel. It used to be old fashioned in a conventional sort of way. Now the downstairs, at least, is modern in a somewhat soulless way. The glass and metal lobby connecting the two old buildings might look better in an airport hotel, and the emerald green of the furnishings will not appeal to all our readers. Nonetheless, it's highly recommendable, and we continue to receive plenty of readers' letters saying just that. Of the two conventional dining rooms, one is less formal than the other and gives on to a terrace with tables and chairs, from which you can enjoy the garden with the river bubbling in the background.

Bedrooms are all different, with bright colour schemes and pleasant, but relatively simple furnishings. No. 36 has a fine view over the garden. Bathrooms are dull, but practical. We can't fault this as a stopover, prices being particularly honest – if not good value – and staff, on our visit, dutiful and friendly. The food is well above average, with *pie au crabe* still a *pièce de résistance*. Breakfast is better than the norm. Ask about the salmon fishing.

~

NEARBY Avranches (11 km); Le Mont-St-Michel (20 km).
LOCATION by the river in the village, on the N176, SE of Avranches; car parking
FOOD breakfast, lunch, dinner
PRICE €
ROOMS 21; 14 double, 5 twin, 1 single, 1 family, all with bath; all rooms have phone; 10 have TV
FACILITIES sitting room, 2 dining rooms, bar, conference room, terrace, garden, salmon fishing **CREDIT CARDS** DC, MC, V
CHILDREN accepted
DISABLED access difficult
PETS not accepted
CLOSED mid-Jan to mid-Feb; restaurant Mon in low season
PROPRIETOR Jean-Pierre Girres

THE NORTH-WEST

✳ LE DONJON ✳
～ SEASIDE HOTEL ～

chemin de Saint Clair, 76790 Etretat (Seine-Maritime)
TEL 02 35 27 08 23 **FAX** 02 35 29 92 24
E-MAIL ledonjon@wanadoo.fr **WEBSITE** www.ledonjon-etretat.fr

THIS EXTRAORDINARY LITTLE HOTEL set on a steep hill used to be one of our favourite places for a short break (it's only half an hour from Le Havre). Unfortunately we were unable to visit it this year, but recent reports suggest that standards of service and food may no longer match the high prices charged.

It is a former hilltop castle, with venerable origins and a secret subterranean channel to the sea, now safely surrounded by the leafy suburbs of Etretat. Inside, all is bright and light, decorated with a Parisian sophistication by Mme Abo-Dib, who runs the hotel with her son. The dining room, candlelit and mirrored, is wonderfully atmospheric; the cocktail bar overlooks Etretat's famous cliffs; and there is an impeccably kept small swimming pool surrounded by sunshades and loungers. But it is perhaps the eight bedrooms which best show off Mme Abo-Dib's creative skills: all are different, and immensely stylish. The largest, almost circular, has an Eastern theme, with black chintz drapes and gigantic mirror; another is in bright Impressionist hues, and one has a large fireplace for real log fires. Bathrooms, some in the turrets, are spacious and elegant in pure white.

The menu offers rather more possibilities for *pensionnaires*, with the option of choosing dishes from the *carte*, as well as the four-course *menu du Gentleman*. We will welcome further reports.

～

NEARBY Fécamp (17 km); Le Havre (28 km). **LOCATION** on hill behind the resort; car parking **FOOD** breakfast, lunch, dinner **PRICE** €€€ half-board obligatory **ROOMS** 11; 9 double, 2 suites, 10 with bath, 1 with shower; all rooms have phone, TV **FACILITIES** sitting room, dining room, bar, garden, swimming pool

CREDIT CARDS AE, MC, V **CHILDREN** accepted **PETS** accepted **DISABLED** access difficult **CLOSED** never **PROPRIETORS** Mme Abo-Dib and M. Abo-Dib

THE NORTH-WEST

✳ CHATEAU DE LA RAPEE ✳
∼ CHATEAU HOTEL ∼

Bazincourt-sur-Epte, 27140 Gisors (Eure)
TEL 02 32 55 11 61 **FAX** 02 32 55 95 65

'A COMFORTABLE STAY, although we found the decoration, with carpets for wallcoverings, rather idiosyncratic,' commented one reporter on this 19thC Gothic mansion. Well, yes: perhaps we should have warned about the carpet; but it is more or less confined (along with the antlers) to the reception area. The rest of this grandly conceived but small-scale period piece is less eccentric.

The château lies in a peaceful setting at the end of a long, rutted forest track from Bazincourt. Inside, original features have been carefully preserved and, although the public areas are rather dark in places, the house has been pleasantly furnished with antiques and reproductions. Some of the spacious, calm bedrooms are quite stately, with fine country views, plenty of antiques and creaky wooden floors; others verge on the eccentric (but are antler-free). Immediately next to the house is a small, pleasant flower-garden.

Pascal and Philippe Bergeron take their cooking seriously – classic dishes, with some regional influences and occasional original flourishes. Further reports would be welcome.

NEARBY Jouy-sous-Thelle (25 km); Beauvais (32 km); riding.
LOCATION in countryside 4 km NW of Gisors; car parking
FOOD breakfast, lunch, dinner
PRICE €€€
ROOMS 13; 12 double and twin, 1 apartment, all with bath or shower; all rooms have phone **FACILITIES** sitting room, 2 dining rooms, bar, banqueting room
CREDIT CARDS AE, MC, V **CHILDREN** accepted by arrangement
DISABLED no special facilities
PETS not accepted
CLOSED Feb, last 2 weeks Aug; restaurant Wed
PROPRIETORS M. and Mme Bergeron

THE NORTH-WEST

✳ CHATEAU DE LOCGUENOLE ✳
～ CHATEAU HOTEL ～

route de Port-Louis en Kerivignac, 56700 Hennebont (Morbihan)
TEL 02 97 76 76 76 **FAX** 02 97 76 82 35
E-MAIL locguenole@relaischateaux.fr **WEBSITE** www.chateau-de-locguenole.fr

OWNED AND RUN BY THE de la Sablière family (son Bruno is the director), this handsome 200-year old château stands in its own extensive wooded park at the head of an arm of the Blavet estuary. A private pontoon allows direct access to the water, and sea-fishing and sailing can be organized on the spot. Rhododendrons and azaleas dot the grounds, walled gardens provide sheltered suntraps to relax in and a heated outdoor pool offers an attractive alternative to the nearby sea.

By almost any measure this is a very grown-up establishment. It has been a hotel now for more than 30 years but has never lost the feel of a comfortable stately home. The antique furniture standing on the glowing parquet floors would cost a prince's ransom today, but you get the distinct feeling that these pieces have been here since they were new. The bedrooms on the first floor are the grandest, but those on the second floor are full of character; one is a 'double-decker' with additional beds in a light and airy loft space. There are seven more bedrooms in the old manor house next door to the château.

The restaurant, dominated by a magnificent tapestry, has a deservedly high reputation – and a wine list to match.

～

NEARBY Lorient (5 km); Ile de Groix; Belle-Ile; golf; sailing. **LOCATION** to the right off the D781 from Hennebont to Port-Louis, before D194 junction, on the Blavet estuary; car parking **FOOD** breakfast, lunch, dinner; room service **PRICE** €€€-€€€€ **ROOMS** 9; 8 double and twin, 1 suite, all with bath; all rooms have phone, TV, minibar, hairdrier **FACILITIES** sitting rooms, restaurant, sauna, terrace, garden, swimming pool, tennis, fishing **CREDIT CARDS** AE, DC, MC, V **CHILDREN** accepted **DISABLED** access difficult **PETS** tolerated **CLOSED** early Jan to early Feb; restaurant closed lunch Mon-Wed and Fri **PROPRIETORS** de la Sablière family

THE NORTH-WEST

✳ LA CHAUMIERE ✳
～ COUNTRY HOTEL ～

route du Littoral, Vasouy, 14600 Honfleur (Calvados)
TEL 02 31 81 63 20 **FAX** 02 31 89 59 23
E-MAIL informations@la-chaumiere.com **WEBSITE** www.chaumiere-honfleur.com

STRICTLY SPEAKING A *chaumière* is a thatched cottage, but the Normans seem to have put tiles on this very handsome half-timbered house tucked into its manicured seaside meadow on the Seine estuary, minutes west of Honfleur. Compared to the stratospherically upmarket Ferme Saint Siméon a mile away, also owned by the Boelen family, it is a smaller, more relaxed establishment with nothing else between it and the sea. Run by a manager, it is a little difficult to forget that this is a business and not a vocation. Standards are high and so are prices, but the position alone goes a long way towards justifying the cost.

There is a cosy beamed and tiled restaurant with a view out over the estuary and a consistently high-class output, strong on seafood and fresh local produce and with a wine list to remember. In summer, tables are set on a sheltered sunny terrace guarded by flower beds and fruit trees. The beamed bedrooms are all decorated in fresh colours, with matching fabrics and wallpapers and sound wooden furniture. One, rather eccentrically, is bathroom and bedroom rolled into one: best avoided by those with a preference for privacy. The Pont de Normandie has cut the journey time from Calais to Honfleur to a couple of hours, making this a very undemanding destination for travellers from England. Golfers will also relish the challenge of two courses within ten miles.

～

NEARBY Deauville (15 km); Pont-l'Evêque (19 km); golf. **LOCATION** W of Honfleur on the D513 to Deauville; car parking **FOOD** breakfast, lunch, dinner **PRICE** €€€ **ROOMS** 9; 8 double and twin, 1 suite, all with bath; all rooms have phone, TV, minibar, hairdrier **FACILITIES** sitting area, restaurant, terrace, garden **CREDIT CARDS** AE, MC, V **CHILDREN** accepted **DISABLED** access difficult **PETS** accepted **CLOSED** 2 weeks Jan, 2 weeks early Dec; restaurant Tues, Wed lunch, Thurs lunch **PROPRIETORS** Boelen family

THE NORTH-WEST

HONFLEUR

LE MANOIR DU BUTIN
~ SEASIDE HOTEL ~

Phare du Butin, 14600 Honfleur (Calvados)
TEL 02 31 81 63 00 **FAX** 02 31 89 59 23
WEBSITE www.le.manoir.com

YOU GET A FIRM IMPRESSION that time runs a little more slowly than usual at this 18thC half-timbered Norman manor tucked into a wooded hillside just outside Honfleur. As well as a view across the Seine estuary, you are offered peace and quiet and the kind of welcoming atmosphere where no one would think it at all remarkable if you took a rug and a book out on to the gently sloping sunny lawn for a sleep after lunch. Veronique Heulot greets all the guests herself and settles them into one of the nine deeply comfortable bedrooms. All of these are individually decorated, each themed to a different colour, and all have excellent bathrooms. The one ground-floor bedroom has no view at all, but has been given a large sunken bath by way of compensation.

There is a sizeable drawing room for residents which, beneath its beams, has a baronial fireplace surmounted by a hunting fresco that chases from one end of the room to the other. On the opposite side of the hall is the light and attractive restaurant, decorated in pale yellow, that offers an excellent regional cuisine on shortish, changing menus as well as a serious selection of old Calvados.

~

NEARBY Deauville (15 km); Pont-l'Evêque (19 km); golf.
LOCATION just W of Honfleur on the D513 to Deauville; car parking
FOOD breakfast, lunch, dinner
PRICE €€
ROOMS 9 double and twin with bath; all rooms have phone, TV, minibar, hairdrier
FACILITIES sitting room, restaurant, terrace, garden
CREDIT CARDS AE, MC, V
CHILDREN accepted
DISABLED access difficult
PETS accepted
CLOSED 2 weeks Jan, 3 weeks Nov; restaurant Wed, Thurs lunch, Fri lunch
MANAGER Veronique Heulot

THE NORTH-WEST

AUBERGE DU CLOS NORMAND
∽ VILLAGE INN ∽

22 rue Henri IV, 76370 Martin-Eglise (Seine-Maritime)
TEL 02 35 04 40 34 **FAX** 02 35 04 48 49

THE OUTSKIRTS OF DIEPPE are only a few minutes' drive away from this charming country inn, but you would never know it. The only real imponderable about this place is whether the dining room is in the kitchen – or the other way round. Either way the result is cosy and cheerful. Scooting around the flagged floor on his chef's stool, M. Hauchecorne has been exercising his culinary skills in public for 23 years. When asked about the staples of his menu, *"Tarte aux moules,* turbot, sole, *barbue, foie gras de canard,"* he beams, "plenty of cream and butter – and the wines of the Loire." A sign on the road says 'Enter lightly', but it's unlikely you will be able to leave in the same fashion. The menu card itself was illustrated by his son, an artist who has a small *atelier* in Dieppe.

Outside, the River Eaulne flows between the large garden and the pasture beyond, and this is the view for all the bedrooms which are in a separate annexe – purpose-built 100 years ago and showing its age a little. The bedrooms themselves are modestly furnished and decorated, clean and comfortable. If you need plenty of room to swing your sponge when bathing, Nos 6 and 10 have outsize bathrooms. On the ground floor is a large sitting room, reserved for the occupants of the rooms.

∽

NEARBY forest of Arques; Côte d'Albâtre; Rouen (50 km).
LOCATION in the village, 5 km SE of Dieppe; car parking
FOOD breakfast, lunch, dinner
PRICE €
ROOMS 9 double and twin with bath or shower; all rooms have phone, TV
FACILITIES sitting room, dining room, terrace, garden
CREDIT CARDS AE, MC, V
CHILDREN accepted
DISABLED access difficult
PETS accepted
CLOSED mid-Nov to mid-Dec; restaurant Mon dinner, Tues
PROPRIETORS M. and Mme Hauchecorne

THE NORTH-WEST

MOELAN-SUR-MER

✳ LES MOULINS DU DUC ✳
∼ CONVERTED MILL ∼

29350 Moëlan-sur-Mer (Finistère)
TEL 02 98 96 52 52 **FAX** 02 98 96 52 53
E-MAIL tqad29@aol.com **WEBSITE** www.moulins-du-duc.com

I N THE WOODED HILLS OF FINISTERE, just above the lowest tidal reaches of the Belon, Les Moulins du Duc is an old mill that is still in the food business but has rocketed upmarket since it became a restaurant, with Thierry Quilfen, who started off as head chef, now the owner as well. You arrive to find manicured gardens round a small lake and apparently no building big enough to house a restaurant, let alone a 27-room hotel. The mill is below the dam which traps the water that used to turn its grindstone and, from a small cottage-like entrance perched on top of the dam, it expands downwards and outwards in an almost extra-dimensional way.

Bare stone, beams and tiled and timbered floors lead you through the bar and down to the lowest level where, almost in the river (big sliding windows open in summer), you can dine very seriously indeed at the pink linen-covered tables. Given its location near the coast, it's not surprising that M. Quilfen majors on seafood. If you need more than a stroll by the lake to work up an appetite, try the indoor pool. All the bedrooms are in two-storey cottages dotted around the grounds, quietly decorated and with better-than-adequate bathrooms.

NEARBY Lorient (23 km); Quimper (45 km).
LOCATION from Quimperlé take the D783 through Baye and follow signs 1.2 km on left; car parking
FOOD breakfast, lunch, dinner; room service
PRICE €€€ **ROOMS** 27; 13 double, 11 twin, 3 family, 22 with bath, 5 with shower; all rooms have phone, TV; some have minibar **FACILITIES** sitting room, dining room, breakfast room, meeting room, bar, sauna, indoor swimming pool, terrace, garden **CREDIT CARDS** AE, DC, MC, V **CHILDREN** accepted **DISABLED** 2 specially adapted rooms **PETS** accepted **CLOSED** Jan-Mar **PROPRIETOR** Thierry Quilfen

THE NORTH-WEST

NOTRE-DAME-D'ESTREES

AU REPOS DES CHINEURS
~ COUNTRY GUESTHOUSE ~

D50, Chemin de l'Eglise, 14340 Notre-Dame-d'Estrées (Calvados)
TEL 02 31 63 72 51 **FAX** 02 31 63 62 38 **E-MAIL** hotel.aureposdeschineurs@libertysurf.fr
WEBSITE www.au-repos-des-chineurs.com

THERE IS A FORMAL *brocante*, which doubles as a tea room, in this 17th and 18thC post house set in deep countryside between Cambremer and Moult. Rugs, china, porcelain, silver, pictures, mirrors and furniture are piled around you. But you can't afford to relax when you leave the *brocante* and walk through to the long, wide flagged hall that runs virtually the length of the house, because everything else here is for sale as well (barring the five cats, the very large dog and the bed you sleep in). Mme Steffen, who owns Le Repos and all the saleable and non-saleable items in it, not only turns her hand to teas and breakfasts but will also whizz up a snack at any other time of the day. If you need weightier fare, there are several restaurants a few minutes' drive away, and telling Mme Steffen what you need is no problem – she learned her English while living in Dallas.

The bedrooms, all with bathrooms, are comfortable and unfussy; those upstairs have floors stained to match the rest of their furnishings and decoration, and those downstairs have tiled floors. Some look up towards a pretty 16thC church perched at the top of the hill. Residents have a small sitting room in which to relax.

~

NEARBY Caen (26 km); Pont-l'Evêque (25 km); Normandy beaches.
LOCATION edge of the village on the D50; car parking on road
FOOD breakfast, light meals from noon to 7 pm
PRICE €-€€
ROOMS 10; 7 double, 3 twin, all with bath or shower; all rooms have phone
FACILITIES tea room, garden
CREDIT CARDS MC, V
CHILDREN accepted
DISABLED not suitable
PETS accepted
CLOSED Jan-Mar (open Sat and Sun by request)
PROPRIETOR Mme Claudine Steffen

THE NORTH-WEST

PAIMPOL

LE REPAIRE DE KERROC'H
~ QUAYSIDE HOTEL ~

29 quai Morand, 22500 Paimpol (Côtes d'Armor)
TEL 02 96 20 50 13 **FAX** 02 96 22 07 46

SET ON THE NORTH COAST of Brittany, famous for its pink granite shoreline,
Paimpol is a prosperous port with a working fishing fleet in one harbour and a bustling yacht marina in the other. Le Repaire de Kerroc'h, built at the end of the 18th century by Corouge Kersau, a famous local corsair, looks out over the latter. The flagged ground floor of this attractive, practical hotel is mostly given up to eating and drinking. At one end there is a fine, cosy restaurant that spills out towards the harbour in summer. Oysters, lobster, *coquilles*, salmon, pork and veal all put in an appearance somewhere on the menu, deftly treated in M. Trebaol's kitchen and well presented by friendly staff. The wine list is extensive but sensibly includes a fine selection of modestly priced wines (reds from Graves and the Loire amongst them). There is also a newly refurbished small bistro at the other end of the hotel that is open both for lunch and for dinner and offers excellent value on a short menu.

The bedrooms vary in size from just big enough to acceptably spacious. There is also a two-bedroomed, two-bathroomed suite that would be ideal for people travelling together. All the bathrooms are very well equipped.

NEARBY Guingamp (31 km); St Brieuc (47 km); golf.
LOCATION in town on quayside opposite yacht marina; car parking
FOOD breakfast, lunch, dinner
PRICE €€€
ROOMS 13; 11 double and twin, 2 suites, all with bath; all rooms have phone, TV, minibar
FACILITIES sitting area, bar, 2 restaurants, meeting room, lift, terrace
CREDIT CARDS MC, V
CHILDREN accepted
DISABLED access possible
PETS accepted
CLOSED never
PROPRIETOR Jean-Claude Broc

THE NORTH-WEST

PERROS-GUIREC

LE MANOIR DU SPHINX
∼ SEASIDE VILLA ∼

chemin de la Messe, 22700 Perros-Guirec (Côtes d'Armor)
TEL 02 96 23 25 42 **FAX** 02 96 91 26 13
WEBSITE www.perros-guirec.com

PERCHED ON THE SHOULDER of a steep headland that shelters it from the fleshpots of Perros-Guirec, Le Manoir du Sphinx is reached by a small seaside lane and looks out across the bay of Tristrignel to the chain of islets that guard it. All the rooms have their own view of the sea – bar and restaurant included. Its steep hydrangea-studded gardens run all the way down to the low cliffs at the high-water mark – or to the edge of the moonscape of rocks revealed by low tide.

There is nothing 'olde-worlde' about the Sphinx. Furniture and fittings are modern, a lift whisks you up to your room, and everything works the first time you press the button. Every bedroom has a little table and a couple of chairs by the window for those who want to put their feet up and read. Fabric-covered walls match the chairs, and bathrooms are first-rate.

The deeply comfortable restaurant, dressed in pale blue linen when we visited, is the shop window for M. Le Verge's excellent (predominantly sea-based) cooking. The Le Verges offer a well-polished, well-furnished, hospitable hotel with a firm emphasis on peace and quiet, and with a sandy beach a short walk away.
∼

NEARBY Lannion (11 km); Guingamp (43 km); St Brieuc (75 km).
LOCATION overlooking the sea beyond the town centre on the D788; car parking
FOOD breakfast, lunch, dinner
PRICE €€€
ROOMS 20; 14 double, 6 twin, all with bath or shower; all rooms have phone, TV, hairdrier, safe
FACILITIES sitting room, restaurant, lift, garden
CREDIT CARDS AE, MC, V
CHILDREN accepted
DISABLED ground-floor rooms available
PETS accepted
CLOSED early Jan to late Feb; restaurant Mon and Fri lunch, Sun dinner in low season
PROPRIETORS M. and Mme Le Verge

THE NORTH-WEST

PONT-AUDEMER

✳ BELLE ILE SUR RISLE ✳
∽ CHATEAU HOTEL ∽

112 route de Rouen, 27500 Pont-Audemer (Eure)
TEL 02 32 56 96 22 **FAX** 02 32 42 88 96
E-MAIL hotel@bellile.com **WEBSITE** www.belleile.com

IF YOUR HEART SINKS SLIGHTLY as you drive along the unpromising suburban road towards Belle Ile for the first time, don't worry: the charming owner, Madame Yazbeck, felt exactly the same. When you cross the little bridge to the romantic setting of a private wooded island, your spirits will lift, and they will positively soar as you step into the elegant interior. Rescued from dereliction, this mid-19thC mansion has become a thoroughly well-equipped hotel without losing the welcoming feel of a private house. Period furniture is mixed with little oriental touches and sofas chosen with comfort firmly in mind.

You can choose between three *salons* to relax in, or head for the conservatory bar that doubles as a sunny breakfast room. The bedrooms are all large and impeccably decorated, with bathrooms to match. The new chef looks very promising, judging by the quality of his first-ever dinner from this kitchen, served in a raised conservatory with a wonderful view of the river at sunset. The wine list is extensive, with rare vintages at appropriate prices and more modest wines at everyday levels. If you feel the need to punish yourself for dinner, there are two swimming pools (one indoors), a small gym (steps, bike and walker), a sauna, a sun bed and a tennis court.

NEARBY Honfleur (25 km); Rouen (47 km); Pont-l'Evêque (26 km). **LOCATION** just E of town on an island in the river Risle; car parking **FOOD** breakfast, lunch, dinner **PRICE** €€€; half-board only in high season and at weekends **ROOMS** 20; 13 double, 7 twin, all with bath; all rooms have phone, TV, minibar; most have hairdrier **FACILITIES** sitting rooms, dining room, conservatory, bar, health centre, terrace, garden, indoor and outdoor swimming pools, tennis **CREDIT CARDS** AE, DC, MC, V **CHILDREN** accepted **DISABLED** access difficult **PETS** accepted **CLOSED** Jan to mid-Mar **PROPRIETOR** Mme Marcelle Yazbeck

THE NORTH-WEST

PONT-AUDEMER

AUBERGE DU VIEUX PUITS
~ TOWN INN ~

6 rue Notre-Dame-du-Pré, 27500 Pont-Audemer (Eure)
TEL 02 32 41 01 48 **FAX** 02 32 42 37 28 **E-MAIL** vieux.puits@wanadoo.fr
WEBSITE www.lerapporteur.fr/vieux-puits

O**UR LATEST REPORT** on this wonderful, half-timbered, 17thC building is
short and to the point: 'Excellent'. It might equally well have said:
'Unchanging'. Sadly though, we have just heard that the owners are retiring in late 2002 and the inn's future is uncertain.

Although war-damaged Pont-Audemer still has a charming historic centre, it is rather dwarfed by the nondescript suburbs which have grown up around it. The Vieux Puits shines out like a beacon – all crooked beams and leaded windows. Inside it is a medievalist's dream, with twisting wooden stairs and dark beams hung with shining copper and ancient pewter.

Jacques Foltz and his charming wife bring out the best in the building, by keeping the style simple and restrained. The small, intimate salon and dining rooms are carefully furnished with antiques, and are decorated with fresh flowers. Three of the bedrooms in the old building have been converted into a family apartment; the other three are quite small but full of character. Across the peaceful, flowery courtyard a modern wing provides six bedrooms – smarter and well equipped, but in keeping.

M. Foltz sees the auberge very much as a restaurant-with-rooms, and those who want to stay are encouraged to have dinner. To do so is hardly a penance, given the kitchen's high standards and the interesting dishes on the seasonal menus and *carte*.

NEARBY Honfleur (25 km); Rouen (47 km); Pont-l'Evêque (26 km).
LOCATION near middle of town; car parking
FOOD breakfast, lunch, dinner
PRICE €
ROOMS 11 double and twin and family, all with bath or shower; all rooms have phone; some have TV
FACILITIES bar/sitting area, restaurants, garden **CREDIT CARDS** MC, V
CHILDREN welome
DISABLED 2 specially adapted rooms **PETS** accepted
CLOSED late Dec to late Jan; restaurant Mon and Tues in low season
PROPRIETORS Jacques and Hélène Foltz

THE NORTH-WEST

QUINEVILLE-PLAGE

✳ CHATEAU DE QUINEVILLE ✳
∼ CHATEAU HOTEL ∼

50310 Quineville-Plage (Manche)
TEL 02 33 21 42 67 **FAX** 02 33 21 05 79

IN A DRAB SEASIDE RESORT at the northern end of Utah Beach, this place has all the ingredients of a smart Relais et Château establishment: a fine, classically proportioned 18thC building (once inhabited by James Stuart), set in 12 hectares, with a tower dating back to the middle ages, an ice-house and *pigeonnier* in the grounds; an enticing swimming pool; a moat with a Giverny-style bridge. But there's a difference: it has not been 'got at'.

Run by a simple family who speak no English, it's both sincere and endearing – if you appreciate the old style of French provincial hotel, warts and all: run-of-the-mill comfort, old-fashioned wallpaper, unstinting puce velveteen in the bedrooms.

The graceful dining rooms, straddling the width of the house, lit from tall windows on both sides, are airy and charming, with original panelling. Here you can savour traditional Normandy cuisine; try to ignore the murals and huge arrangements of artificial flowers.

Forgive the shortcomings in service and housekeeping and rejoice in the quaintness. A cockerel and geese roaming within metres of the house make for a bright and early start to the day.

Golf, riding, tennis and sailing are all a short distance away.

∼

NEARBY Île de Tatihou; Les Iles St-Marcouf; Barfleur (22 km); Normandy beaches.
LOCATION 1 km from sea, in village, near church and town hall; car parking
FOOD breakfast, lunch, dinner **PRICE** €€€ **ROOMS** 26; 24 double and twin, 19 with bath, 5 with shower; 2 suites with bath; all rooms have phone **FACILITIES** 2 sitting rooms, dining rooms, bar, billiards, garden, swimming pool, fishing lake

CREDIT CARDS AE, MC, V
CHILDREN accepted
DISABLED 1 suitable bedroom
PETS accepted
CLOSED early Jan to mid-Mar
MANAGER Mme Ledanois

THE NORTH-WEST

LA ROCHE-BERNARD

✳ AUBERGE BRETONNE ✳
∽ TOWN RESTAURANT-WITH-ROOMS ∽

2 place Duguesclin, 56130 La Roche-Bernard (Morbihan)
TEL 02 99 90 60 28 **FAX** 02 99 90 85 00 **E-MAIL** jacques.thorel@wanadoo.fr
WEBSITE www.relaischateaux.aubbretonne

IF YOU COME TO LA ROCHE-BERNARD from the west, you reach it by crossing a
dizzyingly high bridge over the Brière estuary which takes you into this
partly medieval town. Auberge Bretonne is in the middle, overlooking what
might pass for a town square if it were two or three times bigger. It has
been owned and run by Solange and Jacques Thorel since 1980, and their
priorities are quite simple: offer the finest and rarest wines they can find,
the best possible food to accompany them and then a really comfortable
bed for the night. Hardly surprising, then, that the *auberge* has built up a
wide and dedicated following.

The dining room, pale yellow sponged walls and cool tiled floor, stretches round a little vegetable garden with lettuce, cabbage and onions ready
for the kitchen. Jacques Thorel's cooking is sublime: mackerel pickled
with ginger; a feather light beetroot mousse; *coquilles St-Jacques*
sprinkled with chopped truffles until invisible and then covered with fresh
cream of asparagus; sea bass virtually unadorned; *brochette* of duck served
with dates; strawberries and cream – except the cream turns out to be a
weightless elderflower froth. The wine list is exceptional and although
some of the prices look heavy, you are being offered vintages no longer
available on the open market.

NEARBY Redon (32 km); Château de Rochefort-en-Terre.
LOCATION in the centre of town; car parking
FOOD breakfast, lunch, dinner **PRICE** €€€€ **ROOMS** 8 double and twin with bath;
all rooms have phone, TV **FACILITIES** sitting area, restaurant **CREDIT CARDS** AE, DC,
MC, V **CHILDREN** accepted **DISABLED** 1 specially adapted room **PETS** accepted
CLOSED 2 weeks Jan, early Nov
to early Dec; restaurant Thurs
and lunch Mon, Tues and Fri
PROPRIETORS Solange and
Jacques Thorel

THE NORTH-WEST

ST-ANDRE-D'HEBERTOT

✳ AUBERGE DU PRIEURE ✳
∽ COUNTRY HOTEL ∽

St-André-d'Hébertot, 14130 Pont-l'Evêque (Calvados)
TEL 02 31 64 03 03 **FAX** 02 31 64 16 66

THE MILLETS HAVE EXTENDED their country home so vigorously over the last few years we can't help worrying that they might spoil their retreat simply by being too enterprising.

The former 13thC priory, built of pale stone beneath a steep slate roof, has made a delicious little hotel. Inside, it is all beams, stone walls, country antiques and earthy colours. There is a surprisingly big dining room, with a black-and-white stone-flagged floor and heavy wood tables gleaming with polish. At one end, there are easy chairs before an open fire. On the first floor, a cosy sitting room offers books and board games; next door is a billiard room. Bedrooms in the main house are full of character, and attic rooms are no less spacious than those on the first floor, although rather dark. An annexe accommodates about half the rooms (not sound-proofed), but was 'tired and run-down' according to our most recent report. Outside, a lush garden is surrounded by Norman orchards and meadows, and features a neat heated pool. Traditional food is prepared by Mme Millet and offers one mid-priced menu and a more expansive *carte*. 'Good value accommodation; stiffly-priced dinner,' says a reporter.

∽

NEARBY Pont-l'Evêque (7 km); Honfleur (15 km); Deauville (20 km).
LOCATION by church in village, S of N175, E of Pont-l'Évêque; car parking
FOOD breakfast, lunch, dinner
PRICE €
ROOMS 12 double and twin, all with bath or shower; all rooms have phone, TV,
hairdrier **FACILITIES** sitting room, dining room, billiard room, library, garden,
swimming pool **CREDIT CARDS** MC, V **CHILDREN** welcome

DISABLED ground-floor rooms
available
PETS accepted
CLOSED never; restaurant Wed
PROPRIETORS M. and Mme
Millet

THE NORTH-WEST

ST-PIERRE-DU-VAUVRAY

HOSTELLERIE SAINT-PIERRE
~ RIVERSIDE HOTEL ~

chemin des Amoureux, 27430 St-Pierre-du-Vauvray (Eure)
TEL 02 32 59 93 29 **FAX** 02 32 59 41 93
E-MAIL stpierre@free.fr

'**P**ERFECT FOR A SHORT BREAK,' says one report on this unusual hotel on the banks of the Seine. Could be; we've always seen it as an ideal stopover – consistently well run, and located only a short drive from the Paris-Rouen motorway. It is a bizarre concoction: a modern building, triangular in plan with a turret on one corner, half-timbered like a traditional Norman manor house. It sounds naff, but don't dismiss it.

Not the least of the attractions is the cuisine – classical in style but inventive and light in approach, and of excellent quality, with the emphasis on fish and seafood – witness the enormous tank of *langoustes* and other consumables dominating the heavily decorated dining room (which has big picture windows looking on to the river). The hotel's other public areas are limited, and solid rather than elegant – the baroque/rococo decoration does not suit all tastes – but the bedrooms are comfortable and well equipped, and many have balconies overlooking the river. (For the full flavour of this eccentric establishment, opt for the top room in the turret, with exposed beams and token four-poster.) The garden, which stretches down to the water's edge, is a relaxing place to sit. The hotel is family run; service is friendly.

~

NEARBY Acquigny (10 km); Gaillon (15 km); Giverny (30 km)
LOCATION on edge of the village 8 km E of Louviers, beside Seine; car parking
FOOD breakfast, lunch, dinner
PRICES €€
ROOMS 14; 10 double, 4 twin, all with bath; all rooms have phone, TV; most have minibar
FACILITIES sitting room, dining room, lift, garden **CREDIT CARDS** MC, V
CHILDREN accepted
DISABLED access possible
PETS accepted
CLOSED early Jan to mid-Mar, mid-Nov to late Dec; restaurant Tues lunch
PROPRIETORS Potier family

THE NORTH-WEST

ST-QUENTIN-SUR-LE-HOMME

LE GUE DU HOLME
~ VILLAGE RESTAURANT-WITH-ROOMS ~

14 rue des Estuaires, 50220 St-Quentin-sur-le-Homme (Manche)
TEL 02 33 60 63 76 **FAX** 02 33 60 06 77
E-MAIL gue.holme@wanadoo.fr **WEBSITE** www.le-gue-du-holme.com

IF YOU ARE IN SEARCH of somewhere spectacular, look elsewhere. But if you
want a comfortable place to stay near Mont-St-Michel, to avoid the
crowds, and to get a taste of what real Norman cooking is all about – then
here is your spot. Michel and Annie Leroux (he is the chef) own and run
this spic-and-span restaurant-with-rooms opposite the church in the little
village of St-Quentin. She prides herself on always being the first to open
the doors in the morning and the last to lock up at night; he prides himself
(justifiably) on his devotion to local produce from field, river or, above all,
the sea. On the menu you will find lobster, turbot, bass and most of their
friends and relations, all treated with a light hand to make sure that they
are not robbed of their flavour. The wine list makes just as good reading as
the menu.

The restaurant itself greets you with soft, warm colours, gentle lighting,
starched white linen and fresh flowers. Most of the bedrooms are in a
newer wing, good-sized and furnished in an uncluttered modern style.
These are away from the road and look over a pretty, quiet garden filled
with roses where breakfast is served in summer.

~

NEARBY Mont-St-Michel (22 km); Avranches (5 km).
LOCATION in the village; car parking
FOOD breakfast, lunch, dinner
PRICE €
ROOMS 10; 6 double, 3 twin, all with bath, 1 triple with shower; all rooms have
phone, TV, hairdrier
FACILITIES sitting room, bar, restaurant, garden
CREDIT CARDS AE, DC, MC, V
CHILDREN accepted
DISABLED 1 specially adapted room **PETS** accepted
CLOSED hotel and restaurant Jan; hotel Sun dinner Oct to mid-Apr; restaurant Fri
and Sat lunch Oct to mid-Apr
PROPRIETORS Annie and Michel Leroux

THE NORTH-WEST

HOTEL DE FRANCE ET DES FUCHSIAS
∼ SEASIDE TOWN HOTEL ∼

20 rue Marechal Foch, 50550 St-Vaast-la-Hougue (Manche)
TEL 02 33 54 42 26 **FAX** 02 33 43 46 79
E-MAIL france-fuchsias@wanadoo.fr **WEBSITE** www.france-fuchsias.com

'THE GARDEN IS STILL in good order, as are the fuchsias, and the conservatory where we ate memorable, beautifully presented food is very enticing; friendly and efficient staff.' So says a reporter, confirming that the essential attractions of this perennially popular halt for Cherbourg ferry passengers (French and British alike) are unchanged.

The emphasis is on the restaurant; and the expressions of delight at the superb seafood platters, or the wonderfully presented produce from the Brix family farm, prove that the customers are happy, although one ultra critical and well-travelled couple recently found the food good but unexceptional. The wine list offers plenty of half bottles and good-value options, the service is friendly and efficient, the atmosphere warm − whether in the cosy dining room or in the conservatory, decorated by a local *décorateur anglais*.

At the far end of the delightful English-style garden, where free chamber music concerts are held on the last ten days of August, is the hotel's annexe. Here bedrooms are more spacious and more stylishly decorated than the fairly simple ones in the main part of the hotel. A suite sleeping two or three people and a ground-floor bedroom have been created.

∼

NEARBY Normandy beaches; Barfleur (12 km); Cherbourg (29 km).
LOCATION in quiet street near fishing port and marina; car parking on street
FOOD breakfast, lunch, dinner
PRICE €
ROOMS 33; 32 double, 1 suite, all with bath or shower; all rooms have phone, TV
FACILITIES sitting room, restaurant, garden
CREDIT CARDS AE, DC, MC, V
CHILDREN welcome
DISABLED access possible
PETS tolerated
CLOSED early Jan to late Feb, Mon mid-May to mid-Sep
PROPRIETOR Mme Brix

THE NORTH-WEST

STE-ANNE-LA-PALUD

HOTEL DE LA PLAGE
~ SEASIDE HOTEL ~

boulevard Ste-Barbe, Ste-Anne-la-Palud, 29127 Plonévez-Porzay (Finistère)
TEL 02 98 92 50 12 **FAX** 02 98 92 56 54
E-MAIL laplage@relaischateaux.fr **WEBSITE** www.relaischateaux.fr/laplage

A SEASIDE HOTEL INDEED – metres from the shore, with a vast strand of pale sand just next door. But this is far from being a bucket-and-spade holiday hotel. Although prices might not be quite so high as those of many fellow Relais et Châteaux members, they have gone up recently and are now firmly in our top bracket – way beyond the range of most people's summer-fortnight-with-the-kids budget. And although children are welcome, as usual in France, there are no special facilities for them.

It's as a place for relaxing, pampering breaks with an outdoors element that the Plage wins a place here. The hotel combines its splendid, peaceful seaside setting – plus attractive pool and tennis court – with one of the best kitchens in Brittany (specializing, of course, in seafood), which earns a star from Michelin. Within the manicured grounds is a bar in a separate thatched cottage. Mme Le Coz and her staff generate a welcoming atmosphere; service is sometimes a little slow but always friendly, and details are not overlooked. Bedrooms are comfortable, even if they do tend towards traditional French styles of decoration, and some have stunning views (worth booking ahead).

~

NEARBY Locronan (10 km); Quimper (25 km).
LOCATION in countryside 4 km W of Plonévez; car parking
FOOD breakfast, lunch, dinner
PRICE €€€€
ROOMS 26; 10 double,10 twin, 2 single, 4 family, all with bath; all rooms have TV, phone, minibar
FACILITIES sitting room, dining room, bar, conference room, lift, sauna, garden, swimming pool, tennis
CREDIT CARDS AE, DC, MC, V
CHILDREN welcome
DISABLED access possible
PETS accepted
CLOSED mid-Nov to Apr; restaurant Tues lunch Sep-Jun
PROPRIETOR M. Le Coz

THE NORTH-WEST

AUBERGE DU TERROIR
~ VILLAGE INN ~

Le Bourg, 50170 Servon (Manche)
TEL 02 33 60 17 92 **FAX** 02 33 60 35 26

IF YOU NEED TO STAY somewhere quiet and simple near Mont-St-Michel, and want to avoid the ugly rash of modern-box hotels that have sprung up within sight of the causeway, then leave the N175 to the east of Pontorson and go into Servon. Here you will find Auberge du Terroir, recommended to us by Annie Leroux who runs Le Gué du Holme (see page 55), and you'll be greeted warmly either by Annie or Thierry Lefort.

In Servon the front of each house faces into the village and their back gardens look out over open countryside. The *auberge* occupies two distinct houses: one is the old school house which contains three very satisfactory bedrooms (the one on the ground floor being properly equipped for handi-capped guests), and a reading room advertised with total honesty 'for those Norman days' (ie when the rain is coming down in torrents); the other house has a rather un-Gallic Presbyterian history, and now contains a charming restaurant and three more bedrooms.

The garden, with tennis court, is large enough for the most energetic children. Another bonus is the drive from here to Mont-St-Michel, on back roads virtually all the way.

~

NEARBY Mont-St-Michel (8 km); Avranches (15 km).
LOCATION in village 1 km N of N175 between Pontorson and Précey; car parking
FOOD breakfast, lunch, dinner
PRICE €
ROOMS 6; 5 double, 1 twin, all with bath or shower; all rooms have TV, phone
FACILITIES sitting room, restaurant, terrace, garden, tennis
CREDIT CARDS MC, V
CHILDREN accepted
DISABLED 1 specially adapted room
PETS accepted
CLOSED Feb, late Nov to early Dec
PROPRIETORS Thierry and Annie Lefort

THE NORTH-WEST

MANOIR DE LAN KERELLEC
~ MANOR HOUSE HOTEL ~

22560 Trébeurden (Côtes d'Armor)
TEL 02 96 15 47 47 **FAX** 02 96 23 66 88 **E-MAIL** lankerellec@relaischateaux.fr
WEBSITE www.integra.fr/relaischateaux/lankerellec

L AN KERELLEC IS A GEM. Quietly situated on a wooded promontory to the west of Lannion, it is sheltered from the open sea by its own archipelago of shoals, rocks and islets that curves round it on all three sides. Not content with this stunning position, which guarantees each and every room a view of the sea, it has style as well. Gilles and Luce Daubé started the hotel in 1981 with seven rooms. Since then it has been gradually and sympathetically extended, and the quality of the decoration and furnishings raised. Oriental rugs vie with one another for floor space in the public rooms, even in the conservatory where little groups of immaculately upholstered chairs wait in convivial groups. The timbered roof of the restaurant looks like an upturned boat: come here in winter and you can dine by an open fire and drink your coffee in the *salon* by another one. Winter or summer, you will have been superbly fed and almost certainly have found plenty to tempt you on the wine list.

The fashionably decorated bedrooms all have their fair allocation of fine antiques. They start at a reasonable size and get bigger as they become more expensive. If you are thinking of upgrading a bathroom at home, bring a camera and a notebook: the bathrooms here are superb. One even has the bath positioned so you can enjoy the view.

~

NEARBY Perros-Guirec (15 km); Tréguier (30 km).
LOCATION on promontory just S of resort, overlooking sea; car parking
FOOD breakfast, lunch, dinner
PRICE €€€€-€€€€€
ROOMS 19; 8 double, 11 twin, all with bath; all rooms have phone, TV, minibar, safe
FACILITIES sitting rooms, conservatory, dining room, bar, room, terrace, garden
CREDIT CARDS AE, DC, MC, V **CHILDREN** welcome
DISABLED some suitable rooms **PETS** accepted
CLOSED mid-Nov to mid-Mar
PROPRIETORS Gilles and Luce Daubé

THE NORTH-WEST

TREBEURDEN

✳ TI AL-LANNEC ✳
◞ SEASIDE HOTEL ◟

allée de Mezo-Guen, BP 3, 22560 Trébeurden (Côtes d'Armor)
TEL 02 96 15 01 01 **FAX** 02 96 23 62 14 **E-MAIL** ti.al.lannec@wanadoo.fr
WEBSITE www.pro.wanadoo.fr/ti.al.lannec

HAPPY REPORTS ABOUT this handsome house on the 'pink granite' coast of Brittany suggest that the hotel manages to pamper while at the same time coping with the families who are drawn to this seaside holiday area.

The house stands high above the sea with a path down to the beach; its south-facing terrace has a splendid view over the bay of Lannion. It is a supremely comfortable hotel, with that elusive private-house feel. Bedrooms are thoughtfully decorated, light and airy but cosy, with fresh flowers and books, small tables and table lamps liberally used. Some have terraces or verandas. The dining room has the sea view, and is crisp and fresh with rich drapes and old stone walls. Antique and modern furnishings mix well in the comfortable sitting room, dotted with pot plants.

The house was completely renovated and opened as a hotel in 1978 by Gérard and Danielle Jouanny, and is run by them with a convincing blend of charm, taste and efficiency. Danielle's food is 'consistently delicious', the service 'five-star' and the welcome for children genuine – witness the swing and seesaw on the lawn.

NEARBY Perros-Guirec (15 km); Tréguier (30 km).
LOCATION in wooded grounds above resort, 10 km NW of Lannion; car parking
FOOD breakfast, lunch, dinner
PRICE €€€€-€€€€€
ROOMS 29; 20 double and twin, 2 single, 7 family, all with bath; all rooms have phone, TV
FACILITIES 2 sitting rooms, dining room, bar, billiards room, play room, beauty and fitness centre, lift, garden
CREDIT CARDS AE, MC, V **CHILDREN** welcome **DISABLED** some suitable rooms
PETS accepted
CLOSED mid-Nov to mid-Mar
PROPRIETORS Gérard and Danielle Jouanny

THE NORTH-WEST

LE CLOS
~ MANOR HOUSE HOTEL ~

98 rue de la Ferté-Vidame, 27130 Verneuil-sur-Avre (Eure)
TEL 02 32 32 21 81 **FAX** 02 32 32 21 36
E-MAIL leclos@relaischateaux.fr **WEBSITE** www.relaischateaux.fr/leclos

LE CLOS REMAINS one of our favourite upmarket French hotels – partly because it remains just affordable by ordinary mortals, but also because it avoids the pretension and vulgarity that afflict so many château-style places. A recent report supports this view.

The hotel is on the edge of the pleasant little country town of Verneuil, in a quiet back street – though with a busy bypass visible (and just audible) in the background. It is a rather comical turn-of-the-century building of highly patterned brickwork, with a mock-medieval tower, set in well-kept leafy grounds with lawns and creeping willows that are overlooked by a large terrace. Inside, everything is of the highest quality: smart, antique-style cane chairs, heavy linen tablecloths and huge bunches of flowers in the dining room, neat reproduction armchairs in the *salon*, chintzy drapes in the bedrooms, deep pile carpets everywhere – even in the luxurious bathrooms. The bedrooms are light and airy, and furnished in individual style. The kitchen wins no awards, but produces a range of classical dishes with absolute professionalism and finesse.

~

NEARBY Château de Pin au Haras; Evreux (39 km); Chartres (56 km).
LOCATION on southern edge of town; car parking
FOOD breakfast, lunch, dinner
PRICE €€
ROOMS 10; 4 double, 5 suites, 1 apartment, all with bath; all rooms have phone, TV
FACILITIES sitting room, 2 dining rooms, bar, garden, tennis
CREDIT CARDS AE, DC, MC, V
CHILDREN welcome
DISABLED no special facilities
PETS accepted
CLOSED mid-Dec to mid-Jan; restaurant Mon, except holiday periods
PROPRIETORS Patrick and Colette Simon

THE NORTH-WEST

AUBERGE DU VAL AU CESNE
~ COUNTRY INN ~

Le Val au Cesne, 76190 Yvetot (Seine-Maritime)
TEL 02 35 56 63 06 **FAX** 02 35 56 92 78 **E-MAIL** val-au-cesne@aol.com
WEBSITE www.pageszoom.com/val-au-cesne

IN A QUIET WOODED VALLEY this half-timbered inn springs out at you from an otherwise unremarkable roadside, looking slightly as if the Norman builder had suddenly developed Swiss leanings. It started life as a restaurant, but as its popularity grew Jérôme Carel eventually created five boldly, almost alarmingly, decorated bedrooms. The maid who showed them off to us was particularly delighted by the way the bathroom furniture varied in colour to match the scheme of each bedroom. All in a separate building from the restaurant, four bedrooms are on the ground floor, a kind thought for those for whom stairs might become a challenge after dinner. The largest, which has its own outside staircase to the first floor, has more natural light than the others.

Cats, dogs, ducks, parakeets and prize poultry compare lengthy pedigrees with one another in the flower-filled garden, while inside are beams, log fires in winter, acres of family photos and a cuisine which is both regional and seasonal. A modestly priced *Logis de France* menu is always available too. The original snug dining room flows round a stone chimney breast into another room, and recently space on the first floor has been brought into play to extend the seating capacity of the restaurant.

~

NEARBY Rouen (30 km); Honfleur (67 km); Côte d'Albâtre.
LOCATION 3 km SE of Yvetot on the D5 to Fréville; car parking
FOOD breakfast, lunch, dinner
PRICE €
ROOMS 5 twin with bath; all rooms have phone, TV, hairdrier
FACILITIES bar, restaurant, terrace, garden
CREDIT CARDS AE, DC, MC, V
CHILDREN accepted
DISABLED 1 ground-floor room
PETS accepted
CLOSED never; restaurant Mon, Tues
PROPRIETOR Jérôme Carel

THE NORTH-WEST

BAYEUX

✳ HOTEL D'ARGOUGES ✳

TOWN MANSION

21 rue St-Patrice, 14400 Bayeux (Calvados)
TEL 02 31 92 88 86
FAX 02 31 92 69 16
E-MAIL dargouges@aol.com
FOOD breakfast **PRICE** €€
ROOMS 25
CLOSED never

THE ARGOUGES IS A classically proportioned town house removed from the street – and the hurly-burly of tapestry watchers – in its own courtyard. Now an efficiently run bed-and-breakfast, rooms vary in size but are all decorated in quiet good taste and, for the most part, have larger than average bathrooms. Guests can use a smart, light drawing room and the garden at the back. This is a real oasis in which to relax after a hard day's touring or to lay plans for the day over breakfast. Last but not least, if you arrive by car you will appreciate the value of the hotel's off-street parking.

Book through our travel service – see page 7.

LE MONT-ST-MICHEL

AUBERGE SAINT-PIERRE

TOWN HOTEL

BP16, Grande Rue, 50116 Le Mont-St-Michel (Manche)
TEL 02 33 60 14 03
FAX 02 33 48 59 82
WEBSITE www.mont-st-michel-hotel.com **FOOD** breakfast, lunch, dinner **PRICE** €€ **ROOMS** 21
CLOSED never

MONT-ST-MICHEL'S CROWDS are thinner in the morning and evening, so it makes some sense to stay on the Mont itself, and the 15thC Auberge St-Pierre is one of a handful of hotels at its foot. It is close to the causeway, which is useful since all cars have to be left outside the walls and bags carried in. There is a large and busy restaurant at street level, where breakfast is served; but once on the first floor a pleasantly rustic calm takes over. Bear in mind, if you take a room in the annexe, that you will have many more stairs to climb than in the main building.

THE NORTH-WEST

AUX POMMIERS-DE-LIVAYE

COUNTRY GUESTHOUSE

14340 Notre-Dame-de-Livaye (Calvados)
TEL 02 31 63 01 28 **FAX** 02 31 63 73 63 **FOOD** breakfast, dinner by arrangement **PRICE** € **ROOMS** 5
CLOSED mid-Dec to mid-Mar

IT WOULD BE DIFFICULT to beat the welcome that Germain and Marie-Josette Lambert-Dutrait give guests to their 300-year-old black-and-white Norman farmhouse. She was born in the house, and her choice of decoration is in keeping with its age. As you walk inside, you are struck by the rich gleam of the timbers, the jars and pots arranged in ranks on shelves and the hanging bunches of dried flowers and herbs. Bedrooms are rustic, decked in pink and green, with iron bedsteads.

The generous breakfast and dinner are both served on an enclosed veranda looking out over the fields; menus tend to be a collaboration between the Lambert-Dutraits and their guests.

✳ LE MANOIR DU RODOIR ✳

MANOR HOUSE HOTEL

route de Nantes, Nivillac, 56130 La Roche-Bernard (Morbihan)
TEL 02 99 90 82 68
FAX 02 99 90 76 22 **E-MAIL** manoir.rodoir@wanadoo.fr
FOOD breakfast, lunch, dinner
PRICE €€ **ROOMS** 24
CLOSED never

JEANINE AND DENIS SETTEMBRE'S hotel is a favourite with golfers; they have arranged discounts for their guests at Savenay, La Baule (not high summer), St Laurent, La Bretesche and Caden and will even book tee times for them.

Housed in a long stone building on the outskirts of town, high above a river and looking across to woods, Manoir du Rodoir offers practical well-sized rooms with neat modern furnishings, a busy bar and a modest restaurant with a short, changing menu. Good value. *Book through our travel service – see page 7.*

ILE-DE-FRANCE

HOTELS IN THE ILE-DE-FRANCE

IN THIS SECTION we combine Paris and the surrounding *départements* of Ile-de-France because, for many visitors, they are both parts of the same picture. If you're passing through the area and need a stopover, your instinct will probably be to stay outside the city; but if you're bent on a sightseeing holiday or a romantic break you will probably want to be in the heart of things. However, this is not always true: an overnight stop in Paris can work perfectly well, and a rural base for city sightseeing can be very restful.

Paris is a compact city – much more so than London, for example – and for many visitors choice of location is not critical (from the convenience point of view) unless you intend to spend a great deal of time in one place (the Louvre, say).

From the point of view of atmosphere and charm, location can make a great difference. It pays to know something about the districts (*arrondissements*) that make up the city. The one-digit or two-digit number at the end of Paris postcodes is the number of the *arrondissement*. Thus 75006 is the 6th, for example.

The *arrondissements* are numbered in a clockwise spiral starting in the centre on the Right Bank of the Seine (the northern bank). You will mainly be interested in the first turn of the spiral.

The 1st is an upmarket area extending from the place de la Concorde past the Louvre to Les Halles; we have a couple of entries here. We have none in the 2nd and only one in the 3rd to the east (the luxurious and very expensive Pavillon de la Reine on page 81). But the spiral then turns back towards the Seine, and we have a number of entries in the 4th – in the revitalized Marais, east of the Pompidou Centre, including the original and excellent value Hôtel de Nice (page 79) – and on the alluring little Ile Saint-Louis, where the glossy Hôtel du Jeu de Paume (page 77) is one of a sprinkling of hotels along the main street.

Across the river, the 5th, 6th and 7th make up the Left Bank, with the Boulevard St-Germain its main axis. Between the Jardin des Plantes in the east and the Eiffel Tower in the west, there are more charming small hotels than anywhere else. In the 5th, the Parc St-Séverin contains our favourite bedroom in the city (page 80), and the Degrés de Notre-Dame is a useful, traditional restaurant (page 73). In the 6th and the 7th, our entries range from the chic and pricey (Duc de St-Simon (page 74) and Le Relais St-Germain (page 83) to the down-to-earth and reasonably priced St-Paul (page 86). The spiral then crosses the river again to bring you to the 8th, the Champs Elysées area.

Outside this first central spiral, our other entries are to the north, in the 9th (the Chopin, page 89 – a real find); the 17th (the charming Hôtel de Banville, page 71); and the 18th (Montmartre), where the Ermitage (page 75) is a delightful, if different, choice. For even wider coverage, see our *Charming Small Hotel Guide to Paris*.

Outside Paris, our Ile-de-France recommendations are in Dampierre to the west, in Barbizon and Flagy to the south, and in Germigny-L'Evêque to the east; all within an hour's drive of the capital.

ILE-DE-FRANCE

AUBERGE DU CHATEAU
~ VILLAGE INN ~

1 Grande Rue, 78720 Dampierre (Yvelines)
TEL 01 30 47 56 56 **FAX** 01 30 52 56 95

A TRADITIONAL INN with a calm, prosperous atmosphere which stands in the centre of a stone-built country village. The building dates back to 1650 and has always been a hostelry, probably putting up visitors to the Duc de Luynes, an influential figure in the time of Louis XIII, whose elegant château and surrounding park lie across the road. His descendants still live there.

The layout of the *auberge* bears witness to its age: floors rise and fall at will, there are low-slung beams at every turn, and rickety wooden staircases lead to the bedrooms. These are spacious and decorated in matching floral wallpapers and curtains; the ones at the front have a view of the château and its park; those at the rear overlook the hotel's small garden. Some have stone floors and marble-clad bathrooms. Part of the beamed dining room reaches out to a conservatory-style extension which runs along the front of the building, opening on to a roadside terrace.

Dampierre lies in the heart of the Parc Naturel de la Haute Vallée de Chevreuse, a lovely rural area which seems very far from Paris but is, in fact, only half an hour away by car. Also nearby are châteaux worth visiting, as well as walking and pony trekking.

~

NEARBY Versailles; Montfort l'Amaury.
LOCATION opposite the Château de Dampierre, 36 km SW of Paris, 16 km NE of Rambouillet; car parking
FOOD breakfast, lunch, dinner
PRICE €€
ROOMS 20 double and twin, all with bath; all rooms have phone, TV
FACILITIES sitting room, dining room, terrace, garden
CREDIT CARDS AE, MC, V **CHILDREN** accepted
DISABLED not suitable
PETS accepted
CLOSED hotel never; restaurant Sun dinner, Mon
MANAGER M. Blot

ILE-DE-FRANCE

HOSTELLERIE DU MOULIN
~ CONVERTED MILL ~

2 rue du Moulin, 77940 Flagy (Seine-et-Marne)
TEL 01 60 96 67 89 **FAX** 01 60 96 69 51

OVER THE YEARS, since its inclusion in our first edition, we have received a steady flow of readers' reports approving of this imaginatively converted flour mill an hour from Paris.

The setting, with tables in the grassy garden beside the stream that still gently turns the mill wheel, is idyllic, and creates a blissfully soporific effect. Beyond the neat gardens you look out on to cultivated fields which, until the 1950s, supplied the grain that was milled here. The heavy beams, wheels and pulleys of the mill dominate the cosy sitting room, and the bedrooms, named after cereals, are as quirkily captivating as you would hope in a building of this character; space is at a premium, and low beams lead some guests to move about with a permanent stoop.

The chef specializes mainly in traditional dishes, and the menu and *carte* have English translations, underlying the Moulin's popularity with British travellers. Claude Scheidecker is a charming and friendly host who gives his little hotel, which he has been running for more than 20 years, an exceptionally welcoming atmosphere. And he still manages to keep his prices admirably low.

~

NEARBY Fontainebleau (23 km); Sens cathedral (40 km).
LOCATION in village, 23 km SE of Fontainebleau, 10 km W of Montereau; car parking
FOOD breakfast, lunch, dinner
PRICE (€)
ROOMS 10; 7 double, 3 family, all with bath; all rooms have phone
FACILITIES sitting room, dining room, bar, garden, fishing
CREDIT CARDS AE, DC, MC, V
CHILDREN accepted
DISABLED access difficult
PETS accepted
CLOSED hotel 2 weeks Sep, late Dec to late Jan; restaurant Sun dinner, Mon (except Easter and Whitsun: Mon dinner, Tues)
PROPRIETOR Claude Scheidecker

ILE-DE-FRANCE

HOTEL DE L'ABBAYE
~ TOWN HOTEL ~

10 rue Cassette, 75006 Paris
TEL 01 45 44 38 11 **FAX** 01 45 48 07 86
E-MAIL hotel.abbaye@wanadoo.fr **WEBSITE** www.hotel-abbaye.com

IF WE GAVE AWARDS, this gorgeous hotel would be a very strong contender. Indeed, we find it hard to fault, with the single caveat that the standard bedrooms are fairly small (and feel even smaller compared to the spaciousness of the public rooms); you would do well to upgrade to a larger room if you can afford it. One room on the ground floor has its own terrace, as do the four duplex apartments. You need to book well in advance.

The moment we walked into this skilfully converted former abbey, we felt calmed and cosseted. The hotel has a reputation for attentive yet unobtrusive service which it justly deserves: the courteous staff seem genuinely eager to help. The public rooms are inviting yet chic, newly decorated and filled with fresh flowers, with several sitting areas, the sofas and armchairs attractively upholstered in floral or striped fabrics, lit by huge table lamps; in cool weather there's an open fire. The conservatory-style breakfast room/bar must be one of the most alluring in Paris, with walls covered in trellis and French doors which overlook a large courtyard garden complete with fountain. Here you can have breakfast or a drink in warm weather. Worth every penny.

~

NEARBY Jardin du Luxembourg; St-Sulpice.
LOCATION close to junction with rue de Meziers
FOOD breakfast
PRICE €€€€
ROOMS 42 double and twin, all with bath, 4 duplex apartments; all rooms have phone, TV, air conditioning, hairdrier
FACILITIES 2 sitting rooms, breakfast room/bar, courtyard garden
CREDIT CARDS AE, MC, V
CHILDREN accepted
DISABLED 2 rooms on ground floor
PETS not accepted
CLOSED never
PROPRIETORS M. and Mme Lafortune

ILE-DE-FRANCE

PARIS

HOTEL D'ANGLETERRE
~ TOWN HOTEL ~

44 rue Jacob, 75006 Paris
Tel 01 42 60 34 72 **Fax** 01 42 60 16 93
E-MAIL anglotel@wanadoo.fr

ONE OF THE MOST PEACEFUL, comforting and gracious small hotels in Paris, the Angleterre has a faintly English air, befitting a building which was once the British Embassy. In 1783, Benjamin Franklin refused to enter it to sign the Treaty of Paris because he considered it to be British soil. Had he done so, he would have found well-proportioned rooms, fine mantle-pieces, a beautiful staircase with *trompe l'oeil* murals and a lovely court-yard garden.

The feeling of spacious calm in the recently renovated public rooms is echoed in the bedrooms, which are all roomy, elegant and comfortable, often with splendid bathrooms. One guest reports a de luxe room with one of the largest hotel bathrooms he had seen, all marbled and mirrored glamour, based on one in the London Ritz. Another bathroom has a charming hand-painted suite, with the basin set into a wood and tiled washstand. A couple report that they stayed in the hotel's smallest room – normally let out as a single, but with a double bed so that two can share if they wish. Their verdict? Despite the size, they were happy to enjoy the hotel's benefits at a modest price. Their only quibble: the nose-in-air attitude of the receptionists, though not the manageress.

~

Nearby blvd St-Germain; Musée d'Orsay; Louvre.
Location in the stretch of rue Jacob between rue Bonaparte and rue des Sts-Pères
Food breakfast
Price €€€€-€€€€€
Rooms 24 double and twin, either small, standard or de luxe, all with bath, 3 apartments; all rooms have phone, TV, air conditioning, hairdrier, safe
Facilities sitting room, breakfast room, bar, courtyard garden, lift to some rooms only **Credit cards** AE, DC, MC, V **Children** accepted
Disabled no special facilities
Pets not accepted
Closed never
Manager Mme Michèle Blouin

ILE-DE-FRANCE

PARIS

✳ HOTEL D'AUBUSSON ✳
⌇ TOWN HOTEL ⌇

33 rue Dauphine, 75006 Paris
TEL 01 43 29 43 43 **FAX** 01 43 29 12 62
E-MAIL reservationherve@hoteldaubusson.com **WEBSITE** www.hoteldaubusson.com

WHEN OUR INSPECTOR arrived here on a chilly January afternoon, she was greeted by a log fire crackling in the huge grate, focal point of the sitting room, and a warm welcome from the staff. The go-ahead manager, Pascal Gimel, is committed to offering faultless service while keeping prices at a reasonable level. The hotel occupies a 17thC town house, built of honey-coloured stone and arranged around a large courtyard. A huge pair of double doors, formally a coach entrance, lead from the street into the airy lobby. To the right, Café Laurent – in various incarnations – has attracted the literati and glitterati since 1690, from Voltaire to Brigitte Bardot. Today's crowd are regularly entertained by a pianist. Of the sitting room, our inspector said, '...my favourite in Paris. It manages to be cosy despite its grand proportions'. It has a high-beamed ceiling, Versailles parquet floor and pretty furniture. Appropriately, two Aubusson tapestries hang in the breakfast room next door.

The bedrooms cocoon their inhabitants behind heavy doors in silence and restrained luxury. The most expensive are massive and beamed, but even the smallest are large by local standards.

NEARBY blvd St-Germain; Ile de la Cité; Latin Quarter.
LOCATION corner of rue Christine; car parking
FOOD breakfast, light meals; 24 hr room service
PRICE €€€€
ROOMS 49 double and twin, all with bath; all rooms have phone, TV, air conditioning, minibar, hairdrier, safe **FACILITIES** sitting room, breakfast room, café/bar, courtyard garden, lift **CREDIT CARDS** AE, DC, MC, V

CHILDREN accepted
DISABLED 2 specially adapted rooms
PETS accepted
CLOSED never
MANAGER Pascal Gimel

ILE-DE-FRANCE

✳ HOTEL DE BANVILLE ✳
~ TOWN HOTEL ~

166 blvd Berthier, 75017 Paris
TEL 01 42 67 70 16 **FAX** 01 44 40 42 77
E-MAIL hotelbanville@wanadoo.fr **WEBSITE** www.hotelbanville.fr

THIS 1930s TOWN HOUSE hotel offers an attractive combination of style, comfort and middle-of-the-road prices. Convenient, too, for motorists: finding your way from the Périphérique to boulevard Berthier is easy, and parking is not impossible.

The airy Art Deco building – the work of a celebrated architect, we're told – looks promising, and does not disappoint. Inside, all is tastefully decorated and comfortable, bordering on the luxurious. There is an elegantly furnished sitting area/bar, where a pianist occasionally plays in the evening. Another welcoming sitting room, with antique pieces as well as comfy sofas (which can be closed off for meetings), puts the Banville comfortably ahead of the Parisian norm in this important respect.

Murals create a garden effect in the breakfast room. The bedrooms are attractively decorated in individual styles, with thoughtfully chosen fabrics and antiques dotted throughout. Fresh flowers add a reassuring personal touch, as do such small services as having your bed turned down – a rare thing in the city nowadays. Staff are extremely friendly, and we suspect that this hotel would be far more expensive if it were on the Left Bank.

NEARBY Arc de Triomphe; Champs-Elysées; Palais des Congrès.
LOCATION on service road off blvd Berthier, between rue A. Samain and rue de Courcelles
FOOD breakfast
PRICE €€€ **ROOMS** 42; 39 double and twin, 2 triple, 1 family room, all with bath or shower; all rooms have phone, TV, air conditioning, hairdrier, safe **FACILITIES** sitting area/bar, sitting room, breakfast room, lift

CREDIT CARDS AE, MC, V
CHILDREN accepted
DISABLED no special facilities
PETS accepted
CLOSED never
PROPRIETOR Mme Moreau

ILE-DE-FRANCE

✳ HOTEL DE LA BRETONNERIE ✳
~ TOWN HOTEL ~

22 Rue Ste-Croix-de-la-Bretonnerie, 75004 Paris
TEL 01 48 87 77 63 **FAX** 01 42 77 26 78
E-MAIL hotel@bretonnerie.com **WEBSITE** www.bretonnerie.com

A DISTINCTIVE 17THC TOWN HOUSE, converted with sympathy and style, which, though conveniently placed in the middle of the picturesque and (now) fashionable Marais district, is – as our inspector points out – 'in a rather scruffy street', a little too close to the rowdy atmosphere of the Pompidou Centre. Fortunately, she continues, 'once in the hotel, all is calm and peaceful'.

The exposed beams in the public areas and the upper bedrooms are echoed throughout the house by the sturdy hardwood furniture. The small basement breakfast and sitting rooms attempt a Medieval flavour, with stone-vaulted ceilings, iron light fittings, richly coloured fabrics and polished tiled floors. Considering the apparent size of the hotel, the bedrooms are surprisingly roomy, also comfortable and pretty, and every one is different; some are arranged with the beds on a mezzanine gallery with the 'downstairs' used as a small sitting area. All have a glossy modern bathroom and guests will find no lack of comfort. Good-humoured staff extend a warm welcome, and cope admirably with such crises as the sudden arrival of all their guests at the same time.

NEARBY Hôtel de Ville; Pompidou Centre; Les Halles.
LOCATION between rue des Archives and rue Vieille du Temple
FOOD breakfast
PRICE ⓔⓔ
ROOMS 30; 27 double and twin, 3 suites, all with bath; all rooms have phone, TV, minibar, hairdrier, safe
FACILITIES sitting area, breakfast room, lift

CREDIT CARDS MC, V
CHILDREN accepted
DISABLED no special facilities
PETS not accepted
CLOSED end Jul to end Aug
PROPRIETOR M. Sagot

ILE-DE-FRANCE

PARIS

DEGRES DE NOTRE-DAME
~ TOWN HOTEL AND RESTAURANT ~

10 rue des Grands Degrés, 75005 Paris
TEL 01 55 42 88 88 **FAX** 01 40 46 95 34

ALMOST ALL THE SMALL HOTELS of Paris are without a dining room. Here, however, is an exception – the kind of family-run establishment well known in the French countryside, but rarely found in the city: a restaurant with rooms. The building is charmingly sited on a little tree-filled square, and the restaurant has the feel of a simple *auberge*, serving correspondingly rustic food: nothing special, but honest. This is where guests also have breakfast (served at any time) which, assures the *patron* (who does not speak English), includes the freshest of bread, orange juice squeezed on the spot, and properly made coffee.

A steep wooden staircase (staff carry your bags), decorated with charming murals, leads to the bedrooms, which are good value: well equipped, with beamed ceilings and smart wooden furnishings. Some rooms have views over Notre-Dame; some are tiny; the ones at the front are the largest, most with triple windows on to the street; No. 24 is handsome, with an expansive desk in the centre. In contrast is the attic conversion, which swaps Gallic character for modern decoration, a private bar and a huge contoured bath. Recent readers' reports have been positive, though one warns against taking the 'grim' apartment in a nearby building also owned by M. Tahir.

~

NEARBY Notre-Dame; Musée de Cluny; Ile St-Louis.
LOCATION on tiny square at junction with rue Fréderic-Sauton, close to quai de Montebello
FOOD breakfast, lunch, dinner
PRICE €€
ROOMS 10 double, all with bath; all rooms have phone, TV, hairdrier; some rooms have minibar
FACILITIES restaurant, bar
CREDIT CARDS MC, V
CHILDREN accepted **DISABLED** not suitable **PETS** accepted
CLOSED never
PROPRIETOR M. Tahir

ILE-DE-FRANCE

PARIS

DUC DE SAINT-SIMON
~ TOWN HOTEL ~

14 rue de St-Simon, 75007 Paris
TEL 01 44 39 20 20 **Fax** 01 45 48 68 25
E-MAIL Hotel.Duc.De.Saint.Simon@wanadoo.fr

A STYLISH HOTEL ON A STYLISH STREET, just off the boulevard St-Germain. First glimpsed through two pairs of French windows beyond a pretty courtyard, the interior looks wonderfully inviting; and so it is – there is a warm, beautifully furnished *salon* with the distinctly private-house feel that the Swedish proprietor seeks to maintain, and elegant yet cosy bedrooms, all individually decorated with not a jarring note. The twin bedrooms are more spacious than doubles. Everywhere you look are rich fabrics, gloriously overstuffed pieces of furniture and cleverly conceived paint effects. The kilim-lined lift is a particularly original idea.

The white-painted 19thC house backs on to an 18thC building behind, also part of the hotel, with a tiny secret garden wedged in between. Breakfasts can be had in the courtyard or in the intimate cellar bar; service is smiling and courteous. But as the hotel's own brochure points out, there are two famous cafés (the Deux Magots and the Flore) only a few blocks away.

Prices are high, but not unreasonable, we felt, especially in comparison with other hotels in this category, and Gun Karin Lalisse, the manager, runs the hotel with great charm and efficiency.

NEARBY Invalides; Musée d'Orsay; Musée Rodin.
LOCATION between rue P. L. Courier and rue de Grenelle
FOOD breakfast, light meals
PRICE €€€€
ROOMS 34; 29 double and twin, 28 with bath, 1 with shower, 5 suites with bath; all rooms have phone, hairdrier, safe, TV on request; some rooms have air conditioning
FACILITIES 2 sitting rooms, bar, lift **CREDIT CARDS** AE, MC, V
CHILDREN accepted
DISABLED no special facilities
PETS not accepted **CLOSED** never
PROPRIETOR M. Lindqvist

ILE-DE-FRANCE

PARIS

✳ ERMITAGE ✳
∼ TOWN HOTEL ∼

24 rue Lamarck, 75018 Paris
TEL 01 42 64 79 22 **FAX** 01 42 64 10 33

W E WERE ENTRANCED when we found the Ermitage, tucked away behind Sacré-Coeur. Only a sober wall plaque announces that this is a hotel, the door opening on to a smart little gold and cream lobby, followed by a dark-blue hall with deep-red carpet strewn with rugs. From the reception you can see a charming kitchen with its *faience* stove from Lorraine (breakfast is prepared here and served in your room) and a little terrace beyond. Also on the ground floor: an old-fashioned parlour, with green velvet hangings, filled with antiques, photographs and ornaments. Par for the course so far, you may think, yet the Ermitage has a decorative surprise which starts in the hall and continues all the way up the stairs, on walls, doors, glass panels, skirtings. These are the charming, shadowy paint effects and murals of the artist Du Buc; the sketchy scenes of Montmartre were done in 1986 when he was an old man.

Eclectic and friendly, with an atmosphere of calm familiarity, the Ermitage is the creation of its endearing *patronne*. Bedrooms are by and large light and spacious, decorated with floral wallpapers, lace curtains and large *armoires*. Those on the ground floor benefit from the leafy terrace with views of eastern Paris. Bathrooms are tiny.

NEARBY Sacré-Coeur; Place du Tertre.
LOCATION at E end of rue Lamarck, close to Sacré-Coeur
FOOD breakfast
PRICE ⓔ **ROOMS** 12; 11 double and twin, 1 family room, 11 rooms have bath or mini bath; all rooms have phone, hairdrier
FACILITIES sitting room **CREDIT CARDS** not accepted **CHILDREN** accepted
DISABLED 2 rooms on ground floor
PETS accepted
CLOSED never
PROPRIETOR Maggie Canipel

✳ BOOK THIS HOTEL
✳ BOOK FERRY/EUROSTAR
✳ SAVE MONEY
TEL: (UK) 01892 55 98 66
e-mail: enquiries@chs-travelservice.com

ILE-DE-FRANCE

HOTEL DE FLEURIE
~ TOWN HOTEL ~

32 rue Grégoire-de-Tours, 75006 Paris
TEL 01 53 73 70 00 **FAX** 01 53 73 70 20
E-MAIL bonjour@hotel-de-fleurie.tm.fr **WEBSITE** www.hotel-de-fleurie.tm.fr

A MODEL HOTEL, rightly very popular, where charm, efficiency and up-to-date comforts go hand in hand. Renovated in the 1980s by the Marolleau family, who used to own the well-known Latin Quarter brasserie, Balzar, it combines an immaculate appearance (not least the pretty façade, elegantly lit at night, complete with statues in the niches) with a cosy, intimate feel. The hands-on owners – parents and two sons – are determined to keep it so, and the place always feels fresh, clean and well cared for.

Instantly eye-catching in the terracotta-tiled reception is a delightful *faience* stove picked up by Mme Marolleau in the flea market; the adjoining sitting room, with its exposed beams and section of ancient wall, has a discreet bar and little tables covered in Provençal cloths. The basement *cave*, where a generous breakfast is served, is equally cosy, cleverly lit by uplighters.

The spotless bedrooms do not disappoint. You will find pretty billowing curtains, walls of panelled wood and grasspaper, period style furniture, inviting beds and – a rare touch – fresh flowers. Bathrooms, all in pink-hued marble, are well equipped with thick towels on heated rails and towelling bathrobes.

~

NEARBY blvd St-Germain; St-Sulpice; Jardin du Luxembourg.
LOCATION between blvd St-Germain and rue des Quatres-Vents
FOOD breakfast
PRICE €€€€
ROOMS 29; 19 double and twin, 17 with bath, 2 with shower, 10 single, 5 with bath, 5 with shower; all rooms have phone, TV, air conditioning, minibar, hairdrier, safe
FACILITIES sitting room, bar, breakfast room, lift **CREDIT CARDS** AE, DC, MC, V
DISABLED no special facilities **PETS** not accepted
CLOSED never
PROPRIETORS Marolleau family

ILE-DE-FRANCE

PARIS

✳ HOTEL DU JEU DE PAUME ✳
∼ TOWN HOTEL ∼

54 rue St-Louis-en-l'Île, 75004 Paris
TEL 01 43 26 14 18 **FAX** 01 40 46 02 76
E-MAIL info@jeudepaumehotel.com **WEBSITE** www.hoteldujeudepaume.com

OF ALL THE HOTELS in the delightful rue St-Louis-en-l'Ile, this is the most original. Whereas the others are homely, the Jeu de Paume packs a stylish punch.

As its name implies, the building was the site of a 17thC *jeu de paume* court, built in the days when the 'palm game', forerunner to tennis, was all the rage; when the proprietors acquired it in the 1980s, however, it was a run-down warehouse. M. Prache is an architect and he wrought something of a miracle on the building, opening out the heart of it right up to the roof, exposing all the old timber construction and slinging mezzanine floors around a central well. The impression of light and transparency is reinforced by a glass-walled lift and glass balustrades around the upper floors. Stone walls and all those beams add a reasuringly rustic feel. The sitting area has the appearance of a sophisticated private apartment, with leather sofas, subtle lighting and handsome stone fireplace. Nearby, at the reception desk, the chic, laid-back staff coolly deal with the guests while a modish sheepdog called Enzo pads around.

Bedrooms are smallish, perfectly pleasant, but nothing like as exciting as the rest of the hotel.

∼

NEARBY Marais; Notre-Dame; Latin Quarter.
LOCATION halfway along the island's main street, near the junction with rue des Deux Ponts
FOOD breakfast **PRICE** €€€€ **ROOMS** 32, including suites and duplexes, all with bath and shower; all rooms have phone, TV, minibar, hairdrier **FACILITIES** breakfast room, sitting room, bar, 2 conference rooms, sauna, lift, courtyard garden **CREDIT CARDS** AE, DC, MC, V
CHILDREN accepted
DISABLED access difficult **PETS** accepted **CLOSED** never
PROPRIETORS M. and Mme Prache

ILE-DE-FRANCE

MANSART
~ TOWN HOTEL ~

5 rue des Capucines, 75001 Paris
TEL 01 42 61 50 28 **FAX** 01 49 27 97 44
E-MAIL hotel.mansart@wanadoo.fr **WEBSITE** www.esprit-de-france.com

A STONE'S THROW from the Ritz, spacious bedrooms which recall an earlier, more gracious era, attentive service, fair prices – these are the principal attributes of the excellent Mansart, now in the same ownership as several other Paris hotels, including the Parc St-Séverin (page 80).

When restored, the aged hotel's proportions were left mercifully intact. The large modern lobby, with its expanse of marble floor and walls boldly painted in geometric patterns based on Mansart's drawings for the gardens of Versailles (he was also architect of place Vendôme) is impressive, but it doesn't prepare you for the bedrooms, which you might expect to be similarly contemporary. In fact, though recently decorated, they have a dignified, old-fashioned flavour. We loved No. 205, which feels like a private flat with its own entrance hall opening on to a large room with antique mirrors and regal prints on the white walls, the panelling picked out in gold. All the rooms have new bathrooms, covered from floor to ceiling in Italian tiles, each in a different cheerful colour. A cheaper option, but equally stately, is No. 212, a huge room with large gilt-framed mirrors and panelled walls.

~

NEARBY place Vendôme; Opéra Garnier; Tuileries.
LOCATION on corner of place Vendôme
FOOD breakfast
PRICE €€€
ROOMS 57; 53 double and twin, 50 with bath, 3 with shower, 4 single with bath; all rooms have phone, TV, minibar, hairdrier, safe
FACILITIES sitting room, bar, lift
CREDIT CARDS AE, DC, MC, V
CHILDREN accepted
DISABLED no special facilities
PETS not accepted
CLOSED never
MANAGER M. Dupaen

ILE-DE-FRANCE

PARIS

HOTEL DE NICE
~ TOWN HOTEL ~

42 bis rue de Rivoli, 75004 Paris
TEL 01 42 78 55 29 **FAX** 01 42 78 36 07

HERE IS A WONDERFULLY WACKY two star, every bit as comfortable and twice as enjoyable as many a more expensive three star. We thought it a terrific find, intrigued and not disappointed by what lay behind the vivid turquoise door and up the winding stairs.

The Nice is the enchanting creation of a previously high-flying professional couple who love both collecting and entertaining. The fruits of their hobby are everywhere – masses of period engravings and prints – particularly of Paris – mirrors, old doors, postcards, even a splendid portrait of Lady Diana Cooper. The effect is charming and highly individual – the panelled *salon*, for example, is a harmony of unco-ordinated colours, fabrics and furniture: antique, painted, modern, garden. The use of wallpaper copied from French 18thC designs makes the compact bedrooms feel fresh and pretty, with the off-beat addition of Indian cotton bedspreads, and doors and skirtings boldly painted in turquoise, orange or pillar-box red.

Two attic rooms are particularly charming, with their own little balconies. Others look out on to a pretty square. You'll find only basic amenities here but plenty of character and youthful appeal.

~

NEARBY Musée Carnavalet; place des Vosges; Notre-Dame.
LOCATION near rue Vieille du Temple, on corner of rue de Rivoli and rue du Bourg Tibourg
FOOD breakfast
PRICE €€
ROOMS 23; 17 double and twin, 1 family room, all with bath or shower; all rooms have phone, TV, hairdrier
FACILITIES sitting/breakfast room, lift
CREDIT CARDS MC, V
CHILDREN accepted
DISABLED no special facilities **PETS** accepted
CLOSED never
PROPRIETORS M. and Mme Vaudoux

ILE-DE-FRANCE

✳ PARC SAINT-SEVERIN ✳
∽ TOWN HOTEL ∽

22 rue de la Parcheminerie, 75005 Paris
TEL 01 43 54 32 17 **FAX** 01 43 54 70 71
E-MAIL hotel.parc.severin@wanadoo.fr **WEBSITE** www.esprit-de-france.com

OF ALL THE BEDROOMS in Paris described in this book, No. 70 at the Parc St-Séverin remains this writer's favourite. And although it's an expensive choice, it's far more desirable than, say, a standard double room at the Pavillon de la Reine (page 81) which costs some 140 euros per night more. Overall, of course, the Pavillon is a far superior hotel, but this room is special: a light, sophisticated and beautifully decorated penthouse suite which is entirely encircled by a broad private terrace affording breathtaking views across the rooftops of all the landmark buildings as far as the Eiffel Tower in one direction, Sacré-Coeur in another. Taking breakfast here on a warm summer morning is sheer bliss. Less expensive, but nonetheless very impressive, are two more rooms, each with a broad terrace on three sides. On lower floors, room Nos 12 and 50 both have style and space. The rest are pleasant, unexceptional, pastel-coloured, with predominantly grey modern furniture.

The large ground-floor lobby/breakfast room is a disappointment, another example of contemporary colours – grey, pink, mauve – abstract paintings and minimalist furniture failing to inspire. The hotel is now part of the group that owns the Hôtel Mansart (page 78).

∽

NEARBY Notre-Dame; Musée de Cluny; St-Séverin.
LOCATION in pedestrian area close to St-Séverin and junction with rue des Prêtres St-Séverin
FOOD breakfast **PRICE** €€ **ROOMS** 27; 22 double and twin, 1 family room, 4 single, all with bath; all rooms have phone, TV, minibar, hairdrier, safe; half have air conditioning **FACILITIES** breakfast room, sitting area, lift **CREDIT CARDS** AE, DC, MC, V
CHILDREN accepted
DISABLED no special facilities
PETS not accepted
CLOSED never
MANAGER M. Mulliez

ILE-DE-FRANCE

PARIS

PAVILLON DE LA REINE
~ TOWN HOTEL ~

28 place des Vosges, 75003 Paris
TEL 01 40 29 19 19 **FAX** 01 40 29 19 20
E-MAIL pavillon@club-internet.fr **WEBSITE** www.pavillon-de-la-reine.com

SET BACK FROM THE gloriously harmonious place des Vosges, approached through a calming courtyard garden, the Pavillon de la Reine has our vote for the most perfect location in Paris. It is run with calm professionalism by a dedicated and friendly team, although, like them, perhaps it lacks the intimacy of a true charming small hotel.

The fine 17thC mansion was once the residence of Anne of Austria, wife of Louis XIII. Rescued from near ruin, it now feels more like a baronial country house, with an impressive entrance hall, handsome panelled sitting room with comfy leather sofas and a huge stone fireplace complete with roaring log fire, stone-vaulted breakfast room and two flowery courtyards. For us, the only jarring note was the use of reproduction old masters in some rooms. We were told about the guest of another hotel who removed an expensive original canvas from its frame, replacing it with a copy, but still, we felt it was a misconceived idea.

Upstairs, via a lift cleverly disguised by *trompe l'oeil*, bedrooms and suites contrive to be both smart and pretty, and suitably luxurious. Unlike most other hotels in Paris, prices here have taken an astronomic leap in the past couple of years.

~

NEARBY Musée Carnavalet; Musée Picasso; Ile St-Louis.
LOCATION entrance from N side of place des Vosges; car parking
FOOD breakfast; room service
PRICE €€€€€
ROOMS 55 double and twin, including standard, de luxe and junior suites, all with bath; all rooms have phone, TV, air conditioning, minibar, hairdrier
FACILITIES sitting room, breakfast room, lift, 2 courtyard gardens
CREDIT CARDS AE, DC, MC, V **CHILDREN** accepted
DISABLED ground-floor bedrooms
PETS accepted
CLOSED never
MANAGER Mme Ellinger

ILE-DE-FRANCE

✴ LE RELAIS DU LOUVRE ✴
~ TOWN HOTEL ~

19 rue des Prêtres-St-Germain-l'Auxerrois, 75001 Paris
TEL 01 40 41 96 42 **FAX** 01 40 41 96 44

IN A QUIET SIDE STREET hard by the Louvre and the river, this sophisticated little hotel proves that, in the right hands, even the most featureless of bedrooms can be made to feel charming and welcoming. Most are standard box-shape, no more than adequate in size, although some have the benefit of beamed ceilings and floor-length windows. Ours had a terrific view on to the gables and gargoyles of St-Germain-l'Auxerrois opposite and, though small, felt extremely welcoming and comforting, with its pink hydrangea curtains and matching bedspread, elegant desk and bedside tables, each with a decent-sized lamp. On the walls were pretty 19thC fashion plates, and the television could be popped away in the upholstered box on which it sat. Breakfast is served in your bedroom.

Rooms are cleverly arranged so that a pair can be taken together, closed off behind a communal front door; two rooms on the ground floor have access to a little patio. The manageress, Sophie Aulnette, and her close-knit staff pride themselves on trying to accommodate clients in the best way and to help with budgets wherever possible.

~

NEARBY Louvre; Ile de la Cité; Samaritaine store (rooftop view).
LOCATION in quiet side street parallel to quai du Louvre
FOOD breakfast
PRICE ⒺⒺⒺ
ROOMS 18; 11 double and twin, all with bath, 5 single all with shower, 2 junior suites; all rooms have phone, TV, minibar, hairdrier, safe
FACILITIES sitting area, lift
CREDIT CARDS AE, DC, MC, V

CHILDREN accepted
DISABLED 2 ground-floor bedrooms
PETS accepted
CLOSED never
MANAGER Sophie Aulnette

ILE-DE-FRANCE

PARIS

LE RELAIS SAINT-GERMAIN
~ TOWN HOTEL ~

9 carrefour de l'Odéon, 75006 Paris
TEL 01 44 27 07 97 **FAX** 01 46 33 45 30

IRRESISTIBLE, IF YOU CAN AFFORD IT: a sumptuous 17thC house whose mini-lift and cramped public rooms – albeit artfully mirrored and glossily decorated – give no hint of the wonderfully spacious bedrooms upstairs. Expensive though the Relais undoubtedly is (it has recently – and deservedly – been awarded its fourth star), what is termed a 'standard double' here would be called a 'junior suite' elsewhere. Most 'standard' rooms in Paris give you just enough room to swing a cat. The de luxe rooms are enormous, with two sets of French windows overlooking the street; they are embellished with stunning antiques – mostly French country – plump sofas, lovely fabrics and well-chosen prints and pictures. One is notable for its pair of stone angels culled from a medieval chapel, another for two beautiful matching bookcases. The top-floor suite is a dashing yellow, with black-and-white prints all over the walls, a plethora of ancient sprouting beams and a tiny suntrap terrace.

In the morning, it's hard to choose whether to take breakfast in bed or in the adjoining café, now part of the hotel. Here you can enjoy the ambience of an authentic 1930s café once frequented by Hemingway, Picasso *et al*, married to slick hotel service.

~

NEARBY blvd St-Germain; St-Sulpice; Latin Quarter.
LOCATION just off blvd St-Germain, corner of rue Monsieur Le Prince
FOOD breakfast
PRICE ©©©©
ROOMS 22; 21 double and twin, 1 suite, all with bath; all rooms have phone, TV, video, air conditioning, minibar, hairdrier, safe
FACILITIES 2 small sitting rooms, breakfast room/bar, lift
CREDIT CARDS AE, DC, MC, V **CHILDREN** accepted
DISABLED not suitable
PETS accepted
CLOSED never
PROPRIETOR Alexis Laipsker

ILE-DE-FRANCE

✳ LE SAINT-GREGOIRE ✳
∼ TOWN HOTEL ∼

43 rue de l'Abbé-Grégoire, 75006 Paris
TEL 01 45 48 23 23 **FAX** 01 45 48 33 95
E-MAIL hotel@saintgregoire.com **WEBSITE** www.hotelsaintgregoire.com

A CHIC, IF PRICEY, LITTLE HOTEL in a tall 18thC town house, run with affable charm by manager François de Bené. Le St-Grégoire was designed by Christian Badin of David Hicks – dusty pink walls, maroon carpets, floral peachy curtains, and crisp white linen bedspreads and chair covers – and a warm intimate atmosphere prevails. An open fire blazes in the *salon* on wintry afternoons, a room dotted with antiques and knick-knacks, picked up by Mme Bouvier, the owner's wife, in flea markets and antique shops. Trellis on the walls and large French windows leading on to a tiny enclosed garden, full of flowers and ferns, make the back part of the sitting room feel more like a conservatory.

The colour scheme leads from the ground floor upstairs to equally attractive bedrooms, with beautiful antique chests of drawers, tables and mirrors; two bedrooms have private terraces. Bathrooms are mostly tiled in white; they tend to be small, but are well designed. The ubiquitous cellar breakfast room is a particularly pretty one, with woven floor, rush chairs and baskets decorating one wall.

∼

NEARBY Musée Bourdelle; Jardin du Luxembourg; blvd St-Germain.
LOCATION between rue du Cherche Midi and rue de Vaugirard
FOOD breakfast
PRICE €€€€
ROOMS 20 double and twin, all with bath; all rooms have phone, TV, air conditioning, hairdrier
FACILITIES sitting room, breakfast room, lift
CREDIT CARDS AE, DC, MC, V

CHILDREN welcome
DISABLED no special facilities
PETS accepted
CLOSED never
PROPRIETOR M. Bouvier

ILE-DE-FRANCE

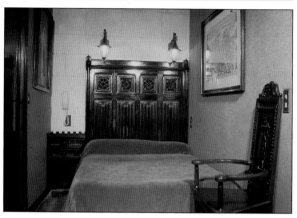

SAINT-MERRY
~ TOWN HOTEL ~

78 rue de la Verrerie, 75004 Paris
TEL 01 42 78 14 15 **FAX** 01 40 29 06 82

ONE OF THE MOST DISTINCTIVE small hotels in Paris, the St-Merry has a church-like, medieval atmosphere all its own, with heavily beamed ceilings, pale stone walls, wrought-iron fittings and splendid carved wood neo-Gothic furnishings. Everything is kept simple: bedrooms and bathrooms are spotless though mostly small; there are no public rooms to speak of, and breakfast, which is brought to your room, is prepared in a tiny galley behind the reception; a spiralling staircase is the only means by which you can reach your room.

This former presbytery of the adjacent church of St-Merri became a private residence after the 1789 revolution, and served for a time as a brothel before it was rescued from decay by its previous owner in the 1960s. He decided on its memorable – if sombre – style after acquiring some neo-Gothic furnishings which were languishing in the basement of the church. The hotel is famous for No. 9, where flying buttresses form a low canopy over the bed, whilst Nos 12 and 17 have remarkable bedheads. Little seems to have changed since the new owner, M. Juin, took over; but we would welcome reports.

~

NEARBY Pompidou Centre; Hôtel de Ville; Marais; Notre-Dame.
LOCATION in pedestrianized zone, on the corner of rue de la Verrerie and rue St-Martin
FOOD breakfast
PRICE €€€
ROOMS 14; 11 double and twin, 2 family, 1 suite, all with bath or shower, 2 without WC; all rooms have phone, hairdrier
FACILITIES small sitting area
CREDIT CARDS AE, V
CHILDREN accepted
DISABLED not suitable
PETS accepted
CLOSED never
PROPRIETOR M. Juin

ILE-DE-FRANCE

✳ SAINT-PAUL ✳
~ TOWN HOTEL ~

43 rue Monsieur Le Prince, 75006 Paris
TEL 01 43 26 98 64 **FAX** 01 46 34 58 60
E-MAIL hotel.saint.paul@wanadoo.fr **WEBSITE** www.hotel-saint-paul.paris.com

THE ST-PAUL, a 17thC building, was renovated in 1987. The public rooms are stylish in an unfussy way with beamed ceilings, a mixture of stone and colour-washed walls, Indian rugs, *haute époque* and good country antiques, dark pink drapes and attractive pink and green checked armchairs. Facing the entrance, a courtyard garden is set behind a glass wall, carefully tended and full of colour year-round. The cellar breakfast room is a particularly elegant variation on the theme, with high-backed tapestry chairs and round wooden tables. If the reception rooms have a rural feel, so do the bedrooms, all of which are differently decorated, with walls covered in grass cloth, Sanderson's paper or enlivened with a dash of colour, and carefully lit bathrooms clad in ginger or reddish marble. Our room under the eaves felt cosy, with views over the rooftops; others have four-posters or antique brass bedsteads. All in all easy-going and well run: a pleasure to stay in. The owner, whose family have been talented hoteliers in France for generations, married an Englishman, and now their friendly and capable daughter, Marianne Hawkins, is in charge, along with the hotel's cat, Sputnik.

NEARBY Latin Quarter; Musée de Cluny; Jardin du Luxembourg.
LOCATION about halfway along the street, between rue Racine and rue de Vaugirard
FOOD breakfast
PRICE €€€
ROOMS 31; 26 double and twin, including suites, duplex and family rooms, all with bath, 5 single, 2 with bath, 3 with shower; all rooms have phone, TV, air conditioning, minibar, hairdrier, safe **FACILITIES** sitting room, breakfast room, lift
CREDIT CARDS AE, DC, MC, V
CHILDREN accepted
DISABLED 1 room on ground floor **PETS** accepted
CLOSED never
PROPRIETORS Hawkins family

ILE-DE-FRANCE

PARIS

✳ LE SAINTE-BEUVE ✳
~ TOWN HOTEL ~

9 rue Ste-Beuve, 75006 Paris
TEL 01 45 48 20 07 **FAX** 01 45 48 67 52
E-MAIL saintebeuve@wanadoo.fr

ALL IS DISCRETION AND understatement at this essentially simple little hotel with luxurious touches: plain cream walls, restrained patterns in the rich fabrics; beds draped in white, simple furniture mixing modern designs with country antiques, attractive pictures, fresh flowers strategically placed. A log fire burns in the classically-styled *salon,* where there is also a bar.

The Ste-Beuve's previous owner, Bobette Compagnon, was responsible for its sense of style, which lifts it from the crowd. She also introduced some pampering extra services, which the new management seems to be continuing. The excellent breakfast – which arrives on a tray beautifully laid with porcelain – can be ordered at almost any time of the day or night, and room service is available up until 10 pm.

During our stay we met someone who had benefited from the hotel's policy of upgrading guests, whenever possible, to a more expensive room than was booked, and another who was accompanied by her three cats – every bit as stylish as their owner – one of which had inadvertently escaped and which we found wandering down the winding staircase – a dizzying sight from the top floor – as we passed.

~

NEARBY blvd du Montparnasse; Jardin du Luxembourg.
LOCATION off blvd Raspail, between places Lafou and Picasso
FOOD breakfast; room service for light meals and drinks
PRICE €€€€ **ROOMS** 23 double and twin, including standard, de luxe, junior suites and 2 bedroom apartments, all with bath; all rooms have phone, TV, air conditioning, minibar, hairdrier, safe **FACILITIES** sitting room, breakfast room, bar, lift **CREDIT CARDS** AE, MC, V

CHILDREN accepted
DISABLED access difficult **PETS** accepted **CLOSED** never
PROPRIETOR Jean-Pierre Egurreguy

ILE-DE-FRANCE

BARBIZON

HOSTELLERIE LES PLEIADES
VILLAGE HOTEL

21 Grande Rue, 77630 Barbizon
(Seine-et-Marne)
TEL 01 60 66 40 25
FAX 01 60 66 41 68 **E-MAIL**
les.pleiades.barbizon@wanadoo.fr
FOOD breakfast, lunch, dinner
PRICE € **ROOMS** 24
CLOSED never

SET BACK FROM the main road leading into the Fontainebleau Forest, this handsome 19thC building was once home to the artist Charles Daubigny, and as a hotel accommodated landscape painters of the Barbizon School. Nowadays, it is a comfortable, down-to-earth three star, combining old-fashioned charm with modern comforts including surprisingly luxurious bathrooms. There is a cosy bar and large elegant restaurant, which a reader rates as, 'one of the best in Barbizon'. He also commends the 'very attentive' housekeeping, 'very friendly' atmosphere and welcome, and 'incredibly personal' service.

GERMIGNY-L'EVEQUE

HOSTELLERIE LE GONFALON
VILLAGE HOTEL

2 rue de l'Eglise, 77910
Germigny-L'Evêque (Seine-et-Marne)
TEL 01 64 33 16 05
FAX 01 64 33 25 59
FOOD breakfast, lunch, dinner
PRICE € **ROOMS** 8
CLOSED Jan, Sun dinner, Mon

THE HOSTELLERIE, which our inspector happened upon as he passed by one day, is set in a lovely wooded position on a bend of the River Marne, overlooked by a tree-shaded terrace, where a menu based on fish and seafood dishes is served in summer – or in the beamed dining room in cooler weather. Germigny-L'Evêque is a quiet residential village, but only 20 minutes from Euro-Disney, making it a perfect spot to escape to after a demanding day in the land of make-believe. Mme Collubi, voluminous and in perennial bloom, has been in charge for nearly 30 years.

ILE-DE-FRANCE

CHOPIN
TOWN HOTEL

10 boulevard Montmartre (46 passage Jouffroy), 75009 Paris
TEL 01 47 70 58 10
FAX 01 42 47 00 70
FOOD breakfast
PRICE €€
ROOMS 36
CLOSED never

DEFINITELY ONE OF OUR TOP Paris two-stars, with perhaps the most charming façade of all. It stands at the end of passage Jouffroy, one of the 19thC glass-and-steel roofed arcades which thread this no-frills shopping and theatre neighbourhood. Our room, No. 412, was one of the best, with coral-coloured walls and a third bed as well as simple furniture and a bright, white bathroom. Tucked under the eaves and approached along a narrow, creaky corridor, the room had the feel of an artist's garret. The continental breakfast was generous, yet reasonably priced.

SAINT-DOMINIQUE
TOWN HOTEL

62 rue St-Dominique, 75007 Paris
TEL 01 47 05 51 44
FAX 01 47 05 81 28 **WEBSITE**
www.hotel-saint-dominique.com
FOOD breakfast
PRICE €€ **ROOMS** 34
CLOSED never

THE HEART OF THIS well-located, reasonably-priced hotel is the delightful reception-cum-sitting-room, always manned by one of a friendly, helpful team, now working for new owners. From here a wooden spiral staircase leads down to a little breakfast room – a white-painted vault with a mixture of Lloyd loom and wicker chairs – where our inspectors found a generous breakfast. The small but well-equipped bedrooms are decorated in a confidently colourful style. Across a flowery courtyard, the annexe rooms tend to be smaller and more modest, but are beautifully quiet.

THE NORTH-EAST

HOTELS IN THE NORTH-EAST

We've made an extra special effort for this edition to discover some new addresses in our North-East region, as we felt we had neglected it a little of late. Although it does of course contain some popular holiday destinations, it is more often a part of France which is driven through rather than lingered in, and our readers are mostly looking for pleasant overnight stops, or bases for short breaks. There are still several *départments* in which we have no recommendations at all, but the region does embrace four areas worth singling out for their touristic interest and the quality of their hotels.

The hinterland of the main Channel ferry ports includes some pleasant rolling countryside, and of course proximity to those ports makes the area – particularly the *départment* of Pas-de-Calais, containing Calais and Boulogne – prime territory for a quick weekend away.

The *départments* of Oise and Seine-et-Marne, respectively to the north and east of the Île de France, contain some tourist highlights (Compiègne, Chantilly, Vaux-le-Vicomte). More or less due east of Paris, where the motorway from Paris to Strasbourg meets that coming down from Calais, is Champagne. Wherever there is wine there is a satisfyingly cultivated landscape, and here there is also the architectural spectacle of Reims, at the heart of the Champagne business as well as the region, of which the cathedral is only one part.

And then there are the forested hills of the Vosges, and beyond, Alsace, at the far eastern end of this region, against the German border. This is another wine region – a hilly one, with some wonderful scenery and the quaintest of prettily painted, half-timbered villages strung out along the so-called Route de Vin. Here, in particular, we have found some delightful new entries, full of local character, where you should sleep soundly and eat well on such German-influenced Alsatian delicacies as *choucroute* and *presskopf*, sausages, black puddings, *foie gras* and *tartes flambées*, washed down by the region's excellent white wines.

THE NORTH-EAST

ARRAS

L'UNIVERS

~ VILLAGE RESTAURANT-WITH-ROOMS ~

3-5 place de la Croix Rouge, 62000 Arras (Pas-de-Calais)
TEL 03 21 71 34 01 **FAX** 03 21 71 41 42
E-MAIL hotelunivers.arras@wanadoo.fr

DON'T MISS OUT ON ARRAS. The famous squares (*places*) in the town centre are amazing, with their beautiful old gabled buildings. They are a good reason to choose the town as a stopping place (Channel Tunnel, less than an hour by car). Another is the Hôtel L'Univers, awkward to find in the backstreets behind the Hôtel de Ville, but as provincial town hotels in Northern France go, more worth the effort than most. Behind an arch off a pretty little square, the handsome hotel buildings form a peaceful rectangle of their own, pleasantly apart from the bustle. Inside, exposed brickwork contrasts with white Picardy stone giving the pleasant striped effect which is traditional hereabouts. The bedrooms we saw were in reasonable taste, uncluttered (clinical, perhaps), one all beiges and grey, the other powder blue. Bathrooms are smart, modern, acceptable, nothing special. Given the shortage of our type of hotel within reach of the Channel, the Univers is recommendable, despite the five conference rooms, housed separately around the courtyard. We counted off-road parking for 16 cars in the courtyard – on the face of it a bonus, but they can fill up quickly, which, we suspect, drives some guests mad – you may not reserve a space.

~

NEARBY Arras places.
LOCATION behind Hôtel de Ville, in own square; ask for directions; car parking
FOOD breakfast, lunch, dinner
PRICE €€
ROOMS 37 double and twin, all with bath, or shower; all rooms have phone, TV
FACILITIES sitting areas, dining room, bar, lift
CREDIT CARDS AE, MC, V
CHILDREN accepted
DISABLED 2 rooms suitable
PETS accepted **CLOSED** restaurant only, Sun dinner
PROPRIETOR M. Durand

THE NORTH-EAST

LE COLOMBIER
~ TOWN HOTEL ~

7 rie de Turenne, 68000 Colmar (Haut-Rhin)
TEL 03 89 23 96 00 **FAX** 03 89 23 97 27
E-MAIL hotel-le-colombier.com

L E COLOMBIER HAS RELATIVELY few bedrooms in a largish building – a former convent, converted seven years ago to a hotel. Original stone features sprout, *de rigueur*, in the public spaces (notably the staircase), but
we thought the bar area showed imagination, with a freestanding wood fire
screened by glass, throwing off dancing flames and a comfortable heat
from a mere three or four logs. Quite original, too, is the breakfast room,
with cane and metal chairs. Upstairs, we tried not to let the aromatherapy
oils wafting through the ventilation system dull our senses. The bedrooms
seemed spacious, certainly well cared for; but the curtains and bedspreads
were dull. The corridors are smart, but, well, like hotel corridors, and the
bedrooms didn't quite dispel that antiseptic feel of town hotels where the
designer has been let loose, no expense spared. Even so, No. 21 is great,
with painted ceiling beams and parquet floor. The price of breakfast can
be a barometer in such places: here, it's a fair one for a buffet with
choices – you can pay more for bad coffee and croissants in humbler
hotels. So, we conclude that Le Colombier is a fair deal, and a good base in
Colmar, home of the amazing Issenheim altarpiece.
~

NEARBY Musée des Cappuchins; Alsace wineries.
LOCATION near town centre, well signposted; car parking in street
FOOD breakfast
PRICE €€
ROOMS 24; 19 double and twin, 3 single, 1 triple, 1 family, all with bath (8 Jacuzzi)
or shower; all rooms have phone, TV, air conditioning, minibar, safe, hairdrier
FACILITIES sitting room, bar, breakfast room, courtyard
CREDIT CARDS AE, DC, MC, V
CHILDREN welcome
DISABLED 2 specially adapted rooms
PETS accepted
CLOSED never
MANAGER Martine Pont-Heck

THE NORTH-EAST

✳ CHATEAU DE COURCELLES ✳
~ COUNTRY HOTEL ~

8 rue du Château, 02220 Courcelles-sur-Vesle (Aisne)
TEL 03 23 74 13 53 **FAX** 03 23 74 06 41 or book through our travel service, see below
E-MAIL reservation@chateau-de-courcelles.fr **WEBSITE** www.chateau-de-courcelles.fr

IN PAST YEARS WE HAVE RATED this expensive Relais & Château hotel as a back-up address rather than a main entry, and that's what it would remain except for consistently good reports from readers. They talk of an especially warm welcome, beautiful rooms and impressive food, and we too think that the management do something quite special here, probably helped by there being only 11 bedrooms, plus four suites and three apartments. It's a graceful, not intimidatingly large, 17thC château set in a small park in a peaceful backwater of the Vesle between Reims and Soissons; and, of course, it has a history – Napoléon and Rousseau were guests. We think the drawing room is somewhat heavy, with much betasseled lampshades, and predictably deep-red, traditionally patterned wallpaper. But the roomy bedrooms have, at their best, a certain freshness, with good use of paint on the panelling; one has an unusual terracotta floor. You could be calm-but-busy here for two or three days – see the list of facilities, and things to do nearby. But expect outside visitors in the evenings - there are three dining rooms.

~

NEARBY Reims; Epernay; Abbaye St Jean-des-Vignes; Laon **LOCATION** from Reims N31 direction Soissons; Courcelles-sur-Vesles is in about 30 km (NB, don't confuse it with Courcelles, 10 km from Reims); signposted in village; car parking **FOOD** breakfast, lunch, dinner; room service **PRICE** €€€ **ROOMS** 18; 11 double and twin, 4 suites, 3 apartments, all with bath; all rooms have phone, TV, minibar, hairdrier **FACILITIES** sitting room, 3 dining rooms, swimming pool, tennis, sauna, jogging track, bicycles

CREDIT CARDS AE, DC, MC, V
CHILDREN welcome
DISABLED 1 specially adapted room **PETS** accepted
CLOSED never
MANAGER Michel Anthonioz

THE NORTH-EAST

L'EPINE

AUX ARMES DE CHAMPAGNE
~ VILLAGE HOTEL ~

avenue de Luxembourg, 51460 L'Epine (Marne)
TEL 03 26 69 30 30 FAX 03 26 69 30 26 E-MAIL contact@auxarmesdechampagne.com
WEBSITE www.auxarmesdechampagne.com

THIS WOODEN-SHUTTERED flower-decked roadside inn has long been, in the capable and caring hands of its owners, Jean-Paul and Denise Pérardel, an outstanding example of its type. The building is attractive but not memorable, the position, though enjoying a fine view of L'Epine's flamboyant Gothic cathedral, is marred somewhat by being on the road, but it's the standards inside that count, and they are notably high. Though it has been continually improved and refurbished over the years, the hotel still exudes a refreshing lack of pretension. Bedrooms, in wings behind the main building, are either fairly small and countrified in style, or larger and more 'country house' style; all are 'comfortable and impeccable'. Sixteen more straightforward rooms are located in a modern annexe 200 metres down the road.

A good night's sleep and a warm welcome notwithstanding, the main attractions of Aux Armes de Champagne are the renowned cuisine and the very fine cellar. Gilles Blandin, from Savoy, has kept up the standards of his predecessor, Patrick Michelin, in the kitchen, and the modern cooking with regional touches is consistently appreciated. This is a popular overnight stopping place, especially for people en route to Alsace and beyond from the Channel Tunnel. ~

NEARBY cathedral; Champagne country.
LOCATION in L'Épine, 8 km E of Châlons-sur-Marne on N3 to Metz; car parking
FOOD breakfast, lunch, dinner
PRICE €€€
ROOMS 37 double and twin, all with bath or shower; all rooms have phone, TV, minibar, hairdrier
FACILITIES sitting room, bar, restaurant, garden, tennis, mini-golf
CREDIT CARDS AE, DC, MC, V CHILDREN accepted
DISABLED no special facilities PETS accepted CLOSED early-Jan to mid-Feb
PROPRIETORS Jean-Paul and Denise Pérardel

THE NORTH-EAST

HOTEL CLERY
~ COUNTRY MANSION ~

rue du Château, 62360 Hesdin-l'Abbé (Pas-de-Calais)
Tel 03 21 83 19 83 **Fax** 03 21 87 52 59

AFTER ONLY A SHORT TIME under the aegis of its previous owners, we were somewhat concerned to hear that the Cléry had changed hands yet again, but an inspection revealed that all was well and still running as smoothly as before.

Properly called the Château d'Hesdin l'Abbaye, a dignified façade dominates the fine tree-lined approach to the house. But there is no need to be intimidated: this is not a stuffy place. There is a very fine Louis XV wrought-iron staircase, but essentially the style is bright and light in harmonious pastel tones, understated and modern.'Public rooms all excellent, with relaxing general atmosphere', runs our latest report.

The hotel already has an established British trade; the excellent golf at nearby Hardelot is an attraction in addition to the proximity to the Channel. Bedrooms are freshly decorated, with plenty of individual touches; don't overlook those in the cottage annexe, especially if you are a family. There is an attractive bar, and a log fire in the sitting room when the weather calls for it. Dinner can be had here on weekday evenings. One reporter talks of 'excellent quality and impeccable service', another that 'the cooking was disappointing and left much to be desired'. What do you think?

~

Nearby Hardelot, golf and beach (9 km); Le Touquet (15 km).
Location in tiny rural village, 9 km SE of Boulogne; 1 km from exit 28 (A16); ample car parking
Food breakfast, dinner
Price €€
Rooms 22 double and twin, all with bath or shower; all rooms have phone, TV
Facilities sitting room, dining room, bar, garden, tennis, bicycles
Credit cards AE, DC, MC, V **Children** welcome
Disabled no special facilities **Pets** not accepted **Closed** Jan
Proprietors M. Lard and M. Durand

THE EAST

HOTEL DES BERGES
~ VILLAGE HOTEL ~

4 rue de Collonges, 68970 Illhaeusern (Haut-Rhin)
TEL 03 89 71 87 87 **FAX** 03 89 71 87 88

THIS IS THE HOTEL that goes with the famous Auberge de l'Ill, one of just three French restaurants that have kept their three Michelin stars for more than 20 years. Hotel and *auberge* stand a little apart in a garden on the little River Ill at the edge of the village. Like most class acts, the Berges is understated. Even the prices – while not cheap – avoid vulgar excess. The softly spoken manager, Marco Baumann, is laid back, in a charming way, but be sure that he knows his business. It's all in superb taste, full of natural materials – kelims, much use of wood, almost nothing metallic or shiny, with admirable attention paid to connecting areas, which are often overlooked. Reception is just a desk in the hall; the computer banished to a side office. It feels, and is, like a private house. The five double bedrooms, all different, use many a fine fabric in soft colours. In summer you can breakfast on a barge in the river. Apart from punting, there's (intentionally) little to do, except mellow out, attended by eight discrete staff, who say they treat everyone (including royalty and presidents) the same. There was piped music in the bar. Marc Haeberlin's food at the *auberge* remains a memorable experience.

NEARBY Alsace wineries; Riquewihr; Colmar.
LOCATION on edge of village; car parking
FOOD breakfast (lunch, dinner in Auberge de l'Ill)
PRICE €€€€
ROOMS 5 double and twin, all with bath, 1 apartment; converted fisherman's cottage; all rooms have phone, TV, video, air conditioning, minibar, safe, hairdrier
FACILITIES sitting areas, bar, lift, terrace, garden, river punt
CREDIT CARDS AE, DC, MC, V
CHILDREN welcome
DISABLED specially adapted apartment
PETS accepted
CLOSED hotel and restaurant closed Mon, Tues; hotel closed Feb
MANAGER Marco Baumann

THE NORTH-EAST

ITTERSWILLER

ARNOLD
~ VILLAGE HOTEL ~

98 route des Vins, 67140 Itterswiller (Bas-Rhin)
TEL 03 88 85 50 58 **FAX** 03 88 85 55 54
E-MAIL arnold-hotel@wanadoo.fr **WEBSITE** www.hotel-arnold.com

HERE IS A CLEVER PACKAGE OF HOTEL, restaurant and shop – a blend of the best of the old and the new, aimed at today's traveller, who appreciates a traditional ambience but wants everything convenient. The accommodation is in a pleasing timber and yellow-painted Alsatian house standing in its own vineyards. There is no restaurant or bar here, just a small breakfast room, and the place feels *sotto* because of it. Bedrooms have rough-cast, yellow-washed plaster walls, some with new panelling and bright cotton bedspreads. Bathrooms are a similar standard. The best have long views of vineyards and hills.

For a happy buzz, just go fifty paces up the road to the Arnold's restaurant, where local residents mingle with hotel guests and the hearty Alsatian food is way above average. Here, as in the hotel, everything seems to run on rails – yet there's nothing functional about it. To achieve this effect you need a head for the market, attention to detail and a liking for people: all of which, not surprisingly, are qualities of the friendly young owner, Bruno Simon. The Arnold has its own wines: try the Oscar Riesling, available in restaurant and shop.

~

NEARBY The Alsatian wine route; Colmar; Strasbourg.
LOCATION on edge of village, with restaurant almost opposite; car parking just off road
FOOD breakfast, lunch dinner
PRICE €€€
ROOMS 29; 24 double and twin, 3 triple, 1 family, 1 apartment, all with bath or shower; all rooms have phone, TV, minibar
FACILITIES sitting room, bar, restaurant, local produce boutique, terrace, small garden, wine tastings
CREDIT CARDS AE, MC, V
CHILDREN welcome
DISABLED 1 specially adapted room
PETS by arrangement
CLOSED hotel Christmas; restaurant Jan, mid-late Feb, 1 week end of Jun
PROPRIETOR Bruno Simon

THE NORTH-EAST

LES ALISIERS
~ COUNTRY HOTEL ~

5, Foudé, 68650 Lapoutroie (Haut-Rhin)
TEL 03 89 47 52 82 **FAX** 03 89 47 22 38
E-MAIL hotel-restaurant.lesalisiers@wanadoo.fr

~

AN ENGLISH COUPLE report that they have been back to this converted farmhouse three times – 'which speaks for itself'. You approach along a narrow, steeply winding road to get a 'wonderful surprise' on arrival. The picturesque building with 'an Alpine feel' has a splendid setting and great views to the village below and across a wooded valley to the Vosges hills.

Food is the strong card, with a 'sophisticated' set menu centred on local ingredients and dishes. Michelin awards a Bib Gourmand for good food at moderate prices. Floor-to-ceiling windows in the dining room exploit the view: try to get the table in the pole position to enjoy this to the full. Rooms are simple – 'comfortably rustic' – and spotlessly clean; but some are small. The Degouys are proud of what they do and go out of their way to make guests feel welcome. Staff are eager to please and prices are very fair.

If you like a relaxed, family atmosphere, with children and dogs in the dining room, then Les Alisiers is for you. A member of the Hôtels au Naturel Group, which believes in respecting the environment and using local ingredients.

NEARBY Vosges walking; cross country skiing
LOCATION in own grounds, off the N415 in direction of St-Die, 3 km from Lapoutroie's centre – signposted from the church; car parking
FOOD breakfast, lunch, dinner
PRICE €
ROOMS 18; 17 double and twin, 1 single, all with bath; all rooms have phone
FACILITIES sitting room, bar, restaurant, terrace, garden
CREDIT CARDS MC, V
CHILDREN welcome
DISABLED some specially adapted rooms
PETS by arrangement
CLOSED Christmas, Jan, 1 week end Jun
PROPRIETORS Jacques and Ella Degouy

THE NORTH-EAST

MONTREUIL

CHATEAU DE MONTREUIL
~ CHATEAU HOTEL ~

4 chaussée des Capucins, 62170 Montreuil (Pas de Calais)
TEL 03 21 81 53 04 **FAX** 03 21 81 36 43 **WEBSITE** www.chateaudemontreuil.com

MONTREUIL, CHATEAU DE: charming host, exceptional food, great advice on local shopping for food and wine. Comfortable, well equipped rooms. Not cheap. Wife of patron: English.' Military man, our reporter; as usual verdict spot on; other readers concur. The latest comment: 'you would go far to find a better place to stay in the north of France'.

This substantial, luxurious country house, dating from the 1930s, is a well-established favourite with British travellers, who make up most of the resident guests. The house is immaculately done out, with great taste throughout. New this year: shower cubicles being added to bathrooms, and a complete refit for the kitchen. Bedrooms are splendid – decorated with flair and furnished with character; those on the top floor are very spacious, but the first floor rooms give better views of the beautiful English-style gardens. There is a snug brick-and-beams bar, an airy glass-fronted sitting room and an elegant dining room. Although you're quite close to the town centre, the setting is quiet, the gardens secluded.

Christian Germain's cooking aims high and hits the target (the restaurant does not rely on English custom but has a loyal French following). Breakfast ('home-made everything') is delicious.

~

NEARBY ramparts (still intact), citadel; Le Touquet (15 km); golf.
LOCATION in quiet part of town, 38 km S of Boulogne, off N1; ample car parking
FOOD breakfast, lunch, dinner; room service
PRICE €€€€
ROOMS 14; 12 double and twin, 2 family, all with bath; all rooms have phone, TV, air conditioning, minibar, safe, hairdrier
FACILITIES sitting room, restaurant, bar, terrace, garden
CREDIT CARDS AE, DC, MC, V
CHILDREN welcome
DISABLED 3 rooms on ground floor
PETS not accepted
CLOSED mid-Dec to end Jan
PROPRIETORS Christian and Lindsay Germain

THE NORTH-EAST

OSTHOUSE

A LA FERME
~ VILLAGE GUESTHOUSE ~

10, rue du Château, 67050 Osthouse (Haut-Rhin)
TEL 03 90 29 92 50 **FAX** 03 90 29 92 51

A BRAND NEW ENTRY FOR THE GUIDE – 2001 was its first full season – and perhaps one of the most interesting new enterprises in Alsace. The former 18thC farm building, its outside painted a brilliant powder blue – a contemporary twist to the traditional Alsatian colour – stands just off the village centre in its garden. Inside, no expense has been spared to turn it into Brigitte and Jean-Philippe Hellmann's ideal modern-traditional lodging. The homely old proportions have been artfully preserved to keep the private house feel. Walls are panelled or roughly plastered with a pale wash. Wooden oak floors smartly pull it all together. Bedrooms – the smallest we saw was spacious – are enticing, with striped cotton fabrics, fat duvets, white-painted furniture: homely but uncluttered rustic-chic. The suite is elegant and roomy, the bathrooms sparkling, all marble. You get a view of old farm buildings from the bedrooms and a big breakfast (special bread, smoked salmon, *presskopf* terrine) at a reasonable charge served in your room, or downstairs. Room rates are presently very cheap – you could pay double for this elsewhere. For lunch or dinner, stroll to the Hellmanns' restaurant, À l'Aigle d'Or, four minutes away, where Jean-Philippe, the chef, offers traditional dishes presented in clean, contemporary style.

~

NEARBY Strasbourg; Alsace vineyards; Colmar.
LOCATION in village; ask hotel for directions; car parking
FOOD breakfast
PRICE €
ROOMS 7; 6 double, 1single, all with bath or shower; all rooms have phone, TV, minibar, safe
FACILITIES sitting area, breakfast room, terrace, garden
CREDIT CARDS MC, V
CHILDREN welcome
DISABLED 2 specially adapted rooms
PETS accepted
CLOSED never; restaurant closed Sun dinner, Mon dinner, Tues
PROPRIETORS Brigitte and Jean-Philippe Hellmann

THE NORTH-EAST

AUX TROIS ROSES
~ VILLAGE HOTEL ~

19, rue Principal, 67290 La Petite-Pierre (Bas-Rhin)
TEL 03 88 89 89 00 **FAX** 03 88 70 41 28
E-MAIL hotel.3roses@wanadoo.fr **WEBSITE** www.aux-trois-roses.com

THIS NEW DISCOVERY is tucked away near the northern border of Alsace, in the Northern Vosges, in the middle of an atmospheric medieval village – but could almost be in the country, so quiet can seem these Alsatian communities. Its (18thC) face to the street is pleasing: creeper-covered, shuttered and balconied, tumbling with geraniums in summer, just the size you might expect of a charming small hotel, and the small-scale feel continues in reception, divided into warmly panelled alcoves. Check curtains and Alpine chalet-style fittings and furnishings are all very cosy and calming. It gets less charming as you move away from the central public area: several spacious dining rooms spread out beyond – and, to one side, an indoor swimming pool with generous lounging-around space (the solarium).

Bedrooms are all in excellent condition (renewed in 2000), again in Alpine chalet style, with pale wooden panelling and pleasant green carpets (inoffensive geometric pattern). Many have the view down the steep little valley on one of whose edges the village perches – others are on the street. Rooms are a notable bargain, given their size and appearance. Going down a level from reception there's a much less attractive, more functional floor, whose extra accommodation helps to make the place larger than it seems – there are 43 bedrooms. A family could be very happy here, flopping by the pool and going on walks.

NEARBY Northern Vosges walking; Alsace wineries.
LOCATION in village main street; car parking in garages and on street
FOOD breakfast, lunch,dinner
PRICE €
ROOMS 43 double, twin and family, all with bath or shower; all rooms have phone, TV, hairdrier
FACILITIES sitting areas, dining rooms, bar, lift, indoor swimming pool, solarium, terrace, table tennis
CREDIT CARDS AE, DC, MC, V **CHILDREN** accepted
DISABLED no special facilities **PETS** accepted **CLOSED** never
MANAGER Philippe Geyer

THE NORTH-EAST

LES AGAPES ET LA MAISON FORTE
~ VILLAGE RESTAURANT-WITH-ROOMS ~

6, place Henriot du Coudray, 55800 Revigny-sur-Ornain (Meuse)
TEL 03 29 70 56 00 **FAX** 03 29 70 59 30

THE RESTAURANT, LES AGAPES, and its rooms in adjacent fortified buildings make a self-confident little group, standing apart up a neat drive. Much has been done to bring out the charm of the 17thC building containing the restaurant: exposed stone walls, beams and oriental rugs from yesterday are the backdrop for today's ironwork dining furniture, modern light fittings and minimalist flower arrangements. Owner-chef Jean-Marc Joblot has a Michelin star and reporters speak of strong flavours in his mainly regional dishes.

Les Agapes is not, however, a temple to food: the atmosphere is warm and relaxed; you're very much the guest of Jean-Marc and his lively wife Daniele. We especially like places such as this where you eat in a room full of buzzing locals. The unpretentious and comfortable style continues into the bedrooms, all different (and with a wide but very reasonable range of prices) – but perhaps a little predictable. Like many a chef in charge of his own establishment, Jean-Marc makes extra effort with breakfast. A useful address in an area where until now we've found nowhere quite right for the guide.

~

NEARBY Champagne country; Bar-le-Duc (18 km).
LOCATION 18 km NW of Bar-le-Duc, in own grounds in village, signposted; ample car parking
FOOD breakfast, lunch, dinner
PRICE €
ROOMS 7 double, twin and triple, all with bath; all rooms have phone, TV
FACILITIES restaurant, terrace, garden
CREDIT CARDS AE, DC, MC, V
CHILDREN accepted
DISABLED not suitable
PETS accepted
CLOSED 1 week Mar, 2 weeks Aug; restaurant closed Sun dinner, Mon lunch
PROPRIETORS Jean-Marc and Daniele Joblot

THE NORTH-EAST

RIBEAUVILLE

SEIGNEURS DE RIBEAUPIERRE
~ VILLAGE HOTEL ~

11, rue du Château, 68150 Ribeauvillé (Haut-Rhin)
TEL 03 89 73 70 31 **FAX** 03 89 73 71 21

SITUATED AT THE EDGE of this picture-perfect wine town, this is a hotel that you will if you enjoy escaping into a warm, enveloping interiors and a hushed atmosphere, where everything runs on rails. Two sisters, Marie-Madeleine and Marie-Cécile Barth, have softened and brightened exposed stone and gnarled beams with classy fabrics at the windows, cheerful tablecloths in the vaulted breakfast room and, in the intimate *salon*, armchairs arranged so that everyone gets their share of the glow from the raised corner fireplace. Bedrooms come in many sizes, adding to the private house feel. There is a sprinkling of antiques, duvet covers in pretty fabrics, and pools of light from well-placed table lamps. In the sitting area of a suite, two sofas overflow with generously stuffed cushions in co-ordinating fabrics. Not the place for a stag party. Some rooms are non-smoking, and, you may not be surprised to hear, *animaux ne sont pas admis*. We think it's probably a fair deal for the prices charged - breakfast is included in the room rate. No restaurant; recommended Ribeauvillé eating places are Winstub Zum Pfifferhuis (serious food, no smoking) and l'Auberge Zahnacker; also Chambard at Kaysersberg.

~

NEARBY Alsace Route de Vin; Hunawihr; Colmar (19 km).
LOCATION from Grand'rue, head for place de la Sinne and bear right; hotel on corner near church of St Grégoire; car parking.
FOOD breakfast
PRICE €€
ROOMS 10; 7 double, 3 suites, all with bath or shower; all rooms have phone
FACILITIES breakfast room
CREDIT CARDS AE, DC, MC, V
CHILDREN welcome
DISABLED access difficult
PETS not accepted
CLOSED Christmas to Mar
PROPRIETORS Marie-Madeleine and Marie-Cécile Barth

THE NORTH-EAST

ST-RIQUIER

✳ JEAN DE BRUGES ✳
~ VILLAGE HOTEL ~

18, Place de l'Eglise, 80135 St-Riquier (Somme)
TEL 03 22 28 30 30 **FAX** 03 22 28 00 69
E-MAIL jeandebruges@wanadoo.fr **WEBSITE** www.somme-tourisme.comJDB.htm

THIS IS WHAT you think a good small French hotel ought to be – and so often isn't. Location: in a big square, right beside a medieval abbey, with amazing façade. Exterior: a smallish, handsome 17thC house in white Picardy stone. Public rooms: full of unpretentious style. Bedrooms: white walls, wrought-iron bedsteads, with homely, painted cane bedside tables, no jarring colour schemes or standard-issue floral wallpaper; even the smallest has the loo separate from the bath or shower. Bathrooms: gleaming. Can there be a catch? It's hard to fault, except perhaps on price, which is not unfair, but pushes at the top end of its range.

Actually, it's not strictly a French hotel, but Belgian. The engaging (and savvy) Bernadette Stubbe-Martens and her lawyer husband came here from Bruges in 1995 and created the place from a ruin. Even if you don't stay, have a drink in the beautifully light *salon de thé*, which doubles as dining room and breakfast room. (English readers, note the grandfather clock showing the time in London.) If warm, spill outside on to the terrace for a better view of that church façade, and explore the town, with its unexpectedly interesting shops.

NEARBY Côte d'Opale; Fôret de Crécy; Somme battlefields.
LOCATION in church square, 10 km NE of Abbeville; car parking
FOOD breakfast, lunch, dinner
PRICE €€€ **ROOMS** 11, 10 double and twin, 1 apartment, all with bath or shower; all rooms have phone, TV, hairdrier, minibar; 2 have air conditioning
FACILITIES sitting room, bar, tea room/dining room, lift, terrace **CREDIT CARDS** AE, DC, MC, V **CHILDREN** welcome
DISABLED no special facilities
PETS accepted
CLOSED Christmas, Jan
PROPRIETOR Bernadette Stubbe-Martens

THE NORTH-EAST

TROYES

LE CHAMP DES OISEAUX
~ TOWN HOTEL ~

20, rue Linard Gonthier, 10000 Troyes (Aube)
TEL 03 25 80 58 50 **FAX** 03 25 80 98 34
E-MAIL message@champdesoiseaux.com **WEBSITE** www.champdesoiseaux.com

THE CITE, OR HISTORIC CENTRE of Troyes, is a symphony of amazing timber-framed buildings dating back to the Middle Ages, and this hotel gives you a ringside seat. It is an exceptionally skilful restoration using traditional techniques of two dwellings dating from the 15th and 16th centuries, on a peaceful cobbled side street.

The courtyard is a charming feature of the interior, where you can eat in warm weather. Looking into it are the bedrooms, artfully carved out of irregular spaces. Here, a bed raised on a platform; there a bathroom slipped in under closely sloping beams, and a loo dramatically perched up flights of steps. Some of the rooms are small, and some guests report noise as other visitors enter or leave their rooms, but all are decorated in clean good taste to contrast with the heavy, beamy features: simple white bedspreads, white-painted tables, and well-judged, emphatically patterned or coloured fabrics. There's a sitting room in the cellar and an artfully decorated breakfast room. No restaurant, but Mme Boisseau will give you the inside track on local eating places.

~

NEARBY cathedral; archbishop's palace with museum of modern art.
LOCATION city centre; garage car parking
FOOD breakfast
PRICE €€€
ROOMS 12; 9 double and twin, 3 suites, 10 with bath, 2 with shower; all rooms have phone, TV
FACILITIES 2 sitting rooms, bar, breakfast room, courtyard
CREDIT CARDS AE, DC, MC, V
CHILDREN accepted
DISABLED 1 specially adapted room
PETS accepted
CLOSED never
PROPRIETOR Monique Boisseau

THE NORTH-EAST

✳ LA TOUR DU ROY ✳
∼ TOWN HOTEL ∼

45 rue Général Leclerc, 02140 Vervins en Thierache (Aisne)
TEL 03 23 98 00 11 **FAX** 03 23 98 00 72
E-MAIL chatotel@chatotel.com **WEBSITE** www.chateauxethotels.com

PLACES LIKE THIS often disappoint, perhaps especially in France: the imposing manor house exterior (in this case commanding the town's ramparts), the historic associations, the romantic fortified tower -- could so easily be gift wrapping for pretentious food and dubious bedrooms. Well, to be honest, some of La Tour's bedrooms are fairly middle-aged and predictable, with jarring colour schemes; but that doesn't stop it being something special. In fact, it has a certain quirky panache: mainly because of the circular bedrooms in the 11thC tower (one approached through the bathroom, with double tub); but also on account of the flowery wash basins; of the lobster tank jostling the solid manor house furniture in the lobby; the huge stained glass windows; the fortified wall exposed in the dining room; and here and there an interesting Art Nouveau chair to contrast with parquet, tapestries, panelling and provincial antiques.

The Desvignes run things with enthusiasm and care. Their assistant manager, the Anglophile Eric de Robaulx, is a character – "Tell your English readers I've got Scottish ancestry – the Beamishes." In 2001, the courtyard was turned into a swimming pool. Your comments on this slightly eccentric, but endearing hotel, would be appreciated.

∼

NEARBY Laon (36 km); St-Quentin (50 km).
LOCATION 36 km NE of Laon, on N2 between Paris and Brussels; underground car parking **FOOD** breakfast, lunch, dinner **PRICE** €€ **ROOMS** 22; 13 double, twin and triple, 8 suites, 1 apartment, all with bath; all rooms have phone, TV, air conditioning, minibar **FACILITIES** sitting room, dining room, swimming pool

CREDIT CARDS AE, DC, MC, V
CHILDREN welcome
DISABLED 2 specially adapted rooms **PETS** accepted
CLOSED never
PROPRIETORS Desvignes family

THE NORTH-EAST

WIERRE-EFFROY

FERME DU VERT
~ FARM GUESTHOUSE ~

62720 Wierre-Effroy (Pas-de-Calais)
TEL 03 21 87 67 00 **FAX** 03 21 83 22 62
E-MAIL ferme.du.vert@wanadoo.fr **WEBSITE** www.fermeduvert.com

There are two farm guesthouses at the village of Wierre-Effroy, the Ferme du Vert and the Ferme Auberge de la Raterie. From the outside, they both have the same sort of charm: farm buildings arranged around a delightful courtyard, dominated by the farmhouse itself, in each case a pleasing, long, low, shuttered building. Animals range freely. Ferme du Vert, however, is our clear favourite because the bedrooms are in simple good taste – white walls, beams, adequate, homely furnishings – rather than jarring colour schemes. No. 16 is good fun, with plenty of space. Ferme du Vert also offers genuine peace – much of the Raterie is given over to conference facilities. There is a homely *salon*, which some might think stark, but we thought it relaxing. M. and Mme Bernard are friendly owners who know their business. Across the courtyard is the simple restaurant, with its big, inviting open fireplace and herbs hanging from the roof beams. Visitors report 'tasty home cooking', singling out the soup and duck cooked in beer. There's plenty to amuse you here, and they make their own cheese. The Bernards are in the process of opening another interesting new place to stay nearby – the former family home of Mme Bernard – leaving the Ferme du Vert to be run by their son. Ask for details.

~

NEARBY Côte d'Opale; Boulogne; Calais.
LOCATION A16 exit Marquise-Rinxent, follow signs to Wierre-Effroy, hotel well signposted up track; car parking
FOOD breakfast, lunch, dinner
PRICE €
ROOMS 16; 11 double, 1 single, four triple/family, all with bath or shower; all rooms have phone, TV; some have minibar
FACILITIES sitting room, bar, breakfast room, dining room, table tennis, putting, short tennis, bicycles
CREDIT CARDS MC, V **CHILDREN** welcome
DISABLED 3 rooms on ground floor
PETS accepted **CLOSED** mid-Dec to mid-Jan
PROPRIETORS M. and Mme Bernard

THE NORTH-EAST

TROIS MOUSQUETAIRES

CHATEAU HOTEL

27 rue du Fort de la Redoute, 62120 Aire-sur-la-Lys (Pas-de-Calais)
TEL 03 21 39 01 11 **FAX** 03 21 39 50 10 **E-MAIL** phvenet@wanadoo.fr
FOOD breakfast, lunch, dinner
PRICE € **ROOMS** 33 **CLOSED** mid-Dec to mid-Mar

AN ECCENTRIC MIXTURE of stone-and-brick stripes and pseudo-timbering beneath a steep slate roof, set in a large wooded garden with ponds and streams, this family-run *hostellerie* has long featured in our guide. On a recent visit we felt that Mme Venet's hotel, though spruce, was becoming somewhat dowdy, and readers' reports confirmed our view that her husband and son's regional food, though very good, was served (from the spotless open-to-view kitchen) without much enthusiasm. The interior is traditionally grand in style, the best of the old bedrooms huge and elegant, although some are much smaller and plainer. Those in the annexe are decorated in various styles – one has a Japanese theme, for example.

CHEZ NORBERT

TOWN HOTEL

9 Grand'rue, 68750 Bergheim (Haut-Rhin)
TEL 03 89 73 31 15
FAX 03 89 73 60 65
FOOD breakfast, Sun lunch, dinner
PRICE €€
ROOMS 12
CLOSED Mar, 1 week Nov

ONE OF OUR MOST knowledgeable reporters recommends this hotel-restaurant on the (rather busy) main street of charming Bergheim. Behind the big wooden gates, you're at once removed from the traffic, in a charming, mellow courtyard: plenty of flowers and greenery, outdoor seating and tables in sunny corners. Inside, the atmospheric restaurant is centre-stage: they reckon on packing the customers in here, under the low-slung beams, on one of which perches a row of bulbous *eau de vie* bottles: The Alsatian cooking is locally popular, and owner Norbert has an interesting wine cellar. Bedrooms are comfortable. A simple inn from which to enjoy Bergheim and surroundings.

THE NORTH-EAST

CHAMPILLON

✷ ROYAL CHAMPAGNE ✷

VILLAGE HOTEL

RN 51, Bellevue, 51160 Champillon (Marne)
TEL 03 26 52 87 11 **FAX** 03 26 52 89 69 **E-MAIL** royalchampagne @relaischateaux.fr **FOOD** breakfast, lunch, dinner; room service **PRICE** €€€€
ROOMS 25 **CLOSED** early to mid-Feb

WE STRAY SOME WAY outside our usual territory to include this conventional hotel with *grand-bourgeois* (Relais et Chateaux) comforts. It has a staggering view over Epernay; there are cosy, timbered public areas, with fabric wall coverings, hung with breastplates and swords (the place is named after the Royal Champagne, a cavalry regiment); and there's a quaintly beamed dining room. The friendly service is a bonus, too. However: none of the bedrooms is in the main hotel building, but in characterless motel-style chalets about a minute's walk away, some down unlovely concrete steps. Best for the middle-aged or elderly.

Book through our travel service – see page 7.

MARLENHEIM

✷ LE CERF ✷

VILLAGE INN

30 rue du Général-de-Gaulle, 67520 Marlenheim (Bas-Rhin)
TEL 03 88 87 73 73
FAX 03 88 87 68 08
E-MAIL info@lecerf.com
WEBSITE www.lecerf.com
FOOD breakfast, lunch, dinner
PRICE €€€
ROOMS 13
CLOSED never; restaurant closed Tues, Wed

ALL THE SIGNS are that the Cerf is as compelling as ever for visitors who like the cooking of Alsace as much as its wines. Michel Husser carries on the gastronomic tradition of father Robert; Michelin awards two stars for such house specialities as *presskopf de tête de veau en croustille, sauce gribiche* and *choucroute au cochon de lait et foie gras fumé*. Bedrooms are not particularly luxurious, but are well furnished and thoroughly comfortable. There is a cobbled courtyard for drinks and breakfast. We hope, given the prices charged, that Le Cerf continues to keep up standards – one reader's letter indicates that they can sometimes slip up. More reports would be welcome.

Book through our travel service – see page 7.

THE NORTH-EAST

AUBERGE LA GRENOUILLERE

RESTAURANT-WITH-ROOMS

La Madelaine-sous-Montreuil,
62170 Montreuil (Pas-de-Calais)
TEL 03 21 06 07 22
FAX 03 21 86 36 36
FOOD breakfast, lunch, dinner
PRICE € **ROOMS** 4
CLOSED Jan, Wed (except Jul,
Aug), Tues

WE'VE RECEIVED a few quibbles of late about this low Picardy-style farm-house, known to many as the Froggery, but hopefully the negative comments reflect no more than hiccups. Positive voices speak of 'delight-ful' lunches taken on the terrace, and Michelin continues to award a star, Gault Millau 16/20 for the food. The spacious gravel terrace is certainly an excellent spot for leisurely lunches, rather overshadowing the gleaming brass and polished wood of the restaurant – complete with frog-motif mural (done by an Englishman of course). Bedrooms are excellent, with well-equipped and very attractive bathrooms. Don't be too put off by all those other English voices: this is a serious French enterprise.

CLOSED Christmas to mid-Jan

BOYER 'LES CRAYERES'

CHATEAU HOTEL

64 boulevard Henry Vasnier,
51100 Reims (Marne)
TEL 03 26 82 80 80
FAX 03 26 82 65 52 **E-MAIL**
crayeres@relaischateaux.com
WEBSITE www.relaischateaux.
com/crayeres
FOOD breakfast, lunch dinner;
room service **PRICE**
€€€€€ **ROOMS** 16

GERARD BOYER (one of the finest chefs in the land) and his wife Elyane had a good starting point: a graceful turn-of-the-century mansion, situ-ated in a spacious park almost at the heart of Reims and surrounded by the *caves* of the famous champagne names. With Elyane's taste in interior decoration, they could hardly go far wrong. There are a grand staircase, enormous windows, marble columns and tapestries, a wood panelled.can-dlelit dining room, and, of course, sumptuous bedrooms, individually deco-rated. As for the superb wines and the food, which continues to merit three Michelin stars: our advise is to starve yourself in preparation.

THE NORTH-EAST

TURCKHEIM

BERCEAU DE VIGNERON

TOWN HOTEL

10 place Turenne, 68230 Turckheim (Haut-Rhin)
TEL 03 89 27 23 55
FAX 03 89 27 41 21
FOOD breakfast
PRICE €
ROOMS 16
CLOSED Jan to mid-Feb

OUR REPORTERS LIKED the location of this new entry to the guide: it's built into the ramparts of the Disneyesque medieval town of Turckheim, by the city gates. The traditional Alsatian building has been completely renovated, to give a smart, if predictable style - clay floors, beams, wooden pillars, rustic furniture and check tablecloths in the breakfast room. The owners, M. and Mme Baur, have entrusted day to day running to Pecci Laurent and Sojka Thomas. Bedrooms are adequately furnished, but a bit dull. A useful back-up, budget address along the Route de Vin. your impressions would be welcome. Breakfast only is served, but there's a restaurant - Auberge du Veilleur - close by.

THE WEST

HOTELS IN THE WEST

O UR WEST OF FRANCE REGION has three major components of interest to visitors. First there is the Loire valley and its immediate surroundings, including the atmospheric Sologne, south of Orléans, as well as the valleys of the Loire's two major tributaries, the Cher and the Indre. Not surprisingly in a region so rich in history and magnificent architecture, with a cultivated landscape, some important vineyards and a fine cuisine, the greatest cluster of charming small hotels is here. The second area of interest is the hilly Limousin, fading into the northern fringes of Périgord, around Angoulême and Limoges. And finally there is the hinterland of the Atlantic coast, including the canals of Poitou-Charente.

The Loire cuts a swathe across the centre of France, linking the important cities of Angers, Tours and Orléans; the last was the country's artistic and intellectual capital in medieval times. Strung out between the three are the famous royal châteaux, including the Renaissance jewels of Chambord and Chenonceau. Some of our Loire hotels are housed in châteaux that are cast in the same mould: Château de Pray at Amboise (page 113), Château des Briottières at Champigné (page 120), Château de Rochecotte at St-Patrice (page 139) and Domaine de la Tortinière at Montbazon-en-Touraine (page 126). They might look intimidating from the outside, but are generally run with the kind of warm informality that particularly appeals to us.

Just because you're in the Loire, however, doesn't mean that you have to stay in a château and there are many more intimate charming small hotels as well: for example, the family-friendly manor house Manoir de Clénord at Mont-près-Chambord (page 125), Le Bon Laboureur, an extended coaching inn at Chenonceaux (page 121) , La Tonnellerie, a solid village house with a country atmosphere in Tavers near Beaugency (page 140) or, further south on the Indre at St-Jean-St-Germain near Loches, the converted mill, Le Moulin (page 137).

There are a couple of magnificent châteaux hotels, de La Verrerie (at Oizon near Aubigny-sur-Nère, page 130) and its smaller neighbour, d'Ivoy (at Ivoy le Pré, page 124) towards the eastern edge of the region on the fringes of the Massif Central. To the south there's another pocket of hotels around Châteauroux including the charming L'Hermitage on the river at Buzançais (page 118), renowned for its excellent food.

Travelling south, in the Limousin, where the hills are gentle precursors to the dramatic landscape of cliffs and gorges of the Massif Central, we recommend another couple of châteaux. De Nieuil is an impressive turreted Renaissance building (at Nieuil, page 129), which has been in the same family for years, and Hostellerie Ste-Catherine at Montbron (page 127), once owned by the Empress Joséphine, is a relaxed place for a short stay, more like a country house than a château.

Finally, to the west, where great rollers break on the long sandy beaches of the windswept Atlantic coast, we have a clutch of hotels, from a useful bed-and-breakfast in La Rochelle (33 Rue Thiers, page 132) to a simple *auberge* in Pons (Auberge Pontoise, page 142), and one of our most satisfactory new finds, Domaine de Rennebourg at St-Denis-du-Pin (page 134), a delightful *chambres d'hôte*, run by a mother and daughter.

THE WEST

AMBOISE

✳ CHATEAU DE PRAY ✳
∼ CHATEAU HOTEL ∼

route de Chargé, 37400 Amboise (Indre-et-Loire)
TEL 02 47 57 23 67 **FAX** 02 47 57 32 50
E-MAIL chateau.depray@wanadoo.fr **WEBSITE** www.praycastel.online.fr

IF YOU ARE FOND OF Loire wines and, by and large, would prefer not to walk up and down hills, then the main road between Amboise and Chargé is just the place for a stroll. Every few yards there are caves hollowed from the soft stone of the bluffs that line the course of the river. Further back, and higher, the Château de Pray's Renaissance façade looks down towards the river, flanked by two stout 13thC turrets. The effect is a little like the belle of the ball sandwiched between a pair of dowager aunts. Managed by chef Ludovic Laurenty and his wife, this is an agreeable, friendly spot in a surprisingly pastoral setting. Monsieur Laurenty's short, seasonal menus, presented in a dining room with an imposing stone fireplace, are a delight and draw in not only locals but also guests staying at a neighbouring *manoir* that has no restaurant of its own.

The bedrooms, all with excellent bathrooms, are smart and appealing. They are not furnished in heavy baronial style (although two or three of them have four-posters) but all have their fair share of antique furniture and walls hung with paintings that are appreciably better than average. The immaculate courtyard is a suntrap and the lawns below the château look a likely place for that aperitif you've been thinking about all day.

∼

NEARBY Tours (25 km); Blois (34 km); Loire châteaux; golf.
LOCATION 3 km E of Amboise on the D751 beyond junction with the N10; car parking
FOOD breakfast, lunch, dinner **PRICE** €€€-€€€€ **ROOMS** 19; 13 double, 3 twin, 2 triple, 1 family, all with bath or shower; all rooms have phone, TV, hairdrier
FACILITIES sitting room, dining room, bar, terrace, garden, swimming pool **CREDIT CARDS** AE, DC, MC, V **CHILDREN** accepted **DISABLED** access difficult **PETS** not accepted **CLOSED** early Jan to mid-Feb; restaurant Tues dinner, Wed **MANAGER** Ludovic Laurenty

✳ BOOK THIS HOTEL
✳ BOOK FERRY/EUROTUNNEL
✳ SAVE MONEY
TEL: (UK) 01892 55 98 66
e-mail enquiries@chs-travelservice.com

THE WEST

LE RELAIS DU LYON D'OR
~ VILLAGE INN ~

4 rue d'Enfer, 86260 Angles sur l'Anglin (Vienne)
TEL 05 49 48 32 53 **FAX** 05 49 84 02 28
E-MAIL thoreau@lyondor.com **WEBSITE** www.lyondor.com

ANGLES SUR L'ANGLIN IS, by any measure, a very attractive village indeed. Perched on a hill, its medieval houses look out over the substantial ruins of both castle and abbey to the river below. Carvings discovered recently in caves near the river show that people have been coming here for around 15,000 years but these early visitors' misfortune was that Guillaume and Heather Thoreau didn't arrive until 1994. They took a semi-derelict post house and transformed it, inside and out, making a delightful hotel with a highly successful restaurant that beats any big-city equivalent with the freshness and quality of its (local) ingredients, and wins the service match hands down with its warmth and friendliness. A large room with a high, beamed ceiling and a baronial stone fireplace at one end, it is still warm and intimate. Local wines are well represented on the short, excellent wine list, and there is a wide selection of half bottles so you can ring the changes.

The decoration is Heather's department, and her art and influence show in every room, where the original architectural features have been painstakingly restored. The bedrooms are all different, decorated in warm colours and with fine fabrics, and all reveal Heather's skill with paint-effects (she runs courses). The bathrooms are works of art themselves.

~

NEARBY La Roche-Posay (12 km); jardin des 'Rosiers'; Poitiers (51 km).
LOCATION in centre of village; car parking
FOOD breakfast, lunch, dinner
PRICE €
ROOMS 11; 8 double and twin, 1 triple, 2 family suites, 5 with bath, 6 with shower; all rooms have phone, TV
FACILITIES sitting room, restaurant, health centre
CREDIT CARDS AE, MC, V
CHILDREN accepted
DISABLED 1 specially adapted suite
PETS accepted **CLOSED** Jan to Mar
PROPRIETORS Heather and Guillaume Thoreau

THE WEST

AUBERGE DU MOULIN DE CHAMERON
~ CONVERTED MILL ~

Bannegon, 18210 Charenton-du-Cher (Cher)
TEL 02 48 61 83 80 **FAX** 02 48 61 84 92
E-MAIL moulindechameron@wanadoo.fr **WEBSITE** www.moulindechameron.free.fr

THE MOULIN DE CHAMÉRON is a curious animal, and difficult to categorize. At the heart of it is the original 18thC watermill – now a combination of country museum, displaying ancient tools of the trade, and charmingly intimate and traditional restaurant, with the old fireplace as its focal point. But the bedrooms are housed across the garden in a pair of unremarkable modern buildings of rather towny appearance – comfortable, but thin on charm. So should it be thought of as a restaurant-with-rooms? We think to do so would be to underestimate its appeal as a place to stay for more than a one-night stopover (though one reporter found the peace marred by the noise of early morning departures) – at least in summer, when the wooded garden and neat pool come into play, along with the restaurant's romantic tented dining terrace beside the mill stream. Jean Merilleau's cooking is excellent: dinner might include trout served with a *fondue* of endives, oxtail cooked in wine, followed by a chocolate *fondant aux aromates*, and we've heard that there is a well-stocked and wide-ranging cellar.

Try for one of the bedrooms with its own small terrace, where in fine weather you can breakfast to birdsong.

~

NEARBY Meillant castle (25 km); Noirlac abbey (30 km).
LOCATION in countryside between Bannegon and Neuilly, 40 km SE of Bourges; car parking
FOOD breakfast, lunch, dinner
PRICE €-€€€
ROOMS 14; 8 double, 5 twin, 8 with bath; 5 with shower, 1 family with bath; all rooms have phone, TV
FACILITIES 2 sitting rooms, bar, 2 dining rooms, garden, swimming pool, table tennis, fishing **CREDIT CARDS** AE, MC, V **CHILDREN** welcome
DISABLED no special facilities **PETS** accepted **CLOSED** mid-Nov to early Mar; restaurant low season Mon and Tues lunch
PROPRIETORS M. Rommel and M. Merilleau

THE WEST

Le Blanc

DOMAINE DE L'ETAPE
⟿ MANOR HOUSE HOTEL ⟿

route de Bélâbre, 36300 Le Blanc (Indre)
TEL 02 54 37 18 02 **FAX** 02 54 37 75 59
E-MAIL domainetape@wanadoo.fr **WEBSITE** www.domainetape.wanadoo.fr

THE DOMAINE DE L'ETAPE IS, quite literally, at the end of the road deep enough in the countryside to satisfy the most desperate need to escape the city. A 19thC mansion in 250 hectares of woods and fields, it also has a large lake, which you're welcome to fish, and, three minutes' walk away, the outbuildings of a home farm, complete with horses and chickens. All this is presided over by Mme Seiller with the kind of genial tranquillity that comes of years of practice (28 of them in her case). The house has been in her family for 120 years, and when she started the hotel she had just seven bedrooms. There are now 35 but within that total there are three distinct types. Those in the hotel itself are undoubtedly the best on offer, comfortably and informally decorated – although one or two will be bidding for a place in the renovation schedule quite soon. Then there is a pleasant two-storeyed modern building, with rooms on the ground floor that open directly to the garden. Lastly there are some very rustic rooms down on the farm, which are long on character, but short on comfort. Hard-wearing and cheap, they tend to be popular with families. Back in the main building there is a panelled dining room that opens out to the terrace and a handsome Louis Philippe *salon*. Family friendly.

NEARBY La Roche-Posay (30 km); jardin des 'Rosiers'; Poitiers (60 km); golf; canoeing.
LOCATION 5 km SE of Le Blanc off the D10 to Bélâbre; car parking
FOOD breakfast, lunch, dinner
PRICE €-€€
ROOMS 35; 14 double, 17 twin, 3 triple, 1 family, 30 with bath, 5 with shower; all rooms have phone, TV, minibar, hairdrier
FACILITIES sitting room, 2 dining rooms, terrace, garden, fishing, riding
CREDIT CARDS AE, DC, MC, V **CHILDREN** accepted
DISABLED access possible
PETS accepted **CLOSED** never
PROPRIETOR Mme Seiller

THE WEST

BRIOLLAY

✳ CHATEAU DE NOIRIEUX ✳
～ MANOR HOUSE HOTEL ～

26 route du Moulin, 49125 Briollay (Maine-et-Loire)
TEL 02 41 42 50 05 **FAX** 02 41 37 91 00
E-MAIL noirieux@relaischateaux.fr

'A GEM OF A HOTEL, situated at the western end of the Loire châteaux-belt; whereas most hotels on the Loire tourist trail are over-priced and under-enthusiastic, this one gets most things right and is thoroughly professional in the nicest way.' So says one of our most conscientious reporters. Since he's started so well, we'll let him finish.

'Dating from the 17th century, with Art Deco additions in 1927, it opened as a hotel in 1991. It is set in magnificent grounds, with views down to the Loire. It is outstandingly comfortable; a good test was that during three days of almost continuous rain we always felt cosseted. The *salons* are beautifully furnished and comfortable, the dining room light and airy, with a terrace for fine weather. Bedrooms are split between the main building and two others – all well furnished, some quite opulently.

'The cuisine is inventive and of a high standard. The wine list is exemplary, with prices that don't take your breath away. We received a warm welcome, and all the staff were unfailingly helpful and courteous. The château is not cheap, but is excellent value in every respect.'

NEARBY Angers (12 km); Loire châteaux; golf.
LOCATION in countryside off D52 (junction 14 off A11); car parking
FOOD breakfast, lunch, dinner
PRICE €€€€-€€€€€
ROOMS 19 double with bath; some rooms have phone, TV, minibar, hairdrier
FACILITIES sitting room/bar, dining room, Jacuzzi, garden, swimming pool, tennis
CREDIT CARDS AE, DC, MC, V
CHILDREN accepted **DISABLED** 2 ground-floor bedrooms
PETS accepted
CLOSED Feb, Nov; restaurant Sun dinner, Mon mid-Oct to mid-Apr
MANAGERS Gérard and Anja Côme

THE WEST

L'HERMITAGE
~ RIVERSIDE HOTEL ~

route d'Argy, 36500 Buzançais (Indre)
TEL 02 54 84 03 90 **FAX** 02 54 02 13 19

ON THE OTHERWISE unremarkable fringe of Buzançais, with its back to the road, lies a small, charming creeper-clad hotel. After turning into the yard (lockable garages are available) you walk under a short, covered land bridge into delightful and unexpectedly large grounds complete with peacocks. Beyond the gravel outside the front door, lawns slope gently down to the shade of the weeping willows on the bank of the Indre – you are welcome to bring your fishing-pole and try your luck. Inside, probably after an effusive greeting from various dogs, the first person you're likely to meet is Mme Sureau. Her husband Claude is the chef, and between them they own and run L'Hermitage. His menus offer tremendous value (count the locals who are keeping you company) and vary not just from season to season but also from day to day depending on what looked tempting in the market that morning. The hotel has two dining rooms, for summer and winter, with the land bridge connecting the summer dining room, in its own attractive (air-conditioned) garden pavilion, to the main building. It has a small terrace outside for those who would rather dine outside. The bedrooms are quite modest in size, but light and fresh and most have a view over the gardens.

NEARBY Châteauroux (27 km); Loches (45 km); golf; riding.
LOCATION on outskirts of town on D11 to Argy, beside the Indre; car parking
FOOD breakfast, lunch, dinner
PRICE €
ROOMS 14; 6 double, 6 twin, 6 with bath, 6 with shower, 2 single with shower; all rooms have phone, TV, hairdrier
FACILITIES sitting area, 2 dining rooms, terrace, garden, fishing
CREDIT CARDS MC, V
CHILDREN accepted
DISABLED not suitable **PETS** accepted
CLOSED 2 weeks mid-Sep
PROPRIETORS M. and Mme Sureau

THE WEST

CANGEY

LE FLEURAY
～ MANOR HOUSE HOTEL ～

Cangey, 37530 Amboise (Indre-et-Loire)
TEL 02 47 56 09 25 **FAX** 02 47 56 93 97
E-MAIL lefleurayhotel@wanadoo.fr **WEBSITE** www.lefleurayhotel.com

WE REVISITED a couple of years ago and appreciated once more Le Fleuray's two key attractions: a warm welcome and relaxed atmosphere, courtesy of the Newingtons, the lively and committed English owners; and the peaceful, indeed isolated, rural setting in open fields. (Keep faith in the signposting from Cangey – it's more than 6 km outside the village.) Combined, these qualities are at a premium in the Loire (major sights and vineyards are within half an hour) and together with fair prices for prettily decorated rooms with views (the best with small outdoor sitting areas) explain the place's obvious popularity. There is a particularly attractive terrace for summer dining, and when we visited in high season there was a good-humoured buzz in the dining room from a cross-section of nationalities. The staff, several English students on long vacation, were at full stretch. Don't expect a 'French eating experience'. Despite positive readers' letters about the cooking, we found that the menu changes little, and that the food, though satisfying, lacks panache.

At certain times, guests are expected to eat dinner in the hotel – check when booking if the obligatory half pension terms are operating.

～

NEARBY Châteaux: Amboise, Chaumont, Chenonceaux, Tours; Vouvray (vineyards).
LOCATION on D74, 12 km NE of Amboise, 7 km from A10 exit 18; car parking
FOOD breakfast, dinner
PRICE €€€
ROOMS 14 double and family, 8 with bath, 6 with shower; all rooms have phone
FACILITIES sitting room, restaurant, terrace, garden
CREDIT CARDS MC, V
CHILDREN welcome
DISABLED specially adapted rooms available
PETS accepted
CLOSED late Feb, late Oct to early Nov, Christmas and New Year
PROPRIETORS Newington family

THE WEST

CHATEAU DES BRIOTTIERES
~ CHATEAU HOTEL ~

49330 Champigné (Maine-et-Loire)
TEL 02 41 42 00 02 **FAX** 02 41 42 01 55
E-MAIL briottieres@wanadoo.fr **WEBSITE** www.briottieres.com

LIFE'S HURLY-BURLY has never made it through the gates, let alone up the wooded drive, of this serene château. Two hundred years of unbroken ownership by the same family have kept the atmosphere as well as the contents and appearance of this house wonderfully intact. François de Valbray, the present relaxed owner, has thought of everybody. If you want the undiluted charm and grace of the château, you can stay in it, dine beneath the gaze of the ancestors (by arrangement), relax in the *grand salon* and generally use the place like home (including a game of billiards after dinner if you're so inclined). Bedrooms and bathrooms vary in size but all offer style and comfort.

If you're travelling in a party, or are worried about how your children and your blood pressure will thrive in this antique-laden environment, then take some or all of the old *fruitier*: this thoroughly comfortable house is close to the main building, and has its own more utilitarian sitting room. Outside there are 40 hectares of woods, lawn and lake to protect you from the farmland beyond. If you just want to get married, you can take the imposing old stable block but expect to have to arrive along the back drive and leave (quietly) the same way to avoid disturbing other guests. A gem.

NEARBY Angers (24 km); abbeys of Solesmes and Fontevrault; Loire châteaux; golf.
LOCATION 3.5 km N of Champigné on the D190; car parking
FOOD breakfast, dinner (by arrangement)
PRICE €€€-€€€€€
ROOMS 15; 10 double and twin with bath, 5 double and twin with shared bath in *gîte*; 10 rooms have phone
FACILITIES sitting rooms, billiards room/library, dining room, terrace, garden, swimming pool
CREDIT CARDS AE, DC, MC, V **CHILDREN** accepted
DISABLED access difficult
PETS accepted **CLOSED** New Year, Feb
PROPRIETORS François and Hedwige de Valbray

THE WEST

✳ LE BON LABOUREUR ✳
∽ VILLAGE HOTEL ∽

6 rue du Docteur-Bretonneau, 37150 Chenonceaux (Indre-et-Loire)
TEL 02 47 23 90 02 **FAX** 02 47 23 82 01
E-MAIL laboureur@wanadoo.fr **WEBSITE** www.amboise.com/laboureur

AFTER 200 YEARS OR SO as close neighbours of the Château de Chenonceau, the Jeudi family knows a thing or two about receiving visitors. The first priority, of course, is to have somewhere to put them. So, as the popularity of this 18thC coaching inn increased (the châteaux of Amboise, Chambord and Chaumont are all close by), it has absorbed several other buildings, expanding sideways and even across to the other side of the road. A swimming pool in the pleasant garden and a tree-shaded terrace for outside dining have increased its appeal, and two sitting rooms and a capacious bar offer plenty of uncrowded space indoors. A pair of dining rooms, one an elegant period room and the other a more relaxed area, gives you a chance to ring the changes and, if travelling with children, to lengthen their leashes a little.

It would be difficult to shorten the supply chain for many of the vegetables used in the hotel's competent kitchen: their own kitchen garden is right next door. Several of the generally light, attractive bedrooms are well set up as family rooms, with those in 'The Manor' furthest from the general bustle of the hotel. An amiable spot.

NEARBY Tours (35 km); Amboise (14 km); Loire châteaux; golf.
LOCATION in the middle of the village, 200 m from the château; car parking
FOOD breakfast, lunch, dinner
PRICE € € € **ROOMS** 28; 24 double and twin, 4 apartments, all with bath or shower; all rooms have phone, TV; some have air conditioning **FACILITIES** sitting room, 2 dining rooms, bar, terrace, garden, swimming pool, helipad **CREDIT CARDS** AE, DC, MC, V **CHILDREN** welcome **DISABLED** 2 specially adapted rooms **PETS** accepted **CLOSED** mid-Nov to mid-Dec, early Jan to mid-Feb; restaurant mid-Oct to Apr Wed lunch, Thurs **PROPRIETORS** M. and Mme Jeudi

THE WEST

CHINON

✳ HOTEL DIDEROT ✳
∼ TOWN MANSION ∼

4 rue Buffon, 37500 Chinon (Indre-et-Loire)
TEL 02 47 93 18 87 **FAX** 02 47 93 37 10
E-MAIL hoteldiderot@wanadoo.fr

SURPRISINGLY FEW HOTELS have been in these pages since the first edition while generating a steady stream of entirely complimentary reports. And we hear that nothing has changed at the Diderot, not even the moderate prices. 'Excellent' and 'superb' are typical verdicts, and the latest visitors, who couldn't have been happier with their 'lovely', 'comfortable', 'bright and airy' room facing the front, will 'definitely return'. The rooms at the back are darker but equally comfortable and attractively decorated.

Creeper-covered and white-shuttered, it is a handsome town house set in a courtyard, which conveys the benefit of convenient private parking. Its exotic collection of trees – including fig and banana – makes the courtyard an appealing spot for sitting out and there are plenty of tables and chairs to encourage you. The French-Cypriot proprietors are charming and unstintingly helpful, and breakfast (served on the shady terrace or in a rustic room with tiled floor and massive beams) is exceptionally tasty – thanks to Madame's home-made preserves, which you can buy to take home with you. Bedrooms are simply furnished, but are spotlessly clean and some have fine views. Some now also have smart new bathrooms.

NEARBY châteaux: Azay-le-Rideau (20 km), Langeais (30 km).
LOCATION in middle of town; car parking
FOOD breakfast
PRICE €
ROOMS 28; 26 double and twin, 2 family, all with bath or shower; all rooms have phone **FACILITIES** bar, breakfast room, courtyard
CREDIT CARDS AE, DC, MC, V **CHILDREN** welcome

DISABLED some ground-floor bedrooms
PETS not accepted
CLOSED 1 week Christmas, mid-Jan to mid-Feb
PROPRIETOR Theo Kazamias

THE WEST

LE CHATEAU DES REAUX
~ CHATEAU HOTEL ~

Chouzé-sur-Loire, 37140 Bourgueil (Indre-et-Loire)
TEL 02 47 95 14 40 **FAX** 02 47 95 18 34
E-MAIL reaux@club-internet.fr **WEBSITE** www.chateaux-france.com/-reaux

O**N THE NORTH BANK** of the Loire, between its confluences with the Indre and Vienne, this was the first Renaissance château to be built in the Valley of the Kings. The builder, Jean Briçonnet, was the first mayor of Tours and his family went on to build Chenonceau and Azay-le-Rideau. Built on the foundations of a 1,000-year-old keep, and surrounded by a moat, alternating brickwork with the white stone of Touraine produced its startling red and white geometric exterior. The plainer neo-classical element was added some 250 years later and the most recent addition, by the great-great-grandfather of the present owners, reverted to the original chequerboard design.

Jean-Luc and Florence de Bouillé obviously cherish this national monument (just look at the care lavished on the glorious *salons*) and have encyclopædic knowledge of its history. Bedrooms may vary in size but not in authenticity, their old, beamed interiors freshened rather than obscured by modern decoration. Whatever else you do, take a walk up the magnificent staircase inside one of the towers – perhaps to work up an appetite before settling down to a dinner designed to show you the best produce the region can offer (only available for groups of 10 people or more, and must be booked in advance). There are four more modest bedrooms in a cottage in the grounds – at cheaper prices.

~

NEARBY Chinon (13 km); Tours (38 km); Saumur (26 km); Loire châteaux; golf; riding; canoeing.
LOCATION just E of Chouzé-sur-Loire off the N152, 4 km S of Bourgueil; car parking
FOOD breakfast; lunch and dinner for groups by arrangement
PRICE €€-€€€€
ROOMS 16; 12 double and twin, 4 suites, all with bath; all rooms have phone, TV, hairdrier **FACILITIES** sitting room, dining room, bar, meeting room, garden, tennis
CREDIT CARDS AE, DC, MC, V **CHILDREN** accepted
DISABLED access difficult **PETS** not accepted **CLOSED** Christmas
PROPRIETORS Jean-Luc and Florence de Bouillé

THE WEST

CHATEAU D'IVOY
~ CHATEAU HOTEL ~

18380 Ivoy-le-Pré (Cher)
TEL 02 48 58 85 01 **FAX** 02 48 58 85 02
E-MAIL chateau.divoy@wanadoo.fr **WEBSITE** www.perso.wanadoo.fr/chateau.divoy

On a damp, cold day at the beginning of April, at the end of a long wet drive through the woods that surround it, and despite its 400-odd years of age, this château was warm. That makes it one of a very select band indeed and also signals the care that Mme Gouëffon-de Vaivre takes with her guests' comfort. The place was built by Lord Drummond, Mary Stuart's Purser, whose family wisely moved in permanently after the Battle of Culloden left Scotland open to the not-so-tender mercies of the English. All the bedrooms are large and they, and their superb bathrooms, look out over the lawns and park at the back of the château. Like the rest of the rooms, they are all stunning examples of Mme Gouëffon-de Vaivre's art: she is a professional interior designer whose first task was to rescue the dining room from the jungle established there by the previous owner as a habitat for his beloved insects. Ferns have now given way to Spode and hearty breakfasts.

Each bedroom is named and themed accordingly. 'Kipling' for example has colonial furniture surrounding a Victorian Anglo-Indian bed draped with a mosquito net. You can almost hear the distant skirl of pipes as you walk into 'Lord Drummond' with its ceiling-scraping four-poster. Downstairs, a grand *salon* and library are yours to enjoy.

~

NEARBY Aubigny-sur-Nère (19 km); Bourges (47 km); Gien (48 km); golf; canoeing.
LOCATION off D12, 5 km E of La Chapelle d'Angillon, through a park, 300 m on the right after the church; car parking
FOOD breakfast
PRICE €€€
ROOMS 6; 5 double, 4 with bath, 1 with shower, 1 twin with bath; all rooms have phone, TV, minibar
FACILITIES sitting room, library, breakfast room, terrace, garden, swimming pool, croquet, helipad **CREDIT CARDS** MC, V **CHILDREN** accepted over 14
DISABLED access difficult **PETS** not accepted **CLOSED** never
PROPRIETORS M. and Mme Gouëffon-de Vaivre

THE WEST

MANOIR DE CLÉNORD
~ COUNTRY BED-AND-BREAKFAST ~

route de Clénord, 41250 Mont-près-Chambord (Loir-et-Cher)
TEL 02 54 70 41 62 **FAX** 02 54 70 33 99
WEBSITE www.clenord.com

A QUIET, FAMILY-FRIENDLY 18thC manor house, surrounded by 25 hectares of woods, with a little river nearby and an attractive swimming pool, makes the Manoir de Clénord a popular spot with people keen to avoid the formality of many of the hotels in the region. The river, Le Beuvron, is a tributary of the Loire and took its name from the native beavers which still live along its course.

Madame Clement-d'Armont has given up offering a *table d'hôte* because of a serious traffic accident, but breakfast (included in the price) is as delicious as ever. With her son Christian's wife, Sylvie, taking over the reins of the business, she is now free to help her husband re-create an 18thC garden in front of the manor. Guests have the run of the house, including the use of a large drawing room (with an open fire in winter) furnished with the emphasis more on comfort than on show, which really sets the style for the rest of the house. The bedrooms are large, for the most part, with fine, old, solid furniture of the sort one's grandparents might have in their spare bedroom – no items of frail elegance playing hostage to childish misfortune.

If you plan to stay here, do something about it in good time: there are plenty of regulars who fill up the diary early in the season.

~

NEARBY Blois (9 km); Loire châteaux; Tours (69 km).
LOCATION in woods 4 km SW of Mont-près-Chambord on the road to Clénord; car parking
FOOD breakfast
PRICE €€
ROOMS 6; 2 double, 2 twin, 2 suites, all with bath or shower
FACILITIES sitting room, breakfast room, terrace, garden **CREDIT CARDS** AE, MC, V
CHILDREN accepted
DISABLED access difficult **PETS** accepted
CLOSED mid-Nov to mid-Mar
PROPRIETOR Christiane Clement-d'Armont

THE WEST

MONTBAZON-EN-TOURAINE

✳ DOMAINE DE LA TORTINIERE ✳
~ CHATEAU HOTEL ~

37250 Montbazon-en-Touraine (Indre-et-Loire)
TEL 02 47 34 35 00 **FAX** 02 47 65 95 70 **E-MAIL** domaine.tortiniere@wanadoo.fr
WEBSITE www.pro.wanadoo.fr/domaine.tortinere

PERCHED HIGH ABOVE the Indre, this attractive, turreted château has a clear view across its own sloping meadows and the river to the tower of Montbazon, and is close to the line of the old Roman road that led from there to Tours. Built in 1866 by the widow of Armand Dalloz (who created France's civil code), it took its name from the old manor that preceded it and first became a hotel in 1955. It is run with charm and energy by Xavier Olivereau and his wife Anne, who show the kind of attention to detail and genuine concern for the comfort of their guests that is almost a forgotten art elsewhere.

The ground-floor hall and *salon* are panelled and plastered, with parquet floors dotted with oriental rugs, empire chairs and generously upholstered, comfortable sofas. The winter restaurant shares this floor and has a cosy section inside one of the house's twin towers. The other tower hides a winding staircase and an underground passage to the spare and cool summer restaurant in the old orangery beneath a formal terrace. In dry weather the tables drift outside under awnings to get the full benefit of the magical setting. Bedrooms are a satisfying combination of taste and money: both elegant and comfortable. Some are not in the château proper but these are, if anything, of an even higher standard.

NEARBY Tours (9 km); Chenonceaux (33 km); Amboise (38 km).
LOCATION 2 km N of Montbazon on the N10 towards Tours and left on the D287; car parking **FOOD** breakfast, lunch, dinner **PRICE** €€€ **ROOMS** 29; 22 double and twin, 7 suites, all with bath; all rooms have phone, TV, hairdrier; some have air-conditioning **FACILITIES** sitting room, 2 dining rooms, terrace, garden, swimming pool, tennis, fishing **CREDIT CARDS** DC, MC, V **CHILDREN** accepted **DISABLED** 2 specially adapted rooms **PETS** accepted **CLOSED** never **PROPRIETORS** Olivereau family

THE WEST

HOSTELLERIE SAINTE-CATHERINE
~ CHATEAU HOTEL ~

route de Marthon, 16220 Montbron (Charente)
TEL 05 45 23 60 03 **FAX** 05 45 70 72 00

THE TARDOIRE VALLEY is a pretty one, but the area around Montbron, east of Angoulême, is off the beaten tourist track and we presume this is why we hear so little from readers about this fine old house, once the residence of the Empress Joséphine.

The approach, along a winding drive through splendid wooded grounds, is appropriately imposing and the house – built in a pale, irregular stone – looks handsome but austere. Inside it is a different story: despite fine furnishings and immaculate housekeeping, there is none of the expected pretension, and a relaxed, informal atmosphere prevails.

Rooms are decorated and furnished with proper regard for both style and comfort: the dining rooms (one leads into the other) have tapestries on the walls, and a carved wooden mantlepiece stands over an old fireplace; the two sitting rooms are inviting and relaxing. Most of the individually furnished and thoroughly comfortable bedrooms have views of the surrounding parkland; they do vary in size, and the prices reflect this. One menu and an 'interesting' *carte* are offered, where the majority of dishes are from nearby Périgord. There has been a change of owner since our last edition, so reports please.

~

NEARBY Angoulême (30 km); Brie (40 km); Rochechouart (40 km).
LOCATION in park off D16, 4 km SW of Montbron, E of Angoulême; car parking
FOOD breakfast, lunch, dinner
PRICE €€
ROOMS 18; 14 double, 4 family, most with bath or shower; all rooms have phone, TV
FACILITIES 2 sitting rooms, 2 dining rooms, bar, garden, swimming pool
CREDIT CARDS AE, DC, MC, V
CHILDREN accepted
DISABLED no special facilities **PETS** accepted
CLOSED never
PROPRIETOR Mme Crocquet

THE WEST

✳ CHATEAU DE LA MENAUDIERE ✳
～ CHATEAU HOTEL ～

BP15-Chissay-en-Touraine, 41401 Montrichard (Loir-et-Cher)
Tel 02 54 71 23 45 **Fax** 02 54 71 34 58
e-mail chat-menaudiere@wanadoo.fr

THERE SEEM TO BE FEW Loire châteaux that are not connected in some way with Jean Briçonnet, the first mayor of Tours, and Menaudière is not one of them. Built originally in 1443 on a rocky outcrop known as La Kaërie (which gave the château its first name), it replaced a manor owned by Briçonnet's family and continued in their ownership until 1624. This association also puts Menaudière in the heartland of the Loire châteaux, with Chenonceau, Amboise, Chambord and Chaumont all within striking distance. It has had its ups and downs, and, architecturally speaking, its additions and subtractions. One surviving element which preserves its charm is a stout, round tower, now completely divorced from the main building, which has three bedrooms served by a stone spiral staircase.

Elsewhere the fairly frequent changes of ownership have gradually worn away the original contents of the château so although the walls are historic, there are few ancestors gazing down from them, and some of the more modern furniture sits a little uneasily in its ancient surroundings. However, the staff are friendly and efficient, the bedrooms spacious and well equipped, and the two in-house restaurants offer the hungry traveller a wide range of choices supported by an extensive wine list.

Nearby Chenonceaux (11 km); Loire châteaux; golf.
Location to the right off the D115, 2 km from Montrichard towards Amboise; car parking
Food breakfast, lunch, dinner **Price** €€€ **Rooms** 27 double, twin and triple, 20 with bath, 7 with shower; all rooms have phone, TV, minibar **Facilities** sitting room, 2 dining rooms, meeting room, bar, terrace, garden, swimming pool, tennis

Credit cards AE, DC, MC, V
Children accepted **Disabled** not suitable **Pets** accepted **Closed** mid-Nov to Mar; restaurant Sun dinner, Mon low season
Proprietor Philippe Viard

THE WEST

NIEUIL

✳ CHATEAU DE NIEUIL ✳
～ CHATEAU HOTEL ～

route de Fontafie, 16270 Nieuil (Charente)
TEL 05 45 71 36 38 **FAX** 05 05 45 71 46 45
E-MAIL nieuil@relaischateaux.fr **WEBSITE** www.relaischateaux.fr/nieuil

'OUR ROOM WAS extremely comfortable, even though it was one of their smaller ones, and one of the best-value rooms of our holiday,' says a reporter on this fairy-tale Renaissance château, making the point that high prices can be worth paying if you get something special in return. Steep-roofed, turreted, and surrounded by parkland stretching away beyond its formal garden and ornamental 'moat', it is the picture of elegance. Inside, it is appropriately furnished, with exquisite antiques, porcelain and tapestries. Some of the bedrooms are exceedingly grand.

It could be embarrassingly pretentious. But the delight of the place is that it is not at all pretentious or intimidating. The château has been in the Bodinaud family for over 100 years, and the hotel is very much a family concern. Mme Bodinaud (an ex-design lecturer) does all the interior decoration and oversees the cooking, earning a Michelin star for her imaginative food, while her husband administers a collection of 300 cognacs.

Quite recently, the Bodinauds opened a 'winter' restaurant, La Grange aux Oies, in converted stables. Their shared interest in art has also led to the opening of a gallery.

～

NEARBY Angoulême (40 km); Limoges (65 km).
LOCATION in wooded park, 2 km E of Nieuil; car parking
FOOD breakfast, lunch, dinner **PRICE** €€€ **ROOMS** 14; 11 double, 3 suites, all with bath; all rooms have phone, TV, minibar, air-conditioning **FACILITIES** sitting room, 2 restaurants, bar, meeting room, garden, swimming pool, tennis, fishing
CREDIT CARDS AE, DC, MC, V **CHILDREN** accepted**DISABLED** access possible to 1 bedroom and suite

PETS welcome
CLOSED Nov to late Apr; restaurant 'La Grange aux Oies' Sun, Mon dinner
PROPRIETORS Jean-Michel and Luce Bodinaud

THE WEST

OIZON

CHATEAU DE LA VERRERIE
~ CHATEAU HOTEL ~

Oizon, 18700 Aubigny-sur-Nère (Cher)
TEL 02 48 81 51 60 **FAX** 02 48 58 21 25
E-MAIL laverrerie@wanadoo.fr **WEBSITE** www.chateau-france.com/-verrerie.fr

IF YOU DRIVE NORTH from Bourges for 50 km, you will arrive at Aubigny-sur-Nère without having encountered a single corner worthy of the name. Long after the Romans left, the Scots arrived in 1422 in the shape of John Stuart, Count of Darnley, on whom a grateful Charles VII of France had bestowed the estates of Aubigny for his help against the English during the Hundred Years' War. Stuart's grandson built the first elements of this handsome château about 80 years later. The Duke of Richmond sold it three and a half centuries after that to an ancestor of the present owner, Count Béraud de Vogüé. This is the house where he was born and where he and his family now live.

Their welcome is as warm as the setting is magical: lawns, lake and woods keep the rest of the world at bay while you hunt, shoot, fish, ride, row, practise archery or just sit under a tree with a book and absorb some of the history that surrounds you through peaceful osmosis. The bedrooms are satisfyingly large, the furniture antique and the decoration fresh. Bathrooms are baronial and guests have a drawing room of their own to use as they please. Breakfast comes to you in your room, and you can take your other meals at the excellent restaurant housed in a 17thC cottage just outside the body of the keep. The wine list reminds you effortlessly that you are between Sancerre and the Loire.

~

NEARBY Gien (29 km); Bourges (45 km).
LOCATION 11 km SE of Aubigny (follow signs) off the D89; car parking
FOOD breakfast, lunch, dinner
PRICE €€€
ROOMS 12; 11 double and twin, 1 suite, all with bath; all rooms have phone, hairdrier **FACILITIES** sitting rooms, library, billiards room, meeting rooms, restaurant, bar, terrace, garden, swimming pool, riding, boating, fishing, hunting, shooting, helipad **CREDIT CARDS** AE, MC, V **CHILDREN** accepted
DISABLED not suitable **PETS** accepted **CLOSED** mid-Dec to mid-Feb; restaurant Tues and Wed lunch
PROPRIETOR Comte Béraud de Vogüé

THE WEST

✳ DOMAINE DES HAUTS DE LOIRE ✳
～ MANOR HOUSE HOTEL ～

41150 Onzain (Loir-et-Cher)
TEL 02 54 20 72 57/02 54 20 83 41 **FAX** 02 54 20 77 32
E-MAIL hauts.de.loire@wanadoo.fr **WEBSITE** www.domainehautsloire.com

THE CRUNCH OF freshly-raked gravel gives you something of a clue as you walk towards the front door of Domaine des Hauts de Loire – and even if you've arrived by helicopter (some do, by the way) you have to walk the last bit like the rest of us. Inside this former hunting lodge, built in 1860, the Bonnigal family have created a very stylish, very luxurious hotel. Travellers on a modest budget should just sigh and pass by. The wooden floors here have a deeper shine, the carpets deeper pile and the oriental rugs lie thicker on the ground than most other places you are likely to visit. A regiment of keen young staff keeps everything just so under the watchful eye of Mme Bonnigal – and this includes maintaining the marked trails through the woods, each with helpful signs to let you know how long it should take to walk. Fresh flowers are everywhere (with a rose on each of the yellow-clad tables in the beamed dining room) and in fine weather the French windows are thrown open to let in the country air.

The food is everything you could hope for, as is the wine list. The smartly decorated, antique-filled bedrooms are divided between the house itself and a nearby row of cottages, where the most spectacular is a beamed loft with a gigantic picture window and a bathroom to die for.

～

NEARBY Blois (20 km); Amboise (20 km); Loire châteaux.
LOCATION 2 km from Onzain off the D1 before Mesland; car parking **FOOD** breakfast, lunch, dinner **PRICE** ⓔⓔⓔⓔ **ROOMS** 33; 19 double, 14 twin, all with bath; all rooms have phone, TV, minibar, hairdrier; some have air-conditioning **FACILITIES** sitting room, dining room, breakfast room, terrace, garden, swimming pool, tennis, helipad **CREDIT CARDS** AE, DC, MC, V **CHILDREN** accepted **DISABLED** access possible **PETS** not accepted **CLOSED** Dec to mid-Feb; restaurant Mon-Tues low season **PROPRIETORS** M. and Mme Bonnigal

THE WEST

LA ROCHELLE

33 RUE THIERS
~ SEASIDE BED-AND-BREAKFAST ~

33 Rue Thiers, 17000 La Rochelle (Charente-Maritime)
TEL *05 46 41 62 23* **FAX** *05 46 41 10 76*
E-MAIL *106510.2775@compuserve.com*

DESPITE A CHANGE in ownership and a rise in rates, this distinctive little guesthouse continues to delight a steady stream of guests, who still pronounce it value for money. The warm welcome makes 33 Rue Thiers a particular favourite, says one reporter. It proved to be the most memorable hotel I stayed in, and one I will certainly visit again, says another. Because of these reports, we are recommending the place for another year, although we were unable to visit it ourselves. New reports would be especially welcome.

33 Rue Thiers is a renovated 18thC townhouse in the heart of La Rochelle. Its former owner and renovator was a half-American/half-French cook-book author, Maybelle Iribe. She opened for business in 1987, the word spread like wildfire and she built up a faithful band of enthusiastic guests who returned year after year. Public rooms have a slightly faded elegance, and are filled with antiques and (mainly) stylish modern furniture. Huge bedrooms are decorated in soothing pastel shades; to say they have been furnished individually is an understatement.

The new owners have stopped serving dinner and the breakfast is very simple, but in summer it is served in the attractive little walled garden.

NEARBY old quarter, port, and lantern tower of La Rochelle; Ile de Rey.
LOCATION in street next to central market; car parking
FOOD breakfast
PRICE €-€€€
ROOMS 6 double and family with bath
FACILITIES sitting room, TV room, breakfast room, garden
CREDIT CARDS not accepted
CHILDREN welcome
DISABLED no special facilities **PETS** accepted **CLOSED** never
PROPRIETOR M. Fonteneau

THE WEST

CHATEAU DE LA VALLEE BLEUE
~ CHATEAU HOTEL ~

route de Verneuil, St-Chartier, 36400 La Châtre (Indre)
TEL 02 54 31 01 91 **FAX** 02 54 31 04 48
E-MAIL valleebleue@aol.com **WEBSITE** www.valleebleue.com

THE YOUNG GASQUETS took over this handsome château in 1985, just in time to make an appearance in the first edition of this guide, and have been assiduously improving it ever since – a barn and stables have been renovated to provide extra space. A report from a British resident in France with three young children sums up the Vallée Bleue precisely: 'Here is complete commitment. Service was friendly and discreet – the children treated like young adults. The restaurant was one of the best we've eaten in.' Another report praises the 'large and airy' rooms and votes it 'the nicest hotel that we stayed in'.

Inside, the atmosphere of the house is, as always, warm and easy. Fresh flowers and a cosy log fire in the spacious entrance hall set the tone, and personal touches are in evidence in every room, including memorabilia of Georges Sand and Chopin, whose doctor built the château. It overlooks gardens front and back, giving all the bedrooms – big, and comfortably furnished with antiques – a pleasant outlook; just visible, beyond cows grazing in the fields, are the terracotta rooftops of the village. Public rooms are gracious and charming, furnished with solid antiques and looking on to the garden. Cooking is regionally based but *nouvelle*-oriented and way above average in execution.

~

NEARBY Tour de la Prison; Sarzay (10 km); Nohant (5 km).
LOCATION just outside hamlet, on D69 9 km N of La Châtre; car parking
FOOD breakfast, lunch, dinner
PRICE €€€
ROOMS 15 double and twin with bath or shower, 1 apartment with bath; all rooms have phone, TV, minibar, hairdrier
FACILITIES sitting room, 2 dining rooms, meeting room, fitness room, garden, swimming pool, bowling
CREDIT CARDS MC, V **CHILDREN** welcome
DISABLED 3 ground-floor rooms **PETS** not accepted **CLOSED** mid-Nov to early Mar
PROPRIETOR Gérard Gasquet

THE WEST

ST-DENIS-DU-PIN

DOMAINE DE RENNEBOURG
∾ COUNTRY GUESTHOUSE ∾

17400 St-Denis-du-Pin (Charente-Maritime)
TEL 05 46 32 16 07 **FAX** 05 46 59 77 38

IN DEEP COUNTRYSIDE, the Domaine de Rennebourg is a mother-and-daughter enterprise born, like so many others, out of a desire to escape the extinction by a thousand divisions that Napoleonic inheritance laws visit on family estates. And what a success it has been. The long stone house forms one side of the classic large grassed courtyard so characteristic of the yeoman farms of the region, and beyond it is a garden big enough to lose yourself in. The rooms inside are as welcoming as Michèle and Florence Frappier themselves. Utterly in keeping with the architecture, they are lifted way above the ordinary by innumerable little flashes of inspiration – artistic and humorous – and all look as if they are wearing their Sunday best.

Inside one of the outbuildings that form a second side of the yard, like a cross between a waxworks and a section of the Victoria & Albert Museum, is Florence's astonishing collection of dresses, accessories and assorted fripperies from the central 40 years of the 19th century. Another houses the sort of wet weather games centre for children that despairing parents elsewhere would go down on bended knee to have access to. You'd think there would have to be a catch somewhere, but Michèle's kitchen apparently effortlessly produces food that is inventive, plentiful and, despite including aperitif and wine, seems to defy rational economic analysis.

∾

NEARBY Niort (38 km); La Rochelle (60 km); tennis.
LOCATION in deep countryside off the N150, 6 km N of St Jean-d'Angély; car parking
FOOD breakfast, dinner
PRICE €
ROOMS 7 double and twin with bath or shower
FACILITIES sitting room, dining room, terrace, garden, swimming pool
CREDIT CARDS not accepted **CHILDREN** welcome
DISABLED access possible **PETS** accepted
CLOSED never **PROPRIETORS** Michèle and Florence Frappier

THE WEST

LE MANOIR DES REMPARTS
~ MANOR GUESTHOUSE ~

14 rue des Remparts, 36800 St-Gaultier (Indre)
TEL and **FAX** 02 54 47 94 87
E-MAIL willem.prinsloo@wanadoo.fr

PEOPLE WHO CHERISH the fond belief that rooms photographed to illustrate interior design magazines don't exist in real life will be forced to change their minds by Ren Rijpstra's treatment of this 18thC manor house. The quiet town has long since flowed round and incorporated the house, but behind high walls it sits in its own green oasis with a gravelled court-yard in front and a walled garden behind. To one side of the yard is a barn that now houses a cool dining room, but the real treat starts inside where, without disturbing the building's original form, furniture, fabrics and light-ing work with carefully considered colours to show the rest of us how it can be done. Floors and fireplaces are original and a particularly fine, broad oak staircase rises in easy stages to the four bedrooms. Nor are creature comforts forgotten: the beds may be old and the fine linen antique, but the mattresses are new, the bathrooms are difficult to leave and the drawing room is a comfortable book-lined haven.

Despite all the thought and energy spent on the house there seems to be an inexhaustible supply left to benefit the guests. Breakfasts are famous: fresh fruit juice, yoghurt, cereals, eggs from their own hens, home-made jams, local cheeses and tea that has never been in a bag. Dinners are by arrangement – and well worth arranging. There's a no smoking rule, even in the garden.

~

NEARBY Châteauroux (30 km); Poitiers (76 km); golf.
LOCATION in town (ask for directions when you book); car parking
FOOD breakfast, dinner (by arrangement)
PRICE €€
ROOMS 4; 3 double, 1 suite, all with bath
FACILITIES sitting room, dining room, terrace, garden **CREDIT CARDS** MC, V
CHILDREN accepted
DISABLED not suitable **PETS** not accepted
CLOSED mid-Dec to early Jan
PROPRIETOR Ren Rijpstra

THE WEST

ST-HILAIRE-DE-COURT

CHATEAU DE LA BEUVRIERE
∾ CHATEAU HOTEL ∾

St-Hilaire-de-Court, 18100 Viezon (Cher)
TEL 02 48 75 14 63 **FAX** 02 48 75 47 62

THE APPROACH IS THROUGH glorious wooded grounds, part of this 11thC château's Cher valley estate, which has survived virtually untouched since the Middle Ages. A splendid example of the period's architecture, its round towers topped by conical slate roofs, the small-scale château is as appealing inside as it is out. Put a foot through the door and you will immediately sense its intimacy and welcome. Château seems too grand a name to describe it. The pleasantly decorated public rooms are filled with family furniture, and our reporter was particularly taken with the mellow dining room with its upholstered Empire armchairs and immaculate tables. Here the food – fish, game and truffles in season – excels.

The peaceful bedrooms overlook the gardens, and although they're all different, each has something to recommend it. Some have beds tucked into wood-panelled alcoves; in others the bed is on a mezzanine floor, with a sitting area below – not suitable for the unsure of foot, as the staircase is steep. Another reporter was enchanted with her room in one of the turrets. She was also impressed by the reasonable prices, but warned that the owners speak little English. Our only disappointment was the siting of the swimming pool, a touch too close to the hotel – but that's a quibble.

∾

NEARBY Bourges (39 km); Viezon (7 km); golf.
LOCATION off the D96 W of St-Hilaire near the Cher; car parking
FOOD breakfast, lunch, dinner
PRICE €
ROOMS 15 double and twin with bath; all rooms have phone; 2 have minibar
FACILITIES sitting area, bar, dining room, terrace, garden, swimming pool, tennis
CREDIT CARDS AE, DC, MC, V
CHILDREN accepted
DISABLED access difficult
PETS accepted
CLOSED late Dec to mid-Mar; restaurant Sun dinner, Mon Sep to June
PROPRIETORS M. and Mme de Brach

THE WEST

ST-JEAN-ST-GERMAIN

LE MOULIN
~ CONVERTED MILL ~

St-Jean-St-Germain, 37600 Loches (Indre-et-Loire)
TEL 02 47 94 70 12 **FAX** 02 47 94 77 98
E-MAIL millstjean@aol.com

IF ASKED WHETHER you stayed with friends or at a hotel on your last trip to France, you would be hard pushed to know how to reply if you had stayed at Le Moulin. Sue Hutton and Andrew Page treat their guests as if they had just struggled ashore after a shipwreck and needed quickly, but in no particular order, a drink, a bath, hot soup, sticking plaster for their cuts, another drink, food, maps, news from home, advice on local shops, shampoo, weather forecast – and just about anything else you can think of. And, as if that weren't enough, like skilled tailors they size you up before deciding which of their appealing, comfortable rooms would suit you best.

The sight of their mill, on its own little tree-lined isthmus at the edge of the village, would bring tears of self-pity to your eyes if it weren't the end of your own journey. Surrounded on all sides by water, and with a little river beach when the winter rains are over, they have nevertheless added a swimming pool for those who prefer not to share with perch and tadpoles. Dinner, cooked with skill and care by Andrew, is usually at a 'club' table where everybody sits together but if you don't feel up to it, you can always have a table of your own in the pretty little conservatory that also does duty in the mornings as a breakfast room.

~

NEARBY Loches (6 km); Tours (45 km); Poitiers (74 km).
LOCATION at the edge the village on an isthmus that juts into the Indre, S of Loches on the N143; car parking
FOOD breakfast, dinner
PRICE €
ROOMS 6; 5 double, 1 twin, 4 with bath, 2 with shower
FACILITIES sitting room, dining room, conservatory/breakfast room, terrace, garden, swimming pool
CREDIT CARDS not accepted **CHILDREN** accepted
DISABLED not suitable **PETS** accepted
CLOSED Dec-Feb
PROPRIETORS Andrew Page and Sue Hutton

THE WEST

ST-MAIXENT-L'ECOLE

LE LOGIS SAINT-MARTIN
～ COUNTRY HOTEL ～

chemin de Pissot, 79400 St-Maixent-l'Ecole (Deux-Sèvres)
TEL 05 49 05 58 68 **FAX** 05 49 76 19 93 **E-MAIL** courrier@logis-saint-martin.com
WEBSITE www.logis-saint-martin.com

L E LOGIS ST-MARTIN is a wonderful surprise. A couple of minutes' drive down a worryingly suburban road leading off the N11 as it leaves St-Maixent-L'Ecole brings you suddenly to the green, wooded bank of the river Sèvre, opposite an island served by a footbridge. For six years Bertrand and Ingrid Heintz have been running this long, low 17thC stone house as a hotel-restaurant of uncompromisingly high standards. Their chef has been with them for two years longer than that. The first thing you will notice is that the hotel staff don't ever appear in the restaurant, and vice versa. Monsieur Heintz would rather his people mastered their trades one at a time, and any confusion would mar his passion for tip-top service.

The beamed restaurant is an enticing room washed in muted yellows and glinting with silver and crystal and there is a steady stream of local people who make a pilgrimage from town, along the river bank, to eat here. This close to Cognac you can easily bring your excellent meal to a satisfactory conclusion; there is also a generous list of teas and coffees to choose from, and the cigars are pretty good as well. The very comfortable well-lit bedrooms are no disappointment – pale yellows and greens predominate and most look out over the peaceful river.

～

NEARBY Niort (24 km); Poitiers (48 km); golf; riding; fishing.
LOCATION on the western edge of town beside the river Sèvre, S of the N11; car parking
FOOD breakfast, lunch, dinner
PRICE ©©
ROOMS 11; 10 double and twin, 1 suite, 5 with bath, 6 with shower; all rooms have phone, TV, hairdrier
FACILITIES sitting room, restaurant, meeting room, terrace, garden, helipad
CREDIT CARDS AE, DC, MC, V **CHILDREN** accepted
DISABLED access difficult **PETS** not accepted
CLOSED Jan; restaurant Mon, lunch on Tues and Sat
PROPRIETORS Bertrand and Ingrid Heintz

THE WEST

✳ CHATEAU DE ROCHECOTTE ✳
~ CHATEAU HOTEL ~

St-Patrice, 37130 Langeais (Indre-et-Loire)
TEL 02 47 96 16 16 **FAX** 02 47 96 90 59
E-MAIL chateau.rochecotte@wanadoo.fr **WEBSITE** www.chateau-de-rochecotte.fr

TALLEYRAND BOUGHT ROCHECOTTE in 1825 for his favourite niece, the Duchess of Dino. Originally a rather stark 18thC castle with glorious views over the Val de la Vienne to the Château d'Usée, she gave it an Italianate look by adding pillars, pergolas and terraces, extended it in the same style to make room for their many friends and even harnessed the hydraulic technology of the moment to pipe water to the suites and kitchens. In 1986 Monsieur Pasquier bought it for his wife and daughters and they have continued faithfully in the house's tradition of 'hands on' hospitality: large though it is, there seems to be at least one member of the family in sight at all times.

Many of the pictures, chandeliers, tapestries and pieces of furniture originally installed by the Duchess are still where she put them, undisturbed by the intervening owners. But this is no museum: the smart *salons* are there to be used and enjoyed and more modern pieces mingle comfortably with the old. The bedrooms are all individually decorated to an exacting standard, with carpets, wall-coverings and fabrics teamed together, and quite sensibly priced by floor area. Talleyrand preferred the calm of Rochecotte to his own, ritzier, Valençay: it's not difficult to see why.

~

NEARBY Langeais (10 km); Tours (24 km); Chinon (32 km).
LOCATION outside village, between Langeais and Bourgueil off the D35; car parking
FOOD breakfast, lunch, dinner
PRICE €€€€-€€€€€ **ROOMS** 35; 32 double and twin, 3 suites, all with bath; all rooms have phone, TV, hairdrier **FACILITIES** 2 sitting rooms, dining room, meeting room, lift, terrace, garden, swimming pool **CREDIT CARDS** AE, DC, MC, V
CHILDREN accepted
DISABLED access difficult **PETS** accepted **CLOSED** 3 weeks Feb, 2 weeks early Dec
PROPRIETORS Pasquier family

THE WEST

TAVERS

LA TONNELLERIE
~ VILLAGE HOTEL ~

12 rue des Eaux-Bleues, Tavers, 45190 Beaugency (Loiret)
TEL 02 38 44 68 15 **FAX** 02 38 44 10 01
E-MAIL tonelri@club-internet.fr **website** www.chateaux-france.com/-latonnellerie

THE FLOW OF READERS' REPORTS on this fine 19thC wine merchant's house has dried to a trickle (perhaps because the cheapest rooms are no longer cheap) but its attractions seem to us to remain undiminished.

The hotel, in the small village of Tavers, close to the Loire and not far from Beaugency, is set around a central courtyard-garden which is at the heart of its appeal. There are shady chestnut trees and a pretty little swimming pool; tables for summer meals stand on the lawn and further away from the house on terrace areas.

The country atmosphere extends indoors to the two dining rooms, both looking on to the garden; one in 'winter garden' style, the other handsomely rustic, with a tiled floor and mellow woodwork. The cooking is *nouvelle* in style but recognizes the traditions of the region, and is above average in its execution.

In recent years Mme Pouey has steadily improved the hotel, adding four 'apartment/suites' (pastel walls, flowery drapes, polished antiques, smart tiled bathrooms) and refurbishing other bedrooms.

~

NEARBY Beaugency (3 km); châteaux: Chambord (25 km), Blois (30 km)
LOCATION in middle of village, W of Beaugency; car parking
FOOD breakfast, lunch, dinner
PRICE €€€
ROOMS 20; 5 double, 7 twin, 3 suites, 5 apartments, all with bath; all rooms have phone, TV, hairdrier
FACILITIES sitting room, 2 dining rooms, lift, garden, swimming pool, tennis
CREDIT CARDS AE, MC, V
CHILDREN welcome
DISABLED ground-floor rooms available
PETS accepted
CLOSED early Jan to Mar
PROPRIETOR Marie-Christine Pouey

THE WEST

TONNAY-BOUTONNE

LE PRIEURE
~ VILLAGE HOTEL ~

17380 Tonnay-Boutonne (Charente-Maritime)
TEL and **FAX** 05 46 58 66 50
E-MAIL AuLeliege@aol.fr

A FEW YEARS AGO we came close to dropping this hotel from the guide through lack of support from readers, but our perseverance has been rewarded by a renewed burst of enthusiastic reports. 'I certainly endorse the inclusion of Le Prieuré,' says one. Another reporter sums it up as 'excellent in every respect,' with 'first-rate food'. Unfortunately we haven't been able to visit the Prieuré since the Lelieges took over, but the early signs are promising and their staff, charming and helpful. Apart from breakfast, other meals are now only provided by prior arrangement. New reports would be especially welcome.

Tonnay-Boutonne is a small, quiet village lying between the old military town of Rochefort and St-Jean-d'Angély, a former wine port. Set slightly back from the (not very busy) main road in a large grassy garden, Le Prieuré is a typical Charentaise building: plain but handsomely symmetrical, with white-shuttered windows. It was the family home of the proprietors before they opened it as a hotel, and retains a friendly atmosphere. The bedrooms and bathrooms have been revamped, leading a reporter to call them 'lovely' and justifying a move from two-star to three-star status a couple of years ago.

~

NEARBY Rochefort (21 km); La Roche Courbon (25 km); Saintes (30 km).
LOCATION in village E of Rochefort; car parking
FOOD breakfast, lunch and dinner (by arrangment)
PRICE €
ROOMS 18; 10 double, 6 twin, 2 family, 15 with bath, 3 with shower; all rooms have phone, TV
FACILITIES reception/sitting area, TV/sitting room, 2 dining rooms, garden
CREDIT CARDS MC, V
CHILDREN welcome
DISABLED no special facilities
PETS accepted **CLOSED** never
PROPRIETORS M. and Mme Leliege

THE WEST

CHAUMONT-SUR-THARONNE

LA CROIX BLANCHE DE SOLOGNE

VILLAGE INN

5 place de l'Eglise, 41600 Chaumont-sur-Tharonne (Loir-et-Cher) TEL 02 54 88 55 12 FAX 02 54 88 60 40 E-MAIL lacroix blanchesologne@wanadoo.fr FOOD breakfast, lunch, dinner PRICE €-€€€ ROOMS 18 CLOSED never

A 200-YEAR-OLD TRADITION of women chefs continues at this cosy *auberge* in a 15thC building, furnished with gleaming country antiques and floral-patterned fabrics. The 'superb' food is the attraction, served in a traditionally rustic dining room, its walls hung with hunting trophies; the style of cooking is largely Périgordian (*foie gras*, *confits*, walnuts, truffles), but with the benefit of a feminine touch. There is a delightful flower-filled garden where food is served in summer. Staff are courteous and friendly, and the country-style bedrooms comfortable, though some of the decoration is a bit heavy-handed. The suites are in an annexe.

PONS

AUBERGE PONTOISE

TOWN HOTEL

23 avenue Gambetta, 17800 Pons (Charente-Maritime) TEL 05 46 94 00 99 FAX 05 46 91 33 40 E-MAIL auberge.pontoise@ wanadoo.fr FOOD breakfast, lunch, dinner PRICE € ROOMS 22 CLOSED 5 weeks Dec to Jan; restaurant Sun dinner and Mon low season

WHEN OUR INSPECTOR ARRIVED at this simple hotel, he found it closed, but we decided to include it on the strength of a comprehensive reader's report. Our reader was most complimentary about the new owners, the Massiots: Hélène, the efficient manageress, responsible for an eager young staff, and her husband Frédéric, the chef, responsible for what our reader describes as 'one of our best dinners in France'. The Massiots are gradually giving the place a much-needed overhaul. The elegant dining room has already received the treatment. The bar, reception, basic bedrooms and small, slightly musty bathrooms are next on the list. It offers terrific value for money – let's hope that doesn't change once the work is completed.

THE EAST

HOTELS IN THE EAST

OUR EASTERN FRANCE region takes in Burgundy, Franche-Comté and most of the Alps, each different in character, but all exceptionally rewarding areas for lovers of food and the great outdoors.

The attractions of Burgundy are well known, especially to the gourmet and wine-lover. If you have begun to suspect that standards have slipped in French cooking of late, your faith will surely be restored in this region, where you will find its famous regional dishes cooked to perfection. There are plenty of glossy, sophisticated hotels in these parts, but also good examples of our favourite sort of places such as the traditional village *auberge* or old coaching inn, where the chef/*patron* is a fine cook (perhaps with a Michelin star) and the bedrooms are spotless, comfortable, unpretentious and inexpensive enough to excuse that bottle of Gevry-Chambertin. Try, for example, the Hôtellerie du Val d'Or in Mercurey (page 165) or the Hostellerie du Château in Châteauneuf-en-Auxois (page 153). For a marvellous gastronomic tour of the cuisine of the whole region, don't miss lunch or dinner at Le Cep in Fleurie-en-Beaujolais (no rooms).

Most people come to Burgundy to tour the world-famous vineyards and to see the Romanesque architecture, but there are peaceful lesser-known corners which have much to offer, such as Fontaine-Française and the Vingeanne valley north-east of Dijon; the Brionnais (see La Reconce, Poisson, page 169) and the rolling pastures and woodland north of Nevers (see Ferme Auberge du Vieux Château, Oulon, page 168).

Franche-Comté comprises the high valley of the Saône whose wide rolling country has a rustic simplicity, and the wild, untamed slopes of the Jura mountains. Amongst the handful of recommendations we have in these parts is a new find, the elegant Hôtel Castan in Besançon (page 150).

In the right hands, Alpine chalets and former farmhouses make perfect charming small hotels: our selection includes sophisticated old favourites such as La Croix-Fry at Manigod (page 163) and the Bois Prin at Chamonix (page 152) as well as much simpler places such as Chalet Rémy at St-Gervais (page 178) and Au Gay Séjour at Faverges (page 176). A summer visit to any of these hotels, when the bustle of winter sports is exchanged for a much more gentle atmosphere, is highly recommended.

THE EAST

✳ VILLA LOUISE ✳
～ MANOR HOUSE HOTEL ～

21420 Aloxe-Corton (Côte-d'Or)
TEL 03 80 26 46 70 **FAX** 03 80 26 47 16 **E-MAIL** hotel-villa-louise@wanadoo.fr
WEBSITE www.hotel-villa-louise.fr

ALL CHANGE AT THIS 17THC MANSION in the tiny village of Aloxe-Corton, a place of pilgrimage for lovers of great white wines. Its symbol is the château of Corton-André, a picturesque building of gleaming coloured tiles and tidy tunnels full of *premiers crus*. Next to it lies the Villa Louise, with old timber work and beamed ceilings, and a large airy *salon* which opens out on to the park and vineyards, and a garden dotted with attractive tables and chairs. "You are very lucky, standing here," laughs new owner Michel Schorwitzel. "This garden should really be given over to vines too. The land is worth a great deal of money." He points out the much-prized Corton Charlemagne vines at the top of the hill as we drink the delicious wine that his wife makes at neighbouring Pernand-Vergelesses with her brother – you can taste and buy in the vaulted cellars below the house. Villa Louise, which has long featured in these pages, was her grandmother's home before becoming a hotel, latterly run down. The Schorwitzels have renovated and redecorated it with great flair, mixing modern with old. It's a pity that bedrooms and bathrooms are all standardized, but they are comfortable, practical and stylish, and there is a happy ambience. Breakfasts are superb. At night, walk through the vineyards to dine in a nearby village.

NEARBY Beaune (3.5 km); Château de Rochepot (25 km). **LOCATION** on edge of village, 3.5 km N of Beaune on N74; ample car parking
FOOD breakfast, light dinner **PRICE** €€ **ROOMS** 10 double and twin, all with bath; all rooms have phone, TV, minibar, hairdrier **FACILITIES** sitting room, wine-tasting cellar, garden, bicycles **CREDIT CARDS** MC, V **CHILDREN** accepted **DISABLED** 1 specially adapted room **PETS** accepted **CLOSED** never **PROPRIETORS** Véronique and Michel Schorwitzel

THE EAST

L'ABBAYE
~ CONVERTED ABBEY ~

15 chemin de l'Abbaye, 74940 Annecy-le-Vieux (Haute-Savoie)
TEL 04 50 23 61 08 **FAX** 04 50 27 77 65
WEBSITE www.lac.annecy.com

ANNECY-LE-VIEUX is not the lovely medieval heart of Annecy, but a sprawling, rather unsightly residential area north of the lake, and to be honest, our inspectors have always fretted about this weak spot in an otherwise appealing, (though idiosyncratic) hotel. In keeping it in the guide, we are influenced by the reader who summarizes it as a 'very attractive hotel with delightful bedrooms,' with no niggles about the location. A room overlooking the attractive garden is recommended.

L'Abbaye was indeed an ancient abbey. A stone archway leads into a quaint cobbled courtyard surrounded by a wooden balcony. The dining room is a splendid vaulted room sporting a motley array of decoration: gold mythological masks, chandeliers, Renaissance fresco, Indian print napkins. In summer, tables are set up in the shade of huge trees. The bedrooms and suites are luxuriously furnished in a variety of styles, with every modern convenience.

It's rather surprising to find a disco in a hotel like this, but it is separate and does not disturb the peace. The food is good and well priced; service is casual in terms of dress, but effective.

~

NEARBY Roman church of Annecy-le-Vieux; lake; town centre.
LOCATION in rural/residential setting 2 km NE of Annecy; car parking
FOOD breakfast, dinner; room service
PRICE €€€
ROOMS 18; 15 double and twin, 2 suites, 1 apartment, all with bath; all rooms have phone, TV, minibar, hairdrier
FACILITIES dining room, bar, terrace, garden
CREDIT CARDS AE, DC, MC, V
CHILDREN welcome
DISABLED no special facilities
PETS accepted **CLOSED** restaurant only, Mon
PROPRIETORS M. Menges and M. Burnet

THE EAST

ARNAY-LE-DUC

CHEZ CAMILLE
~ TOWN HOTEL ~

1 place Edouard-Herriot, 21230 Arnay-le-Duc (Côte-d'Or)
TEL 03 80 90 01 38 **FAX** 03 80 90 04 64
E-MAIL chez-camille@wanadoo.fr **WEBSITE** www.chez-camille.fr

ARMAND POINSOT'S EXCELLENT COOKING (traditional but light) is only one attraction of this captivating hotel whose position on a north/south, east/west axis at a crossroads in the centre of Arnay makes it the town's most notable feature. The dark, dull corridors give no hint of the appeal of the bedrooms, which come as a delightful surprise: some are compact, others spacious; many are beamed and all are full of character: antiques, pretty floaty curtains, armchairs. Bathrooms are simple, but acceptable. One family room has two bedrooms; another room in the roof is tiny but appealing. Cheaper rooms are available in the Claire de Lune annexe.

Downstairs there is a large, comfortable lobby/sitting room, but the heart of the hotel is its dining room, fashioned, conservatory-style, from a covered coutyard, with a leafy tree in the middle. To one side is the kitchen, open to view, and adjoining, the *pâtisserie*. "It's interesting for the guests to see the kitchen staff at work", says M. Poinsot, "and just as interesting for the staff to see the guests." His team appears to be fault-less: one feels he has perfected the art of running a traditional French restaurant. The waitresses wear long white aprons and floral skirts, the food is delicious, the service smooth. This is the France we love to find.

~

NEARBY Beaune (36 km); Saulieu (29 km).
LOCATION in town centre; car parking and garage
FOOD breakfast, lunch, dinner
Price €
ROOMS 11 double and twin, all with bath; all rooms have phone, TV, minibar, hairdrier
FACILITIES 2 sitting rooms, restaurant, cellar
CREDIT CARDS AE, DC, MC, V
CHILDREN welcome
DISABLED no special facilities **PETS** accepted **CLOSED** never
PROPRIETOR Armand Poinsot

THE EAST

AUXERRE

PARC DES MARECHAUX
~ TOWN MANSION ~

6 avenue Foch, 89000 Auxerre (Yonne)
TEL 03 86 51 43 77 **FAX** 03 86 51 31 72
E-MAIL info@ch-demeures.com **WEBSITE** www.ch-demeures.com

THIS SUBSTANTIAL 1850s house, restored from near-dereliction by Espérance Hervé and her doctor husband, enjoys clear support from readers, not least because it offers excellent value.

The Hervés have cut no corners: the welcoming ambience, confident style and solid comfort of the house would do credit to any professional hotelier. For a bed-and-breakfast establishment, the public rooms are exceptionally comfortable; as well as the sitting room, the smart little bar looking over the garden is appreciated.

The large bedrooms are beautifully done out in restrained colours, and handsomely furnished using warm wooden beds and chests in traditional styles. Although the rooms on the noisy roadside have been soundproofed of late, one overlooking the garden – the secluded, leafy 'park' from which the hotel takes its name – is preferable. Some have French windows opening directly on to the garden.

Breakfast, which can be taken outside in summer – as an alternative to the pretty breakfast room – is 'excellent', and includes fresh orange juice and 'more copious options to bread and croissants, should you wish'. Light meals served in your room are also available.

~

NEARBY cathedral, abbey church of Saint-Germain; Chablis (20 km).
LOCATION signposted in Auxerre, close to middle of town; car parking
FOOD breakfast, light meals
PRICE €€
ROOMS 24; 19 double and twin, 2 single, 3 family, all with bath; all rooms have phone, TV
FACILITIES sitting room, bar, dining room, lift, garden
CREDIT CARDS AE, DC, MC, V
CHILDREN welcome
DISABLED 3 rooms on ground floor
PETS accepted **CLOSED** never
PROPRIETOR Espérance Hervé

THE EAST

AVALLON

CHATEAU DE VAULT DE LUGNY
~ COUNTRY HOTEL ~

11 rue du Château, 89200 Avallon (Yonne)
TEL 03 86 34 07 86 **FAX** 03 86 34 16 36
E-MAIL hotel@lugny.com **WEBSITE** www.lugny.com

PRESS A BUTTON and the iron gates open automatically; once through, the front door comes into view across the sweep of lawn. Standing there on the steps is the amiable butler and a maid; they take your cases and show you to your room. Have no fears: this is understated, friendly service such as guests once might have experienced at large country houses. You will be at ease.

Inside, this ambience is faithfully preserved: it's a very handsome house, but Elisabeth Audan's good taste has kept the decoration not too smart, not too informal: it has the feel of a private home. There are two rather grand bedrooms, filled with impressive antiques; the rest are more homely, but spacious and comfortable.

Dinner is taken house-party style at a table large enough to allow a couple to talk amongst themselves, but if you prefer to sit at a separate table for complete privacy, you can. The food is rich and delicious, and presented in restrained good taste: not dolled up, but in the style of authentic home cooking. If in doubt, try the classic Burgundy menu.

The extensive, well-wooded grounds include a stretch of trout fishing, a tennis court and a medieval defensive tower.

~

NEARBY Avallon (4 km); Vézelay (10 km).
LOCATION 4 km W of Avallon, 1 km N of Pontaubert, on D427 outside village of Vault de Lugny; ample car parking
FOOD breakfast, lunch, dinner; room service
PRICE €€€€
ROOMS 12 double and twin, all with bath; all rooms have phone, TV, minibar, hairdrier, safe
FACILITIES sitting room, bar, dining room, garden, tennis, fishing
CREDIT CARDS AE, MC, V **CHILDREN** welcome
DISABLED rooms on ground floor **PETS** accepted **CLOSED** mid-Nov to Apr
PROPRIETOR Elisabeth Audan

THE EAST

MOULIN DES TEMPLIERS
~ BED-AND-BREAKFAST CONVERTED MILL ~

Vallée du Cousin, Pontaubert, 89200 Avallon (Yonne)
TEL 03 86 34 10 80 **FAX** 03 86 34 10 80
E-MAIL jean.liberatore@freesbee.fr **WEBSITE** www.hotel-moulin-des-templiers.com

WHEN WE LAST TURNED UP HERE we were met by a sorry sight: the place had been flooded during a freak deluge, and the waters of the Cousin still lapped menacingly close to the sodden walls of the building. If you ask, Anne and Jean will doubtless show you how high the water reached, but by now there will be few other signs of the havoc it caused.

We have always felt affection for this modest stopover, now in the capable hands of new young owners, the Liberatores. They have freshened the quaint bedrooms, which have white rough plastered walls, flowery wallpaper on the ceilings, dark old polished doors, and tiny bathrooms (with separate loos) tucked into odd corners. Bedrooms on the first floor are compact – the smallest is minute – while those on the second floor are slightly larger.

Records of a mill on this spot as far back as the 12th century can be found in the National Archives. It was used by the Templars as a resting place on the pilgrimage to Santiago della Compostella, but was burned by the Huguenots in 1571, along with the Templars' chapel. Today it makes an idyllic spot on the banks of the normally charming little river, which runs along an unspoiled wooded valley. Breakfast is served in one of two tiny rooms, or on the riverside terrace on fine days.

~

NEARBY Avallon (4 km); Vézelay (13 km).
LOCATION just outside Pontaubert, signposted, in Cousin valley; with car parking across road
FOOD breakfast
PRICE €
ROOMS 15 double and twin, all with bath (small) or shower; all rooms have phone
FACILITIES 2 breakfast rooms, sitting room, bar, terrace
CREDIT CARDS AE, DC, MC, V **CHILDREN** accepted
DISABLED not suitable **PETS** accepted **CLOSED** Dec to mid-Feb
PROPRIETORS Anne and Jean Liberatore

The East

BESANCON

CASTAN
~ TOWN HOTEL ~

6 square Castan, 25000 Besançon (Doubs)
Tel 03 81 65 02 00 **Fax** 03 81 83 01 02
E-MAIL art@hotelcastan.fr **WEBSITE** www.hotelcastan.fr

AN EXEMPLARY HOTEL with lovely, individually furnished bedrooms that are full of elegance and character, with antiques, oil paintings, gilt mirrors, chandeliers, and parquet floors strewn with rugs. Each one is displayed on the excellent website; you are invited to fax or phone your booking stating your preferred choices – a tough decision. For those without internet: all ten are lovely, but of the cheaper ones (which are a bargain) we particularly like Trianon, with original panelling, Bonaparte and Victor Hugo (who was born in this lovely town). The building is an 18thC *hôtel particulier* with a verdant courtyard, filled in summer with flowers, palms and climbing plants, around which its three wings are wrapped. It was bought in a derelict state by dentist Gérard Dintroz and his wife as their private home, but being larger than they needed, they decided to turn part of it into a small hotel. Madame Dintroz is in charge, along with a small friendly staff, while her husband continues to work on the town's teeth. His passion for collecting antiques, and particularly old armour, is a bonus for his guests. Breakfast, served on charming china, either in your bedroom or in the panelled breakfast room, lives up to expectations with home-made jams and other products.

~

NEARBY Vieille Ville; Citadelle; Natural History Museum.
LOCATION on small square in town centre; follow signs for Vieille Ville and La Citadelle; limited private car parking
FOOD breakfast
PRICE €€€
ROOMS 10 double and twin, all with bath; all rooms have phone, TV, minibar, hairdrier; half have air conditioning
FACILITIES sitting area, breakfast room, courtyard
CREDIT CARDS AE, MC, V **CHILDREN** accepted
DISABLED 2 rooms on ground floor **PETS** accepted
CLOSED Christmas and New Year, first 3 weeks Aug
PROPRIETOR Gérard Dintroz

THE EAST

CHAGNY

✳ LAMELOISE ✳
∼ TOWN HOTEL ∼

36 place d'Armes, 71150 Chagny (Saône-et-Loire)
TEL 03 85 87 65 65 **FAX** 03 85 87 03 57
E-MAIL reception@lameloise.fr **WEBSITE** www.lameloise.fr

JACQUES LAMELOISE AND HIS WIFE maintain with ease the reputation of this calm, shuttered house, established by his father Jean, as one of the best restaurants in France. A haven of sophisticated yet low-key luxury, it comes as something of a surprise in the middle of workaday Chagny (despite its proximity to the Côte d'Or, wine is not produced in Chagny). Entering from the scruffy place d'Armes, you are suddenly amongst bronzed people in designer clothes and gold jewellery. The refurbished reception lobby is modern and slick, with red sofas and soft lighting. The bedrooms are very attractive and comfortable, no two the same, and furnished with charming fabrics and antiques, with the obligatory marble bathrooms.

The classical, dignified, yet not exorbitant restaurant, is of course at the heart of things, and still retains three Michelin stars and 19/20 from Gault et Millau. You are hardly likely to be staying in the adjoining hotel unless you are treating yourselves to lunch or dinner here. The food is rooted in the cuisine of Burgundy, with the best Burgundy wines to accompany. Breakfast, as you can imagine, is superior. Despite its elevated status and its sophistication, Lameloise, which began humbly enough, retains its solid and traditional roots.

∼

NEARBY Beaune (16 km); Côte de Beaune.
LOCATION in town centre; car parking and garage
FOOD breakfast, lunch, dinner **PRICE** €€€ **ROOMS** 17 double and twin, all with bath; all rooms have phone, TV, hairdrier; most have air conditioning **FACILITIES** sitting room, bar, restaurant, lift **CREDIT CARDS** AE, DC, MC, V **CHILDREN** accepted **DISABLED** access possible **PETS** accepted **CLOSED** mid-Dec to mid-Jan; hotel and restaurant closed Wed, Thurs until 5 pm; restaurant closed Mon lunch **PROPRIETORS** Lameloise family

THE EAST

✳ AUBERGE DU BOIS PRIN ✳
∼ CHALET HOTEL ∼

69 chemin de l'Hermine, Les Moussoux, 74400 Chamonix (Haute-Savoie)
TEL 04 50 53 33 51 **FAX** 04 50 53 48 75 **E-MAIL** boisprin@relaischateaux.fr
WEBSITE www.boisprin.com

DESPITE INCREASING COMPETITION, the Bois Prin remains our favourite spot in, or at least near, Chamonix. This is partly because of the stunning views – the kind that would have driven the 19thC Romantics crazy – across the valley to the spires and glaciers of Mont Blanc, but also because (as recent visits attest), it is a deeply cosseting place to stay.

The Bois Prin is a traditional, dark-wood chalet, in a pretty, flowery garden close to the foot of the Brévent cable-car, on the north side of the deep, steep-sided Chamonix valley. The Carriers have run the hotel since it was built (by Denis Carrier's parents) in 1976. The first impression may be of a surprising degree of formality, with crisply dressed staff. But in fact you quickly find that the informal and friendly approach of the young owners sets the tone. Bedrooms face Mont Blanc, and are lavishly furnished, with rich fabrics, carved woodwork (much of it Denis's own work) and a sprinkling of antiques; the best have private terraces. Food is excellent, with a good choice of menus and a 'wonderful' cheeseboard. 'Luxurious...yet at the same time homely and cosy' praises a recent guest.

∼

NEARBY Mont Blanc and Le Brévent.
LOCATION on hillside, NW of town; ample car parking and garages
FOOD breakfast, lunch, dinner; room service
PRICE €€€
ROOMS 11; 9 double and twin, 2 family, all with bath; all rooms have phone, TV, minibar, hairdrier
FACILITIES dining room, lift, sauna, spa, terrace, garden
CREDIT CARDS AE, DC, MC, V **CHILDREN** welcome

DISABLED no special facilities
PETS accepted
CLOSED mid-April to early May, Nov
PROPRIETORS Denis and Monique Carrier

THE EAST

CHATEAUNEUF-EN-AUXOIS

HOSTELLERIE DU CHATEAU
~ VILLAGE HOTEL ~

Châteauneuf-en-Auxois, 21320 Pouilly-en-Auxois (Côte d'Or)
TEL 03 80 49 22 00 **FAX** 03 80 49 21 27 **E-MAIL** hostellerie-du-chateau@hostellerie-chateauneuf.com **WEBSITE** www.hostellerie-chateauneuf.com

THIS PICTURESQUE *hostellerie*, cleverly converted from a 15thC presbytery close to the château, is in keeping with the delightful, and very quiet, medieval village around it: old stone walls, quiet rustic rooms and terraced gardens. In the beamed, picture-windowed restaurant, wholesome Burgundian dishes are the order of the day. 'Very good value', says a recent report. Another enthusiastic reader tells us that they felt relaxed and at ease as soon as they walked through the door on a cold, snowy day. 'Warm and welcoming...small, brick-walled reception/bar, warming log fires and a comfortable seating area. In the dining room I ate a Charolais steak good enough to kill for. Our large family room was attractively decorated and overlooked the château. It was clean and the bathroom was perfectly adequate'.

Another reader endorses these comments. 'A delightful hotel. The surrounding village is most picturesque, and there are lovely views over the plain from its hilly vantage point. The staff were helpful and the accommodation comfortable. The food was delicious – perhaps the best meal of our trip.' Please note that the hotel is closed on Mondays and Tuesdays, except in July and August.

~

NEARBY Pouilly-en-Auxois (10 km); Dijon (45 km).
LOCATION in hamlet, next to château, 10 km SE of Pouilly-en-Auxois; street car parking
FOOD breakfast, lunch, dinner
PRICE (€)
ROOMS 17; 15 double and twin, 1 single, 1 suite, all with bath; all rooms have phone
FACILITIES 2 sitting rooms, dining room, terrace, garden
CREDIT CARDS AE, DC, MC, V **CHILDREN** welcome
DISABLED no special facilities **PETS** accepted
CLOSED Dec to mid-Feb, Mon, Tues except July, Aug
PROPRIETOR André Hartmann

THE EAST

CHAUBLANC

✳ MOULIN D'HAUTERIVE ✳
～ CONVERTED MILL ～

Chaublanc, 71350 St-Gervais-en-Vallière (Côte-d'Or)
TEL 03 85 91 55 56 **FAX** 03 85 91 89 65
E-MAIL hauterive@aol.com **WEBSITE** www.moulin-etape.com

THE WHEELS WERE STILL TURNING at the Moulin d'Hauterive 40 or so years ago. Only since 1977 has it enjoyed a new lease of life as an unusual country hotel – offering a blend of rural seclusion (it is delightfully isolated), good living and a wealth of amenities. It is a handsome, creeper-clad building, three stories high, surrounded by a collection of lower outbuildings. Beyond them are the little pool (with a lift-up cover/roof which is doubtless a great aid to child safety and energy conservation when the pool is not in use, but diminishes the pleasure of swimming) and tennis court.

When M. and Mme Moille, new then to the hotel game, first opened the Moulin to guests, the interior must have seemed the epitome of rustic chic. Indeed we thought so – we raved about it. Now, such is the fickleness of fashion, it seems dated and cluttered. If it stays the same, it will become a period piece. Most of the rooms are apartments or suites; in ours, which was comfortable and homely (with a walk-in clothes cupboard, iron and ironing board), the lavender loo seat, carpet on the side of the bath and artificial fruit were reminders of a bygone age.

Christiane Moille is the chef, while her husband operates front of house. We dined well in a restaurant that was animated and busy, with correct, efficient service.

～

NEARBY Beaune (16 km); archéodrome (10 km). **LOCATION** 16 km SE of Beaune, off D970; in grounds with ample car parking **FOOD** breakfast, lunch, dinner **PRICE** €€€€ **ROOMS** 20; 5 double, 14 apartments/suites, 1 single, all with bath or shower; all rooms have phone, TV, minibar, hairdrier **FACILITIES** 2 dining rooms, bar, billiards, spa, sauna, solarium, fitness room, terrace, garden, swimming pool, tennis, heliport
CREDIT CARDS AE, DC, MC, V
CHILDREN accepted **DISABLED** 1 suitable room **PETS** accepted
CLOSED Jan, Feb **PROPRIETORS** Michel and Christiane Moille

THE EAST

CURTIL-VERGEY

LE MANASSES
~ VILLAGE HOTEL ~

rue Guillaume de Tavanes, 21220 Curtil-Vergey (Côte-d'Or)
TEL 03 80 61 43 81 **FAX** 03 80 61 42 79

WHAT BETTER WAY to spend an overnight stop in Burgundy than in the heart of a working vineyard in the Hautes Côtes de Nuits? Indeed the Prince of Wales saw fit to stay here for several days, painting and walking (see the little display cabinet). And several readers have recently written to us, warmly recommending Le Manassès.

The Chaley family opened the hotel ten years ago. It is all very *propre*: neat as a pin and furnished with great care and taste, and offers excellent value for money. Most of the rooms are located in the same building as the reception/ breakfast room, while five more luxurious – and larger – rooms have recently been added in a converted stone building across the court-yard. These are excellent, decorated with charming co-ordinated fabrics. All the rooms have marble bathrooms. Back in the main building the Chaleys have installed a wine museum, where tools and bottles from the past are displayed, and where, each evening, wine tastings are conducted for their guests. Breakfast is exemplary, with local jams and cheeses, *assiette charcuterie, jambon persillé*, and *pain d'épices*, even a glass of wine if you should wish. Perhaps best of all is the view: green valley, wooded hillside, no other buildings in sight. No dinner, but the Chaleys will recommend good restaurants.

~

NEARBY Beaune (24 km); abbeys of St Vivant and Citeaux.
LOCATION in village, 24 km NW of Beaune; car parking
FOOD breakfast
PRICE €-€€
ROOMS 12 double and twin, all with bath; all rooms have phone, fax, TV, air conditioning, minibar, hairdrier
FACILITIES breakfast room, wine museum
CREDIT CARDS AE, DC, MC, V **CHILDREN** accepted
DISABLED not suitable **PETS** accepted **CLOSED** Dec to Mar
PROPRIETORS Yves, Françoise and Cécile Chaley

THE EAST

CHATEAU DE FLEURVILLE
~ VILLAGE HOTEL ~

71260 Fleurville (Saône-et-Loire)
TEL 03 85 33 12 17 **FAX** 03 85 33 95 34
E-MAIL fleurville@chateauxhotels.com **WEBSITE** www.chateauxhotels.com/fleurville

WELL-PLACED FOR A STOPOVER on the route south, equidistant between Tournus and Mâcon, Fleurville is hemmed in on one side by the A6 *autoroute*, and on the other by the N6 main road, with the railway line running alongside, and yet the hotel is peaceful and pleasant enough for more than just a night's stay. Surrounded by a wooded park, with pretty flowerbeds dotted around green lawns, it is a fine 16th and 17thC residence built by the Counts of Fleurville. Unlike so many château hotels, however, it is not a formal luxury establishment – the place is relaxed and it is reasonably priced. Many of the original features have been retained, and despite modernizations, there is a genuine atmosphere of times past. An enthusiastic reader comments that it was 'delightful...the staff were very sweet and the pool and grounds make up for the room being a bit small and the decor a bit '70s. The food was fine but not spectacular. It's a wonderful place to come back to after a hot day touring the vineyards, and good for families with children because of the relaxed atmosphere'.

The hotel has recently changed hands. The new owner, Pascal Lehmann, is refurbishing all the rooms 'with old furniture' and there are plans for a 'fitness pool house'. Reports would be welcomed.

~

NEARBY Tournus (15 km); Mâcon (15 km); vineyards; Romanesque churches and abbeys.
LOCATION just off RN6, halfway between Tournus and Mâcon; car parking
FOOD breakfast, lunch, dinner
PRICE €€
ROOMS 15; 14 double and twin, 1 suite, all with bath; all rooms have phone, TV; refurbished rooms have minibar, hairdrier
FACILITIES sitting room, dining room, breakfast room, bar, terrace, garden, swimming pool, bicycles **CREDIT CARDS** AE, DC, MC, V **CHILDREN** welcome
DISABLED access possible **PETS** accepted **CLOSED** Jan to Mar
PROPRIETOR Pascal Lehmann

THE EAST

GEVRY-CHAMBERTIN

LES GRANDS CRUS
~ VILLAGE HOTEL ~

route des Grands Crus, 21220 Gevry-Chambertin (Côte-d'Or)
TEL 03 80 34 34 15 **FAX** 03 80 51 89 07

THE WALLS ARE VERTICAL and plastered, the exposed beams are straight and smooth, the windows are easily opened casements: this is a modern hotel, built as recently as 1977, and so not as immediately charming as many older places in these pages. But the Grands Crus has been done out in traditional Burgundian style, with quarry-tiled floors, lime-washed walls, tapestry fabrics and a carved-stone fireplace, and it drips with geraniums in summer – so to a degree at least it combines the charm of the old with the comfort of the new. The welcome, however, could be improved: never exactly ebullient, it can involve a fair amount of Gallic *froideur*.

The bedrooms are not the last word in stylish decoration, but they are peaceful, spacious and thoughtfully furnished, and look out over the famous Gevry-Chambertin vineyards, which sweep away in all directions. A better-than-average breakfast is served in the small flowery garden in fine weather; if you're confined indoors, there may be delays because of a shortage of space in the breakfast room, off reception.

There are plenty of restaurants nearby for other meals, including some notably good ones.

~

NEARBY Dijon (10 km); Beaune; abbeys of St-Vivant and Citeaux.
LOCATION in village, 10 km SW of Dijon; car parking
FOOD breakfast
PRICE €
ROOMS 24 double and twin, all with bath; all rooms have phone, hairdrier
FACILITIES sitting room, garden **CREDIT CARDS** MC, V **CHILDREN** welcome
DISABLED no special facilities **PETS** accepted
CLOSED Dec to Mar
PROPRIETOR Marie-Paule Farnier

THE EAST

GOUMOIS

TAILLARD
∼ CHALET HOTEL ∼

25470 Goumois (Doubs)
TEL 03 81 44 20 75 **FAX** 03 81 44 26 15
WEBSITE www.hoteltaillard.com

A N INTERMITTENT FLOW of appreciative comments about this pretty chalet in a wooded valley on the Swiss border continues to arrive in our office. They like the wonderful views, the delightful garden, the comfortable, affordable rooms, the friendly atmosphere, and (not least) the food. 'Delicious, if slightly repetitive', is the latest word on the latter subject, while others have been unqualified in their praise of the 'beautifully presented' dishes. The dining room makes the most of the view, with elegantly laid tables placed around bay windows, thrown open in summer. The colourful garden gives way to green pastures and then thickly forested hills which stretch over the border. In summer you can take in the breathtaking view over a coffee and croissants on the terrace, eyeing up the inviting swimming pool while you do so.

The house has its roots in the 18th century, and has been owned and run as a hotel by the same family since 1875. The present M. Taillard is an artist, and some of his paintings decorate the walls. Bedrooms are comfortable and carefully furnished with a mixture of pieces, some antique. The welcome, as one reader comments, is 'low-key but genuine'.

NEARBY Switzerland; Mombaillard (45 km).
LOCATION in elevated position in Doubs valley overlooking Goumois; car parking
FOOD breakfast, lunch, dinner
PRICE €€
ROOMS 22; 14 double and twin, 8 family, all with bath; all rooms have phone, TV
FACILITIES sitting room, dining room, billiards room, fitness/Jacuzzi, terrace, garden, swimming pool
CREDIT CARDS AE, DC, MC, V **CHILDREN** welcome
DISABLED no special facilities **PETS** accepted **CLOSED** mid-Nov to mid-Mar
PROPRIETORS Taillard family

THE EAST

CHATEAU D'IGE
~ CHATEAU HOTEL ~

71960 Igé (Saône-et-Loire)
TEL 03 85 33 33 99 **FAX** 03 85 33 41 41
E-MAIL ige@relaischateaux.fr **WEBSITE** www.ige@relaischateaux.com

THIS TURRETED, creeper-covered *château*, fortified in 1235 and built by a little river on the edge of the Mâcon hills, has preserved its medieval atmosphere despite its conversion into a luxury Relais & Châteaux hotel. Spiral staircases winding up into the turrets, stone-flagged floors, a huge open hearth in the massively beamed dining room, dark, narrow corridors, vast old beds and antique furnishings all contribute to the sense of time standing still. For a Relais et Châteaux hotel, the atmosphere is remarkably unstuffy too – 'welcoming and informal' is how one reader describes it – although other aspects were felt to be a bit below par, such as poor quality sheets and towels, and bathrooms in need of attention. The food, however, receives unqualified praise: 'copious and traditional, well-suited to the surroundings. We ate lunch outside on a warm day and it was perfect – *foie gras de canard* with a *confiture* of green tomatoes, *escargots* with *pain d'épices,* and a delicious *volaille à la d'Albufera.*' The *château* is surrounded by lovely flowery gardens, and breakfast is taken in a splendid light-filled conservatory overlooking them.

~

NEARBY Mâcon (15 km); Cluny (13 km); Romanesque churches and abbeys; vineyards.
LOCATION in village, signposted, 15 km NW of Mâcon; ample car parking and garage
FOOD breakfast, lunch, dinner; room service
PRICE €€€
ROOMS 13; 7 double and twin, 6 suites, all with bath; all rooms have phone, TV, hairdrier
FACILITIES sitting room, bar, 2 dining rooms, terrace, garden
CREDIT CARDS AE, DC, MC, V
CHILDREN welcome
DISABLED no special facilities
PETS accepted
CLOSED Dec to Mar; restaurant closed Tues lunch
PROPRIETOR Françoise Germond-Lieury

THE EAST

LE PARC
~ VILLAGE BED-AND-BREAKFAST ~

Levernois, 21200 Beaune (Côte-d'Or)
TEL 03 80 24 63 00 **FAX** 03 80 24 21 19
E-MAIL hotel.le.parc@wanadoo.fr

BEAUNE HAS A DEARTH of reasonably priced accommodation, and so Le Parc, just five kilometres away, is an especially welcome address. In a pleasant rural setting, it's an attractive old white shuttered *maison bourguignonne*, its walls thickly draped in creeper. Here is the cosy little reception area, with wicker armchairs, fringed lampshades and potted plants, with a bar behind. There is also a breakfast room, although in fine weather you can sit at tables in the pretty gravelled courtyard, flanked on the other side by another attractive building. This houses some of the hotel's 25 bedrooms, larger than those in the main part. All the bedrooms are simple but prettily decorated, with odd bits of furniture picked up here and there – nothing standardized – and rather low, skimpy looking beds.

From the outside, the hotel is lent a deceptively smart, even exclusive appearance by the long white wrought-iron fence which runs along the village pavement between the two buildings. At the rear, the courtyard opens on to a large, peaceful and informal garden.

Mme Oudot is friendly and efficient. She is opening a new hotel, Le Clos, at Montigny-les-Beaune, which is sure to be another useful address in the Beaune area.

~

NEARBY Beaune (5 km); Côtes de Beaune.
LOCATION in village, 5 km SE of Beaune; ample car parking
FOOD breakfast
PRICE €
ROOMS 25 double and twin, 6 with bath, 19 with shower; all rooms have phone, TV
FACILITIES sitting area, bar, breakfast room, courtyard, garden **CREDIT CARDS** MC, V
CHILDREN welcome
DISABLED 5 rooms on ground floor **PETS** not accepted
CLOSED Dec, Jan
PROPRIETOR Christiane Oudot

THE EAST

LA TOUR ROSE
~ TOWN HOTEL ~

22 rue du Boeuf, 69005 Lyon (Rhône)
TEL 04 78 37 25 90 **FAX** 04 78 42 26 02
E-MAIL chavent@asi.fr

PHILIPPE CHAVENT is a Lyon chef with a Michelin star – and something of a Renaissance man. In St-Jean, the old quarter, he has recreated the atmosphere of the residences of the great Florentine bankers and merchants by turning a 17thC building into something extraordinary. There are 12 spectacular bedrooms, each designed to illustrate a period in the long history of Lyon's silk industry. One is decorated with Fortuny pleats, another with Art Deco patterns designed by Dufy, and all are draped, from floor to ceiling, in silk, taffeta, velvet and other textiles. (Bathrooms are modern, with stone floors and walls, and are fitted with shiny stainless steel wash basins.)

The heart of the hotel is a pink tower and there are balustraded galleries, ornamental ponds with waterfalls, and terraced gardens. The fireplace in the bar was rescued from a condemned château and there is an original 13thC wall of a *jeu de paume* (real tennis) court. Panelling in the bar comes from the law courts at Chambéry. The dining room is in the 13thC chapel of what used to be a convent, with a cobbled terrace and a fabulous glass extension which opens to the sky in the summer.

~

NEARBY Vieux Lyon.
LOCATION in the heart of Vieux Lyon, with car parking; ask hotel for details of car access
FOOD breakfast, lunch, dinner
PRICE €€€€€€
ROOMS 12; 6 double and twin, 6 suites, all with bath; all rooms have phone, TV, minibar, hairdrier
FACILITIES 3 sitting rooms, bar, dining room, lift, terraces
CREDIT CARDS AE, DC, MC, V **CHILDREN** accepted
DISABLED no special facilities **PETS** accepted
CLOSED never
PROPRIETOR Philippe Chavent

THE EAST

LE CASTEL
~ VILLAGE HOTEL ~

place de l'Eglise, 89660 Mailly-le-Château (Yonne)
TEL 03 86 81 43 06 **FAX** 03 86 81 49 26

HVING HAD MIXED REPORTS of late on this pleasant old *maison bourgoise*, we recently returned for a careful look. Our verdict: although its old-fashioned demeanour may not suit everyone, we were once again beguiled. A modest hotel (a two-fireplace Logis de France), it offers rooms and food at remarkably attractive prices. But because the house and its name are rather grand, some visitors perhaps expect too much. On the contrary, we think that the value offered here is exceptional.

Built at the end of the 19th century, Le Castel is a large shuttered house lying in the shadow of the village church. It has a well-kept garden and a flowery terrace shaded by lime trees where you can breakfast or take drinks in warm weather.

There are two dining rooms, separated by a small *salon* and a handsome fireplace. Bedrooms vary widely – from spacious ones with touches of grandeur such as chandeliers and drapes over the bedheads, to much smaller and simpler rooms. These rooms are all endearingly dated, with eclectic touches; other rooms have been recently renovated, mostly using *toile de jouy* fabrics, with new enclosed showers. Renovation continues. M. Breerette is a character and a good cook, and Madame is 'the perfect hostess'.

NEARBY Vézelay (24 km); Chablis (45 km).
LOCATION in village centre, opposite church, 30 km S of Auxerre; car parking
FOOD breakfast, lunch, dinner
PRICE €
ROOMS 12; 10 double and twin, 7 with (tiny) bath, 2 with shower, 2 family with bath; all rooms have phone
FACILITIES 2 dining rooms, sitting room, terrace, garden
CREDIT CARDS MC, V **CHILDREN** accepted **DISABLED** 1 ground-floor bedroom
PETS accepted
CLOSED mid-Nov to mid-Mar
PROPRIETORS M. and Mme Breerette

THE EAST

MANIGOD

CHALET HOTEL DE LA CROIX-FRY
~ CHALET HOTEL ~

rue du Col de la Croix-Fry, Manigod, 74230 Thônes (Haute-Savoie)
TEL 04 50 44 90 16 **FAX** 04 50 44 94 87
WEBSITE www.hotelchaletcroixfry.com

'ABSOLUTELY GORGEOUS' was the verdict of one of our reporters, and a recent visit confirms the star rating of this wooden mountain chalet at the highest point of an alpine col, with a terrace overflowing with flowers. Run, with great pride, by a third generation of Veyrats – the chalet was once shared in the summer by the family and their cows – the hotel is cosy and welcoming. A wood fire burns on cool evenings and the sofas and armchairs gathered around the hearth are covered in sheepskin. The bedrooms are attractively rustic – even in the modern annexe-chalets, which provide adaptable family accommodation with kitchenettes. But what really impresses us is the evident pride of the family and their endless efforts to maximize a guest's stay. The Veyrats love running their hotel and the pleasure shows.

The restaurant, serving nourishing mountain food, has spectacular views of peaks and valleys. Mme Guelpa-Veyrat's brother, Marc, is one of Savoy's culinary celebrities, but the *tarte aux myrtilles* has many admirers. In summer the Veyrat's invite their guests to picnic in the pastures with their cows; in winter the invitation is to ski.

NEARBY Vallée de Manigod; Thônes (10 km); Annecy (26 km).
LOCATION on the col, 5 km NE of Manigod, on D16, 6 km S of La Clusaz; car parking
FOOD breakfast, lunch, dinner
PRICE €€€
ROOMS 10; 5 double, 4 one bedroom suites, 1 two bedroom suite, all with bath (suites with Jacuzzi bath); all rooms have phone, TV, terrace or balcony
FACILITIES sitting room, bar, gym, terrace, garden
CREDIT CARDS AE, MC, V
CHILDREN accepted
DISABLED no special facilities
PETS not accepted
CLOSED mid-Sep to mid-Dec, mid-Apr to mid-Jun
PROPRIETOR Marie-Ange Guelpa-Veyrat

THE EAST

LE COIN DU FEU
~ CHALET HOTEL ~

route du Rochebrune, 74120 Megève (Haute-Savoie)
TEL 04 50 21 04 94 **FAX** 04 50 21 20 15
E-MAIL contact@coindufeu.com **WEBSITE** www.coindufeu.com

IT'S DIFFICULT TO KNOW which of the Sibuet's Megève hotels to highlight, but our inspector picks out this one, citing it as the 'most authentic'. You could also stay at Les Fermes de Marie (tel 04 50 93 03 10) or Le Mont Blanc (tel 04 50 21 20 02) and experience the same exclusive sense of rustic sophistication; here you have the advantage of being a little away from the hustle and bustle of the attractive and elegant village centre. It feels like a private chalet, and makes a seductive place to return to after a day's skiing or walking in the mountains: in fact it's rather difficult to leave in the first place.

Le Coin du Feu has all the right ingredients for a fantasy about living in the mountains: masses of old wood – walls, floors, beamed and panelled ceilings, even a carved wooden fireplace in the sitting room – pretty fabrics (smart checks and tartans mixed with Provençal), soft lighting, snug, duvet-covered beds hidden in alcoves behind curtains (as was the tradition in these chalets), indulgent afternoon tea in front of a crackling fire, friendly and efficient service, and good honest food served in the popular restaurant. A slick interpretation of Alpine charm for the smart set.

NEARBY skiing; walking; Chamonix valley.
LOCATION on outskirts of town, near Rochebrune téléphérique, signposted; car and garage parking
FOOD breakfast, lunch, dinner
PRICE €€€
ROOMS 23 single, double and twin and suites, all with bath; all rooms have phone, TV, minibar, hairdrier
FACILITIES sitting room, dining room, bar, lift, terrace
CREDIT CARDS AE, DC, MC, V
CHILDREN welcome
DISABLED no special facilities **PETS** accepted
CLOSED Apr to mid-Jul, late Aug to mid-Sep
PROPRIETORS M. and Mme Sibuet

THE EAST

MERCUREY

HOTELLERIE DU VAL D'OR
~ VILLAGE INN ~

Grande-Rue, 71640 Mercurey (Côte-d'Or)
TEL 03 85 45 13 70 **FAX** 03 85 45 18 45
E-MAIL valdor.cogney@infonie.fr **WEBSITE** www.hotellerie-val-dor.com

A RECENT RETURN VISIT confirmed our long-held feelings of affection for this early 19thC coaching inn, situated on the main street of the prestigious but rather dull wine village of Mercurey. Still in the capable hands of chef/*patron* Jean-Claude Cogny and his equally gentle wife Monique, it is a modest place which does its job well, with simple but impeccable accommodation and good food. It's easy to see what brings the customers back, especially in a region of culinary excellence and exorbitant prices where many are daunted by the formal (or even pretentious) style of most hotels, and long to find some village-inn simplicity. The friendly Val d'Or obliges, and the tradition begun by Jean-Claude's great aunt in 1910 continues unbroken.

Downstairs, there are two dining rooms, one rustic, with beamed ceiling, large fireplace and pretty floral curtains, the other more intimate and elegant, and a bar with neat tables and chairs. The simple, impeccable bedrooms, thoughtfully decorated by Mme Cogny, are all different and all pleasing, though some are rather small. M. Cogny's cooking is also a cut above: he has a Michelin star for such dishes as *millechou d'escargots et pied de porc au beurre rouge* and *la pochouse de sandre, grenouilles et ecrevissses à ma façon.*

~

NEARBY Château de Germolles (10 km); Buxy (20 km).
LOCATION in middle of village, 9 km S of Chagny; car parking
FOOD breakfast, lunch, dinner
PRICE €€
ROOMS 13; 10 double and twin, 2 family, 1 single, all with bath or shower; all rooms have phone, TV, hairdrier; 10 have air conditioning
FACILITIES 2 dining rooms, sitting room/bar, garden
CREDIT CARDS MC, V **CHILDREN** accepted
DISABLED no special facilities **PETS** not accepted **CLOSED** Mon and Tues lunch
PROPRIETOR Jean-Claude Cogny

THE EAST

LES CHARMES
~ TOWN HOTEL ~

10 place du Murgur, 21190 Meursault (Côte-d'Or)
TEL 03 80 21 63 53 **FAX** 03 80 21 62 89

ON THE FACE OF IT, the charm of Les Charmes is mostly in the shady walled garden, so big it's almost a small park. At the far end, or by the pool, you could be far from it all, instead of at the heart of this world-famous Burgundy town. But there's more. This 18thC *maison bourgeoise* is a world of its own, once you're through the gates. The outside breakfast area, hard by the front door, under a glass and metal awning is, well, charming. The breakfast room just inside is tiny and the only indoor sitting space also contains the reception desk. But somehow it all hangs together: the patina of the creaky parquet, the neat tiled entrance passage, the antiques and quality repros all quietly tell you that things are done nicely here, in a spinsterish sort of way. Les Charmes is a charming small hotel in the sense that its negative features, such as the dark warren of upstairs corridors, don't spoil things much. One small bedroom we looked at was bleakish; another borderline; another (large, with exposed beams) full of character: be sure to ask for a *chambre meublée à l'ancienne*, rather than *en moderne*. If you like integrity and a genuine French experience, you'll like Les Charmes.

~

NEARBY Beaune (8 km); Côte de Beaune; Château de Rochepot.
LOCATION in town centre; car parking
FOOD breakfast
PRICE €€€
ROOMS 14 double and twin, all with bath; all rooms have phone, TV, minibar
FACILITIES sitting room, breakfast room, terrace, garden, swimming pool
CREDIT CARDS MC, V **CHILDREN** accepted
DISABLED 1 specially adapted room **PETS** not accepted
CLOSED Dec to Mar
PROPRIETOR Marie-Luce Haut

THE EAST

LES MAGNOLIAS
~ TOWN HOTEL ~

8 rue Pierre Joigneaux, 21190 Meursault (Côte-d'Or)
TEL 03 80 21 23 23 **FAX** 03 80 21.29 10
E-MAIL lesmagnolias@mageos.com **WEBSITE** www.les-magnolias.fr

I N A PLEASANTLY QUIET LOCATION, but only a few minutes' walk from the centre of the village celebrated for its white wine, Les Magnolias is a polished and unusually stylish bed-and-breakfast hotel.

Opened 12 years ago by Englishman Antonio Delarue (sadly we didn't meet him, although we are told he is charming), Les Magnolias consists of a group of old houses – once the home of a local *vigneron* – set behind high entrance gates around a small gravelled courtyard full of magnolias, old roses and fig trees. Reception is in one corner; while the bedrooms are located in two separate buildings, three rooms and a suite in one, eight rooms in another. Downstairs is a sweet little sitting room – the only public room in the hotel (breakfast is laid out at a circular table in your room). The bedrooms are a delightful surprise, with the feel of a private house. Each one is large and pretty, and individually decorated with some panache – a chaise-longue here, a carved armoire there, flowery fabrics, floaty curtains, plates and prints on the walls. There are fresh flowers in the bedrooms and little posies in the bathrooms. In fine weather you can take breakfast in the courtyard.

~

NEARBY Beaune (8 km); Côte de Beaune; château de Rochepot.
LOCATION close to town centre; car parking
FOOD breakfast
PRICE €€
ROOMS 12;11 double and twin, 1 suite, 10 with bath, 2 with shower; all rooms have phone, hairdrier
FACILITIES sitting room, courtyard
CREDIT CARDS AE, MC, V **CHILDREN** accepted
DISABLED 2 rooms on ground floor **PETS** not accepted
CLOSED Dec to Mar
PROPRIETOR Antonio Delarue

THE EAST

FERME AUBERGE DU VIEUX CHATEAU
～ FARM GUESTHOUSE ～

58700 Oulon (Nièvre)
TEL 03 86 68 06 77

W E DON'T INCLUDE MANY *fermes auberges* in our guide: they are often too uncomfortable; but we can't resist this one. You won't find much more basic accommodation than offered here – not only are the bedrooms small, but they are unpleasantly box-like and lack anything much more than a bed and a place to put your clothes. But the farm itself and the setting is simply idyllic, and it's unlikely that you would ever find this beautiful, undulating corner of Burgundy unless you were heading here.

The turreted old farm lies just outside the charming village of Oulon in a fold of green hills that stretch out on all sides. We arrived unannounced one lunchtime and were treated to one of those simple but perfect French meals that are becoming more and more of a memory than a reality. In the beamed, stone-walled dining room, we were presented with the family's own *foie gras*, as well as *côte d'agneau, pommes dauphinoise*, a tray of cheese and home-made crystallized fruit; at the next door table, farmworkers were enoying their lunch, too. Afterwards, seduced by the place, we walked in the countryside and, despite the bedrooms, decided to stay the night. Before leaving we bought a bottle of home-made *crème de cassis*. This is a great place for young children, with farm animals, a swimming pool, and outdoor dining in summer.

～

NEARBY Nevers (35 km); Vézelay (60 km).
LOCATION just outside Oulon, 7 km NE of Prémery; car parking
FOOD breakfast, lunch, dinner
PRICE €
ROOMS 9; 8 double,1 family, 3 with shower and W.C., 3 with shower only, 3 with communal bathroom
FACILITIES dining room, courtyard, terrace, swimming pool
CREDIT CARDS MC, V **CHILDREN** welcome
DISABLED not suitable **PETS** accepted **CLOSED** Dec to Mar
PROPRIETORS Fayolle-Tilliot family

THE EAST

✳ LA RECONCE ✳
∼ VILLAGE HOTEL ∼

Le Bourg, 71600 Poisson (Saône-et-Loire)
TEL 03 85 81 10 72 **FAX** 03 85 81 64 34
E-MAIL LaReconce@wanadoo.fr

THE STRANGELY-NAMED VILLAGE of Poisson lies on the borders of Charolais (famous for its white cattle) and Brionnais (noted for its Romanesque churches), both beautiful, little visited stretches of rolling countryside. When farmers walked their cattle to market in St Christophe-en-Brionnais (still held every Thursday), they stopped to rest at the village inn, La Poste, which for the past 27 years has been the restaurant, specializing in Charolais beef and fish, of Denise and Jean-Noel Dauvergne. Seven years ago they bought the handsome house next door and converted it into a small hotel. The parquet flooring in each room is original; apart from that, however, the rooms are standardized and modern, but with more comfort and attention to detail than one expects at this price. Lavatories are separate from bathrooms, and there are desks and plenty of mirrored cupboard space, with well-equipped bathrooms.

A door in the lobby of La Reconce connects with the bar of La Poste, where locals gather. The restaurant is altogether more *soignée*, with apricot walls, pale wicker chairs and white tablecloths, and a tank of tropical fish. In summer it is delightful to eat in the little garden under the shade of paulownia trees. The hands-on chef, M. Dauvergne, rarely emerges from the kitchen, while dainty and elegant Madame runs things at the front.

NEARBY Romanesque churches in Brionnais; Charolais. **LOCATION** in village centre, opposite church, 8 km S of Paray-le-Monial; car parking **FOOD** breakfast, lunch, dinner **PRICE** € **ROOMS** 7; 6 double and twin, 1 suite, 3 with shower, 4 with bath; all rooms have phone, TV, minibar, hairdrier **FACILITIES** breakfast room, bar, dining room, verandah, garden **CREDIT CARDS** AE, MC, V **CHILDREN** accepted **DISABLED** 1 specially adapted suite **PETS** accepted **CLOSED** Mon, Tues, except Aug **PROPRIETORS** Dauvergne family

THE EAST

SAINT-BOIL

AUBERGE DU CHEVAL BLANC
~ VILLAGE HOTEL ~

71390 Saint-Boil (Saône-et-Loire)
TEL 03 85 44 03 16 **FAX** 03 85 44 07 25

IN LOVELY COUNTRYSIDE close to the Charolais region, a good stopover en route between the vineyards of Burgundy and Beaujolais. The owners, Martine and Jany Cantin (he is Burgundian, but spent time at the famous Closerie de Lilas in Paris before opening up here 12 years ago) have augmented the village *auberge* (where there are three very simple bedrooms) by providing further bedrooms in a handsome *maison bourgeoise* across the road. In its grounds is an attractive swimming pool surrounded by a swathe of green lawn. Although the house is charming, with a lovely wooded staircase, bedrooms unfortunately pay little attention to its 18thC period. They are perfectly acceptable, but without much character. Those on the top floor have exposed beams and two have *oeil de boeuf* windows. Downstairs is the breakfast room for hotel guests. In a little separate building there is a useful apartment, again functional, consisting of two bedrooms, kitchenette and bathroom (adapted for use by the disabled).

Back across the road, the restaurant, which has a good local reputation, is soothing and sophisticated, decked in pale green and cream, with a shady courtyard where you can dine in summer.

~

NEARBY Cluny (28 km); Côte Chalonais vineyards.
LOCATION on D981, on main street in village between Chalon and Cluny; with car parking
FOOD breakfast, lunch, dinner
PRICE €€
ROOMS 13 double and twin, 10 with shower, 3 with bath, 1 apartment with bath; all rooms have phone, TV
FACILITIES sitting room, breakfast room, bar, restaurant, courtyard, swimming pool
CREDIT CARDS AE, DC, MC, V **CHILDREN** accepted
DISABLED apartment specially adapted **PETS** accepted
CLOSED mid-Feb to mid-Mar; restaurant closed Wed
PROPRIETORS Jany and Martine Cantin

THE EAST

LE HAMEAU DE BARBORON
~ COUNTRY HOTEL ~

21420 Savigny-les-Beaune (Côte-d'Or)
TEL 03 80 21 58 35 **FAX** 03 80 26 10 59
WEBSITE www.hameau-barboron.com

THIS MUST BE THE MOST lost and alone hotel in Burgundy, yet Beaune is only ten kilometres away. To reach the converted 16thC farmhouse, you drive along a single-track road through a narrow wooded valley, which finally opens out into a wide grassy meadow. Barboron lies amidst a vast *domaine de la chasse*, and wild boar are hunted here, as they have been for centuries, every Saturday between October and February.

The lovely old farm buildings, grouped around a courtyard, have been impeccably restored, as has the interior. It's all in magazine-perfect, rustic-chic good taste – perhaps too perfect. Even the staff kitchen, seen through glass doors from the reception hall, looks like a carefully arranged set piece. A table in reception is artfully strewn with glossy magazines, all opened at pages showing other perfect rustic chic interiors. There are stone walls, exposed beams, natural fabrics and lovely unusual floors – wood and terracotta tiles, with a hunting horn motif engraved on each of the terracotta ones. Bedrooms are spacious, elegant and restful. It's a long way to go, and a lot of money, for what amounts to a simple bed-and-breakfast place, however chic, but the peace and sense of isolation are hard to beat. And to give yourselves something to do in the evening you drive off in search of that perfect restaurant.

~

NEARBY Beaune (10 km); Côte de Beaune.
LOCATION 3 km from Savigny-les-Beaune, follow signs in village; car parking
FOOD breakfast
PRICE €€€
ROOMS 12; 9 double and twin, 3 duplex sleeping 4, all with bath; all rooms have phone, TV, minibar
FACILITIES breakfast room, terrace **CREDIT CARDS** AE, MC, V **CHILDREN** accepted
DISABLED 1 specially adapted room **PETS** accepted
CLOSED never
PROPRIETOR Odile Nominé

THE EAST

LE PONTOT
~ TOWN MANSION ~

place du Pontot, 89450 Vézelay (Yonne)
TEL 03 86 33 24 40 **FAX** 03 86 33 30 0

MOST VISITORS to this rambling fortified house – the only hotel inside the walls of the old town of Vézelay, just a short walk from the famous basilica – are captivated by its combination of character and luxury. Rebuilt after the Hundred Years War, it was added to in the 18th century. Since 1984 the American owner, architect Charles Thum, and manager Christian Abadie have skilfully converted the building into a rather special bed-and-breakfast. (Who needs a restaurant when the famous Espérance lies just down the road?) The bedrooms include a large Louis XVI apartment, with canopied beds, fireplace and private dressing room; and another with stone paving, 16thC beamed ceiling and antique, country-style furnishings.

Breakfast is served on gold-encrusted, royal blue Limoges porcelain. On cool days it is eaten in front of a blazing fire in the handsome, panelled Louis XVI *salon*; but in summer you sit outside in the delightful walled garden. We have had a report that the grandeur does not compensate for some skimping on the food at breakfast and the comforts in the house, and would welcome further comments.

~

NEARBY St-Père-sous-Vézelay (2 km); Avallon (15 km).
LOCATION in middle of town, with car parking
FOOD breakfast
PRICE €€
ROOMS 9 double and twin, 1 single, all with bath; all rooms have phone
FACILITIES sitting room, bar, breakfast room, terrace, garden
CREDIT CARDS DC, MC, V
CHILDREN accepted over 10
DISABLED not suitable
PETS accepted
CLOSED Nov to Easter
MANAGER Christian Abadie

The East

La Lucarne aux Chouettes
~ Restaurant-with-rooms ~

quai Bretoche, 89500 Villeneuve-sur-Yonne (Yonne)
Tel 03 86 87 18 26 **Fax** 03 86 87 22 63
E-mail lesliecaron-auberge@wanadoo.fr **Website** www. lesliecaron-auberge.com

THOSE WHO REMEMBER the delectable *Gigi* will have perked up when reading the e-mail and website addresses of this hotel, and indeed it is the actress Leslie Caron who owns 'The Barn Owl's Window'. She noticed the riverside property – a row of four 17thC derelict houses by the side of a graceful old bridge – on her way in and out of town from her nearby home, and renovated and opened them as a restaurant with four rooms in 1993. It makes a reasonable, moderately priced place in which to stop the night, not least because of the interesting little town of Villeneuve-sur-Yonne and the tranquil riverside setting.

There are just four rooms: three suites and a double room. They are all different and all decorated by Miss Caron, with pretty fabrics, canopied beds, an assortment of furniture, some antique, beamed walls, rugs on the floors, and nooks and crannies. They are, however, we felt, showing signs of wear and tear in places. Some are reached by dramatically steep old staircases, and the sense of being in a really old building predominates (Americans love it). The restaurant, in a 17thC warehouse with high vaulted ceiling, stone walls, roaring fire and fabric-covered chairs, is the heart of the operation (and you can eat by the river under large white parasols). The chef, Daïsuke Inagaki, is Japanese, but sticks to mainly French cuisine, with a few oriental touches.

~

Nearby Porte de Joigny; Sens (14 km); Auxerre (45 km).
Location in middle of town, by bridge, 14 km S of Sens; car parking
Food breakfast, lunch, dinner
Price €€
Rooms 4; 3 suites, 1 double, all with bath; all rooms have phone, TV
Facilities bar, restaurant, terrace, bathing, fishing, boating, bicycles
Credit cards MC, V
Children accepted
Disabled not suitable **Pets** accepted
Closed Sun dinner, Mon except July, Aug
Proprietor Leslie Caron

THE EAST

LE CEP

TOWN HOTEL

*27 rue Maufoux, 21206 Beaune
(Côte-d'Or)*
TEL 03 80 22 35 48 **FAX** 03 80 22 76
80
E-MAIL hotel-le-cep@wanadoo.fr
WEBSITE www.slh.com/hotelcep/
FOOD breakfast, lunch, dinner
PRICE €€
ROOMS 56
CLOSED never

ALTHOUGH IT IS somewhat larger than our usual limit, we include Le Cep because it is a good hotel with plenty of character, and the best address in the centre of Beaune. A stone's throw from the Hôtel-Dieu, it has sumptuously furnished public rooms and attractive – though mostly quite small – bedrooms, with antique furniture and beams. Breakfast ('excellent; much more than just croissants') is served in the vaulted former wine cellar or, in summer, in the pretty arcaded Renaissance courtyard. Although only breakfast is served, most guests dine in the restaurant next door. The Bernard family and their staff are genuinely friendly and hospitable.

CHATEAU DE BELLECROIX

CHATEAU HOTEL

71150 Chagny (Saône et Loire)
TEL 03 85 87 13 86 **FAX** 03 85 91
28 62 **E-MAIL** info@chateau-
bellecroix.com **WEBSITE**
www.chateau-bellecroix.com
FOOD breakfast, lunch, dinner;
room service **PRICE** €€€ **ROOMS**
20 **CLOSED** mid-Dec to mid-Feb,
Wed Oct to end May; restaurant
Wed, Thurs lunch

IMPRESSIVELY TOWERING, mellow exterior walls, covered with creeper; a charming hostess, Delphine Gautier, who has recently taken over from her mother; a roomy but friendly dining room, whose good reproduction panelling gives it a Scottish baronial feel; just off it is a snug little sitting room, done in smart contemporary papers and fabrics. The larger of the bedrooms have massive walls, antique tiled floors and eclectic furnishings. If you like the 'castle experience', these will probably outweigh the drawbacks: some dull smaller bedrooms and traffic noise from the adjacent main road – though only heard outside.

THE EAST

CHAROLLES

HOTEL DE LA POSTE

TOWN HOTEL

place de l'Eglise, 71120 Charolles (Saône-et-Loire) **TEL** 03 85 24 11 32 **FAX** 03 85 24 05 74 **E-MAIL** hotel-de-la-Liberation-DOUCET@wanadoo.fr **FOOD** breakfast, lunch, dinner **PRICE** € **ROOMS** 14 **CLOSED** mid-Nov to Dec, Sun dinner, Mon

A PRIME EXAMPLE of a provincial hotel and restaurant doing a sound job. Its long-time chef/*patron*, moustachioed Daniel Doucet, has now been joined by his son Frédéric in the kitchen, which dishes out a mean *côte de boeuf charolais à deux temps*. The white-painted building is immaculately maintained, as is the smart bar/*salon*, and the pale yellow panelled dining room is postively ritzy by small town standards. It is also possible to dine in the flowery internal courtyard.

    Bedrooms, recently renovated, are unexceptional but smartly done out, with an occasional lapse of taste here and there. A useful address if you are passing.

CLUNY

HOTEL DE BOURGOGNE

TOWN HOTEL

place de l'Abbaye, 71250 Cluny (Saône-et-Loire) **TEL** 03 85 59 00 58 **FAX** 03 85 59 03 73 **E-MAIL** hotel.bourgogne @wanadoo.fr **FOOD** breakfast, lunch, dinner **PRICE** €€ **ROOMS** 19 **CLOSED** Feb to mid-Mar, Nov; restaurant Tues, Wed lunch

A FTER MANY YEARS, this is still our favourite Cluny hotel. It's close to the abbey (in fact it was built in 1817 on abbey ground), facing Cluny's large main square. We particularly like the calm but friendly atmosphere. There's a charming, long, low-ceilinged sitting room with a creaky polished floor, and a graceful dining room with large open fire and an arresting black-and-white tiled floor. The three menus offering mainly Burgundian specialities draw many a non-resident. Off reception is a neat little bar, and a sunny courtyard gives yet another dimension to the public areas. Bedrooms are generally unexceptional, but comfortable. Owners Nathalie and Michel Colin are young and friendly.

✳ THE EAST ✳

ECHENEVEX

AUBERGE DES CHASSEURS

COUNTRY HOTEL

Naz Dessus, 01170 Echenevex (Ain)
TEL 04 50 41 54 07
FAX 04 50 41 90 61
FOOD breakfast, lunch, dinner
PRICE €€€ ROOMS 15
CLOSED mid-Nov to mid-Apr

AT THE FOOT of the Jura mountains, facing the Alps (with views over Lake Geneva to Mont Blanc), this is an attractive converted farmhouse with a warm welcome. It has been in the family of its owner, Dominque Lamy, since the mid-19th century, and thanks to the attentions of a Swedish decorator is now dressed in a Scandinavian-inspired coat of paint effects which includes patterned beams, painted ceilings, and doors adorned with flowers and inscriptions. The satisfying food in the stylish dining room is complemented by an excellent, well-priced wine list. The pool, the lovely flowery terrace and the very reasonable prices are a bonus.

Book through our travel service – see page 7.

FAVERGES

AU GAY SÉJOUR

COUNTRY HOTEL

Le Tertenoz de Seythenex, 74210 Faverges (Haute-Savoie)
TEL 04 50 44 52 52
FAX 04 50 44 49 52 E-MAIL
gaysejour@chateauxhotels.com
WEBSITE www.chateauxhotels.com
FOOD breakfast, lunch dinner
PRICE € ROOMS 12 CLOSED mid-Nov to mid-Dec; restaurant Sun dinner, Mon

A SIMPLE, honest and much admired inn which stands in a secluded spot not far from Lac d'Annecy en route to the major ski resorts. The sturdy 17thC former farmhouse has been in the dedicated hands of the Gay family for generations; chef/*patron* Bernard Gay was taught to cook by his grandmother and will one day hand over the running of the place to his son, who is training as a chef. Food is at the heart of the house, with plenty of fish dishes, both from local lakes and the sea, as well as local specialities such as truffles in season. Bedrooms are simple and spotless, with pine panelled walls and straightforward modern furnishings. There are beautiful views from the terrace; peace and quiet is assured.

THE EAST

L'ANGE SOURIANT

VILLAGE BED-AND-BREAKFAST

rue Voltaire, 21150 Flavigny-sur-Ozerain (Côte d'Or)
TEL 03 80 96 24 93
FAX 03 80 96 24 93 **E-MAIL** ange-souriant@wanadoo.fr **WEBSITE** www.ange-souriant.com **FOOD** breakfast **PRICE** € **ROOMS** 4
CLOSED Nov to Apr

WE WERE ALERTED by a couple of enthusiastic readers' letters to this new B&B in the lovely fortified village of Flavigny, location for the movie *Chocolat*. Owned by Will Barrueto, a naturalized Peruvian-American, it has four double bedrooms, two of which can be connected to make a family suite sharing a bathroom. All the rooms are decorated with antiques, with flowing fabrics and a private home feel (no telephones or televisions). The atmosphere, says one of our nominators, is 'friendly, relaxing and romantic'. Breakfast is taken in the dining room, or on fine mornings in the charming courtyard. 'Fresh bread from the local monastery served with wonderfully brewed coffee', we are told.

LA TOUR DE PACORET

COUNTRY HOUSE HOTEL

Montailleur, 73460 Gresy-sur-Isère (Savoie)
TEL 04 79 37 91 59
FAX 04 79 37 93 84
E-MAIL Albapacore@aol.com
FOOD breakfast, lunch, dinner
PRICE €€
ROOMS 9 **CLOSED** Nov to May

THERE ARE FINE mountain views from the upper windows of this old stone watchtower – built on the summit of a hill in the 13th century for the Dukes of Savoy and later passed on to the Duc de Pacoret. All the bedrooms have views over the Isère valley and the fields of corn which surround it. It's a truly peaceful spot (Relais de Silence) run by informal young owners. A fine staircase leads up to the rather dull but individually decorated bedrooms, and there is a smartish dining room on the ground floor. Best of all is the vine-clad terrace, its tables covered in Provençal cloths, and the large garden with tempting swimming pool.

THE EAST

PULIGNY-MONTRACHET

MONTRACHET

TOWN HOTEL

10 place des Marronniers, 21190
Puligny-Montrachet (Côte-d'Or)
TEL 03 80 21 30 06
FAX 03 80 21 39 06
E-MAIL info@le-montrachet.com
WEBSITE www.le-montrachet.com
FOOD breakfast, lunch, dinner
PRICE €€ **ROOMS** 32
CLOSED Dec

THE CENTRE of Puligny-Montrachet, place des Marronniers, is laid to grass and surrounded by chestnut trees and by the outlets of local wine-growers. The handsome stone-built hotel overlooks the square, and though the interior lacks character, and (we thought) is priced somewhat on the high side, it makes a useful stopover while touring the vineyards. Opened 15 years ago it is furnished in a smart though rather functional way, with the same chairs (modern version of the traditional tapestry) used throughout the public rooms. 22 rooms are located in the main building, the others in a separate building across the street. The spacious, calm restaurant, serving local specialities, has a Michelin star. In summer you can sit on the pretty front terrace.

SAINT-GERVAIS

CHALET REMY

CHALET HOTEL

Le Bettex, 74170 St-Gervais
(Haute-Savoie)
TEL 04 50 93 11 85
FAX 04 50 93 14 45
FOOD breakfast, lunch, dinner
PRICE €
ROOMS 19
CLOSED never

IN SHARP CONTRAST to the glossy chalet hotels of nearby Megève (see page 164), this chalet is as simple – and as genuine – as you could hope to find, with all the associated charm and character. With breathtaking views across to Mont Blanc, it's a traditional stone and log 18thC farmhouse which retains its original woodwork. The interior seems to have been frozen in time for at least 50 years. A central staircase leads to a rectangular gallery off which the bedrooms lead. These, all wood, are tiny and very simple but warm, with comfortable beds, and the communal bathrooms are *très propre*. Traditional, satisfying dishes are served in a candlelit dining room, and there's a fine terrace with views overlooking the garden and the mountains.

THE EAST

VAL-DE-MERCY

AUBERGE DU CHATEAU

VILLAGE RESTAURANT-WITH ROOMS

3 rue du Pont, 89680 Val-de-Mercy (Yonne)
TEL 03 86 41 60 00
FAX 03 86 41 73 28
E-MAIL delfontainej@wanadoo.fr
FOOD breakfast, lunch, dinner
PRICE €€ **ROOMS** 5 **CLOSED** mid-Jan to Mar; restaurant Sun dinner, Mon

WE INCLUDE this hotel in a little riverside village deep in the quiet countryside in the hope that it is as nice as it looks from the outside ... We were recommended it *en passant* while in the area, but sadly when we turned up it was unexpectedly closed. Still, a good poke round gave us every intention of returning – it looked very promising, stylish yet informal, with an elegant restaurant fashioned from two rooms and a pretty courtyard for summer dining. Bedrooms, we are told, have parquet floors, old roses on the curtains and a good smattering of antiques. The menu looked tempting ... the chef/*patron* proudly told us (on the phone) that he had been trained by Michel Roux in England ... reports please.

VEYRIER-DU-LAC

LA DEMEURE DE CHAVOIRE

LAKESIDE HOTEL

route d'Annecy-Chavoire, 74290 Veyrier-du-Lac (Haute-Savoie)
TEL 04 50 60 04 38
FAX 04 50 60 05 36
WEBSITE www.demeuredechavoire.com
FOOD breakfast, snacks
PRICE €€€
ROOMS 13 **CLOSED** never

WE LACK recent feedback on this hotel, situated on the shores of Lake Annecy and, conveniently, on the main road to the ski resorts. On our last visit, we found it an impeccably kept, charming place set in a pretty garden, a happy combination of traditional elegance and modern comforts. Every room has been thoughtfully and richly furnished, and the bedrooms are all individually decorated in romantic style. They are named after local beauty spots and famous writers – you may sleep in the Jean-Jacques Rousseau suite. Reception rooms have marquetry floors, panelled walls and embossed ceilings. Plenty of good taste and calm.

THE SOUTH-WEST

HOTELS IN THE SOUTH-WEST

THE LIMOUSIN HILLS represent the watershed between the basins of the Charente and the Loire, to the north, and that of the Garonne and its tributaries, to the south; and the start of our South-West region.

For many visitors, the valleys of the Dordogne and the Lot represent an ideal, not only of France but of life itself – life in a kind climate and a fertile landscape. Correspondingly, our concentration of hotels here is second only to that of Provence. Our recent researches for this edition have revealed a welcome stability amongst these hotels; old favourites – for example, the Moulin de l'Abbaye (page 187) and Domaine de la Roseraie at Brantôme (page 186), Manoir de Hautegente at Coly (page 192), La Pélissaria at St-Cirq-Lapopie (page 208) and Domaine de la Rhue at Rocamadour (page 206) – remain consistent, while we have added some interesting new addresses, such as Le Jardin d'Eyquem at St-Michel-de-Montaigne (page 215) and Domaine de St-Géry at Lascabanes (page 198). Further south, the peaceful, rolling countryside of Gascony, its gastronomic delights and its fortified *bastides* have become much better known to holidaymakers of late and this is reflected in the number of interesting hotels we have discovered there: Domaine de Bassibé (page 218) and Château de Projan (page 204) to name but two.

Only a handful of addresses in the Bordeaux wine region and the strange, immense expanses of the Landes, but useful ones. In the marvellous landscape of the Pyrenees, we again find consistency, with such old favourites as Arcé at St-Etienne-de-Baïgorry still on top form after five generations in the same hands (page 212) and Arraya at Sare after three (page 217). A useful new address in Biarritz: Maison Garnier (page 185).

The hotels in this guide represent the pick of the region, but there are many other excellent addresses. For wider coverage, see our *Charming Small Hotel Guide to Southern France.*

THE SOUTH-WEST

AGNAC

CHATEAU DE PECHALBET
~ COUNTRY HOUSE HOTEL ~

47800 Agnac (Lot-et-Garonne)
TEL and FAX 05 53 83 04 70
E-MAIL pechalbet@caramail.com **WEBSITE** www.eymet-en-perigord.com

WHEN HENRI PEYRE and his wife, Françoise, fled from the crowded shores of the Riviera in 1995 in search of somewhere quiet in the country, their initial idea was to provide *chambres d'hôte* with breakfast only. But they found that guests were most reluctant to tear themselves away from the huge rooms and peace of this beautiful 17thC château to go out to eat in restaurants at the end of the day and last year Mme Peyre gave in to pressure and now cooks dinner. 'It's very pleasant,' says her husband. 'We all gather on the terrace to watch the sunsets, then eat by candlelight and talk and talk. It's sometimes very difficult to get our guests to bed.' Prices are kept deliberately low to encourage people to come for several days, or even weeks, at a time. There is a huge amount of space – rooms, furnished with charming antiques, are enormous and all open on to the terrace – and the house has an intriguing history. Sheep graze in the park, when autumn comes around logs crackle in the massive stone fireplace and there is mushrooming in the woods. For guests M. Peyre has his own list of what he claims are entirely secret places that he has discovered himself to be visited nearby, and he and his wife offer the warmest of welcomes. Reports please.

~

NEARBY Eymet (4 km); Bergerac (25 km).
LOCATION on 40-hectare country estate; signposted S of Eymet on D933 to Miramont; ample car and garage parking
FOOD breakfast, dinner
PRICE €
ROOMS 5 double and twin, all with bath or shower
FACILITIES 2 sitting rooms, billiard room, bar, dining room, terrace, gardens, swimming pool **CREDIT CARDS** not accepted **CHILDREN** welcome
DISABLED no special facilities **PETS** accepted **CLOSED** Dec to Apr
PROPRIETOR Henri Peyre

THE SOUTH-WEST

AINHOA

OHANTZEA
~ VILLAGE HOTEL ~

64250 Aïnhoa, (Pyrénées-Atlantiques)
TEL 05 59 29 90 50 **FAX** 05 59 29 89 70

A WARM WELCOME AWAITS in this unpretentious, seriously Basque hotel dating back to the 17th century and in the same family for the past three centuries. The timbered and shuttered building in the centre of a picturesque village is typical of the region. Inside, you step back in time, with bare, worn wooden flooring, beamed ceilings, old pictures, shelves of antique kitchen utensils, copper kettles, pewter jugs – and no concession to modern materials or ornament. French windows look out on to the garden from the spacious dining room. Bedrooms are large and convey the same mood of established solidarity and family farmhouse comfort. Mme Ithurria modestly explains that 'this is not a modern house and we have no formula, except to provide the atmosphere of a family home and fair prices'. It is not surprising that it is much patronized by our readers. The food, too, caters to old-fashioned tastes with large helpings of succulent baby lamb and other local products. Great value for money.

The area is renowned for its mild climate; Edmond Rostand, author of *Cyrano de Bergerac*, came here to take the spa waters and liked it so much that he built a house nearby, Villa Arnaga (open to visitors on the D932).

~

NEARBY Spanish border (2 km); Villa Arnaga; St-Pée-sur-Nivelle (10 km); Sare (10 km).
LOCATION in middle of village, 10 km SW of Cambo-les-Bains; car parking
FOOD breakfast, lunch, dinner
PRICE €
ROOMS 10; 8 double and twin, 2 family, all with bath; all rooms have phone
FACILITIES sitting room, dining room, garden
CREDIT CARDS AE, DC, MC, V
CHILDREN welcome
DISABLED no special facilities
PETS accepted
CLOSED mid-Nov to mid-Feb
PROPRIETOR Marcel Ithurria

THE SOUTH-WEST

LE SQUARE
~ VILLAGE HOTEL ~

5/7 place de la Craste, 47220 Astaffort (Lot-et-Garonne)
TEL 05 53 47 20 40 **FAX** 05 53 47 10 38 **E-MAIL** Latrille.Michel@wanadoo.fr
WEBSITE www.latrille.com

WARM OCHRE AND SIENNA-WASHED EXTERIORS, blue shutters and striped awnings on a little *place* filled with roses and pergolas really make you feel you are heading south. There have been recent improvements at this charming little hotel since Agen chef Michel Latrille and his wife, Sylvie, took over. Now there is a satisfying combination: M. Latrille's excellent traditional local cuisine and stylish, comfortable, spacious bedrooms with shining bathrooms, all set off by Mme Latrille's vivacity. No expense has been spared on the high quality renovation of two adjoining houses and the smart Kenzo fabrics, painted furniture, modern uplighting and glistening tiled bathrooms are pleasingly fresh and uplifting. This little hotel is just the right size and the Latrilles have created an easy informality, while assuring that there are no slips in their standards. Nooks and crannies of the hotel are filled with interesting detail; a small Moorish-style patio with olive tree helps to give the impression you are not far away from the road to Spain and there's a large, leafy outside terrace on the first floor for eating on summer evenings. Outside, dogs bark, old men play *boules* and children scamper in the square.

~

NEARBY Agen (18 km); *bastides*; Garonne river.
LOCATION in village centre; garage and street car parking
FOOD breakfast, lunch, dinner
PRICE €€€
ROOMS 14; 12 double and twin, 2 suites, 11 with bath and 3 with shower; all rooms have phone, TV, air conditioning, minibar, safe, hairdrier
FACILITIES sitting room, dining room, lift, terrace **CREDIT CARDS** AE, DC, MC, V
CHILDREN accepted
DISABLED 1 specially adapted room **PETS** accepted **CLOSED** 15 days in Jan; 1 week in Nov
PROPRIETORS Michel and Sylvie Latrille

THE SOUTH-WEST

BARCUS

CHEZ CHILO
~ VILLAGE HOTEL ~

64130 Barcus (Pyrénées-Atlantiques)
TEL 05 59 28 90 79 **FAX** 05 59 28 93 10
E-MAIL martine.chilo@wanadoo.fr

IT IS WELL WORTH making a detour to enjoy the delights of this small hotel on the borders of the verdant Basque and Béarn country. The expertise of three generations has created a place of welcome, comfort and wonderful food. The attractive building harmonizes with the surrounding village, with a delightful garden and children's play area, and a discreetly located swimming pool with mountain views. The rooms have all been recently refurbished, and are bright and friendly without extravagance. Downstairs is an L-shaped dining room with open fireplace, a large sitting room with a bar, reminiscent of an English country inn, and a main dining room with picture windows on to the garden. This is the setting for a memorable meal. Early each morning the freshest and best of local produce is delivered straight from the market, ready to be transformed by Pierre Chilo into dishes of exceptional refinement and quality. This is a refreshing, reasonably-priced, efficient and very enjoyable stopping-place for the traveller and Martine and Pierre Chilo specialize in a warm Basque welcome. Note that they have recently acquired another hotel, the Bidegain, with period Basque interior, in nearby Mauléon (tel 05 59 28 16 05).

NEARBY Pau (50 km); the Spanish border.
LOCATION in village, on D24 between Oloron Ste-Marie and Mauléon; ample car parking
FOOD breakfast, lunch, dinner
PRICE €
ROOMS 10; 7 double and twin, 3 family, 6 with bath (3 Jacuzzi), 4 with shower
FACILITIES sitting room/TV room, bar, restaurant, terrace, garden, swimming pool
CREDIT CARDS AE, DC, MC, V
CHILDREN welcome
DISABLED 1 specially adapted room
PETS accepted
CLOSED Jan
PROPRIETORS Pierre and Martine Chilo

THE SOUTH-WEST

MAISON GARNIER
~ TOWN GUESTHOUSE ~

29 rue Gambetta, 64200 Biarritz (Pyrénées-Atlantiques)
TEL 05 59 01 60 70 **FAX** 05 59 01 60 80
E-MAIL maison-garnier@hotel-biarritz.com **WEBSITE** www.hotel-biarritz.com

A SHORT WALK up from the two main beaches brings you to an old part of the town which belongs to the locals and seems unconnected with surfers and seaside congress venues. It is here that Jean-Christophe Garnier has transformed a neglected old family hotel into the pleasantest place to stay in Biarritz at a reasonable price. With a background in hotel administration, he has applied his professional skill and experience down to the smallest detail with the result that you will find everything you need and nothing you don't. The rooms are uncluttered, with comfortable beds, fittings which are in the right place and work, superb showers (always a triumph to find showers which work perfectly), practical storage facilities.

The dining room is light and pleasant; only breakfast is served but this starts with freshly pressed orange juice and includes a buffet selection of fresh breads and croissants, jams and coffee, so that you don't have to wait or ask for more. The sitting area is stylishly different with a fireplace and interesting pictures on the walls. Wooden floors, white walls and light fabrics lend an almost colonial air which is very attractive. Monsieur Garnier knows what he is doing, and is doing it well.

~

NEARBY market; seafront; golf; town centre.
LOCATION follow signs for Centre Ville, place Clémenceau, then left by Bank Inchauspé (large white building) into rue Gambetta; car parking in street
FOOD breakfast
PRICE €-€€
ROOMS 7 double and twin, all with shower; all rooms have phone, TV
FACILITIES sitting room, dining room
CREDIT CARDS AE, DC, MC, V
CHILDREN accepted
DISABLED no special facilities
PETS accepted
CLOSED never
PROPRIETOR Jean-Christophe Garnier

THE SOUTH-WEST

❋ DOMAINE DE LA ROSERAIE ❋
∽ COUNTRY HOTEL ∽

route d'Angoulême, 24310 Brantôme (Dordogne)
TEL 05 53 05 84 74 **FAX** 05 53 05 77 94 **E-MAIL** domaine.la.roseraie@wanadoo.fr
WEBSITE www.domaine-la-roseraie.com

IT IS SOME TIME since the Domaine de La Roseraie looked like a 17thC monastery and the courtyard surrounded by restored one-storey buildings is now almost swamped by flowers and plants. There are roses in abundance, as the name implies, and everywhere you look there are little troughs and pots full of blooms, which give the air a heavy scent. Evelyne Roux is fastidious about her *domaine*, constantly doing her rounds to check that all is in place and there is nothing that guests might find less than perfect. All her rooms face south, have old family furniture, spotless bathrooms and independent entrances. The most popular, Bagatelle, is turned out in yellow *toile de Jouy* – and is charming. In one room Mme Roux painted the *trompe l'oeil* herself and when she made a mistaken blob on another wall artfully turned that into a butterfly. Her taste will suit those who appreciate high, comfortable beds, immaculate bathrooms, prettiness, and peace and quiet. The swimming pool is discreetly hidden behind greenery and breakfast can be taken outside at little tables. M. Roux's local cooking is served in the evenings in the beamed dining room with stone fireplace and picture windows, or among the roses on the terrace. For nature lovers.

NEARBY Brantôme (1 km); Bourdeilles; Richemont; Puyguilhem.
LOCATION in countryside on 4 hectares of gardens and grounds; ample car parking
FOOD breakfast, dinner
PRICE €€ **ROOMS** 9 double and twin, all with bath and shower; all rooms have phone, TV, hairdrier; 2 have air conditioning **FACILITIES** sitting room, dining room, bar, terrace, garden, swimming pool **CREDIT CARDS** AE, MC, V **CHILDREN** welcome **DISABLED** 1 specially adapted room **PETS** not accepted **CLOSED** mid-Nov to mid-Mar **PROPRIETORS** Evelyne and Denis Roux

THE SOUTH-WEST

✳ MOULIN DE L'ABBAYE ✳
∼ CONVERTED MILL ∼

1 route de Bourdeilles, 24310 Brantôme (Dordogne)
TEL 05 53 05 80 22 **FAX** 05 53 05 75 27 **E-MAIL** moulin@relaischateaux.com
WEBSITE www. relaischateaux.com

'ALTHOUGH WE ARRIVED rather late (8.30 pm), without a booking and clad in leather, we were welcomed with open arms. We stayed in one of their buildings across the river, and were upgraded to a junior suite (without asking) on the top floor which had a fabulous view to the Moulin. There was a huge bathroom with a circular marble bathtub. The room was tastefully decorated in colonial style. We would love to have stayed there longer and felt it was worth the money.' So write a very satisfied pair of motorcyclists about this exquisite little mill.

The setting is the thing. The shady riverside terrace, illuminated in the evening, is an idyllic place for a drink or a meal while admiring Brantôme's unusual angled bridge, the tower of the abbey or the swans gliding by. Wonderful views over the river and the old houses of one of the prettiest villages in France are also to be had from many of the bedrooms – all comfortably furnished, some with four-poster beds and antiques, others in more modern style.

Traditional Périgord dishes with a creative touch earn the restaurant 16/20 from Gault-Millau and a star from Michelin. The dining room makes a pleasant setting for this excellent cuisine in cooler weather, although we can raise no enthusiasm for the 'Monet-style' colour scheme.

∼

NEARBY Antonne-et-Trigonant (3 km); Bourdeilles (10 km).
LOCATION on edge of town, 20 km N of Périgueux; garage parking across road
FOOD breakfast, lunch, dinner; room service **PRICE** €€€€-€€€€€ **ROOMS** 17 double and twin, 3 apartments, all with bath; all rooms have phone, TV, air conditioning, minibar, hairdrier **FACILITIES** sitting room, restaurant, terrace

CREDIT CARDS AE, DC, MC, V
CHILDREN welcome
DISABLED no special facilities
PETS accepted **CLOSED** Nov to May
MANAGER Bernard Dessum

THE SOUTH-WEST

CHEZ MARCEL
~ VILLAGE INN ~

rue du 11 Mai 1944, 46100 Cardaillac (Lot)
TEL 05 65 40 11 16 **FAX** 05 65 40 49 08

BUILT AS AN *auberge* and stables in the mid-19th century and now the local bar-restaurant of a small village north of Figéac, this has been run for the past three years by Bernard Marcel, who took it over on the death of his father, André. Time has barely touched it and from the minute you find yourself among the red-and-white gingham tablecloths and lace curtains of the handsome ground-floor rooms you are enveloped by the authentic rustic charm of days long gone by. The barely believable prices and unspoiled simplicity of the place have proved a winner for the Marcel family, but some very small changes are planned, though nothing that could be described as radical. Mme Marcel, Gisèle, who speaks English, is slowly adding to the delightful collection of country antiques in the bedrooms and her husband is contemplating the possibility of replacing the plastic curtain in the shower with a glass door, but he's not in any hurry. Nothing to frighten the horses, so Chez Marcel fans, of which there are many, will not get any unwelcome shocks when they return. The chef, Jacky Fabre, has been there for 22 years and bread comes in fresh from the baker just up the road. There's plenty of life in the bar in the evenings and a pretty little village to visit.

~

NEARBY Figéac (9 km); Cahors (60 km); valley of the Lot.
LOCATION in country village; car parking in large public car park and street
FOOD breakfast, lunch, dinner
PRICE €
ROOMS 5; 4 double and 1 triple; all rooms have washbasins and share shower and WC on landing
FACILITIES restaurant, bar, terrace **CREDIT CARDS** MC, V **CHILDREN** accepted
DISABLED no special facilities **PETS** accepted
CLOSED 15 days in Feb
PROPRIETOR Bernard Marcel

THE SOUTH-WEST

HOSTELLERIE FENELON
~ VILLAGE INN ~

46110 Carennac (Lot)
Tel 05 65 10 96 46 **Fax** 05 65 10 94 86

Mme Raynal was, with her characteristic attention to detail, busy gardening and planting out geraniums in the plentiful window boxes on this jolly-looking, family-run, colourful *logis*, with red roof and red-and-white striped awnings, when we called. She likes the place to be a riot of flowers and her warm welcome and the friendly and unobtrusive service of her staff have won her many admirers among our readers. Traditionalists will be happy to know that son, Philippe, is now in the kitchen and continues his father's highly commended and generous *cuisine du terroir*. In the middle of the Haut-Quercy, Carennac is a delightful, riverside medieval village, full of charm, and quite a few of Mme Raynal's neat, clean bedrooms – conventionally decorated with reproduction furniture and flowery prints – look over the pointed Périgordan roof of a little gingerbread house on the banks of the Dordogne river. The beamed restaurant, too, overlooks the river, though meals are served, as well, on the paved terrace at the front of the hotel, which is shielded from the quiet road by a tall hedge. Use of the swimming pool is reserved for guests. Excellent value for money and a homely ambience make this a perfect staging post for touring the area.

~

Nearby Carennac priory; Rocamadour (30 km); Gouffre de Padirac (10 km).
Location in village centre; ample car parking
Food breakfast, lunch, dinner
Price €
Rooms 15 double and twin, all with bath or shower; all rooms have phone, TV
Facilities sitting room, dining room, bar, terrace, garden, swimming pool
Credit cards DC, MC, V
Children accepted
Disabled access difficult
Pets accepted
Closed mid-Jan to mid-Mar
Proprietors M. and Mme Raynal and sons

THE SOUTH-WEST

✳ LE MOULIN DU ROC ✳
∾ CONVERTED MILL ∾

24530 Champagnac-de-Bélair (Dordogne)
TEL 05 53 02 86 00 **FAX** 05 53 54 21 31 **E-MAIL** moulinroc@aol.com
WEBSITE www.moulin-du-roc.com

THIS DELECTABLE OLD WALNUT-OIL MILL with its Michelin-starred restaurant belongs to that rare breed of hotels that gives you the sense of being pampered without costing a fortune. The setting on the banks of the Dronne is truly romantic: the gardens are lush, secluded, shady and bursting with colour. A Japanese-style bridge crosses the river to a grassy area with scattered seating and discretely positioned swimming pool and tennis court. Inside the rough-stone 17thC building, oak beams, stone fireplaces, mill machinery, rich fabrics and a wealth of antiques – oil paintings, silverware and solid Périgord dressers – combine with abundant flower arrangements to create an intimate yet highly individual style. Some may find it slightly heavy. The same cannot be said of the food: in the land of *foie gras*, Alain Gardillou manages to build on culinary traditions to produce remarkably light and inventive dishes. Breakfasts, too, are a treat, with home-baked rolls, fresh fruit, eggs and yoghurt, beautifully served. Bedrooms vary in size, but do not disappoint. Many are pretty, cosy and filled with their share of antiques; several have four-posters. Others have recently been redesigned to create fewer, more spacious rooms, including large and immaculate bathrooms.

NEARBY Brantôme (6 km); Bourdeilles (15 km).
LOCATION in village, on D82 and D83, 6 km NE of Brantôme; car parking **FOOD** breakfast, lunch, dinner **PRICE** €€€-€€€€ **ROOMS** 13; 8 double and twin, 4 junior suites, 1 suite, all with bath or Jacuzzi; all rooms have phone, TV, minibar, hairdrier, 8 rooms have air conditioning **FACILITIES** sitting room, restaurant, terrace, garden, covered swimming pool, tennis **CREDIT CARDS** AE, DC, MC, V **CHILDREN** welcome **DISABLED** 2 rooms on ground floor **PETS** accepted **CLOSED** Jan to Mar **PROPRIETORS** M. and Mme Gardillou

THE SOUTH-WEST

CIBOURE

LEHEN TOKIA
~ SEASIDE GUESTHOUSE ~

chemin Achotarreta, 64500 Ciboure (Pyrénées-Atlantiques)
TEL 05 59 47 18 16 **FAX** 05 59 47 38 04
E-MAIL info@lehen-tokia.com **WEBSITE** www.lehen-tokia.com

THE UNUSUAL NAME means 'first house' in the strange language of the
Basques, whose origins still baffle the experts. A splendid example of
neo-Basque architecture, it was built in 1925 by the architect Hiriart who
is credited with coining the expression 'Art Deco'. The house embodies
many features in this style, notably stained glass windows by Jacques
Grüber, and is a *Monument Historique*. It is certainly special.

On a recent visit we found that the new proprietor, Yan Personnaz, has
done much to make the house lighter, fresher and more welcoming and
comfortable without sacrificing any of its spirit or charm. It still feels like
a home, an atmosphere enriched by its display of personal belongings,
books and paintings. All the rooms have been refurbished, and each one is
different (see the hotel's excellent website). Only breakfast is served, but
other meals can be delivered by a local caterer. The rose garden and pretty
summerhouse and terrace look out to the ocean whilst retaining an intimate seclusion. Ideal for golfing enthusiasts: there are seven courses within a radius of 15 kilometres, and golfing trips can be organized.

~

NEARBY St-Jean-de-Luz; Spanish border; Biarritz (16 km).
LOCATION in Ciboure, across river Nivelle from St-Jean-de-Luz, well signposted in
residential street withing walking distance of beach and town centre; street car
parking
FOOD breakfast
PRICE €€
ROOMS 7; 6 double and twin, 1 suite, 5 with bath, 2 with shower; all rooms have
phone, TV, minibar
FACILITIES sitting rooms, terrace, garden, swimming pool
CREDIT CARDS AE, DC, MC, V
CHILDREN accepted
DISABLED access difficult
PETS not accepted
CLOSED mid-Nov to mid-Dec
PROPRIETOR Yan Personnaz

THE SOUTH-WEST

MANOIR D'HAUTEGENTE
~ MANOR HOUSE HOTEL ~

Coly, 24120 Terrasson (Dordogne)
TEL 05 53 51 68 03 **FAX** 05 53 50 38 52
E-MAIL hotel@manoir-hautegente.com **WEBSITE** www.manoir-hautegente.com

A READER ONCE DESCRIBED this creeper-clad manor house as 'so good that I wouldn't tell you about it if it were not already in the guide'. The house, set in beautiful wooded grounds in the heart of the Périgord Noir, has been in the Hamelin family for about 300 years, and is now run by Edith Hamelin and her son Patrick. It was built as a forge in the 13thC, later became a mill (using the stream that runs beside it), was then embellished and turned into a family residence and was finally converted into a hotel – but with the feeling of a private house skilfully retained. Public rooms and the spacious, comfortable bedrooms are imaginatively decorated with family antiques and paintings.

Dinner in the pretty vaulted dining room is a five-course affair – 'first-class cooking' which inevitably includes home-produced *foie gras*, another of the Hamelins' commercial successes. The present chef, Bernard Villain, is a particular find. Wines are reasonably priced.

In the pleasant grassy grounds there is a smart pool that gets plenty of sun. There is also a pond, and fishing is available on the local river. The Hamelins are natural hosts and a warm welcome awaits guests to their family home.

~

NEARBY châteaux; Lascaux (15 km); Sarlat (25 km).
LOCATION in countryside, 6 km SE of Le Lardin on D62, in own grounds; ample car parking
FOOD breakfast, dinner
PRICE ⓔⓔⓔ
ROOMS 15 double and twin, all with bath; all rooms have phone, TV, hairdrier
FACILITIES sitting room, dining room, terrace, garden, swimming pool
CREDIT CARDS MC, V
CHILDREN welcome
DISABLED 1 ground-floor room
PETS accepted **CLOSED** Nov to Easter
PROPRIETORS Edith Hamelin and Patrick Hamelin

THE SOUTH-WEST

CONDOM

TROIS LYS
~ TOWN HOTEL ~

38 rue Gambetta, 32100 Condom (Gers)

THIS BEAUTIFULLY RESTORED 18thC town house is an old favourite of ours for its restrained elegance both externally and within. It is a real oasis of calm and quiet despite its location in the centre of a busy market town. Its new owner, Pascal Miguet, is as dedicated as his predecessor and draws on long experience working in international hotels. A charming new dining room gives a feeling of space and at the same time initimacy, as does the friendly new bar. The hotel is now air-conditioned throughout. In summer the entrance courtyard which leads off the pedestrian precinct is decorated with shrubs and flowers, and set with chairs and tables. You can eat here when the weather permits. The kitchen specializes in fresh local produce cooked with care and expertise, but without pretension.

Despite another new feature, a fully-equipped meeting room, the Trois Lys continues to feel more like a home than a hotel. All is light and restful, with Versailles parquet floors, original moulded wood panelling – and a perfect wide stone staircase with wrought iron balustrade. The bedrooms are in keeping, each with a different colour scheme, with antique or reproduction furniture. Outside there is a large swimming pool and terrace, discreetly hidden behind a wall, and shaded.

~

NEARBY Cathédrale St-Pierre; Musée d'Armagnac.
LOCATION in town centre, car parking
FOOD breakfast, lunch, dinner
PRICE €€€
ROOMS 10; 9 double and twin, 1 single, 8 with bath, 2 with shower; all rooms have phone, TV, air conditioning, hairdrier
FACILITIES dining room, terrace, swimming pool
CREDIT CARDS V
CHILDREN welcome
DISABLED access difficult
PETS accepted
CLOSED never
PROPRIETOR Pascal Miguet

THE SOUTH-WEST

LES EYZIES-DE-TAYAC

LE MOULIN DE LA BEUNE
∼ VILLAGE HOTEL ∼

24620 Les Eyzies de Tayac (Dordogne)
TEL 05 53 06 93 39 **FAX** 05 53 06 94 33

LES EYZIES can be a crowded place – one of the most visited villages in France, so it is said – but signs to the Moulin take you down a track and under the bridge that is the main road to a hidden leafy little enclave on the banks of the Beune, where all you can hear is the sound of rushing water. This is an elegant little hotel, where with simple good taste, Mme Soulié puts together old and new with charming results. In the red-tiled entrance hall, logs crackle in the large stone fireplace to mingle with the sound of the river; there are umbrellas by the door for guests. You look out on to a verdant, shaded, waterside terrace. Rooms are decorated with light, restful colours and there are architectural prints of Versailles on the walls of the corridor. For those who absolutely must see a TV, there is one in the small breakfast room downstairs. The visitors' book is full of tributes: 'everything one loves to encounter – courtesy, good taste, style, high standards and warmth...an enchanted place'. In the evenings, you walk over a little bridge to the restaurant in another part of the restored water mill, where the old wheel still turns and M. Soulié prepares his *Perigordan* specialities. Budget prices, a sublime setting, and easy parking make this a perfect base.

∼

NEARBY National Museum of Prehistory; caves; troglodytic village;
bastides.
LOCATION in village centre; car parking
FOOD breakfast, lunch, dinner
PRICE €
ROOMS 20 double and twin, 14 with bath, 6 with shower; all rooms have phone
FACILITIES small sitting room, dining room, terrace, garden
CREDIT CARDS AE, MC, V **CHILDREN** welcome
DISABLED no special facilities **PETS** accepted
CLOSED Nov to Apr
PROPRIETORS Annick and Georges Soulié

THE SOUTH-WEST

✳ CHATEAU DE FOURCES ✳
~ CHATEAU HOTEL ~

32250 Fourcès (Gers)
TEL 05 62 29 49 53 **FAX** 05 62 29 50 59
E-MAIL chatogers@aol.com **WEBSITE** www.chateau_Fources.com

THE ORIGINS OF THIS FORTIFIED CASTLE are traced back to the 12th century. It stands guarding the entrance to a circular *bastide* (very popular with tourists in summer) with typical half-timbered houses and covered arcades near the river Azoue. Thanks to the energy, dedication and flair of its present owner, Patrizia Barsan, it has been meticulously restored and transformed into a delightful hotel which successfully blends the requirements of modern man into an ancient setting. The massive stone masonry of the high walls and turret – in excellent condition – dominate, but they are softened by Renaissance mullion windows which allow in plenty of light. The central square spiral staircase was one of the first to be built in France. By some miracle an efficient lift has been installed, and leads to charmingly arranged bedrooms. A sitting room opening on to a terrace has vestiges of an old wine press. Stairs lead down to a spacious dining room where a good choice of menus is on offer. Breakfast can be served in your room if you wish. The château is surrounded by a park bordering the river which is fringed by magnificent stands of weeping willow. The swimming pool sits beside a covered terrace. Mme Barsan is a memorable hostess. Reports please.

~

NEARBY Condom (13 km); *bastides.*
LOCATION 5.5 km NE of Montréal via RD29; car parking
FOOD breakfast, lunch, dinner
PRICE €€€-€€€€ **ROOMS** 17; 12 double and twin, 5 suites, all with bath; all rooms have phone, TV, minibar, safe **FACILITIES** sitting room, bar, dining room, billiard room, lift, terrace, swimming pool, fishing

CREDIT CARDS AE, DC, MC, V
CHILDREN accepted
DISABLED no special facilities
PETS accepted
CLOSED Oct to Dec
PROPRIETOR Mme Barsan

THE SOUTH-WEST

PAIN ADOUR ET FANTAISIE
~ RIVERSIDE HOTEL ~

14-16 place des Tilleuls, 40270 Grenade sur l'Adour (Landes)
TEL 05 58 45 18 80 **FAX** 05 58 45 16 57
E-MAIL pain.adour.fantaisie@wanadoo.fr

WHEN DIDIER OUDILL left for the Café de Paris, Biarritz, he was succeeded as chef/*patron* of this distinguished hotel/restaurant by Philippe Garret, who has worked here since its creation. Both served under Michel Guérard at Eugénie-les-Bains and this tutelage is evident as much in the taste and quality in the design and furnishings of the rooms as in the refinement and authority of the cuisine and service. One half of the building was an 18thC *maison de maître* and boasts a superb stone staircase and fine oak panelling and carved fireplace in part of the dining room. The other half is 17th century, with original arcading on to the market square and half-timbered walls. Much care has gone into selecting appropriate antique furniture and the atmosphere is enhanced with original paintings and fine mirrors. On the south side is a handsome wide terrace overhanging the river: a very romantic setting for a summer's evening, with elegantly-laid tables and green-and-white parasols. Bedrooms are spacious; the best are furnished in a modern style and have views over the river, and whirlpool baths. They have fanciful names, such as Clair de Lune. The food is much vaunted – M. Garret has a Michelin star.

NEARBY Pau (60 km); Mont-de-Marsan (14 km); Biarritz.
LOCATION 15 km SE of Mont-de-Marsan on river Adour; car parking and garage
FOOD breakfast, lunch, dinner
PRICE €€€-€€€€
ROOMS 11 double, all with bath; all rooms have phone, TV, hairdrier; 8 have air conditioning, minibar, safe, whirlpool bath
FACILITIES sitting room, restaurant, terrace
CREDIT CARDS AE, DC, MC, V
CHILDREN accepted
DISABLED 1 ground-floor room
PETS accepted
CLOSED 2 weeks Feb, Sun dinner, Mon in winter
PROPRIETOR Philippe Garret

THE SOUTH-WEST

LACAVE

CHATEAU DE LA TREYNE
～ CHATEAU HOTEL ～

Lacave, 46200 Souillac (Lot)
TEL 05 65 27 60 60 **FAX** 05 65 27 60 70
E-MAIL treyne@relaischateaux.com **WEBSITE** www.relaischateaux.com/treyne

W E'VE HAD OUR EYE on this little château beside the Dordogne since an
inspector came back a few years ago with a report littered with
emphatically underscored adjectives – 'gorgeous... impeccable... exceptionally comfortable'. Of course, it is not cheap; perhaps we should be
grateful that elevation to Relais et Châteaux status has not pushed prices
up further.

Michèle Gombert-Deval's house has made a splendid small hotel. It
starts with the advantage of a beautiful position, in woods on a low cliff cut
by the meandering river Dordogne. But the compelling attraction of the
château is the near-ideal balance struck between the impressiveness of a
fortified manor house and the intimacy of a genuine home. The building
dates from the early 14th century, but was substantially rebuilt in the
1600s; it is now tastefully equipped with a happy mix of furnishings –
comfy sofas in front of an open fire, as well as grand antiques.

There are long walks to enjoy in the grounds, and a very beautiful formal garden before which you can take breakfast. Excellent regional food is
served – on the delightful terrace perched above the river in good weather.

～

NEARBY Souillac (6 km); Rocamadour; Sarlat.
LOCATION 3 km W of village on D43, 6 km SE of Souillac; in large grounds beside
river; ample car parking
FOOD breakfast, lunch, dinner; room service
PRICE €€€€
ROOMS 16; 14 double and twin, 2 suites, all with bath; all rooms have phone, TV,
air conditioning, hairdrier
FACILITIES 3 sitting rooms, dining room, bar, billiard room, lift, terrace, garden,
swimming pool, tennis
CREDIT CARDS AE, DC, MC, V
CHILDREN welcome
DISABLED access difficult **PETS** accepted
CLOSED mid-Nov to Easter
MANAGER Philippe Bappel

THE SOUTH-WEST

LE DOMAINE DE SAINT-GERY
~ COUNTRY GUESTHOUSE ~

46800 Lascabanes (Lot)
TEL 05 65 31 82 51 **FAX** 05 65 22 92 89
E-MAIL duler@saint-gery.com **WEBSITE** www.saint-gery.com

FROM THE MOMENT you are welcomed into M. and Mme Duler's captivating *maison d'hôte* you know that this is going to be a special experience. The Dulers go out of their way to ensure that their guests feel completely at ease, far from the cares of the world. Nothing is too much trouble.

The farm buildings – constructed of gleaming white limestone, typical of the Quercy Blanc region – have been painstakingly restored over the years. Likewise, the guest rooms are decorated with great flare; they retain their rustic charm, but this is very gracious country living. One room occupies a vaulted, stone cave, while another features an inglenook fireplace. All are endowed with family heirlooms of distinction.

The Domaine is no longer a working farm. Instead the Dulers now concentrate on preparing top quality local produce, including prize-winning *foie gras* and succulent cured hams and sausages, which they proudly serve at their dinner table. Meals are taken together, usually at a magnificent table on the balcony, where M. Duler eagerly shares his passion for food and wine. To work up a suitably robust appetite, there are 12 km of footpaths around the property and a good-sized swimming pool.

~

NEARBY Lauzerte (18 km); Cahors (18 km).
LOCATION on estate 500 m from Lascabanes; ample car parking
FOOD breakfast, dinner
PRICE €€; half-board obligatory
ROOMS 5; 4 double and twin, 1 duplex suite, all with bath; all rooms have phone
FACILITIES sitting room, terrace, grounds, swimming pool, farm shop
CREDIT CARDS V
CHILDREN welcome
DISABLED no special facilities
PETS accepted
CLOSED Oct to May, except New Year
PROPRIETORS M. and Mme Duler

THE SOUTH-WEST

HOTEL DE BASTARD
~ COUNTRY TOWN MANSION ~

rue Lagrange, 32700 Lectoure (Gers)
TEL 05 62 68 82 44 **FAX** 05 62 68 76 81
E-MAIL hoteldebastard@wanadoo.fr **WEBSITE** www.hotel-de-bastard.com

LECTOURE RISES ON A HILL overlooking the beautiful valley of the Gers. It is a town of rich archaeological finds and fine architecture. So it is fitting that its best hotel stands proudly displaying all its 18thC elegance as a former private mansion. A paved upper terrace is a lovely setting for summer meals. Protected by a semi-circle of warm stone buildings, it has views over the unspoiled countryside. A lower level includes a swimming pool, and plenty of room to relax around it, with a new *salon*/bar in a separate building. Judiciously placed trees, shrubs and flowers add to the picture.

Gascony has a well-deserved reputation for its local produce – *foie gras*, duck and goose in all its forms, vegetables, fruit (including superb melons and prunes) – but rarely are they presented with such imagination and variety as here. 'The best place to eat for miles around', says one knowledgeable local resident. The dining room is made up of three *salons*, each opening into the other and full of light.

Inside the hotel is decorated in sympathy with its 18thC character, with polished wood floors and pretty antique furniture. Bedrooms are mostly small; ask for one on the first floor (*premier étage*), rather than on the second, with its mansard roof. They are, however, along with the food, very good value for money.

~

NEARBY Musée Lapidaire; tannery; *bastides*; Auch (35 km)
LOCATION in town, 35 km N of Auch; car parking and garage
FOOD breakfast, lunch, dinner
PRICE €
ROOMS 29; 24 double and twin, 3 triple, 2 suites, all with bath or shower; all rooms have phone, TV, hairdrier
FACILITIES sitting room, bar, restaurant, terrace, swimming pool
CREDIT CARDS AE, DC, MC, V
CHILDREN welcome
DISABLED no special facilities **PETS** accepted **CLOSED** mid-Dec to Feb
PROPRIETOR Jean-Luc Arnaud

THE SOUTH-WEST

✳ RELAIS SAINTE-ANNE ✳
~ VILLAGE HOTEL ~

rue de Pourtanel, 46600 Martel (Lot)
TEL 05 65 37 40 56 **FAX** 05 65 37 42 82
E-MAIL Relais.Sainteanne@wanadoo.fr **WEBSITE** www.relais-ste-anne.com

OCCUPYING A FORMER GIRL'S CONVENT SCHOOL, the Relais Ste-Anne is one of those understated hotels which you could quite easily walk past without noticing its presence. Inside the arched entrance – marked by a discrete sign on a narrow backstreet – lies a delightfully shaded and flower-filled courtyard with some fine specimen trees and plenty of room to spread out between the neatly clipped box hedges.

The same attention to detail is echoed in the bedrooms scattered among the 18thC buildings and a modern, but unobtrusive annexe. Each room is individually styled, from dusky tones to warm Provençal yellows and blues, or the 'English' room with its cosy floral prints, striped wallpaper and plump cushions. Several have individual terraces or balconies and most are generously proportioned, with king-size beds, although the cheapest rooms above reception are on the small side.

The owners are considering opening a restaurant across the road, but for the moment concentrate their energies on providing a top-notch breakfast with local walnut bread and homemade jams. Or, if you want more, eggs, cheese and *charcuterie*. In fine weather breakfast is served on a raised terrace overlooking the gardens – an idyllic setting.

~

NEARBY Souillac (14 km); Rocamadour (20 km).
LOCATION on S side of village; car parking
FOOD breakfast
PRICE ⓔⓔⓔ **ROOMS** 15; 13 double and twin, 1 single, 1 triple, all with bath or shower; all rooms have phone, TV, hairdrier **FACILITIES** sitting room, terrace, garden, swimming pool

CREDIT CARDS AE, DC, MC, V
CHILDREN accepted
DISABLED 1 specially adapted room **PETS** accepted
CLOSED mid-Nov to Apr
PROPRIETOR M. Bettler

THE SOUTH-WEST

MAUROUX

HOSTELLERIE LE VERT
~ FARMHOUSE HOTEL ~

Mauroux, 46700 Puy l'Evêque (Lot)
TEL 05 65 36 51 36 **FAX** 05 65 36 56 84

LE VERT goes from strength to strength. The attractions of this secluded 17thC farmhouse have been greatly increased by the construction of a swimming pool. Whatever the changes, however, it will doubtless remain the kind of hotel you look forward to returning to at the end of the day; it also looks set to become the kind you're disinclined to leave at all.

There is just a small side door to lead you inside. Within, all is original stone walls and beams ('just about perfect', comments a reader). The dining room opens out on to a terrace with wide views; through an arch at one end is a small sitting room – ideal for an aperitif. The bedrooms are all comfortably and tastefully modernized, and have lovely views. The largest are quite grand and furnished with antiques. But the most attractive are in the little annexe a couple of yards from the entrance – the lower one stone-vaulted, the upper one beamed, with a marble floor. The garden has chairs and tables, and is improving in colour despite dry summers. The owners are a friendly and hard-working couple – M. Philippe cooks (interestingly and competently), Mme Philippe serves (and also speaks excellent English).

NEARBY Bonaguil (15 km); Biron (35 km); Monpazier (50 km).
LOCATION in countryside, off D5 10 km SW of Puy-l'Evêque, 10 km SE of Fumel; ample car parking
FOOD breakfast, lunch, dinner
PRICE €
ROOMS 7 double and twin, all with bath or shower; all rooms have phone, TV
FACILITIES sitting room, dining room, terrace, garden, swimming pool
CREDIT CARDS AE, MC, V
CHILDREN welcome
DISABLED no special facilities
PETS accepted
CLOSED mid-Nov to mid-Feb
PROPRIETORS Eva and Bernard Philippe

THE SOUTH-WEST

MIMIZAN

AU BON COIN DU LAC
~ LAKESIDE HOTEL ~

29 avenue du Lac, 40400 Mimizan (Landes)
TEL 05 58 09 01 55 **FAX** 05 58 09 40 84

WE ARE HAPPY TO REPORT that we continue to see no sign of slippage in the high standards of Jean-Pierre Caule, the third generation of his family to run Au Bon Coin, or, indeed, the exacting standards of Mme Caule, who oversees things front of house. There is no pretence here – everything is genuine and it starts with the smile with which Madame greets you on arrival – it clearly comes from within.

Beside a large freshwater lake away from the noise and bustle of the seaside town, the hotel is a refuge of calm and repose, yet less than a kilometre from the sandy dunes and beaches for which this region is known. It is the gastronomic Mecca for this part of the Landes and amply justifies its reputation. Our inspector's dinner was 'a delight of refined dishes of an individuality not without surprises'. M. Caule, who has a Michelin star, buys his own fish in nearby Arcachon. The dining room is light and welcoming, with a terrace outside shaded by trees and awning, all looking over a smooth green lawn to the water, rowing boats and ducks. Bedrooms are unobtrusively furnished, cosy and restful. Ideal for those who want solicitous treatment, a relaxed atmosphere and excellent food.

~

NEARBY Bordeaux (98 km); Arcachon (65 km); Dax (70 km).
LOCATION on edge of lake, 2 km N of Mimizan; car parking
FOOD breakfast, lunch, dinner
PRICE €-€€
ROOMS 8; 4 double and twin, 4 suites, all with bath; all rooms have phone , TV, fridge, hairdrier
FACILITIES sitting room, restaurant, terrace, garden
CREDIT CARDS AE, MC, V
CHILDREN accepted
DISABLED rooms on ground floor
PETS not accepted
CLOSED never
PROPRIETORS Jean-Pierre and Jacqueline Caule

THE SOUTH-WEST

✳ CHATEAU CORDEILLAN-BAGES ✳
～ CHATEAU HOTEL ～

route des Châteaux, 33250 Pauillac (Gironde)
TEL 05 56 59 24 24 **FAX** 05 56 59 01 89 **E-MAIL** cordeillan@relaischateaux.com
WEBSITE www.relaischateaux.com/cordeillan

THE RESTAURANT AND TERRACE at Cordeillan-Bages look directly out on to rows of vines – neighbours are Latour, Lafite, Mouton-Rothschild and many other distinguished names in the history of wine. Built in the purest 17thC style, the château is in the heart of the Médoc. (There's a small boutique selling good vintages.) The lovely, pale-stone, well-proportioned single-storey house was completely restored in 1989 and the decoration is stylish and restful. There is something of the feel of an English country house about the intimate sitting rooms and elegant dining room. The bedrooms are very comfortable, with the sure hand of the interior designer given free rein. In the kitchen, chef Thierry Marx uses his skills to create new dishes based on seasonal produce, as well as traditional regional food. The wine list is encyclopaedic. The château is home to the École de Bordeaux, which offers a wide choice of courses for both professional and amateur wine lovers and organizes visits to other vineyards in the area. The hotel slightly lacks the character it might have in private hands, but it is a charming house and the high standard of service lives up to its four star expectations.

～

NEARBY Château Mouton-Rothschild (5 km); Bordeaux (40 km).
LOCATION in own vineyards, in wine village on D2, 40 km N of Bordeaux; ample car parking **FOOD** breakfast, lunch, dinner; room service **PRICE** €€€€-€€€€€
ROOMS 25; 24 double and twin, 1 suite, all with bath; all rooms have phone, TV, minibar, safe, hairdrier **FACILITIES** sitting rooms, dining room, boutique, lift, terrace, garden **CREDIT CARDS** AE, DC, MC, V **CHILDREN** accepted
DISABLED access possible
PETS accepted
CLOSED mid-Dec to Feb; restaurant closed Mon, Sat dinner
MANAGER Thierry Marx

THE SOUTH-WEST

PROJAN

CHATEAU DE PROJAN
~ CHATEAU GUESTHOUSE ~

32400 Projan (Gers)
TEL 05 62 09 46 21 **FAX** 05 62 09 44 08 **E-MAIL** chateaudeprojan@libertysurf.fr

WHEN GLOBETROTTING art lover Bernard Vichet acquired this historic château he had a dream of creating something which would bring a breath of life into hotel-keeping. His key words are 'welcome, art and conviviality'. An entry in the guest book reads 'from the moment we entered I knew I was in a very special home – the cultural quality was so exciting for me', indicating how he has succeeded. The setting is magnificent, with panoramas of timeless natural beauty, the château sedate and sure in its classic grace. Inside all is light and airy, and harmoniously juxtaposes the old with the new. One enters a hall to be faced by a superb antique wooden staircase hung with highly colourful modern paintings and a floor featuring bright comtemporary mosaic in marble and granite of symbolic geese taking flight. For conviviality there is a grand piano, a lovely terrace and belvedere for dancing, and a library of art books open to all. The bedrooms each display original paintings by different modern artists. The château is run with expertise by Christine Poullain. In autumn, her husband Richard runs weekend courses on how to buy and prepare fattened ducks for the table – appropriate for the home of *foie gras*.

NEARBY Aire sur l'Adour (15 km); Eugénie-les-Bains; Pyrenees.
LOCATION in own grounds, on rocky spur overlooking the two Lees valleys, 15 km S of Aire sur l'Adour, signposted off D134 to Sarron; car parking
FOOD breakfast, dinner on request
PRICE €-€€
ROOMS 9 double and twin, 4 with bath or shower, 5 sharing shower room
FACILITIES sitting room, restaurant, library, terrace, garden
CREDIT CARDS MC, V
CHILDREN accepted
DISABLED no special facilities
PETS accepted
CLOSED Fri Jan to May
MANAGER Christine Poullain

THE SOUTH-WEST

PUYMIROL

✳ LES LOGES DE L'AUBERGADE ✳
VILLAGE HOTEL

52 rue Royale, Puymirol (Lot-et-Garonne)
TEL 05 53 95 31 46 **FAX** 05 53 95 33 80
E-MAIL trama@aubergade.com **WEBSITE** www.aubergade.com

'*EXCELLENCE PAR EXCELLENCE*' enthused a visitor to this handsome former residence of the Counts of Toulouse, dating from the 13th century and in a little fortified village. The lodestones to Puymirol are chef Michel Trama (two Michelin stars) for his superb food, wine and cigars, and his wife Maryse, with whom he has created this international-class hotel-restaurant. The building has stone walls, high ceilings, beams, a 17thC oak staircase and is decorated with impeccable style. The extensive kitchens are impressive and full of activity with M. Trama very much in personal charge. A special feature is a large smoking room with a glass-fronted, fully humidified cabinet containing a collection of the very best Cuban cigars – not for show but for smoking.

A terrace garden, leading off the dining room, has attractive canvas sun-shades and is discreetly illuminated through trees and bushes after dark. Bedrooms, in contemporary style, are large and elegant, and bathrooms have whirlpool baths. The overall feeling inside is one of light and airiness, predominantly white (much original stone), with white furniture offset with green and the colours of the abundant floral decorations.

NEARBY Agen (17 km); Moissac (32 km); Villeneuve-sur-Lot (31 km).
LOCATION in middle of small fortified village, 20 km E of Agen; car parking and garage **FOOD** breakfast, lunch, dinner; room service
PRICE €€€-€€€€ **ROOMS** 10 double and twin, all with whirlpool bath or massage shower; all rooms have phone, TV, video, air conditioning, minibar, hairdrier
FACILITIES sitting room, restaurant, terrace **CREDIT CARDS** AE, DC, MC, V **CHILDREN** accepted **DISABLED** 2 rooms on ground floor **PETS** accepted **CLOSED** 5 weeks Feb-Mar **PROPRIETORS** Michel and Maryse Trama

THE SOUTH-WEST

ROCAMADOUR

✳ DOMAINE DE LA RHUE ✳
∼ CONVERTED STABLES ∼

46500 Rocamadour (Lot)
TEL 05 65 33 71 50 **FAX** 05 65 33 72 48 **E-MAIL** domainedelarhue@rocamadour.com
WEBSITE www.rocamadour.com/us/hotels/LaRhue/index.htm

O**N OUR MOST RECENT VISIT** we came away more enthusiastic than ever about this truly charming place. A former stable block next to the handsome, family-owned château, it's set in peacefully rolling countryside, down a long drive, where you're assured complete silence. Above all, the Jooris are exceptional hosts: they have time for everyone, even when demands press in. Helpful and good humoured, they never intrude: the atmosphere is always good.

Their formula is simple: they serve no meals other than breakfast and light lunches (on request) by the pool, but guests are welcome to make themselves at home and spend the day relaxing by the pool if they feel like it. There's a proper reception area and large sitting areas for guests' use. Rooms are comfortable and pretty; several are ideal for families, some with kitchenettes and their own garden entrances.

Eric Jooris is a hot-air balloon pilot and will take guests for flights, weather permitting. With Gallic nonchalance, he calmly pushes away branches as the basket brushes against them on the way up out of Rocamadour's deep gorge. But he's very safe. If you like that sort of thing, don't miss a flight. In short, a brilliant place.

∼

NEARBY Rocamadour (7 km); Padirac (15 km); Carennac (20 km).
LOCATION in countryside, on N140 7 km N of Rocamadour; car parking
FOOD breakfast, light lunch **PRICE** €€ **ROOMS** 14; 12 double and twin, 2 family, 12 with bath, 2 with shower; all rooms have phone, fan; some rooms have minibar, kitchenette, hairdrier
FACILITIES sitting room, terrace, swimming pool **CREDIT CARDS** MC, V **CHILDREN** accepted **DISABLED** no special facilities **PETS** accepted **CLOSED** mid-Oct to Easter **PROPRIETORS** M. and Mme Jooris

THE SOUTH-WEST

CHATEAU LARDIER
~ COUNTRY HOUSE HOTEL ~

route de Sauveterre, Ruch, 33350 Castillon-la-Bataille (Gironde)
TEL 05 57 40 54 11 **FAX** 05 57 40 72 35
E-MAIL chateau.lardier@free.fr **WEBSITE** www.chateau.lardier.free.fr

THE PAGES PRODUCE their own AOC Bordeaux Rouge and Rosé (bottles attractively displayed everywhere and available to accompany your own supper cooked on the barbecue by the pool) from the vineyards that surround this elegant 17th/18thC house, with its rows of white shutters and long ivy-clad stone façade. Relaxed and informal, it is the kind of place that is immediately welcoming, with spacious, airy ground-floor rooms, bedrooms with views over neat rows of vines and a pleasant garden area at the rear next to the pool. If you don't want to go out in the evenings to eat locally, there's a communal barbecue under the chestnut tree and swings for children. Rooms, reached up a wide, stone staircase, are simple and basic, but antique beds have pretty cotton covers and tables have marble tops. There's a good choice of sleeping arrangements, with extra beds available, and it is hard to beat for value, given the swimming pool and the other amenities. Peace, quiet and birdsong are in abundance. A set of large sitting and games rooms is set aside on the ground floor for guests. There are plenty of country lanes to explore and walks through the vineyard at the end of a long, hot day by the pool.

~

NEARBY Castillon-la-Bataille (10 km); Dordogne river; St-Emilion (20 km).
LOCATION among vineyards; ample car parking
FOOD breakfast
PRICE €
ROOMS 7; 5 double and twin, 2 triple, 3 with bath, 4 with shower; all rooms have phone, TV
FACILITIES 2 sitting rooms, billiard room, terrace, garden, swimming pool
CREDIT CARDS MC, V
CHILDREN welcome
DISABLED no special facilities
PETS accpeted
CLOSED Nov to Mar
PROPRIETORS Jean-Noël and Evelyne Pagès

THE SOUTH-WEST

ST-CIRQ-LAPOPIE

LA PELISSARIA
~ VILLAGE INN ~

St-Cirq-Lapopie, 46330 Cabrerets (Lot)
TEL 05 65 31 25 14 **FAX** 05 65 30 25 52
E-MAIL lapelissariahotel@minitel.net **WEBSITE** www.quercy.net

RECENT REPORTS LEAVE US IN NO DOUBT that the Matuchets' distinctive little hotel is as compelling as ever. The 13thC house clings to the steep hillside on the edge of the lovely medieval hilltop village of St-Cirq-Lapopie. It was lovingly restored by the Matuchets themselves, and its quirky character is such that you descend the stairs to the bedrooms which look out on to the tiny garden and enjoy stunning views over the Lot valley. The bedrooms – two of them detached from the house, down the garden – are light, airy and comfortable, with close attention to detail in the furnishings. Three large bedrooms, with two double beds in each, are located in an old house next door to the main one. The place is simply and artistically decorated, its thick stone walls painted white, with old wooden beams and tiled floors.

Although Mme Matuchet no long cooks dinner, there are plenty of good restaurants in St-Cirq-Lapopie to which the couple will direct you. Breakfast is served *alfresco* or in your room if you prefer.

M. Matuchet, who is a musician, provides a pleasant musical background with tapes of his own music. The *salon* is graced by a piano and various stringed instruments.

~

NEARBY Peche-Merle caves and museum; Cahors (35 km).
LOCATION in village, 30 km E of Cahors; car parking difficult
FOOD breakfast
PRICE €€
ROOMS 10; 8 double and twin, 6 with bath, 2 with shower, 2 suites with bath; all rooms have phone, TV
FACILITIES sitting room, dining room, terrace, garden, small swimming pool
CREDIT CARDS MC, V **CHILDREN** welcome
DISABLED 1 suitable bedroom **PETS** accepted
CLOSED mid-Nov to Apr
PROPRIETORS Marie-Françoise and François Matuchet

THE SOUTH-WEST

St-Cirq-Lapopie

AUBERGE DU SOMBRAL
~ VILLAGE INN ~

place Sombral, St-Cirq-Lapopie, 46330 Cabrerets (Lot)
TEL 05 65 31 26 08 **FAX** 05 65 30 26 37

A LITTLE DOLL'S HOUSE of a hotel in this romantic medieval village on a crag overlooking the river, which is one of the major beauty spots of the Lot valley and proud of its reputation as 'Pearl of the Quercy'. Mme Hardeveld is normally to be found behind her desk in the entrance hall, which is also a cosy small *salon* for guests with a bar. Delicious smells waft out of M. Hardeveld's kitchen and copious duck and truffle dishes are served in the beamed restaurant, where table lamps and a wood fire cast a warm glow on the copper saucepans and paintings by local artists hanging on the walls. Rooms, reached by a twisting wooden staircase, are simple, smallish and unpretentious; there are pansies in the window boxes and glimpses through the curtains of narrow cobbled alleyways and stone and half-timbered buildings. Mme Hardeveld, who has been running her little *auberge* for 30 years, says there is just no room for televisions or fancy fittings to the bathrooms. But the essentials are there and they are pretty and spotlessly clean. Staff are friendly. Drinks and cups of coffee may be enjoyed at the metal tables on the pavement terrace along the front of the building. But – a warning – parking can be frustrating here.

~

NEARBY Cahors (30 km); Château de Cénevières (1 km).
LOCATION in village centre; public car parking in square
FOOD breakfast, lunch, dinner
PRICE €
ROOMS 8 double and twin, all with bath or shower; all rooms have phone
FACILITIES small sitting room, restaurant, bar, terrace
CREDIT CARDS DC, MC, V
CHILDREN welcome
DISABLED no special facilities
PETS accepted
CLOSED mid-Nov to Apr
PROPRIETORS Monique and Gilles Hardeveld

THE SOUTH-WEST

ST-CYPRIEN

L'ABBAYE
~ VILLAGE HOTEL ~

rue de l'Abbaye, 24220 St-Cyprien (Dordogne)
TEL 0553 29 20 48 **FAX** 05 53 29 15 85
E-MAIL hotel@abbaye-dordogne.com **WEBSITE** www.abbaye-dordogne.com

THE NEARBY ABBEY OF THE AUGUSTINS gave this handsome, large, stone, 18thC house its name and you enter through an archway off the street. Mme Schaller is anxious to explain that anyone with a car should drive straight in and will then be shown the way to the private car park behind the main house. St-Cyprien is another of the little jewels of the Périgord Noir and rooms at the front of the hotel have views down towards the Dordogne and across the roofs of the village. The Schallers have been welcoming guests to the Abbaye for 30 years and are delightful hosts. M. Schaller is an expert on local history and takes groups of guests out on guided tours. But there is much history in the house itself – the sitting room was once the 16thC kitchen and still has its original sink and bread oven. The big, bright, red-tiled, yellow dining room and small breakfast room open on to the south-facing terrace, where you can sit at small tables under the lime and acacia trees. Madame likes her antique French beds and there's an assortment of Louis-styles to choose from. Most rooms are in the main house; those at the front have the best views, those at the back or in two smaller, buildings (reached through gardens) may be quieter.

~

NEARBY Perigueux (55 km); Sarlat; Le Bugue; châteaux.
LOCATION in medieval village; car parking
FOOD breakfast, lunch, dinner
PRICE €€
ROOMS 23 double and twin, 13 with bath, 10 with shower; all rooms have phone, hairdrier, some have TV
FACILITIES sitting rooms, dining room, bar, terrace, garden, swimming pool
CREDIT CARDS AE, MC, V **CHILDREN** accepted
DISABLED not suitable **PETS** accepted
CLOSED mid-Oct to mid-Apr
PROPRIETORS Yvette and Marcel Schaller

THE SOUTH-WEST

HOSTELLERIE DE PLAISANCE
~ VILLAGE HOTEL ~

place du Clocher, 33330 St-Emilion (Gironde)
TEL 05 57 55 07 55 **FAX** 05 57 74 41 11
E-MAIL hostellerie.plaisance@wanadoo.fr **WEBSITE** www.hostellerie-plaisance.com

NEWLY RENOVATED, this creamy stone hotel in the immaculately preserved wine village of St-Emilion had been open only a few months when we visited; landscaping of the terrace was not yet finished but it has aspirations, we learned, to be a Relais et Château hotel and the new owners also have a *premier grand cru classé* vineyard. The setting – in a little square with terrace and garden looking over old stone houses to vines beyond – is perfect, though parking is liable to be a headache in the high season. The comfortable surroundings, however, should alleviate some of the pain, and the china alone – all Limoges – makes this exquisite little place worthy of note. Bathrooms are – of course – spanking new, with glossy taps, a bath pillow, fresh freesias, piles of fluffy towels, bathrobes, heated towel rail and generous helpings of toiletries (even a nail file). Rooms – some have terraces – have matching wallpaper and fabric, good quality lamps and reproduction furniture, but our inspector was dismayed to find no lining paper in the chest of drawers. First-rate breakfasts with freshly squeezed orange juice and huge white cups of coffee. Manager M. Rizzotti is from the Oustau de Beaumanière in Les Beaux-de-Provence. Reports, please.

NEARBY Bordeaux (40 km); vineyards; Dordogne region (40 km).
LOCATION in upper section of village; free parking outside hotel from 6.30 pm to 11 am, otherwise in public parking spaces
FOOD breakfast, lunch, dinner; room service
PRICES €€€
ROOMS 14; 13 double and twin, 1 single; 12 with bath, 1 with shower; all rooms have phone, TV, air conditioning, hairdrier; some have minibar, safe
FACILITIES sitting room, dining room, bar, lift, terrace
CREDIT CARDS AE, DC, MC, V
CHILDREN welcome
DISABLED no special facilities
PETS accepted
CLOSED Jan
MANAGER M. Martial Rizzotti

THE SOUTH-WEST

✳ ARCE ✳
～ RIVERSIDE HOTEL ～

64430 St-Étienne-de-Baïgorry (Pyrénées-Atlantiques)
TEL 05 59 37 40 14 **FAX** 05 59 37 40 27
E-MAIL hotel-arce@wanadoo.fr **WEBSITE** www.hotel-arce.com

A FAVOURITE OF OUR INSPECTORS AND OUR READERS, recently redecorated and refurbished to maintain its impeccable standards. The setting – by a river in a typical Basque village – is a magical one, best appreciated from the dining terrace, which juts out over the water and is sheltered by a canopy of chestnut trees. Nestled there, one feels both intimate and secluded and nothing could be more pleasant than a relaxed breakfast by the water's edge. Inside, the public rooms are spacious: a smart dining room with picture windows, and a beamed library with books in a variety of languages. The green, white and red colours of the Basque flag predominate. Some of the bedrooms are impressively large, with apartment-sized sitting areas; others open on to small terraces with mountain views. A sizeable blue-tiled swimming pool is hidden in a green enclosure on the far side of a wooden bridge across the river.

Management of the hotel is now in the capable hands of the fifth generation of the family Arcé. The much-appreciated cooking emphasizes fresh local ingredients, with an interesting wine list at reasonable prices. There is plenty to do in the area – walking, fishing, cycling, riding, canoeing – and the Atlantic coast is only half an hour away.

～

NEARBY Pyrenees; Spanish border; Atlantic coast.
LOCATION in village, 10 km W of St-Jean Pied-de-Port; car parking
FOOD breakfast, lunch, dinner
PRICE ⓔⓔ **ROOMS** 23; 22 double and twin, 20 with bath, 2 with shower, 1 single with shower; all rooms have phone, TV, hairdrier **FACILITIES** sitting rooms, dining room, library, games room, terrace, garden, swimming pool, tennis

CREDIT CARDS DC, MC, V
CHILDREN welcome
DISABLED 1 ground-floor room
PETS accepted
CLOSED mid-Nov to mid-Mar
PROPRIETORS Arcé family

THE SOUTH-WEST

LA DEVINIERE
~ SEASIDE GUESTHOUSE ~

5 rue Loquin, 64500 St-Jean-de-Luz (Pyrénées-Atlantiques)
TEL 05 59 26 05 51 **FAX** 05 59 51 26 38

L A DEVINIERE is discreetly tucked away in a pedestrian precinct with nothing more than a modest signboard artistically spelling out the name in Basque green. Other than that, there is little to betray that this house is in fact a hotel. Its owners describe it as a 'charming old English hotel', and that's how it feels, an elegant and traditional privately owned town house in the centre of this historic and picturesque resort. The spell is cast as soon as you enter the beautifully furnished reception area with shelves of leather-bound books and a view through to a sitting room with comfortable chairs and a grand piano. It is the creation of former lawyer Bernard Carrère and his wife, an expert in antiques.

Although there is no restaurant, a fairly new addition is that of a delightful tea room in complete harmony with the rest of the house and the concept of a hotel as a private home, surrounded by personal things. It may be for the discriminating, but nevertheless it has an air of freshness and warm welcome. A small garden lies behind the house. There is parking close by but final access is by foot – well worth the small effort.

~

NEARBY Spanish border; Biarritz (15 km).
LOCATION in pedestrian precinct in town centre; car parking nearby
FOOD breakfast
PRICE €€
ROOMS 8 double and twin, all with bath; all rooms have phone
FACILITIES sitting room, library, tea room, garden
CREDIT CARDS AE, DC, MC, V
CHILDREN welcome
DISABLED not suitable
PETS accepted
CLOSED mid-Nov to Dec
PROPRIETORS M. and Mme Carrère

THE SOUTH-WEST

ST-JEAN-DE-LUZ

PARC VICTORIA
~ TOWN MANSION ~

5 rue Cepé, 64500 St-Jean-de-Luz (Pyrénées-Atlantiques)
TEL 05 59 26 78 78 **FAX** 05 59 26 78 08
WEBSITE www.relaischateaux.com/parcvictoria

THE OWNER – once a neighbour – of this gleaming white 19thC villa rescued it from demolition and spent four years restoring the house and garden to their former glory. The place is now immaculate; the predominant feeling is of space, light and colour, both inside and out. The park that gives the house its name has neat lawns, formal flower beds and magnificent mature cedar, pines and other specimen trees. M. Larralde scoured antique shops to find furnishings and fittings to make his dream come true and the hotel is filled with charming pieces. The elegant *salon* of the main house is in the Napoléon III style, complete with chandeliers. Alongside the generous terrace of the swimming pool stands a veranda-style dining room and relaxation area with sunbeds and exercise equipment. Bedrooms are furnished with antiques, with contemporary marble bathrooms. Two magnificent new suites, clearly designed for the rich and famous, have recently been added. The hotel is perhaps too grand for our purposes, but it does its job very well, with exacting standards and an ambience of lightness and calm. Dining in the Ivy Garden restaurant is a delightful experience, and the food and wine are delicious

~

NEARBY Spanish border; Biarritz (16 km).
LOCATION exit St-Jean-de-Luz Nord from A63; at fourth traffic light, turn right, direction Quartier du Lac; car parking
FOOD breakfast, lunch, dinner; room service
PRICE €€€€€
ROOMS 12; 10 double and twin, 2 suites, all with bath; all rooms have phone, TV, air conditioning, minibar, safe, hairdrier
FACILITIES sitting room, 2 dining rooms, bar, lift, terrace, gardens, swimming pool
CREDIT CARDS AE, DC, MC, V **CHILDREN** accepted
DISABLED access possible **PETS** accepted
CLOSED mid-Nov to mid-Mar
PROPRIETOR M. Larralde

THE SOUTH-WEST

St Michel-de-Montaigne

LE JARDIN D'EYQUEM

~ CASTLE HOTEL ~

24230 St Michel-de-Montaigne (Dordogne)
TEL 05 53 24 89 59 **FAX** 05 53 61 14 40 **E-MAIL** jardin-eyquem@wanadoo.fr
WEBSITE http://perso.wanadoo.fr/jardin-eyquem

AN UNUSUAL RECOMMENDATION for us, but this is such a well thought-out idea that we felt we should not leave it out. The Le Morvans – he was a pilot, she a teacher – moved here from Paris 10 years ago to provide for others what they always hoped to find for themselves on their travels – somewhere pretty, small, calm and somewhere with a small kitchen, so that if you wanted to stay in all day you could. Both passionate about Montaigne, they have converted a farmhouse in the village where the great philosopher was born and named it after his family; in winter you can see through the trees the château of Montaigne's brother. A delightful, thoughtful air prevails. The house faces south and the swimming pool among the vines is in full sun all day. The largest apartment is the old beamed hayloft, but all are spacious with the kitchen section hidden behind cotton curtains made by Danièle, tables, chairs and even egg cups for meals, and painted furniture. When we visited, any fabrics in what could be considered dull colours were being thrown out and replaced by yellow; "for the gaiety of life" said Madame. Breakfast is served in a large ground-floor room with handsome stone fireplace.

House rule: The pool must always be a quiet, peaceful place.

~

NEARBY Montaigne's Tower (short walk); St Emilion (18 km); *bastides* of Ste-Foy and Libourne.
LOCATION among vineyards on edge of village; ample car parking
FOOD breakfast
PRICE €€
ROOMS 5 apartments, double or twin, 3 with bath, 2 with shower; all rooms have phone, TV, kitchenette
FACILITIES sitting room, library, breakfast room, terrace, garden, swimming pool
CREDIT CARDS MC, V **CHILDREN** welcome
DISABLED 1 suitable apartment **PETS** not accepted **CLOSED** Nov to Apr
PROPRIETORS Danièle and Christian Le Morvan

THE SOUTH-WEST

HOSTELLERIE SAINT-JACQUES
~ VILLAGE INN ~

24470 St-Saud-Lacoussière (Dordogne)
TEL 05 53 56 97 21 **FAX** 05 53 56 91 33

THE MORE WE LEARN about the Babayous' enterprise, the more thoroughly impressed we are by their sure understanding of holidaymakers' needs and priorities.

The front of the creeper-clad 18thC building gives little clue to what lies within – or, more to the point, what lies behind: the Babayous' 'summer sitting room', which consists of lovely sloping gardens, with masses of colourful flowers, a fair-sized pool, tennis court and plenty of shade and space for children. Inside there is an unusually large dining room/bar decorated in bright blue and yellow, with big windows which open on to the terrace above the garden. All the bedrooms are comfortable, spacious and attractively decorated; several can accommodate families.

The food is rich and varied; even the basic menu is probably enough to satisfy most appetites. A buffet breakfast/brunch is served in the garden or by the pool. Occasionally there are lively evenings with dancing and games, or communal dinners devoted to exploration of regional cuisine. Not your cup of tea? Just give it a try: you might be surprised.

~

NEARBY Château de Richemont; Montbrun (15 km); Brantôme (30 km); Rochechouart (45 km).
LOCATION in quiet village, 30 km N of Brantôme; car parking
FOOD breakfast, lunch, dinner
PRICE ⓔ
ROOMS 22 double and twin, 2 suites, all with bath or shower; all rooms have phone; some have TV, minibar
FACILITIES 2 restaurants, bar, TV room, terrace, garden, swimming pool, tennis
CREDIT CARDS AE, MC, V **CHILDREN** welcome
DISABLED no special facilities **PETS** accepted
CLOSED Nov to Mar and Sun dinner, Mon
PROPRIETOR Jean-Pierre Babayou

THE SOUTH-WEST

ARRAYA
⌇ RIVERSIDE HOTEL ⌇

64310 Sare (Pyrénées-Atlantiques)
TEL 05 59 54 20 46 **FAX** 05 59 37 40 27
E-MAIL hotel@arraya.com **WEBSITE** www.arraya.com

WITH ITS TIMBERED, white-painted houses adorned with red or green shutters, Sare can claim to be the prettiest of all the extremely pretty Basque villages. In the heart of the village, this 17thC house was once an overnight resting place for pilgrims on their way across the Pyrenees to Santiago de Compostela. Behind the slightly severe frontage on the main road lies a country-style hotel of great character, now run by the third generation of the charming Fagoaga family. Inside all is spick and span and immaculately cared for – clean, airy and light, with much old, dark, burnished wood. The beamed sitting room and dining room – and every nook and cranny on stairways and landings – are filled with glorious old Basque furniture; sofas and chairs are comfortable and inviting, and flowers are everywhere.

A handsome curved wooden staircase leads to bedrooms of different sizes (some border on the small), all expertly decorated using colourful fabrics and bedspreads made by a member of the family. Some look out over the verdant garden, others have a view of the village square. The restaurant is excellent, with a well-chosen wine list; in summer meals are taken on the terrace. A new boutique on the ground floor sells local products, including delicious *gâteau basque*

⌇

NEARBY Aïnhoa (10 km); St-Jean-de-Luz (14 km); Biarritz (29 km).
LOCATION in middle of village, 14 km SE of St-Jean-de-Luz; car parking
FOOD breakfast, lunch, dinner
PRICE €-€€€
ROOMS 22; 20 double and twin, 19 with bath, 3 with shower; all rooms have phone, TV, safe, hairdrier
FACILITIES sitting room, restaurant, boutique, terrace, garden
CREDIT CARDS AE, DC, MC, V
CHILDREN welcome
DISABLED ground-floor rooms **PETS** not accepted
CLOSED mid-Nov to Apr; restaurant closed Sun dinner, Mon lunch
PROPRIETORS Fagoaga family

THE SOUTH-WEST

✳ DOMAINE DE BASSIBE ✳
~ COUNTRY HOTEL ~

32400 Ségos (Gers)
TEL 05 62 09 46 71 FAX 05 62 08 40 15 E-MAIL bassibe@relaischateaux.com
WEBSITE www.relaischateaux.com/bassibe

So MANY RELAIS ET CHATEAUX hotels can't resist exuding a superior air,' comments our first inspector to this new entry, ' but here one feels very much wrapped-up and safe'.

One simply has to admire the flair and taste of Sylvie and Olivier Lacroix, and their success in providing their guests with all the comforts of a first-class hotel in the ambience of a private and very friendly country house. Set in a park and garden run riot with cascades of flowers, the main house is an 18thC *maison de maître* with a long two-storeyed wing which was originally stabling but is now fitted out with delightful suites. Alongside stands the former *chai* – another lovely stone building – once a centre of activity in this huge agricultural *domaine* and now housing the kitchens, restaurant and wine stock. In the garden a newer construction in white and blue, La Maison des Champs, contains more rooms and suites, each decorated in different colours, all bright and light. Close by a stand of impressive centenarian oaks (the oldest more than 300 years old) is a large open-air pool with terrace and enclosed fitness area. The food is exceptional as is the carefully selected wine list. In short – a place where the best is offered with simplicity and warmth. No wonder the extravagant wistaria flowers no less than three times a year.

~

NEARBY Aire-sur-l'Adour (8 km); Pau (30 km).
LOCATION on large farming estate, signposted from Ségos; car parking
FOOD breakfast, lunch, dinner; room service PRICE €€€ ROOMS 18; 11 double and twin, 7 suites, all with bath; all rooms have phone, TV FACILITIES sitting room, restaurant, fitnesss centre, terraces, garden, swimming pool CREDIT CARDS AE, DC, MC, V CHILDREN welcome
DISABLED no special facilities
PETS accepted
CLOSED Jan to Apr
PROPRIETORS Sylvie and Olivier Lacroix

THE SOUTH-WEST

TRÉMOLAT

✳ LE VIEUX LOGIS ✳
∼ VILLAGE HOTEL ∼

24510 Trémolat (Dordogne)
TEL 05 53 22 80 06 **FAX** 05 53 22 84 89 **E-MAIL** vieuxlogis@relaischateaux.com
WEBSITE www.relaischateaux.com/vieuxlogis

WE CONTINUE TO LIST this glorious old hotel, one of the most civilized in a region with many attractive hotels, despite a recent postbag of readers' letters, which, though broadly complimentary, had some niggles too. On the complimentary side, all our correspondents marked out for special praise the 'happy and smiling, well-trained staff' and the warm atmosphere they engendered. The food, too, was praised, including the 'spectacular' buffet breakfast. Irritations included problems with hot water on a couple of occasions, tired decoration in the bedroom and bathrooom, and an exorbitant charge for a single brandy. All our correspondents, however, said they would return.

Owners, the Giraudel-Destords, have lived in this complex of farm and village houses for nearly 400 years. The part which is now the dining room once held pigs and wine barrels. Now all has been designer-decorated to produce comfort of a high degree. Bedrooms, some with four-posters, are done in a cosy sophisticated-rustic style; public rooms (some little used) are elegant and comfortable, with plenty of quiet nooks. The open fire in the small *salon* is much appreciated by guests. The galleried dining room looks out on to the green and flowery garden where you can breakfast.

∼

NEARBY Les Eyzies-de-Tayac (25 km); Monpazier (30 km); Beynac (30 km).
LOCATION in village, 15 km SW of Le Bugue; car and garage parking
FOOD breakfast, lunch, dinner; room service
PRICE €€€€ **ROOMS** 24; 18 double and twin, 6 suites, all with bath; all rooms have phone, TV, minibar, hairdrier
FACILITIES 3 sitting rooms, 2 dining rooms, bar, terrace, garden, swimming pool
CREDIT CARDS AE, DC, MC, V
CHILDREN welcome
DISABLED 1 specially adapted room **PETS** accepted **CLOSED** never
MANAGER Didier Bru

THE SOUTH-WEST

BRANTOME

LE CHATENET
MANOR HOUSE HOTEL

24310 Brantôme (Dordogne)
TEL 05 53 05 81 08
FAX 05 53 05 85 52
E-MAIL chatenet@wanadoo.fr
FOOD breakfast
PRICE €€
ROOMS 10
CLOSED Nov to Apr

WHEN WE VISITED this lovely 17thC riverside manor house to update its entry for this edition, we were sad to hear its owners, the Laxtons, tell us that they were about to hand over, after 20 years or more, to new owners. Just before going to press, however, they informed us that they had had a change of heart and decided to stay 'forever': happpy news. The beauty of this noble stone *gentilhommière* (with yards of walnut panelling and a *pigonnier*) and the Laxtons' warm, welcoming ways have won them – and their dog – many friends. They have thought of everything: heated swimming pool; barbecue and garden room; linen room with washing machine; antique-filled, fabric-lined bedrooms, and excellent bathrooms.

LE BUGUE

AUBERGE DU NOYER
COUNTRY HOTEL

'Le Reclaud' 24260 Le Bugue (Dordogne) **TEL** 05 53 07 11 73
FAX 05 53 54 57 44 **E-MAIL** aubergedunoyer@perigord.com
WEBSITE www.perigord.com/ aubergedunoyer **FOOD** breakfast
PRICE € **ROOMS** 10 **CLOSED** mid-Oct to Easter

A VENERABLE WALNUT TREE presiding over the gravelled forecourt gives this attractive stone-built 18thC coaching inn its name. The new proprietors no longer offer meals, but the tranquil and relaxed atmosphere remains intact.

Beams, exposed stone walls and pretty floral or Dutch-style fabrics lend the rooms their rustic charm, while the books and magazines scattered around add a pleasantly homely touch. All the beds and bedding have recently been replaced and several bathrooms upgraded – though the rest are perfectly adequate and spotlessly clean. Some rooms have their own small, private terrace. A generous breakfast buffet of cereals, freshly-squeezed orange juice, fruit and assorted croissants and breads is served.

THE SOUTH-WEST

LA DAILLE

FARMHOUSE GUESTHOUSE

Florimont-Gaumiers, 24250
Domme (Dordogne)
TEL 05 53 28 40 71
FOOD breakfast
PRICE €€
ROOMS 3
CLOSED Oct to May

THIS UNUSUAL PLACE, in deep countryside, is one of those Dordogne establishments that combines the best of France and Britain – if you can find it (check directions in advance). The Browns have been busy buying up land around their stone farmhouse set among very English gardens, where they've been for more than 25 years; they now have 18 private hectares of woods and fields (with orchids) for visitors to enjoy. Rooms (south-facing) are unfussy, comfortable, clean, with big cupboards, bathrooms and terraces in a modern outbuilding across the garden from the house – clean towels every day and clean sheets on third or fourth. Perfect for walkers. Good teas.

LE MOULIN DE SAINT-AVIT

COUNTRY GUESTHOUSE

St-Avit, 47150 Gavaudun (Lot-et-Garonne)
TEL 05 53 40 86 80
FAX 05 53 40 98 20
E-MAIL moulin.st.avit@wanadoo.fr
WEBSITE www. perso. wanadoo.fr/ moulin.st.avit **FOOD** breakfast, dinner **PRICE** € **ROOMS** 5
CLOSED never

THE WINNING FEATURES of this former mill in the secluded Lède valley are the relaxed family atmosphere and the exceptionally warm welcome; it is the sort of place whose hidden charms grow on you. With its large pool and shady garden it is particularly suitable for children; there are also 12 donkeys which can be hired as pack animals to take on country hikes.

Rooms are rural rather than rustic, smallish, but neat and tidy, with simple pine furniture and assorted knick-knacks brought back from family holidays in Morocco and Turkey. Mediterranean and North African flavours also feature in Lionel's hearty home cooking. Meals are convivial (you mustn't mind being chatty with strangers) with everyone eating together under the old chestnut trees.

THE SOUTH-WEST

LE CHATEAU

RIVERSIDE HOTEL

24150 Lalinde (Dordogne)
TEL 05 53 61 01 82
FAX 05 53 24 74 60
FOOD breakfast, lunch, dinner
PRICE €€
ROOMS 7
CLOSED mid-Dec to mid-Feb

SQUEEZED ONTO THE EDGE of the Dordogne, with dense green woods on the opposite bank, the setting of this odd little turreted castle (mainly 19th century with palm tree and red shutters) is spectacular. Most of the comfortable rooms look down into the fast-running waters of the river – some have their own small balconies – and the decor is quirky and modernistic. One bathroom has a triangular bath. M Gensou, the owner/chef, rides a motorbike and stuffs snails with *foie gras* and walnut butter. We have heard the tiled entrance hall described as dowdy, but still propose Le Château for those who like water and something with a difference.

LE RIPA ALTA

VILLAGE HOTEL

3 place de l'Eglise, 32160
Plaisance (Gers)
TEL 05 62 69 30 43
FAX 05 62 69 36 99
E-MAIL ripaalta@aol.com
FOOD breakfast, lunch, dinner
PRICE € **ROOMS** 15
CLOSED never; restaurant closed
Mon in winter

NO FRILLS HERE BUT A WARM WELCOME awaits at this country town hotel which harbours a famous chef, Maurice Coscuella, who trained alongside Bocuse and Troisgros. For more than thirty years he has regaled his guests with creative cooking using only the best of local produce. This is wine country – good quality at reasonable prices. Bedrooms are adequate (one with balcony) and quiet, except on Saturday nights when the nearby disco is on. The hotel attracts a steady stream of foreign visitors and is very popular with customers of Brittany Ferries. Plaisance is a convenient base from which to explore Gers, the land of the Musketeers, and it has a leisure park with a lake for swimming, sailing and fishing.

THE SOUTH-WEST

ST-MARTIAL VIVEYROLS

✻ HOSTELLERIE LES AIGUILLONS

COUNTRY HOTEL

Le Beuil, 24320 St-Martial-Viveyrols (Dordogne)
TEL 05 53 91 07 55 **FAX** 05 53 91 00 43 **E-MAIL** aiguillons@aol.com **WEBSITE** www.hostellerieles aiguillons. com **FOOD** breakfast, lunch, dinner **PRICE** €
ROOMS 8 **CLOSED** Dec to Apr

THIS LITTLE *LOGIS* was built in 1993 on the ruins of a farmhouse set among the woods and fields of the Périgord Blanc – and in easy driving distance of a string of picturesque villages with Romanesque churches. Once dug in here, however, guests seem reluctant to leave the swimming pool and terrace where breakfast is served to the sound of birdsong, Christophe Beeuwsaert, who speaks English, is a dedicated, much-loved patron and there are many tributes to him – and his cooking – on the theme of 'came for one night, stayed for six' in his visitors' book. Rooms are comfortable; bathrooms are large. For those looking for high standards and tranquillity.

Book through our travel service – see page 7.

VALENCE-SUR-BAISE

LA FERME DE FLARAN

COUNTRY HOTEL

32310 Valence-sur-Baise (Gers)
TEL 05 62 28 58 22
FAX 05 62 28 56 89
E-MAIL fermedeflaran@minitel.net
WEBSITE www.gascogne.com/ guide.hotels/fermeflaran.htm
FOOD breakfast, lunch, dinner
PRICE € **ROOMS** 15 **CLOSED** mid-Nov to mid-Dec, Jan

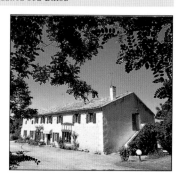

A DECENT PIT STOP on a convenient road for travellers. Typical farmhouse architecture and decoration are executed with a smart touch and plenty of efficiency. In past times the farm belonged to the community of Cistercians in the adjacent abbey which dates back to the 12th century and is now a beautifully kept venue for concerts and art exhibitions. The restaurant is always busy. Why? It serves food of above average quality at attractive prices. Meals can also be taken on the terrace in view of the well-proportioned swimming pool. Rooms are unpretentious: choose one away from the road if you can, as there can be traffic noise.

MASSIF CENTRAL

HOTELS IN MASSIF CENTRAL

FOR MANY BRITISH VISITORS, the Massif is 'unknown France' – the high, remote area between Périgord on the west and the Rhône valley on the east. For guidebook purposes, it is a rather problematic region, particularly if (like all our regions) it is defined in terms of *départements*. The points where you might consider the physical Massif to begin and end don't always coincide happily with governmental boundaries (the *département* of Ardèche, for example, falls in our South of France region, but includes territory that is physically very much part of the Massif). There is also a good case for considering this 'unspoiled France'. Of course tourism has had an impact, but it is slight compared with the impact on the much better-known areas. There are bargains to be found as a result.

The region is distinctive for the grandeur of its scenery, produced by long-extinct volcanoes, from rocky outcrops to the magnificent mountain ranges of Monts Dômes, Monts Dore and Monts du Cantal; a landscape threaded by rivers, lakes and hot springs, around which spa towns have grown up over the centuries. Tamer, more rolling country lies to the north-west, where two of our hotels are in the *département* of Allier: Château de Boussac at Target (page 239) and Le Chalet at Coulandon (page 242). Travelling south, through the Massif's principal town of Clermont-Ferrand, where you can see one of the finest of the area's many Romanesque churches, we have discovered a unique hotel, Les Deux Abbesses (page 237), which almost is the tiny medieval village of Saint-Arcons-d'Allier. From here, a short drive east brings you to Le Puy-en-Velay with its spectacular trio of craggy peaks. To the east lies Cantal, where, after positive reports, we've upgraded the friendly Auberge la Tomette in Vitrac (page 240) from a short to a long entry.

Further south the dramatic Gorges de l'Aveyron and the Gorges du Tarn cleave the landscape, with their scattering of villages that cling precariously to the sheer rock faces. One of our hotels, Longcol (page 235), is set in a valley of the Gorges de l'Aveyron near Najac. There's a new recommendation in Belcastel to the north-west, Hotel Restaurant du Vieux Pont (page 225), with a fine kitchen and comfortable rooms. In Tarn, we feature a favourite from our Southern France guide, Cuq-en-Terrasses in Cuq-Toulza (page 230). Lozère to the east is the *département* at the heart of the Cévennes, where La Lozerette is a terrific new find in Cocurès (page 227), a village on the route taken by Robert Louis Stevenson and his donkey Modestine.

MASSIF CENTRAL

BELCASTEL

HOTEL RESTAURANT DU VIEUX PONT
~ RESTAURANT-WITH-ROOMS ~

12390 Belcastel (Aveyron)
TEL 05 65 64 52 29 **FAX** 05 65 64 44 32
E-MAIL hotel-du-vieux-pont@wanadoo.fr

THE NAME REFERS TO A medieval cobbled bridge linking the two components of this much-lauded restaurant-with-rooms. On one side of the
river stands a solid rough-stone house, the Fagegaltier sisters' childhood
home, now the restaurant; on the other side, the sisters have rescued a
tumbledown building next to the church to create seven comfortable, stylish bedrooms. Above, Belcastel's picture-postcard houses cling to a cliff
with a castle crowning its summit.

Michèle Fagegaltier is the manager, while her sister Nicole and Nicole's
husband Bruno Rouquier are responsible for the cooking. Their imaginative versions of local dishes, such as *boeuf de l'Aubrac à la réduction de
banyuls*, served with *un concassé de pommes de terre à la ventrèche et
au roquefort*, have won them much praise, including a Michelin star and a
Gault Millau heart and 16 points. 'Impeccable service; altogether very
good news,' writes a reader. Through picture windows, diners can spot
trout rising if the Aveyron isn't flowing too fast.

The sisters have imparted some of their own elegance to both restaurant and hotel, and nowhere is this more evident than in the bedrooms.
They are just the kind we like; simply decorated, some with cream walls,
bedspreads and curtains and French windows on to the small garden; all
furnished with handpicked antiques.

~

NEARBY Rodez (23 km); Sauveterre-de-Rouergue (26 km).
LOCATION in the village beside the river, 8 km SE of Rignac; car parking
FOOD breakfast, lunch, dinner
PRICE €
ROOMS 7 double and twin with bath or shower; all rooms have phone, TV, air
conditioning, minibar, hairdrier
FACILITIES restaurant, garden, fishing **CREDIT CARDS** MC, V **CHILDREN** accepted
DISABLED 1 specially adapted room **PETS** accepted **CLOSED** Jan to mid-Feb;
restaurant Mon, Sep to Jun Sun dinner
PROPRIETORS Michèle and Nicole Fagegaltier

MASSIF CENTRAL

CASTELPERS

CHATEAU DE CASTELPERS
~ MANOR HOUSE HOTEL ~

Castelpers, 12170 Léderques (Aveyron)
TEL 05 65 69 22 61 **FAX** 05 65 69 25 31

YOLANDE TAPIÉ DE CELEYRON, of the old and distinguished family that owns this beautiful house, handed over the reins to her daughter, Mme de Saint-Palais, after 30 years. Our inspector found it a 'real delight' to share their home full of memories and objects of continuous history. On the stairs is a portrait of Mme Tapié's great-grandfather, an *'intendant militaire'* of Napoléon. Her grandfather (an engineer who pioneered the building of dams to harness water power and whose car licence plate was 9) restored and built on to the remains of a 17thC mill at the end of the 19th century. The result is not a grandiose château but something more like an unspoiled country house, kept as it has matured and been lived in. Its rooms are full of fine old furniture and pictures. Many of the beds are four-posters.

The taste is timeless; the charm effortless. The park is enchanting – tall trees shading a long stretch of lawn running between a river and a stream. There are swings for children. It is a 'peaceful, timeless place, happy to be just itself', in the words of our inspector. His dinner and choice of wine were excellent. The inexpensive prices, especially for weekend breaks, are an added appeal.

~

NEARBY Château du Bosc; Sauveterre-de-Rouergue (20 km).
LOCATION in countryside 9 km SE of RN88, 10 km S of Naucelle; car parking
FOOD breakfast, lunch, dinner (residents only)
PRICE €-€€€
ROOMS 8; 2 double, 4 twin, 2 family, 3 with bath, 5 with shower; all rooms have phone; some have TV
FACILITIES sitting room, 2 dining rooms, garden, fishing
CREDIT CARDS AE, DC, MC, V **CHILDREN** welcome if well behaved
DISABLED 1 ground-floor room
PETS accepted
CLOSED mid-Oct to mid-Apr; restaurant occasional dinner or lunch
PROPRIETOR Mme de Saint-Palais

MASSIF CENTRAL

COCURES

✳ LA LOZERETTE ✳
～ VILLAGE INN ～

48400 Cocurès (Lozère)
TEL 04 66 45 06 04 **FAX** 04 66 45 12 93
E-MAIL lalozerette@wanadoo.fr

THE DRIVING FORCE behind this village inn is the charming Pierrette
Agulhon, the third generation of her family to own and run it. Her
grandmother opened the house as an *auberge*, and clearly passed her
hotel-keeping skills on to her granddaughter, who manages La Lozerette
with calm efficiency, helped by an able, friendly staff. Although it's on
a fairly busy road (by day) on the historic route taken by Robert Louis
Stevenson and his donkey Modestine, the wild mountainous landscape
of the Cévennes National Park surrounds it, with signs of cultivation –
vineyards and orchards – dotted here and there. The best of the views are
from the large, wood-floored bedrooms. Painted in spring colours, with co-
ordinating floral, checked or striped fabric, they are never fussy, but clean-
cut and fresh-looking.

Several downstairs rooms have been knocked together to make the
large dining room, the heart of the hotel, which, with its wood-panelled
ceiling, cane chairs and cheerful yellow curtains, is cosy despite its size.
The menu is regional – you might find *foie-gras de canard, chataignes,
charcuterie de pays*, river trout or *ceps* on the menu – and so highly
regarded that it keeps the restaurant almost permanently full. Leave your
choice of wines to Pierrette, who – in addition to her other talents – is a
qualified *sommelier*.

NEARBY corniche des Cévennes; gorges du Tarn; Mende (42 km).
LOCATION in village, 6 km NE of Florac; car parking **FOOD** breakfast, lunch, dinner
PRICE € **ROOMS** 21; 20 double and twin, 1 single, all with bath or shower; all
rooms have phone, TV **FACILITIES** 2 sitting rooms, restaurant, bar, garden

CREDIT CARDS AE, DC, MC, V
CHILDREN accepted
DISABLED 1 specially-adapted
room **PETS** accepted **CLOSED**
early Nov to Easter
PROPRIETOR Pierrette Agulhon

MASSIF CENTRAL

CONQUES

GRAND-HOTEL SAINTE-FOY
～ VILLAGE HOTEL ～

Conques, 12320 St-Cyprien-sur-Dourdou (Aveyron)
TEL 05 65 69 84 03 **FAX** 05 65 72 81 04
E-MAIL hotelsaintefoy@hotelsaintefoy.fr **WEBSITE** www.hotelsaintefoy.fr

HOTEL STE-FOY is a lovingly restored, partly timbered 17thC inn which takes its name from the great abbey church directly opposite (with a remarkable tympanum and treasury). It is in the lovely, old village of Conques, and for centuries it has been one of the main stopping places for pilgrims on the route to Santiago.

Marie-France and Alain Garcenot have been the proprietors since they took over from an aunt in 1987. In 1993 it was promoted to four stars. Today they are justifiably proud of their achievement, but the facilities that allow its four-star rating are not the sole basis of the hotel's appeal.

The house has been beautifully furnished with close attention to detail and to preserving the character of the building. Glowing wood is everywhere. The large two-part sitting room is particularly well furnished with antiques. Bedrooms are highly individual, tasteful and large, with views either over the church or the flowery courtyard garden.

You can dine here or in the intimate but pleasantly spacious rooms inside. The increasingly inventive cooking (daily changing menus) gets impressive reviews, although recent guests bemoan the fact that the dinner menu did not vary during their stay.

～

NEARBY Rodez (36 km); Figeac (44 km).
LOCATION in the heart of the village; car parking
FOOD breakfast, lunch, dinner; room service
PRICE €€€-€€€€
ROOMS 17; 15 double, 2 suites, all with bath; all rooms have phone, hairdrier; suites have air conditioning; TV on request
FACILITIES sitting room, 3 dining rooms, bar, conference room, interior patio, 2 terraces
CREDIT CARDS AE, DC, MC, V
CHILDREN accepted **DISABLED** 1 specially adapted room
PETS accepted **CLOSED** mid-Oct to Easter
PROPRIETORS Marie-France and Alain Garcenot

Massif Central

Cordes-sur-Ciel

Le Grand Ecuyer
~ MEDIEVAL INN ~

79 Grand Rue Raimond VII, 81170 Cordes-sur-Ciel (Tarn)
TEL 05 63 53 79 50 **FAX** 05 63 53 79 51
E-MAIL grand.ecuyer@thuries.fr **WEBSITE** www.thuries.fr

AT THE INSTIGATION OF the novelist Prosper Mérimée, this former hunting lodge of the Counts of Toulouse was classified as a historic monument in the 19th century. It has been transformed into a comfortable and dependable hotel, with stone walls, beamed ceilings and paved floors. It is furnished with heavy oak antiques and tapestry-upholstered furniture, oil paintings, suits of armour, paved floors, rich damask and velvet wall coverings, blackamoor lampholders and four-poster beds. Parts of it are rather gloomy, though the bedrooms are quiet and inviting (if you like monumental stone fireplaces), with modern bathrooms.

Cordes-sur-Ciel – a remarkably preserved 13thC fortified hilltop village, with little cobbled streets and a busy tourist attraction – is the gastronomic domain of pastry chef Yves Thuriès, who has a Michelin star and is something of a celebrity. Le Grand Ecuyer is his base, though recent visitors feel he might be doing less in the kitchen now than in the past. The service is excellent and the chandeliered, plum-coloured dining room has been conceived as a prestigious setting for his cuisine. Our reporter dined well, and was struck by the helpfulness and knowledge of the wine waiter.

NEARBY Fôret Grésigne; Albi (27 km); Villefranche-de-Rouergue (47 km).
LOCATION in middle of village; car parking nearby
FOOD breakfast, lunch, dinner
PRICE €€
ROOMS 13; 10 double, 2 triple, 1 suite, all with bath; all rooms have phone, TV; some rooms have air conditioning
FACILITIES sitting room, 2 dining rooms, breakfast room, bar
CREDIT CARDS MC, V
CHILDREN accepted
DISABLED no special facilities
PETS accepted
CLOSED mid-Oct to Apr; restaurant lunch Mon to Fri
PROPRIETOR Yves Thuriès

MASSIF CENTRAL

CUQ-TOULZA

CUQ-EN-TERRASSES
∾ COUNTRY HOTEL ∾

Cuq Le Château, 81470 Cuq-Toulza (Tarn)
Tel 05 63 82 54 00 **Fax** 05 63 82 54 11
E-MAIL Cuq-en-Terrasses@wanadoo.fr **WEBSITE** www.cuqenterrasses.com

I N 1990 TWO LONDON DESIGNERS, Tim and Zara Whitmore, bought a semi-abandoned old presbytery and spent the next few years hard at work on the conversion which produced this successful hotel. The house, in a hilltop village square, is on a series of south-facing levels – from the street downwards – with more terraces of garden tumbling down the hillside below. Although Tim and Zara sold up in 2000, the new owners continue to run the hotel in much the same way, confirmed by a spate of complimentary readers' letters. Our latest reads: 'We were captivated by this charming location and hotel. We had a wonderful dinner and were extremely comfortable there.'

The entrance hall leads to the upstairs rooms via a balustraded staircase and a superb beamed ceiling, uncovered during the building work. Kitchen, dining room and beautiful outside terrace (with barbecue) for summer meals are two floors down. The swimming pool is on another terrace. All quite stunning. The decoration and furnishing are original without eccentricity – clean, fresh and colourful.

The view, particularly from the terraces, is breathtaking. It's not hard to see why the local name for this small pocket of fertile country is Le Pays de Cocagne (the land of plenty). An ideal place in which to relax and enjoy the peace.

∾

NEARBY Castres (35 km); Toulouse (37 km).
LOCATION in a hilltop hamlet by the church, 3 km from Cuq-Toulza; car parking
FOOD breakfast, lunch, dinner (by reservation)
PRICE €€€
ROOMS 8; 7 double, 1 family, 6 with bath, 2 with shower; all rooms have phone, TV
FACILITIES dining room, terraces, garden, swimming pool, badminton
CREDIT CARDS AE, DC, MC, V **CHILDREN** accepted
DISABLED no special facilities **PETS** accepted
CLOSED early Jan to early Apr
PROPRIETORS Philippe Gallice and Andonis Vassalos

MASSIF CENTRAL

DEMEURE DE FLORE
~ COUNTRY HOTEL ~

106 Route Nationale, 81240 Lacabarède (Tarn)
TEL 05 63 98 32 32 **FAX** 05 63 98 47 56
E-MAIL demeure.de.flore@hotelrama.com **WEBSITE** www.hotelrama.com/flore

THIS HOTEL IN THE FOOTHILLS of the Haut-Languedoc was opened in 1992 by Monike and Jean-Marie Tronc to realize their dream of creating a perfect hotel. Having done that, in 1999 they decided to sell to a sophisticated Italian, Francesco Di Bari, who has spent almost a million francs on redecoration, creating a new restaurant, and landscaping the garden.

The 19thC *maison de maître* may be an undistinguished building, but it sits prettily in a mature, wooded *jardin anglais*, far enough from the passing RN112 to feel secluded. And within, there is a delightful ambience, mercifully unchanged since M. Di Bari took over. Stylish floral prints are set against warm, plain backgrounds. The house is full of floor-to-ceiling windows, and the general impression is light and fresh. Carefully chosen antiques and ornaments give the feel of a lived-in but cared-for family home. The eleven bedrooms are individually furnished in the same careful way, with knick-knacks and fresh flowers. You could easily be staying with friends.

Perhaps not surprisingly the cooking combines Provençal and Italian styles, and the menu changes every day depending on what's in season. In summer, 'a bite of lunch' can be had by the smart little pool or on the terrace overlooking the garden. More reports please.

~

NEARBY Castres (35 km); Albi (60 km); Toulouse (100 km);
Mediterranean beaches.
LOCATION opposite service station on outskirts of village on RN112 between St-Pons and Mazamet; car parking
FOOD breakfast, lunch, dinner
PRICE ©©
ROOMS 11; 10 double, 1 suite, all with bath; all rooms have phone, TV, hairdrier
FACILITIES sitting room, restaurant, meeting room, garden, swimming pool
CREDIT CARDS MC, V **CHILDREN** accepted
DISABLED 1 specially adapted room **PETS** accepted **CLOSED** 3 weeks Jan
PROPRIETOR Francesco Di Bari

MASSIF CENTRAL

LA MALENE

MANOIR DE MONTESQUIOU
~ MANOR HOUSE HOTEL ~

48210 La Malène (Lozère)
TEL 04 66 48 51 12 **FAX** 04 66 48 50 47
E-MAIL montesquiou@de-lozere.com **WEBSITE** www.manoir-montesquiou.com

SET DRAMATICALLY between two sheer rock faces in the Gorges du Tarn, this attractive family-run castle-like 15thC manor house offers historical interest as well as excellent value for money. When Louis XIII ordered all rebel fortresses to be razed, the noble Montesquiou family saved their home by carrying out 'special favours' for the king, but worse misfortunes were to follow. A later fire destroyed part of the house and, during the Revolution, Gabriel de Montesquiou was imprisoned and his terrified wife hid herself in a cave; when she re-emerged she was blind.

Today, the house is having happier times. Heavily creepered, it has an inner courtyard and bedrooms in the turret, with stunning views. Larger ones have four-poster canopied beds and rich velvet upholsteries. There's much highly-polished dark furniture, which suits the surroundings, but it is an unassuming, comfortable hotel and guests are well looked after, with good humour and consideration, by owners M. and Mme Guillenet, who have been running the place and providing tasty regional fare for more than 30 years. 'Good-sized rooms, good food, very good views', reports a contented reader.

NEARBY river trips; fishing; bathing; Ste-Enimie (15 km).
LOCATION small village in the Gorges du Tarn; car parking
FOOD breakfast, lunch, dinner
PRICE €€
ROOMS 12; 10 double and twin, 2 suites, 7 with bath, 5 with shower; all rooms have phone, TV; hairdrier on request
FACILITIES sitting room, 2 dining rooms, bar, garden, 2 terraces
CREDIT CARDS DC, MC, V
CHILDREN accepted
DISABLED access difficult
PETS accepted
CLOSED Nov to early Apr
PROPRIETORS M. and Mme Guillenet

MASSIF CENTRAL

✴ CHATEAU D'AYRES ✴
~ COUNTRY HOTEL ~

48150 Meyrueis (Lozère)
TEL 04 66 45 60 10 **FAX** 04 66 45 62 26
E-MAIL Alliette@wanadoo.fr **WEBSITE** www.chateau-d-ayres.com

THE LOVELY, STONE, mainly 18thC, white-shuttered château stands on the site of a 12thC Benedictine monastery, now in the heart of the Cévennes National Park and in its own beautiful wooded grounds, with mature sequoias and oaks. Inside it is handsome, with walnut and chestnut panelling in some rooms, vaulted ceilings and a profusion of good antiques and pictures. Bedrooms are well appointed, with elegant, traditional furniture and carved mouldings. Some of the larger rooms have interesting bathrooms – extended into round towers or elevated on a mezzanine. Staff are friendly and helpful. The food is excellent. The chef, Jacqui Joubin, specializes in Languedoc cooking using plenty of local produce. M. de Montjou is a knowledgeable *sommelier*.

The house has a relaxed, convivial atmosphere and is extremely quiet. The garden is superb, with a lake, tennis court, swimming pool made out of local stone, a small whirlpool bath, and five horses, kept specially for guests to ride. There are plenty of alluring, shady places to which you can retreat with a chair and a book on long, hot afternoons – at 750 metres, the air is fresh and pure.

~

NEARBY Meyrueis (1 km); Gorges du Tarn; Mont Aigoual (1,387 m).
LOCATION 1 km SE of Meyrueis; car parking
FOOD breakfast, lunch, dinner
PRICE €€€€ **ROOMS** 27; 21 double and twin, 6 suites, 24 with bath, 3 with shower; all rooms have phone, TV, hairdrier
FACILITIES sitting room, library, 3 dining rooms, garden, terrace, swimming pool, tennis, riding **CREDIT CARDS** AE, DC, MC, V
CHILDREN accepted
DISABLED no special facilities
PETS accepted
CLOSED mid-Nov to late Mar
PROPRIETOR M. de Montjou

MASSIF CENTRAL

MOUDEYRES

LE PRE BOSSU
~ FARMHOUSE HOTEL ~

43150 Moudeyres (Haute-Loire)
TEL 04 71 05 10 70 **FAX** 04 71 05 10 21

MOUDEYRES IS A REMOTE village of thatched stone cottages and farm buildings, high (1,200 m) in the volcanic Mézenc massif, surrounded by fields of wild flowers in the spring and mushrooms in the autumn. It is a long way off the beaten track, but our inspector found it well worth the journey: 'Rarely have I seen a more beautiful location.' It is very rugged and difficult to get to.

The conscientious Flemish owners, the Grootaerts, have worked extremely hard to create an attractive and comfortable house. To original beams, wooden floors and old-fashioned, open fireplaces, they've added antique dressers, lace curtains, wild flowers when they are available – dried flowers when they are not – and books. Pots of home-made jam and artisan products are (subtly) for sale.

Some of our reports suggest that the hospitality may occasionally lack warmth, while others enthuse over the comfort and high standard of the food. By Easter 2002, M. Grootaert should have completed his project to knock together some of the ten original bedrooms to create five splendid large double rooms and one family room. Picnic baskets are provided for lunching out. Smoking is not allowed in the dining room.

~

NEARBY Le Puy-en-Velay (25 km); Yssingeaux (35 km).
LOCATION on the edge of the village, SE of Le Puy, beyond Laussonne; car parking
FOOD breakfast, lunch (Sun only), dinner
PRICE €
ROOMS 6; 5 double and twin, 1 family, all with bath or shower; all rooms have phone
FACILITIES bar, TV room, dining room, garden
CREDIT CARDS AE, MC, V
CHILDREN accepted
DISABLED no special facilities **PETS** accepted
CLOSED Nov to Easter; restaurant lunch Mon-Sat
PROPRIETOR Carlos Grootaert

MASSIF CENTRAL

NAJAC

❋ LONGCOL ❋
∼ COUNTRY HOTEL ∼

La Fouillade, 12270 Najac (Aveyron)
TEL 05 65 29 63 36 **FAX** 05 65 29 64 28
E-MAIL longcol@relaischateaux.fr **WEBSITE** www.relaischateaux.fr/longcol

THIS SPLENDID TURRETED restored medieval farmhouse – with added buildings in the same bell-shaped slate-roofed style – is set in isolated grandeur in a forested valley of the Gorges de l'Aveyron.

Solid and dignified, the overall effect is delightful. Much skill and taste has gone into the architecture, fittings and furnishings and there are antiques in every room. Quite a few of the pieces are European, but mostly they are from Asia: huge carved and studded Indian doors, exotic wood carvings and bronzes from India, Burma and Thailand, Indian miniature paintings on silk and ivory, all cleverly lit and displayed. One could be in a luxury hotel in India. The original Belgian owner, Fabienne Luyckx, began work on the site in 1982 with her mother (who died before completion) and, although she is no longer in charge, it was her passion for Asian art and antiques that dictated the hotel's style.

Added to all this is a sense of great comfort and professionalism. Seafood and regional dishes are served in a light and airy dining room or on the little walled terrace in summer – or by the angular swimming pool, which has views of woods. Food is taken seriously and there is an excellent wine list.

∼

NEARBY Najac (5 km); Villefranche-de-Rouergue (20 km).
LOCATION between Monteils and La Fouillade on D638, NE of Najac; car parking
FOOD breakfast, lunch, dinner
PRICE €€€ **ROOMS** 19 double, 17 with bath, 2 with shower; all rooms have phone, TV, minibar **FACILITIES** sitting room, dining room, billiard room, garden, terrace, swimming pool, tennis court **CREDIT CARDS** DC, MC, V **CHILDREN** welcome
DISABLED no special facilities
PETS welcome
CLOSED Nov to Easter; restaurant Mon, Tues and lunch Wed
PROPRIETORS Luyckx family

MASSIF CENTRAL

PONT-DE-L'ARN

LA METAIRIE NEUVE
~ FARMHOUSE HOTEL ~

81660-Pont-de-l'Arn (Tarn)
TEL 05 63 97 73 50 **FAX** 05 63 61 94 75
E-MAIL metairieneuve@aol.com

ALTHOUGH THE VILLAGE of Bout-du-Pont-de-l'Arn is beginning to expand, this old fortified farmhouse is set in a peaceful three-hectare oasis of well-manicured gardens sheltered by mature trees, and its mellow stone walls, creeper-clad in places, are gentle on the eye. Mme Tournier is steadily refurbishing the bedrooms in individual, smart country style, but has been careful not to lose the friendly feel of a private house. There are a host of little touches to help you feel very much at home here, the furniture is a happy combination of ancient and modern, and the bathrooms are all new. Three of the bedrooms are in a renovated farm workers' cottage.

Instead of a formal *salon* there are several little sitting rooms, giving you an above-average chance of getting some space of your own to relax in. In winter the beamed dining room has an open fire, and in summer it expands into a large open-sided barn looking out over the swimming pool and garden but protected from unseasonal downpours. The cooking is principally regional, concentrating on local produce as it comes into season, and of a consistently high standard.

Don't miss the splendid collection of Spanish art in the Goya Museum in nearby Castres.

~

NEARBY Castres (19 km); Le Sidobre (30 km); Albi (60 km); golf.
LOCATION at the edge of the village just N of the N112, 3 km E of Mazamet; car parking
FOOD breakfast, dinner
PRICE €
ROOMS 14 double and twin with bath; all rooms have phone, TV, minibar
FACILITIES sitting rooms, 2 dining rooms, garden, swimming pool
CREDIT CARDS DC, MC, V **CHILDREN** accepted
DISABLED access difficult
PETS accepted
CLOSED mid-Dec to late Jan; restaurant Sun
PROPRIETOR Mme Tournier

MASSIF CENTRAL

ST-ARCONS-D'ALLIER

LES DEUX ABBESSES
~ VILLAGE HOTEL ~

Le Château, 43300 St-Arcons-d'Allier (Haute-Loire)
TEL 04 71 74 03 08 **FAX** 04 71 74 05 30
E-MAIL direction@les-deux-abbesses.fr **WEBSITE** www.les-deux-abbesses.fr

ONCE YOU ARRIVE in St-Arcons-d'Allier, a picturesque medieval village perched above the river which gives it the second half of its name, there's no point in asking where the hotel is because you are already standing in the middle of it. Laurence Perceval and Bernard Massas have breathed new life into a well-nigh abandoned village by converting six of the houses into 10 bedrooms for their hotel centred on the château whose origins stretch back more than a thousand years. The streets are cobbled with stones taken from the river bed and, as visitors' cars are excluded to preserve the peace and undeniable charm of the village, you and your luggage will be taken to your lodging by Mini Moke.

The restoration has been done sensitively, and creature comforts have been installed without marring the pleasing simplicity of the buildings. The traditional plantings in the gardens, warm stonework and glimpses of the countryside beyond the village all contribute to the atmosphere of rustic peace. Breakfast and dinner are civilized meals, eaten in the château; the latter by candlelight in the baronial dining room. Dishes at dinner are prepared using fresh local produce, flavoured with herbs from the hotel's own garden. An elegant but comfortable *salon* offers a place to linger after dinner before you walk home.

~

NEARBY Le Puy-en-Velay (47 km); St-Flour (57 km); riding; golf.
LOCATION 6 km SE of Langeac left off the D585 to Saugues; car parking
FOOD breakfast, dinner (by reservation only)
PRICE €€€-€€€€€; 2-night minimum stay Fri to Sun
ROOMS 10; 5 double, 1 twin, 3 triple, 1 family, 9 with bath, 1 with shower
FACILITIES sitting room, dining room, terraces, garden, swimming pool
CREDIT CARDS AE, MC, V **CHILDREN** accepted over 10
DISABLED not suitable
PETS accepted
CLOSED never
PROPRIETORS Laurence Perceval and Bernard Massas

MASSIF CENTRAL

St-Jean-du-Bruel

HOTEL DU MIDI-PAPILLON
～ RIVERSIDE HOTEL ～

12230 St-Jean-du-Bruel (Aveyron)
TEL 05 65 62 26 04 **FAX** 05 65 62 12 97

EVERY YEAR WE RECEIVE a long hand written bulletin from Jean-Michel Papillon, the fourth generation of Papillons to run this old coaching inn, reporting on the latest developments. Readers share our enthusiasm for the place, telling us that nothing changes, the food remains 'wonderful', the welcome 'faultless', the value 'outstanding'. 'No attention to detail has been overlooked.' Our inspector, to his pleasure, finds everything just right: 'The Papillons go on doing what they have been doing for the last 150 years – providing a lively welcome, lodging and food to grateful travellers.' The hotel still bears features of its past and is the sort of traditional unpretentious *auberge* that is getting harder and harder to find; this one stands out for the quality of its food and the warmth of the welcome. There is an excellent dining room – the domain of Mme Papillon – and a view from most tables of the river and a little medieval stone humpbacked bridge. There is also a terrace (though sometimes one may not always be able to sit where one wishes). Jean-Michel Papillon cooks with vegetables from the garden and home-raised poultry, and makes his own jam, croissants, and *charcuterie*. This is the rural, family-run inn at its best. 'Oh, how we love this one,' runs our latest report

NEARBY Gorges de la Dourbie (10 km); Montpellier-le-Vieux.
LOCATION by river, in village on D991, 40 km SE of Millau; car parking
FOOD breakfast, lunch, dinner
PRICE €
ROOMS 19; 8 double, 5 twin, 1 suite, 1 single, 4 family, all with bath or shower; all rooms have phone
FACILITIES sitting room, TV room, 3 dining rooms, bar, terrace, garden, swimming pool, Jacuzzi
CREDIT CARDS MC, V **CHILDREN** welcome
DISABLED access difficult **PETS** accepted
CLOSED mid-Nov to Easter
PROPRIETORS Papillon family

MASSIF CENTRAL

TARGET

CHATEAU DE BOUSSAC
~ CHATEAU HOTEL ~

Target, 03140 Chantelle (Allier)
TEL 04 70 40 63 20 **FAX** 04 70 40 60 03
E-MAIL longueil@club-internet.fr **WEBSITE** www.chateau-de-boussac.com

INCREASED PUBLIC EXPOSURE – now in other British hotel guides as well as this one – has not affected the delicate balancing act conducted by the Marquis and Marquise de Longueil, who continue to welcome guests into their home with captivating charm.

The Château de Boussac lies between Vichy and Moulin, tucked away in the Bourbonnais – quite difficult to find. Solid, turreted and moated, the château could be a tourist sight in its own right; it is built around a courtyard, and the main reception rooms, furnished with Louis XV antiques and chandeliers, open on to a vast terrace with an ornamental lake and formal gardens. But the château is very much lived-in. By day the Marquis dons his overalls and works on the estate, but comes in to cook at least one course of the evening meal and chat to his guests. His wife looks after the rooms with care – there are fresh flowers everywhere, and the antiques are highly polished. Dinner *en famille* can be a rather formal affair, but the food is hard to fault and the Marquis, who speaks English, will make you feel at home. One reader was enchanted, and proclaimed it 'one of the highlights of our two-week trip'.

~

NEARBY Chantelle (12 km); Souvigny (35 km); Vichy (50 km).
LOCATION in countryside, off D42, NW of Chantelle; car parking
FOOD breakfast, dinner
PRICE €€
ROOMS 5; 1 double, 3 twin, 1 suite, all with bath
FACILITIES sitting room, dining room, terrace, garden
CREDIT CARDS AE, MC, V
CHILDREN accepted if well behaved
DISABLED no special facilities
PETS accepted
CLOSED Nov to Feb (except by reservation in advance)
PROPRIETORS Marquis and Marquise de Longueil

MASSIF CENTRAL

AUBERGE LA TOMETTE
~ VILLAGE INN ~

15220 Vitrac (Cantal)
TEL 04 71 64 70 94 **FAX** 04 71 64 77 11
E-MAIL latomette@wanadoo.fr **WEBSITE** www.auberge-la-tomette.com

'THIS HOTEL HAS ALL THE QUALITIES of peace, welcome, attractive setting and very good food that characterize your selections,' a reader said of La Tomette – a jolly whitewashed and shuttered inn, much expanded and improved over the past 18 years, without the loss of its essential appeal. In an exceptionally pretty village in the middle of the chestnut groves of the southern Cantal, it makes a perfect base for a family holiday, with its large garden, where trees and parasols provide plenty of shade, lawns for running around, and covered and heated swimming pool. There's also a health centre with Jacuzzi, sauna and steam room.

Wood-panelling gives a rustic feel to the cosy dining room, where every day a vase of freshly picked garden flowers is placed on each of the pink-covered tables. In summer, meals are served on a lovely terrace, part of which is covered for those who prefer to eat in total shade. In a separate building, the bedrooms are modern and clean but otherwise unexceptional. There is one duplex with a convenient lay-out for families.

~

NEARBY Maurs (21 km); Aurillac (22 km); Figeac (43 km).
LOCATION in village, 5 km S of St-Mamet-la-Salvetat; car parking
FOOD breakfast, lunch, dinner
PRICE €
ROOMS 15; 14 double and twin, 1 family, all with bath or shower; all rooms have phone, TV
FACILITIES sitting room, dining room, sauna, terrace, garden, health centre, swimming pool
CREDIT CARDS AE, MC, V
CHILDREN accepted
DISABLED no special facilities
PETS accepted
CLOSED Jan to Apr
PROPRIETORS Odette and Daniel Chausi

MASSIF CENTRAL

YDES

CHATEAU DE TRANCIS
~ CHATEAU HOTEL ~

15210 Ydes (Cantal)
TEL 04 71 40 60 40 **FAX** 04 71 40 62 13
E-MAIL trancis@wanadoo.fr **WEBSITE** www.trancis.com

ACCORDING TO THE BROCHURE, if paradise existed it ought to resemble the Château de Trancis. But this originally rather ordinary Auvergnat *maison de maître*, transformed at the turn of the century into an Italian Renaissance château, bristling with turrets, may not be everyone's vision of heaven.

Its former English owners brought great panache and dedication to the decoration. (Restoration began in 1990; some of the shutters hadn't been opened for 40 years.) The style is grand and ornate; gilded mirrors, chandeliers, a Louis XIV *salon*, a 'German' dining room and an 'English' library. Our inspector felt the whole was more a homage to a 19thC industrialist than to an aristocratic ideal. 'Apparently, the decoration appeals to the Europeans for its Englishness,' he noted.

The house is now run by a Dutch couple, the van Beymas, who continue to make improvements, and have won awards both for their work on the grounds, and for their food. A house-party atmosphere still prevails, although the five-course dinners are also available to non-residents, so booking in advance is advisable. Two luxurious apartments can be rented in the stable block.

~

NEARBY Dordogne gorges; Parc Régional des Volcans d'Auvergne.
LOCATION on D15, off D22, 2 km N of village of Saignes, 3 km E of Ydes; car parking
FOOD breakfast, dinner
PRICE €€€
ROOMS 9; 6 double, twin and single, 3 suites, all with bath or shower; all rooms have phone, TV, minibar, hairdrier
FACILITIES 3 sitting rooms, 2 dining rooms, 2 terraces, garden, swimming pool
CREDIT CARDS AE, MC, V **CHILDREN** accepted
DISABLED access difficult **PETS** accepted
CLOSED Jan; restaurant Tues
PROPRIETORS Pieter and Roberta van Beyma

MASSIF CENTRAL

COULANDON

LE CHALET
COUNTRY HOTEL

03000 Coulandon (Allier)
TEL 04 70 44 50 08
FAX 04 70 44 07 09
E-MAIL hotelchalet@cs3i.fr
FOOD breakfast, lunch, dinner
PRICE €
ROOMS 28
CLOSED mid-Dec to Feb

WE FIRST VISITED this modest, traditional hotel on a summer evening when its secluded, wooded, park-like garden seemed idyllic. The big fish pond (where guests are welcome to fish) is still perfect for strolling around, drink in hand, before dinner. Rooms (in the chalet-style building itself, and in converted outbuildings) vary in style and size; none is notably stylish, but the best are cheerfully comfortable (with exposed beams and bright wallpaper). Service is amiable in the dining room, where the fare includes some interesting regional specialities; Saint-Pourçain and Sancerre are special features of the wine list.

ST-MARTIN-VALMEROUX

HOSTELLERIE DE LA MARONNE
MANOR HOUSE HOTEL

Le Theil, 15140 St-Martin-Valmeroux (Cantal)
TEL 04 71 69 20 33
FAX 04 71 69 28 22
E-MAIL hotelmaronne@cfi15.fr
WEBSIT www.cfi15.fr/hotelmaronne **FOOD** breakfast, lunch, dinner **PRICE** €€
ROOMS 21 **CLOSED** Nov-Mar

WITH ITS POOL and tennis court surrounded by lovely gardens and sweeping countryside, this elegantly furnished 19thC *hostellerie* makes a fine retreat whether you're in search of peace or of outdoor exercise. Much has changed during Alain de Cock's tenure: a smart dining room has been built into the hillside; new bedrooms have replaced the least attractive of the old ones, and a change of lighting, carpets and seating has revived the public rooms. The improvements continue; the latest being gleaming new bathrooms for each of the bedrooms, and a lift. Food is taken seriously, with 'excellent' results. There is a range of set menus (reaching up to *gastronomique* levels) as well as a reasonable *carte*.

THE SOUTH

HOTELS IN THE SOUTH

MEDITERRANEAN FRANCE: sea, sun, wine, flowers, fruit, mountains, Roman remains. Heaven on earth – and with more hotel recommendations in this book than any other region of France. Our South section stretches from the border with Italy and the foothills of the Alps across Provence and the southern part of the Rhône valley into Languedoc-Roussillon to the Pyrenees, and covers the following *départements:* Alpes-Maritimes, Alpes-de-Haute-Provence, Var, Bouches-du-Rhône, Vaucluse, Gard, Drôme, Ardèche, Aude, Hérault and Pyrénées-Orientales.

Set between the wild Cévennes mountain range, the Pyrenees and the Mediterranean, Languedoc-Roussillon bears many similarities to Provence – on the other side of the Rhône – being a sun-baked land of vineyards, olive groves and dry, scrubby *garrigue.* Romanesque buildings, Roman remains and palaces of popes and cardinals are among its architectural treasures, and rugby pitches and bullrings are evidence of local passions. Far fewer good hotels here than east of the Rhône, but nevertheless we have unearthed one or two interesting new addresses.

The allure of Provence and the Côte d'Azur – sparkling sea, blue skies, the easy Mediterranean way of life, and a light that has inspired painters through the centuries – continues to work its magic. Not surprisingly, our largest concentration of recommendations is here, and the editors of this edition spent arduous (well, fairly arduous) weeks scouring its hotels, rejecting contenders (of which there were many) which, however beautifully decorated and *à la mode*, lacked personality, in favour of ones with real individuality and charm. The region is becoming ever smarter and more crowded with holidaymakers – witness the wild Lubéron, east of Avignon, now dotted with carefully restored villages, boutique hotels and slick restaurants – but it is still possible to find oases of calm even close to the tourist hotspots, as the following pages reveal. For even wider coverage, see *Charming Small Hotels and Restaurants, Southern France*, also published by Duncan Petersen, now with restaurant recommendations as well as hotels.

THE SOUTH

MAS D'ENTREMONT
~ FARMHOUSE HOTEL ~

Montée d'Avignon, 13090 Aix-en-Provence (Bouches-du-Rhône)
TEL 04 42 17 42 42 **FAX** 04 42 21 15 83
E-MAIL entremont@wanadoo.fr **WEBSITE** www.francemarket.com/mas_dentremont

THIS IS ONE OF OUR FAVOURITE HOTELS and a visit not long ago confirms our earlier impressions. The hosts here are the charming M. Marignane and his family – his brother owns the Relais de la Magdeleine at Gémenos, about which we are equally enthusiastic (see page 269). Low, red-roofed buildings are clustered around a courtyard – modern constructions, but using old materials. Within are wooden beams and pillars, rustic furniture, tiled floors and open fireplaces. Bedrooms are also rustic in style and comfortable. Many of the rooms are spread around the grounds in bungalows.

The setting is peaceful and the gardens a delight – with a big swimming pool shielded by cypresses, plenty of secluded corners, and a pond with a fountain, lilies and a number of lazy carp. Overlooking this is a beautiful summer dining room, with windows that slide away, effectively creating a roofed terrace – to which underfloor heating has now been added, allowing you to eat out even on a chilly day.

The food is excellent, with the emphasis on fish, fresh vegetables and a strong Provençal influence (although the chef is from Strasbourg).

~

NEARBY Aix-en-Provence; Abbaye de Silvacane (25 km).
LOCATION just off the RN7, 2 km from the centre of Aix, in large garden and grounds; car parking
FOOD breakfast, lunch, dinner
PRICE ⓔⓔⓔ
ROOMS 17; 15 double and twin, 2 family, all with bath; all rooms have phone, TV, air conditioning, minibar, hairdrier, safe
FACILITIES restaurant, gym, lift, terrace, garden, swimming pool, tennis
CREDIT CARDS MC, V
CHILDREN welcome
DISABLED ground-floor rooms available
PETS accepted
CLOSED Nov to mid-March; restaurant Sun dinner
PROPRIETORS Marignane family

THE SOUTH

AIX-EN-PROVENCE

HOTEL DES QUATRE DAUPHINS
~ TOWN HOTEL ~

54 rue Roux Alphéron, 13100 Aix-en-Provence (Bouches-du-Rhône)
TEL 04 42 38 16 39 **FAX** 04 42 38 60 19

THIS ATTRACTIVE LITTLE 19THC *maison bourgeoise*, on a quiet corner near the pretty Place des 4 Dauphins, opened as a family-run hotel more than eight years ago.

The dark green front door sports four brass dolphins and bright red geraniums grow in window boxes behind the wrought-iron bars on the ground floor. Built on three floors, there is no lift; it is simple, charming and excellent value for money. Some original features have remained – the lovely tiled terracotta floors – and there are some nice antique pieces throughout the house, such as handsome big mirrors, little wooden tables and a pine chest in the breakfast room. The plain decoration in the rooms is very pleasing: walls are painted in pale pastel shades and bedspreads and curtains are in Provençal prints. Furniture is minimal, mainly painted wood. Bathrooms are well equipped and spotless. Large, framed Impressionist posters hang in the corridors. The only public room is the breakfast/sitting room in a gentle pale yellow, with large painted wooden Provençal-style armchairs, big ceramic pots, dried flowers and pretty tablecloths.

Perfect for visiting Aix on a budget.

~

NEARBY place des 4 Dauphins; Cours Mirabeau.
LOCATION in town centre; car parking in street
FOOD breakfast
PRICE €
ROOMS 13; 9 double, 3 single, 1 triple, 8 with bath, 5 with shower; all rooms have phone, TV, minibar
FACILITIES breakfast/sitting room
CREDIT CARDS DC, MC, V **CHILDREN** welcome
DISABLED not suitable
PETS accepted
CLOSED never
PROPRIETORS M. Juster and M. Darricau

THE SOUTH

AIX-EN-PROVENCE

✳ VILLA GALLICI ✳
∾ TOWN VILLA ∾

avenue de la Violette, 13100 Aix-en-Provence (Bouches-du-Rhône)
TEL 04 42 23 29 23 **Fax** 04 42 96 30 45
E-MAIL villagallici@wanadoo.fr **WEBSITE** www.villagallici.com

MANY PEOPLE CONSIDER the four-star Relais et Châteaux Villa Gallici to be the best hotel in Aix; a recent inspection confirms its place at the top. It is certainly beautiful, and interior-designed down to the last curtain hook. Everything, inside and out, is perfect – gardens, terraces, pool, enormous terracotta pots overflowing with flowers, white umbrellas and plenty of wrought iron. A terrace, adjoining the villa, shaded by plane trees has been converted to an outside sitting room with deep-cushioned sofas and chairs. Bedrooms are sumptuous, with marvellous French wallpapers and fabrics and elegant 18thC furniture. Most of the bathrooms are classic, and pristine white. Downstairs, a series of small, welcoming, intimate sitting rooms are filled with colour and light, prints, paintings, coffee-table books and pieces of porcelain.

Our reporter noted that the guests were as beautiful as the hotel; this is not a place for the much-loved old grey T-shirt. Perhaps there is something just a little intimidating about the grand style of the Villa Gallici for it to be entirely relaxing, but that, as always, is a matter of taste.

NEARBY Avignon (82 km); Marseille (31 km).
LOCATION in a quiet suburb, 500 m from cathedral; car parking
FOOD breakfast, lunch, dinner
PRICE €€€€€
ROOMS 22; 18 double and twin, 4 suites, all with bath; all rooms have phone, TV, video, air conditioning, minibar, hairdrier, safe
FACILITIES sitting rooms, dining room, terrace, garden, swimming pool
CREDIT CARDS AE, DC, MC, V **CHILDREN** welcome
DISABLED 1 specially adapted room
PETS welcome
CLOSED never
PROPRIETORS M. Jouve, M. Dez and M. Montemarco

THE SOUTH

CALENDAL
~ TOWN HOTEL ~

5 rue Porte de Laure, 13200 Arles (Bouches-du-Rhône)
TEL 04 90 96 11 89 **FAX** 04 90 96 05 84
E-MAIL contact@lecalendal.com **WEBSITE** www.lecalendal.com

THIS BUSY, FRIENDLY HOTEL offers the best of both worlds: a location right next door to the great Roman arena – our inspector's room had a little balcony looking on to it – and a surprisingly large courtyard garden, a shady haven of trees (including a 400-year-old nettle tree), where on a hot day you can retreat from the dusty city. The building is 18th century, which shows through as features of the decoration, for example the rough stone walls and exposed beams downstairs. Here all the rooms have been knocked through to make one huge open-plan space, supported by pillars, with arches and steps marking the divisions between sitting and eating areas. The cosy sitting area, centred on the fireplace, is a perfect place for waiting, with armchairs and foreign-language newspapers on rods brasserie-style. You help yourself to the buffet breakfast and light lunch, which is still on offer at 5 pm.

One can't imagine being glum for long in this hotel. The colourful decoration would lift the blackest of moods. The bedrooms are different variations on a theme, mixing blues and yellows, yellows and reds or reds and greens, with pretty co-ordinating Provençal fabrics. Though small, they are well designed, with TVs on high brackets or shelves and cleverly added bathrooms, full of the fluffiest, brightest yellow towels

~

NEARBY arena; St-Trophîme; place du Forum.
LOCATION opposite Roman arena; car parking (reserve in advance)
FOOD breakfast, light lunch, tea
PRICE €
ROOMS 38 double, twin, triple and family, all with bath; all rooms have phone, TV, air conditioning, hairdrier
FACILITIES sitting area, dining areas, garden
CREDIT CARDS AE, DC, MC, V **CHILDREN** accepted
DISABLED 3 specially adapted rooms **PETS** welcome
CLOSED 3 weeks Jan
MANAGER Mme Jacquemin

THE SOUTH

ARLES

✳ GRAND-HOTEL NORD-PINUS ✳
~ TOWN HOTEL ~

place du Forum 13200 Arles (Bouches-du-Rhône)
TEL 04 90 93 44 44 **FAX** 04 90 93 34 00
E-MAIL info@nord-pinus.com **WEBSITE** www.nord-pinus.com

A STUNNING EXAMPLE of how a former cult hotel can, in the right hands, live again with its spirit intact but its amenities altered to suit the modern age. Anne Igou's imaginative and extravagant renovation (now 10 years old) has given back the Nord-Pinus its Bohemian past, recalling the post-war days when artists such as Picasso and Cocteau as well as bullfighters were entertained by its charismatic owners, a cabaret dancer and her husband, a famous tightrope-walking clown. The famous yellow bar, in particular, remains a homage to those times. There are other mementoes, too, including a cabinet of souvenirs, huge posters advertising bullfights around the fine stairwell, as well as chandeliers, gilded mirrors and all the original wrought-iron beds. The lobby has a dramatic, slightly Moorish feel; the restaurant, a traditional brasserie, leads off it, although it is not currently owned by Anne Igou.

Bedrooms come in three sizes: the smallest are compact but charming, with Provençal fabrics and antique wardrobes; larger ones are very spacious; and the six suites are enormous, worth splashing out on, especially No. 10, the 'bullfighters' suite', from the window of which legendary matador Dominguín would greet the crowds below. The hotel is run in a laid-back but professional way.

~

NEARBY Arena, Théâtre Antique; St-Trophîme; Les Alyscampes.
LOCATION in town centre (follow hotel signs); garage car parking
FOOD breakfast **PRICE** €€€ **ROOMS** 25; 19 double and twin, 6 suites, all with bath; all rooms have phone, TV, air conditioning, minibar, hairdrier
FACILITIES sitting room, bar, adjoining restaurant, breakfast room, lift, terrace

CREDIT CARDS AE, DC, MC, V
CHILDREN accepted
DISABLED access possible **PETS** accepted
CLOSED never
PROPRIETOR Anne Igou

THE SOUTH

LA MIRANDE
~ TOWN HOTEL ~

4 place de Mirande, 84000 Avignon (Vaucluse)
TEL 04 90 85 93 93 **FAX** 04 90 86 26 85
E-MAIL mirande@la-mirande.fr **WEBSITE** www.la-mirande.fr

A CLASSIC HONEY-COLOURED late 17thC façade by Pierre Mignard transformed La Mirande, which was built on the 14thC foundations of a cardinal's palace, into a *hôtel particulier*. Right opposite the Palais des Papes, in a quiet cobbled square, it was seized on by the Stein family and, since 1990, has been a sumptuous hotel that looks and feels as if it had been lived in for generations by a single family endowed with money and good taste. Tiled and parquet floors, smart Provençal fabrics and chintzes, wall coverings, paint, panelling, pictures, mirrors, and furniture all come together in serene period harmony. The good news doesn't stop there: the staff are kind and courteous as well.

The central courtyard, dotted with plants and sculptures, has been covered over with a glass roof, and is surrounded by a series of public rooms any one of which you'd like to wrap up and take home with you. The bedrooms vary in size (those on the first floor being the largest) but not in their uniformly high quality. From the second-floor balconies you are treated to rooftop views across the city. Last but not least are the treats in store in the dining room: Daniel Hébet draws eager gourmets from far and wide. And, yes, there is a garage for your car.

NEARBY Petit-Palais; Notre-Dame-des-Doms; Calvet museum.
LOCATION opposite the Palais des Papes; car parking
FOOD breakfast, lunch, dinner
PRICE €€€€€€
ROOMS 20; 19 double and twin, 1 suite, all with bath; all rooms have phone, TV, air conditioning, hairdrier
FACILITIES sitting rooms, bar, restaurant, lift, terrace, garden
CREDIT CARDS AE, DC, MC, V **CHILDREN** accepted
DISABLED 1 specially adapted room
PETS accepted
CLOSED never; restaurant Jan
PROPRIETOR M. Achim Stein

THE SOUTH

LES BAUX-DE-PROVENCE

AUBERGE DE LA BENVENGUDO
~ COUNTRY HOTEL ~

Vallon de l'Arcoule, 13520 Les Baux-de-Provence (Bouches-du-Rhône)
TEL 04 90 54 32 54 **FAX** 04 90 54 42 58

THE BEAUPIED FAMILY's creeper-clad hotel, just outside the village of Les Baux, remains compelling – and much more affordable than most places in the area. Rooms have the style of a private country house: a cosy sitting room with beams, an intimate dining room and, although some of the newly-decorated bedrooms are a little brash for our taste, others are homely with pretty patterned curtains.

A surgeon came over to our inspector from the swimming pool to say: "This is absolutely my idea of a charming small hotel. Just the place to spend a quiet, gentle relaxing week or 10 days. And the food is marvellous." Young Bocuse-trained chef Sebastien Beaupied has come home to manage the hotel for his parents – and, of course, to cook. Typical dishes are fresh monkfish with garlic and herbs, and roast duckling with apples. The menu changes every day according to what is in the market. Although the garden adjoins the road, there are no complaints of noise. The bedrooms are in a separate building; some have balconies.

The garden is delightful; there are olive groves and views of the natural stone outcrops of the Alpilles, the 'little Alps' of this part of Provence. Good walking country.

~

NEARBY St-Rémy-de-Provence (10 km); Arles (21 km).
LOCATION just outside the village of Les Baux-de-Provence on D78 to Fontvieille; car parking
FOOD breakfast, dinner
PRICE ©©-©©©
ROOMS 20; 14 double, 6 twin, all with bath; all rooms have phone, TV, air conditioning
FACILITIES sitting room, dining room, terrace, garden, swimming pool, tennis
CREDIT CARDS AE, MC, V **CHILDREN** accepted
DISABLED access possible **PETS** accepted
CLOSED Nov to early Mar; restaurant Sun and Mon Oct to Jun
PROPRIETORS Beaupied family

THE SOUTH

LES BAUX-DE-PROVENCE

✳ MAS D'AIGRET ✳
∽ COUNTRY HOTEL ∽

13520 Les Baux-de-Provence (Bouches-du-Rhône)
TEL 04 90 54 20 00 **FAX** 04 90 54 44 00
E-MAIL masdaigret@aol.com **WEBSITE** www.masdaigret.com

THERE ARE SEVERAL HOTELS dotted peacefully below Les Baux; we include this one, the closest to the ruined fortress and its vertiginous village, for the first time. It's a fairly simple place with some notable features, not least the secluded enclosed swimming pool and tranquil surrounding gardens. Lounging here – but for the rumble of traffic on busy days – you are a world away from the tourist hub of Les Baux: you can glimpse the bright colours of the tour buses through gaps in the foliage, but a real sense of privacy pervades. As for bedrooms, go for the special ones, such as No. 16, which has a private terrace and a troglodyte bathroom incorporating a large slab of rock face, or the family apartment with a perfect little room for children. Other bedrooms in the main house are pretty if a little worn, and many have blue-shuttered French windows and balconies with wonderful views over the Provençal landscape. Downstairs, the reception rooms are *à la mode*, if not quite chic. The rock face into which the hotel is built makes another dramatic appearance in the dining room.

∽

NEARBY St-Rémy-de-Provence (10 km); Arles (18 km); the Alpilles.
LOCATION on D279, 300 m below Les Baux; car parking
FOOD breakfast, lunch, dinner
PRICE €€€
ROOMS 17; 16 double, twin and triple, 1 apartment, all with bath; all rooms have phone, TV, air conditioning, minibar
FACILITIES sitting room, bar, dining room, terrace, garden, swimming pool
CREDIT CARDS MC, V
CHILDREN welcome

DISABLED not suitable
PETS accepted
CLOSED 2 weeks Jan
PROPRIETORS Frédérik Laloy and Vincent Missistrano

THE SOUTH

BEAULIEU

LA SANTOLINE
～ CONVERTED HUNTING LODGE ～

07460 Beaulieu (Ardèche)
TEL 04 75 39 01 91 **FAX** 04 75 39 38 79
E-MAIL contacts@santoline.com **WEBSITE** www.lasantoline.com

RESIDENTS OF NEARBY VILLAGES still speak of the big, old, stone Santoline as '*le château*' – a reference to its 15thC origins. As time passed, it was used as a hunting lodge and remains a secluded place well off the beaten track. With no television or other disruptions, there is little to disturb except birdsong and the occasional braying of a donkey. It is difficult to imagine a more relaxed setting. In the evenings, guests dine outside on the flower-filled terrace and watch the sun set behind the Cévennes.

Since opening their hotel in 1991, the Espenels have gathered a very loyal clientele by striking the right balance between easy-going conviviality and discreet attentiveness. Outsiders use the restaurant providing a menu of regional fare which changes daily, and affordable wines of the Ardèche. (The inside dining room has a fine stone-vaulted ceiling and tiled floor.) Bedrooms are pretty and simple in design, with much use of natural, rustic textures – tiled or pine floors, wicker furniture, some iron bedsteads, and white plastered walls. There are thick towels in the bathrooms. Most have exhilarating views of mountains.

NEARBY Vallon-Pont-d'Arc (22 km); Gorges de l'Ardèche.
LOCATION off the D104 at La Croisée de Jalès, then the D225, 2 km from Beaulieu; car parking
FOOD breakfast, lunch, dinner
PRICE €€; half-board obligatory Jul to Sep
ROOMS 8; 7 double, 1 suite, all with bath; all rooms have phone, minibar; 2 have air conditioning
FACILITIES sitting room, restaurant, terrace, garden, swimming pool
CREDIT CARDS MC, V
CHILDREN accepted
DISABLED no special facilities
PETS accepted
CLOSED Oct to late Apr
PROPRIETORS M. and Mme Espenel

THE SOUTH

BEAUMONT-DU-VENTOUX

LA MAISON
~ VILLAGE RESTAURANT-WITH-ROOMS ~

84340 Beaumont-du-Ventoux (Vaucluse)
TEL 04 90 65 15 50 **FAX** 04 90 65 23 29

FROM THE OUTSIDE, La Maison looks like dozens of other pretty Provençal houses – creeper-covered stone walls, blue window-shutters and doors, white wrought-iron tables and chairs, parasols and plants in terracotta pots on a shady front terrace – but a surprise lies in store. The restaurant, opened by Michèle Laurelut in June 1993, four years before she started letting rooms, is as chic as the owner herself with the kind of sophistication that you would hardly expect to find on the edge of a sleepy rural village like Beaumont-du-Ventoux. The decoration is stylishly simple: ochre-washed plaster walls, terracotta-tiled floor and heavy cream curtains at the windows. It is furnished like a private house, with massive table lamps, cushions to sit on, well-spaced tables, and artfully arranged pictures and ornaments. The focal point is an immense stone fireplace, where a fire burns on chilly autumn nights, to be replaced by a bank of hydrangeas when the weather improves.

Michèle offers a short seasonal menu, which we considered good value at 160 francs, and you can keep your bill down if you stick to the excellent local wine. To save driving home after dinner, you could stay in one of the large, modest bedrooms (two connect), which are immaculately kept but lack the dining room's panache.

~

NEARBY Vaison-la-Romaine (12 km); Avignon (47 km).
LOCATION in village, turn left at sign just before Mairie; car parking
FOOD breakfast, lunch, dinner
PRICE €
ROOMS 4; 2 double, 2 twin, 3 with shower
FACILITIES restaurant, terrace, garden
CREDIT CARDS MC, V
CHILDREN accepted **DISABLED** not suitable **PETS** accepted
CLOSED Nov to Apr; restaurant Mon and Tues Apr to Jun, Sep and Oct; lunch Mon to Sat Jul and Aug
PROPRIETOR Michèle Laurelut

THE SOUTH

BONNIEUX

AUBERGE DE L'AIGUEBRUN
~ COUNTRY HOTEL ~

Domaine de la Tour, RD 943, 84480 Bonnieux (Vaucluse)
TEL 04 90 04 47 00 **Fax** 04 90 04 47 01

SYLVIE BUZIER IS WARM, pretty and talented (she can paint as well as cook and decorate). Her staff are equally charming, easy-going and unobtrusively hip (her co-chef is friendly Francis Motta), They are a happy, well-knit team, and along with the hotel's setting, they engender a rare sense of peace and well-being in their beautiful house.

The hotel lies on its own in a green oasis at the end of a steep track by a waterfall in the river Aiguebrun, the only natural water in this barren region. 'When Sylvie (who previously owned a much loved restaurant near Avignon) bought it, she transformed the interior, which is now a delightful, personalized version of current Provençal decoration. Rooms are full of light: the white and cream dining room with its fresh green leaf curtains is surrounded by windows overlooking the river; the sitting room is a lovely yellow, with a well-stocked drinks tray, comfy sofas and a minah bird in an antique cage; the bedrooms are similarly full of light and colour (the family suite is excellent, with two bedrooms, one perfect for children).

The food is a highlight: a simple, delicious set menu with one or two choices using organic meat and vegetables and wild fish. Herbs and salads come from the *potager*. There is a lovely pool.

~

NEARBY Bonnieux (6 km); Lourmarin (10 km); Aix-en-Provence (45 km).
LOCATION in valley, 6 km E of Bonnieux, down a steep rutted track signposted off Bonnieux to Boux road; car parking
FOOD breakfast, lunch, dinner
PRICE €€€
ROOMS 8; 4 double and twin, 1 single, 3 suites, all with bath; all rooms have phone, TV, hairdrier
FACILITIES sitting room, dining room, terrace, garden, potager, swimming pool bar
CREDIT CARDS MC, V **CHILDREN** accepted
DISABLED not suitable **PETS** not accepted **CLOSED** mid-Nov to mid-Mar; restaurant Tues, Wed lunch
PROPRIETOR Sylvie Buzier

THE SOUTH

BONNIEUX

HOSTELLERIE DU PRIEURE
~ VILLAGE HOTEL ~

84480 Bonnieux (Vaucluse)
TEL 04 90 75 80 78 **FAX** 04 90 75 96 00
E-MAIL hotelprieur@hotmail.com

THIS ATTRACTIVE HOTEL at the foot of the ramparts of one of the showpiece Luberon villages has been in our Southern France guide for many years and, after our latest inspector gave a favourable report, we decided to include it in this guide too. The Prieuré's new manager, Michèle Cadillon is down-to-earth and kindly, fostering the warm, relaxed ambience for guests that her predecessor, Caroline Coutaz, made her trademark.

What is so refreshing about this former hospital – an 18thC *hôtel-Dieu* – is that it has escaped the vogue for prettification, and remains little changed since our first visit. Through massive oak doors, a splendid wide, red-tiled staircase leads up to the balustraded landing. (The former chapel is now used for storage.) What were once rooms for the patients are light with beams, antique furniture and endearingly old-fashioned wallpaper and curtains. Some overlook the pretty walled garden at the rear, where apricot and plum trees give shade from the heat, and are quieter than those at the front, which face the road going up into the village. Food is served on the covered terrace or in the dining room where the original hearth takes up an entire wall. In the spacious bar there is a wonderful antique glass case with replicas of Paris theatres in miniature, designed so that theatre-goers could choose their seats.

~

NEARBY Avignon (51 km); Aix (40 km); the villages of the Luberon.
LOCATION on a lower road of the village; car parking
FOOD breakfast, lunch, dinner
PRICE €€
ROOMS 10; 6 double, 4 twin, 9 with bath, 1 with shower; all rooms have phone
FACILITIES sitting room, dining room, bar, terrace, garden
CREDIT CARDS MC, V **CHILDREN** accepted
DISABLED not suitable **PETS** accepted
CLOSED early Nov to Mar; restaurant lunch Tues to Fri, Oct to May Wed, lunch Tues and Thurs
MANAGERS Michèle Cadillon and Rémi Chapotin

THE SOUTH

CASSIS

LE CLOS DES AROMES
~ TOWN HOTEL ~

10 rue Paul Mouton, 13260 Cassis (Bouches-du-Rhône)
TEL 04 42 01 71 84 **FAX** 04 42 01 31 76

THIS IS A VERY PRETTY SMALL HOTEL, in a quiet street near the old port and run and completely redecorated by the young, friendly and informal Bonnets, who took over from the previous owners seven years ago. The hotel's history goes back 50 years and in the dining room there is a little oil painting of it as it was.

It is a bright, sunny place, entered either off the street into a large, attractive dining room or through the delightful paved garden. The dining room has old terracotta tiles on the floor, stripped wooden panelling on the walls, a big stone fireplace at one end, little tables with blue and yellow cloths and painted blue chairs.

Bedrooms are on the two floors above, up steep stairs. Behind simple white-painted doors, the rooms are small, but very pretty. Each one has a different colour scheme: fabrics, wallpapers and paintwork are carefully co-ordinated. Furniture is quality country-style reproduction. Bathrooms are smallish, but spotlessly clean and sparkling white. There are two tiny rooms, with double beds, but usually let as singles. They offer hardly any room to move, but are nonetheless very appealing. The Provençal menu here is very reasonably priced.

~

NEARBY Marseille (20 km); Aix-en-Provence (35 km).
LOCATION in a quiet side street in the old town, near the port; car parking
FOOD breakfast, lunch, dinner
PRICE €
ROOMS 8; 5 double, 2 single, 1 family, 3 with bath, 5 with shower; all rooms have phone
FACILITIES dining room, terrace, garden
CREDIT CARDS AE, MC, V **CHILDREN** accepted
DISABLED not suitable
PETS accepted
CLOSED Oct to late Dec, Jan to mid-Feb
PROPRIETOR M. Fabrice Bonnet

THE SOUTH

CERET

LE MAS TRILLES
~ COUNTRY HOTEL ~

Le Pont de Reynes, 66400 Céret (Pyrénées-Orientales)
TEL 04 68 87 38 37 **FAX** 04 68 87 42 62

LASZLO BUKK IS A Lithuanian-born, Swiss-trained hotelier, whose experience includes spells working in Canada and Australia. He and his Breton wife, who has carried her artistic and design talents into the world of refined cuisine, make an accomplished team. In a labour of love, they transformed this 17thC *mas* into a delightful, welcoming hotel – blending past and present and endowing it with their own very personal aura. The massive warm stone structure overlooks the fast-flowing River Tech – a tiny path brings you down to a stretch between two bends where the clear water looks almost still – an unspoiled natural sanctuary. A terrace beside the house leads down to a delightfully uncomplicated garden with lawn and swimming pool, mature trees and flowering shrubs.

Bedrooms are practical, immaculately kept and all have either a terrace or a small private garden. The atmosphere in the public rooms is informal and relaxed, so guests feel very much at home in them.

The menu for dinner is chalked up on a board but Mme Bukk is always willing to provide alternative dishes for those with special requirements. She is justifiably proud of her kitchen.

~

NEARBY Perpignan (26 km); Castelnou (30 km); beaches.
LOCATION in countryside on the D115, 2 km from Céret; car parking
FOOD breakfast, dinner
PRICE €€
ROOMS 10 double with bath; all rooms have phone, TV
FACILITIES sitting room, dining room, garden, swimming pool, table tennis
CREDIT CARDS MC, V
CHILDREN accepted
DISABLED 1 specially adapted room
PETS accepted
CLOSED mid-Oct to Easter
PROPRIETORS M. and Mme Bukk

THE SOUTH

CÉRET

❋ LA TERRASSE AU SOLEIL ❋
⟨ COUNTRY HOTEL ⟩

route de Fontfrède, 66400 Céret (Pyrénées-Orientales)
TEL 04 68 87 01 94 **FAX** 04 68 87 39 24
E-MAIL terrasse-au-soleil.hotel@wanadoo.fr **WEBSITE** www.la.terrasse-au-soleil.com

THE ORIGINAL PART OF THE HOTEL was an 18thC *mas* but already a hotel when the present owners acquired it in 1980. Since then two annexes have been added for extra bedrooms and suites. The setting is lovely, higher up the mountains than nearby Céret, with splendid views over unspoiled hills.

Bedrooms vary in size, but the biggest are very spacious and all are tastefully furnished and decorated (some have their own private verandas). There is plenty of individuality in the interior design – much of it the legacy of Charles Trenet (the house at one time belonged to his agent and was a haunt of show-business personalities): unusual terracotta and ceramic tiling and imported African wood carvings, as in the huge bar. Colour and warmth in abundance introduce intimacy and cosiness not normally found in four-star hotels. Picasso is said to have sat on the terrace to enjoy the views of Mont Canigou.

The restaurant, La Cerisaie, has an enviable reputation and a young chef from Paris. At lunchtime, there is a tempting *carte brasserie* as a lighter alternative to the more serious food served at dinner.

NEARBY Perpignan (26 km); Castelnou (30 km); beaches.
LOCATION in Pyrenean foothills above the town, SW of Perpignan; car parking
FOOD breakfast, brunch, dinner; room service
PRICE €€€€ **ROOMS** 21; 14 double, 7 suites, all with bath; all rooms have phone, TV, air conditioning, minibar, hairdrier **FACILITIES** sitting room, restaurant, bar, garden, swimming pool, tennis, table tennis, helipad, petanque, golf practice area **CREDIT CARDS** AE, DC, MC, V **CHILDREN** accepted

DISABLED some specially adapted rooms
PETS accepted
CLOSED never
PROPRIETOR M. Leveille-Nizerolle

THE SOUTH

CHATEAU-ARNOUX

✳ LA BONNE ETAPE ✳
∽ TOWN INN ∽

chemin du Lac, 04160 Château-Arnoux (Alpes-de-Haute-Provence)
TEL 04 92 64 00 09 **FAX** 04 92 64 37 36 **E-MAIL** bonneetape@relaischateaux.com
WEBSITE www.bonneetape.com

'**E**XCEPTIONAL FOOD, impeccable service, beautiful pool and rooms – worth every franc.' says a recent customer of this 'good stopover' – a former coaching inn in an unremarkable small town. Outside, it gives little hint of what lies within – one of the most satisfactory blends of refinement and hospitality to be found in the region. Although the kitchen lost its second Michelin star, we would re-award it if we could. Chefs Pierre and Jany Gleize (father and son) make innovative and stylish use of largely home-grown ingredients. A house speciality is Sisteron lamb (raised on mountain pastures): try it with a deep-red Vacqueyras Côtes du Rhone. Tables in the formal dining room have fresh flowers; Bach plays in the background. There are serious eaters here, many alone. The atmosphere is slightly hushed, but the waiters are helpful and friendly. There is a charming bar with painted beams. But this is no restaurant-with-rooms. Bedrooms are luxuriously comfortable – beautifully decorated with a tasteful mix of modern and antique pieces. Some have marble bathrooms. The Gleize family are warmly welcoming hosts, happily committed to their work; they also own a simpler restaurant nearby.

NEARBY Eglise St Donat; Sisteron (14 km).
LOCATION just off main RN85, 14 km SE of Sisteron (motorway 3 km); car parking and garage **FOOD** breakfast, lunch, dinner; room service
PRICE €€€ **ROOMS** 19 double and twin, all with bath; all rooms have phone, TV, air conditioning, minibar, hairdrier **FACILITIES** sitting room, dining room, terrace, garden, swimming pool **CREDIT CARDS** AE, DC, MC, V **CHILDREN** accepted
DISABLED access possible **PETS** accepted

CLOSED mid-Nov to mid-Dec, Jan to mid-Feb; restaurant closed Tues lunch and Mon Oct to Mar
PROPRIETORS Gleize family

THE SOUTH

COLLIOURE

CASA PAIRAL
~ SEASIDE TOWN HOTEL ~

impasse des Palmiers, 66190 Collioure (Pyrénées-Orientales)
TEL 04 68 82 05 81 **FAX** 04 68 82 52 10
E-MAIL hotelsmascasa@wanadoo.fr **WEBSITE** www.roussillhotel.com

TUCKED AWAY IN A SMALL *impasse,* this quiet, elegant hotel has a magical situation just 150 metres from the busiest part of Collioure, close to the harbour and main beach with their many seaside cafés, restaurants, and narrow packed streets winding up the hill. A period-piece Catalan-style house built in the mid-19th century, it has a lush, picturesque interior garden with 100-year-old palm trees and pines shading a courtyard with tables and chairs and (somewhat apart) a swimming pool. The attractive ground-floor *salon* has a tiled floor and looks out to the courtyard and a fountain backed by oleanders and a huge magnolia. There is also a larger 1930s-style *salon* with a television and card table. The breakfast room (down a stone staircase) is captivating – and surprising; in one corner is the trunk of a vast oak tree which grows out through the roof, while opposite, large windows frame beautiful views of the garden.

Bedrooms in the main house combine old-world charm in the sleeping area with modern bathroom facilities. Our inspector was overcome by nostalgia: 'It reminded me of how good hotels used to be, but with all the up-to-date comforts. A place full of charm.'

NEARBY Port-Vendres (4 km); Argelès-sur-Mer (6.5 km); Perpignan (27 km).
LOCATION in the centre of town 150 m from the port and beach; car parking
FOOD breakfast
PRICE €
ROOMS 28 double and twin; 23 with bath, 5 with shower; all rooms have phone, TV, air conditioning, minibar
FACILITIES 2 sitting rooms, breakfast room, garden, swimming pool
CREDIT CARDS AE, DC, MC, V
CHILDREN accepted
DISABLED some ground-floor rooms
PETS accepted
CLOSED Nov to Apr
PROPRIETOR Mme de Bon

THE SOUTH

CORNILLON

LA VIEILLE FONTAINE
~ HILLTOP VILLAGE HOTEL ~

30630 Cornillon (Gard)
TEL 04 66 82 20 56 **FAX** 04 66 82 33 64
E-MAIL vieillefontaine@libertysurf.fr

BUILT WITHIN THE WALLS of the ruined château of a medieval fortified village, with cobbled streets and ivy-clad ramparts, this little hotel is full of charm. *Patron* and chef, M. Audibert, is a Marseillais; his *gratinée de langoustines* and *chou farci à la provençale*, accompanied by the local Tavel rosé, have long been the restaurant's attractions. The hotel is the creation of Mme Audibert, a native of this once semi-abandoned village. Inspired by the Louvre pyramid, she has, with great flair, clad the exterior circular staircase to the bedrooms with an elegant glass structure, at which one can gaze in wonder over breakfast in the courtyard.

Her decorating style is simple and pretty: tiled bathrooms, Provençal fabrics, furniture from local *antiquaires*. One room contains a great chunk of the old château wall. Most have terraces; Nos 7 and 8 have views way over the top of the castle wall to the south. A steep flight of stone steps through terraced gardens leads to the pool: water gushes down from the hillside, and it is like bathing in a mountain stream.

The welcome is spontaneous and warm, and dinner on the terrace looking over the hills and vineyards of the Gard is a delight.

~

NEARBY Orange (44 km); Avignon (45 km); Gorges de l'Ardèche.
LOCATION in the heart of the village, with limited access by car; car parking outside village
FOOD breakfast, lunch, dinner
PRICE €€
ROOMS 8 double with bath; all rooms have TV, phone
FACILITIES sitting room, dining room, terrace, garden, swimming pool
CREDIT CARDS AE, DC, MC, V
CHILDREN welcome
DISABLED not suitable **PETS** accepted
CLOSED mid-Dec to mid-Mar
PROPRIETORS M. and Mme Audibert

THE SOUTH

CRILLON-LE-BRAVE

✳ HOSTELLERIE DE CRILLON LE BRAVE ✳
∼ VILLAGE HOTEL ∼

place de l'Eglise, 84410 Crillon-le-Brave (Vaucluse)
TEL 04 90 65 61 61 **FAX** 04 90 65 62 86
E-MAIL crillonbrave@relaischateaux.fr **WEBSITE** www.crillonlebrave.com

'**D**ELIGHTFUL', ENTHUSES one satisfied visitor to this luxurious hotel occupying the old vicarage in a hilltop village. 'Very good restaurant, excellent service, a lovely setting and charming *patron*.' Another more recent guest is not so complimentary, sensing 'an air of complacency' in the housekeeping. He also finds the Provençal cooking 'disappointing, not in quality but in the absence of a menu change or a *plat du jour*.' However, he praises the wine list, which 'offered excellent value', and a summer bistro has just opened, which gives guests a choice for dinner.

The rambling 16thC stone-built house is solid and calm, but most of the credit for the resounding success of the hotel must go to the aforementioned *patron*, Peter Chittick, a Canadian lawyer with exceptionally clear ideas about hotelkeeping. A considerable share goes also to the perched location, giving uninterrupted views of a heavenly landscape of olive groves and vineyards. The central trick that Mr Chittick and his collaborator Craig Miller have pulled off is to provide luxury without erasing character. Despite the designer fabrics, fitted carpets and smart bathrooms, the exposed beams, white walls and rustic furniture dominate both in the sitting rooms and the spacious bedrooms (13 of which have recently been added). You eat beneath stone vaults, or out on the pretty terrace.

NEARBY Mont Ventoux; Orange (35 km); Avignon (35 km). **LOCATION** in village NE of Avignon, on D138 off D974; car parking **FOOD** breakfast, lunch (Sat and Sun only), dinner, snacks **PRICE** €€€€ **ROOMS** 32 double, twin and suites, all with bath or shower; all rooms have phone, minibar, hairdrier **FACILITIES** 3 sitting rooms, dining room, terrace, garden, swimming-pool **CREDIT CARDS** AE, DC, MC, V **CHILDREN** welcome **DISABLED** access difficult **PETS** accepted **CLOSED** Jan to Mar; restaurant lunch Mon to Fri; bistro Tues, lunch Mon to Fri **PROPRIETORS** Peter Chittick and Craig Miller

THE SOUTH

ENTRECHAUX

LA MANESCALE
~ COUNTRY HOTEL ~

route de Faucon, Les Essareaux, 84340 Entrechaux (Vaucluse)
TEL 04 90 46 03 80 **FAX** 04 90 46 03 89

THE KING OF BELGIUM has slept here. No doubt, like so many others, he was charmed by all he found in this remote former shepherd's house up in the hills. The thoughtfulness of owners, M. and Mme Warland, permeates what could be described as a pocket-sized hotel with every comfort, and the emphasis on the privacy of guests. The smallest details are attended to here, from towels for the swimming pool to a small library for serious readers and helpfully labelled light switches.

The house is beautifully decorated with the Warlands' own books, paintings, *objets d'art* and furniture. Stone steps and pathways connect the main building to the garden rooms, each giving privacy and views of the forest and hillsides. Two rooms are named after M. Warland's favourite painters, Tiepolo and Dali. A place for lovers of quiet and of nature, there are numerous paths through the woods for long walks. Classical music plays on the terrace at aperitif time; the views across the vineyards and valleys to Mont Ventoux in the distance are superb.

It's a steep, if short, walk from the car park to the hotel; a luggage trolley is provided.

~

NEARBY Vaison-la-Romaine (7 km); Côtes du Rhône vineyards.
LOCATION 3 km N of Entrechaux, signposted off D205 road to Faucon; car parking
FOOD breakfast
PRICE €€
ROOMS 5 double and twin, 2 with bath, 3 with shower; all rooms have phone, TV, minibar, hairdrier
FACILITIES sitting room, breakfast room, terrace, garden, swimming pool
CREDIT CARDS AE, DC, MC, V
CHILDREN accepted over 12
DISABLED not suitable
PETS accepted
CLOSED end Oct to Easter
PROPRIETORS M. and Mme Warland

THE SOUTH

EYGALIERES

AUBERGE PROVENCALE
~ VILLAGE INN ~

place de la Mairie, 13810 Eygalières (Bouches-du-Rhône)
TEL 04 90 95 91 00

IN DELIGHTFUL EYGALIERES, this 18thC former coaching inn has a paved courtyard with trees and potted plants and small marble-topped tables and is well-known locally for its Provençal dishes. The horses' stone drinking troughs remain and guests' cars are safely locked away for the night in the magnificent coach house, which has a great arched gateway on to the street. There is also a spacious bar, deliberately and charmingly evocative of the 19th century.

Owner and chef Didier Pézeril and his young family extend their hospitality to rooms, some of which look out on to the courtyard, and all of which are exceptional. There are just four: quantity has been sacrificed for space and quality – simple and stylish in the best, least fussy Provençal manner, some with huge bathrooms, some with huge bedrooms. Our inspector's room had blue-washed walls, rough white cotton curtains and a paisley cover on the bed and a view out of the window of the lively Progrès café opposite. Tiled floors are attractively uneven and some rooms have traditional cupboards set in the walls. M. Pézeril's philosophy is correspondingly down-to-earth: 'We're an *auberge*, we don't have pretensions to being anything else'. The whole place oozes character.

~

NEARBY St-Rémy-de-Provence (13 km); Les Baux (23 km); the Alpilles
LOCATION in village, with car parking
FOOD breakfast, lunch, dinner
PRICE €€
ROOMS 4 double and twin, all with bath; all rooms have phone, TV
FACILITIES bar, restaurant, courtyard, terrace
CREDIT CARDS MC, V
CHILDREN welcome
DISABLED not suitable
PETS accepted
CLOSED mid-Nov to mid-Dec; restaurant closed Wed, Thurs lunch
PROPRIETORS Pézeril family

THE SOUTH

MAS DE LA BRUNE
~ COUNTRY HOUSE BED-AND-BREAKFAST ~

13810 Eygalières (Bouches-du-Rhône)
TEL 04 90 90 67 67 **FAX** 04 90 95 99 21
E-MAIL MasBrune@Francemarket.com **WEBSITE** www.Francemarket.com/brune/

IT'S A REAL PRIVILEGE to stay at Mas de la Brune, a *monument historique* and a rare example of a Renaissance mansion built in the countryside rather than a town – in this case, St-Rémy-de-Provence. Here you will find (expensive) luxury accommodation with plenty of character. The façade is embellished with stone carvings, corbels, cornices and mullioned windows, there is a spiral stone staircase with mysterious carved capitals (it's thought that the original 16thC owner may have been an alchemist), and the house sits in its own beautifully kept estate. Mme Larouzière, who with her husband has been the proprietor for the past 10 years, is a keen gardener; the pristine landscaped grounds – including a lovely swimming pool – have fabulous views of Eygalières and the Alpilles. Their latest venture is an Alchemist's Garden, open to the public in summer.

Bedrooms are decorated in perfect country house taste, with attractively tiled bathrooms. The suite is impressive; another room incorporates the corner turret, with views across gardens and cypress trees to the village beyond, perched on its hill. The owners are charming, the staff assiduous, and the atmosphere one of calm privacy.

~

NEARBY St-Rémy-de-Provence (12 km); Avignon (27 km).
LOCATION 2 km N of Eygalières, signposted off the road to St-Rémy; car parking
FOOD breakfast
PRICE €€€€
ROOMS 10; 9 double and twin, 1 suite, all with bath; all rooms have phone, TV, air conditioning, minibar, safe, hairdrier
FACILITIES sitting room, breakfast room, terrace, garden, swimming pool, Alchemist's Garden
CREDIT CARDS MC, V **CHILDREN** welcome
DISABLED not suitable
PETS accepted
CLOSED Nov to Jan
PROPRIETORS Alain and Marie de Larouzière

THE SOUTH

EZE

CHATEAU EZA
~ COAST HOTEL ~

rue de la Pise, 06360 Eze (Alpes-Maritimes)
TEL 04 93 41 12 24 **FAX** 04 93 41 16 64
E-MAIL chateza@webstore.com **WEBSITE** www.slh.com/chateza

W HEN AMERICAN OWNERS Patti and Terry Giles took over Château
Eza, once the private home of Prince William of Sweden, they completely redecorated from top to toe. They went, in keeping with the
(much-visited) village, for the medieval look, and the result – exposed
brick, wrought iron, dark wood, red velvet, tapestries, brocade, suits of
armour – is luxurious and not a little kitsch. A couple of donkeys, stabled
in front of the hotel's reception at the bottom of the village, take your bags
up to the top (your car will be parked for you), but be warned, access for
anyone even vaguely infirm is arduous. Here is your bedroom, most likely
with a private entrance from the street as if it were a village house, and
with a private terrace overlooking the jumble of old roofs. All the rooms
have views and wood-burning stoves for cool evenings. They are not especially light or spacious – they have thick stone walls, old beams, stone pillars and village house proportions – but they lack for nothing as far as decoration and comfort are concerned: draped four-poster or otherwise fancy
beds, original paintings, fine antiques, splendid, perfectly equipped bathrooms. The glass-walled restaurant ('fabulous' food) is romantic, and terraces tumble down the hillside as if into the sea below. A favourite with
U.S. readers. Wildly expensive.

~

NEARBY Nice (12 km); Monte Carlo (8 km).
LOCATION on N7 Moyenne Corniche between Nice and Monaco; hotel approached
on foot; valet car parking at edge of village
FOOD breakfast, lunch, dinner; room service
PRICE €€€€€
ROOMS 10; 7 double and twin, 3 suites, all with bath; all rooms have phone, TV,
video, CD player, air conditioning, minibar, safe, hairdrier
FACILITIES restaurant, sitting rooms, bar, terraces
CREDIT CARDS AE, DC, MC, V **CHILDREN** accepted
DISABLED not suitable **PETS** accepted **CLOSED** Nov to Apr
MANAGER Jesper Jerrik

THE SOUTH

FONTVIEILLE

LA REGALIDO
~ CONVERTED MILL ~

rue Frédéric-Mistral, 13990 Fontvieille (Bouches-du-Rhône)
TEL 04 90 54 60 22 **FAX** 04 90 54 64 29
E-MAIL regalido@avignon.pacwan.net **WEBSITE** www.relaischateaux.fr/regalido

WE CONTINUE TO BE FOND of this 19thC oil mill, a Relais et Chateaux place which manages to remain informal and friendly despite its elegant furnishings, pricey boutique and high rates – largely thanks to the presence at almost all hours of the welcoming and helpful Jean-Pierre Michel, chef-proprietor.

The Régalido has been converted into a fine *auberge* in a thoroughly Provençal style, decorated with great flair by Mme Michel. There is a charming sitting room full of flowers, and a log fire lit on chilly days. Tables are beautifully set in the elegant, peaceful, stone-vaulted dining room, and there is an atmosphere of well-being which suits the excellent cooking of Jean-Pierre. His style is classic, but he has a penchant for Provençal dishes (seafood, olive oil, herbs and garlic) – and terracotta or cast iron pots appear alongside the silver salvers.

Bedrooms are individually decorated, and very comfortable, with lots of extras in the well-equipped bathrooms. Friendly staff and a pretty, flowery garden – with a terrace surrounded by mimosa and shaded by fig and olive trees – complete the picture.

~

NEARBY Montmajour Abbey; Arles (10 km); the Camargue (10 km); Tarascon (15 km).
LOCATION in middle of village, 9 km NE of Arles; with gardens and ample car parking
FOOD breakfast, lunch, dinner
PRICE €€€€€
ROOMS 15 double and twin, 13 with bath, 2 with shower; all rooms have phone, TV, air conditioning, minibar, hairdrier, safe
FACILITIES 2 sitting rooms, dining room, bar, terrace
CREDIT CARDS AE, DC, MC, V
CHILDREN accepted
DISABLED 1 specially adapted room **PETS** accepted
CLOSED Jan to mid-Feb; restaurant Mon, Tues and lunch on Sat
PROPRIETOR Jean-Pierre Michel

THE SOUTH

FOX-AMPHOUX

AUBERGE DU VIEUX FOX
～ VILLAGE INN ～

place de l'Eglise, Fox-Amphoux, 83670 Barjols (Var)
TEL 04 94 80 71 69 **FAX** 04 94 80 78 38

OUR MOST RECENT ATTEMPT to revisit this old favourite ended in failure: it was cut off by snow – in spring! Reports continue to be satisfactory, however.

Fox-Amphoux, a charming little village, rich in history, has nothing to do with foxes – the name comes from its Roman origins. The inn was once a priory attached to the 12thC church, headquarters of the Knights Templar. Where owner, M. Staudinger, now has his reception desk was a sacristy, with a door leading directly into the church, the bells of which ring out every half hour. M. Staudinger is normally to be found here in his beamed reception area with his cat, and happy to talk about the life and times of Fox-Amphoux and the surrounding area.

Bedrooms are carpeted and some renovation has been carried out (satellite TVs have recently been installed); curtains and bedspreads are in fresh, bright colours. Two small rooms in the tower were once monks' cells. Bathrooms are spotless. There are comfortable leather armchairs in the *salon*; there is also a library and a billiard table. The dining room is full of character and the outside terraces have fine views over Aix and the Alpes de Haute-Provence. Fish is delivered from Marseille and there is an emphasis on fresh farm produce and country cooking, with huge helpings.

NEARBY Lac de Sainte-Croix; Gorges du Verdon; Thoronet Abbey.
LOCATION in centre of small perched village, 32 km N of Brignoles, 37 km W of Draguignan; public car parking in square
FOOD breakfast, lunch, dinner
PRICE €€
ROOMS 8 double and twin, 6 with bath, 2 with shower; all rooms have phone, TV, hairdrier
FACILITIES sitting room, dining room, library, billiards, 2 terraces
CREDIT CARDS AE, MC, V **CHILDREN** accepted but not encouraged
DISABLED no special facilities **PETS** accepted **CLOSED** never
PROPRIETORS Rudolph and Nicole Staudinger

THE SOUTH

GEMENOS

RELAIS DE LA MAGDELEINE
~ COUNTRY HOTEL ~

13420 Gémenos (Bouches-du-Rhône)
TEL 04 42 32 20 16 **FAX** 04 42 32 02 26
WEBSITE www.relais-magdeleine.com

'WE SIMPLY COULD NOT FAULT IT; the atmosphere, welcome and service could not have been better and the food was excellent. Even though we had one of the more expensive rooms at the front, we felt it was very good value.' So begins the latest eulogy on this lovely old *bastide*, a sentiment strongly echoed by our most recent inspector. For those of us who can't or won't pay the prices (or don't like the style) of Relais & Châteaux places, a gracious country house like this is quite a find.

It is a family affair. Daniel Marignane's mother opened the hotel in 1932, and he and his wife have run it with great dedication, charm and good humour for many years. Now their three sons work alongside them, one as the (excellent) chef. Improvements are being made all the time. Many of the bedrooms have been (charmingly) redecorated and all – even the cheapest – are in elegant country taste, with delightful fabrics (often on the walls, too) and antiques and pictures collected by the Marignanes.

On the airy, spacious ground floor, one of the three dining rooms has been sandblasted to expose vaultings and beams in a lovely, light honey-coloured wood. In summer you eat on the romantic gravelled terrace. There's a pool – and a donkey – in the garden, and children will enjoy the giant chessboard and the ping-pong table. It is worth going miles out of one's way to be so warmly welcomed to such a beautiful house.

~

NEARBY Cassis (15 km); Marseille (23 km); Aix-en-Provence (25 km).
LOCATION on the edge of town; ample car parking
FOOD breakfast, lunch, dinner
PRICE €€€-€€€€
ROOMS 24 double, twin and family, all with bath or shower; all rooms have phone, TV
FACILITIES sitting rooms, dining room, lift, terrace, garden, swimming pool, table tennis **CREDIT CARDS** MC, V **CHILDREN** accepted
DISABLED no special facilities **PETS** accepted
CLOSED Dec to mid-Mar
PROPRIETORS M. and Mme Marignane

THE SOUTH

LES FLORETS
∽ COUNTRY INN ∽

route des Dentelles, 84190 Gigondas (Vaucluse)
TEL 04 90 65 85 01 **FAX** 04 90 65 83 80

Flowers abound at Les Florets: all around the hotel on the nearby hills in spring, in pots and vases on the terrace and in the dining room, on the curtains, the lampshades and the pretty hand-painted plates, each one different. The setting, alone in a fold of wooded hills east of Gigondas and facing the dramatic Dentelles de Montmirail, is delightful, and the ambience is loved by everyone who has a hankering for traditional, family-run places. The Bernard family, who bought the hotel in 1960, have long been respected for their honest, straightforward approach, and for the good value food served in the animated dining room or on the lovely leafy terrace in summer. Now they have refurbished all the bedrooms and the once dim corridors, making this a very comfortable place in which to stay for a few days. The bedrooms remain appropriately sober but the bathrooms are a surprise – very opulent for a two-star establishment, with particularly comfortable baths, expensively tiled walls, good towels and intelligent lighting. The rooms in the garden annexe are pleasantest, with little terraces in front for breakfast; one of them is perfect for a family.

The Bernards are also wine-growers; they keep an excellent cellar, or you can drink a bottle of their own Gigondas or Vacqueras for dinner. Good walking country.

∽

NEARBY Côtes-du-Rhône vineyards; Vaison-la-Romaine (15 km).
LOCATION in hills, 2 km E of Gigondas; car parking
FOOD breakfast, lunch, dinner
PRICE €€€
ROOMS 15 double and twin, 1 family, all with bath; all rooms have phone, TV, hairdrier
FACILITIES sitting room, bar, restaurant, terrace
CREDIT CARDS AE, DC, MC, V **CHILDREN** welcome
DISABLED access possible **PETS** accepted
CLOSED Jan, Feb; restaurant Wed
PROPRIETORS Bernard family

THE SOUTH

GINCLA

HOSTELLERIE DU GRAND DUC
~ VILLAGE HOTEL ~

2 route de Boucheville, 11140 Gincla (Aude)
TEL 04 68 20 55 02 **FAX** 04 68 20 61 22
E-MAIL host-du-grand-duc@ataraxie.fr

THE GRAND DUC IS THE EAGLE OWL, presiding (stuffed) over the fireplace in the beamed dining room of this delightful, modest little *logis*. A refurbished *maison de maître* (the *maître* made his living from the surrounding forests), it was opened more than a decade ago as a restaurant by the son of the Bruchet family, a chef, whose father is a wine inspector from Burgundy. The wide central hallway has original stone walls and the fine old staircase has terracotta tiles with oak nosings and wrought-iron balustrade. There's a large dining room and a superb modern kitchen with the latest German electronic oven, where they make their own bread.

The bedrooms are large, but somewhat disappointing with fussy wallpaper, which comes as an aesthetic let-down after the fine, clean lines and whitewashed walls of the dining room.

Admirers return year after year to write flattering remarks in the visitors' book: 'Gets better all the time – everything, reception, service, food and comfort is excellent.' Our inspector – wallpaper excepted – found it charming. There's a pleasant terrace, looking on to a fountain and old lime trees; in summer, you dine outside by candlelight.

~

NEARBY Perpignan (63 km); Quillan (23 km); Forêt de Fanges.
LOCATION in the village NW of Perpignan; car parking
FOOD breakfast, lunch, dinner
PRICE €
ROOMS 12 double, twin and family, all with bath or shower; all rooms have phone, TV, hairdrier, safe
FACILITIES sitting room, bar, dining room, terrace
CREDIT CARDS MC, V
CHILDREN accepted
DISABLED no special facilities
PETS accepted
CLOSED mid-Nov to mid-Mar
PROPRIETORS M. and Mme Bruchet

THE SOUTH

GRIMAUD

LE VERGER
~ COUNTRY HOTEL ~

route de Collobrières, 83360 Grimaud (Var)
TEL 04 94 43 25 93 **FAX** 04 94 43 33 92

THIS IS A VERY UNPRETENTIOUS HOTEL: relaxed, informal and quiet, with attractive bedrooms, a delightful hostess in Anne Zachary, and mostly good food (reports conflict on this, also a complaint about high prices, although on a recent visit our inspector had no complaints).

Only a short distance from the massed traffic jams of the Ste-Maxime–St-Tropez road, Le Verger is a haven of peace and green, with wonderful smooth lawns, mature walnut trees, hydrangeas and even a little stream. There's plenty of shade where you can sit and look up at the surrounding dry hills. The house is typically Provençal, low, pale pink, white-shuttered, with a shallow tiled roof and on two storeys. French windows from ground-floor bedrooms open directly on to the lawn – and then to the pool. Upstairs rooms have private balconies. Decoration is simple: white walls, Provençal prints, antique country furniture and big beds. The largest of the double rooms is notably glamorous, and there is a delightful triple room. Food is served outside in summer, on a wisteria-covered terrace looking out to woods and hills. In cooler weather, you eat before an open fire in the large dining room, with conservatory-style extension.

~

NEARBY St-Tropez (12 km).
LOCATION on D14, off D558, in countryside 1 km outside Grimaud; car parking
FOOD breakfast, lunch, dinner
PRICE €€-€€€€
ROOMS 9 double and twin, 7 with bath, 2 with shower; all rooms have phone, TV; 4 have air conditioning
FACILITIES dining room, terrace, garden, swimming pool
CREDIT CARDS DC, MC, V
CHILDREN accepted over 15
DISABLED rooms on ground floor
PETS accepted
CLOSED Nov to Easter
PROPRIETORS M. and Mme Zachary

THE SOUTH

✷ LE CAGNARD ✷
~ MEDIEVAL INN ~

rue Pontis-Long, Haut-de-Cagnes, 06800 Cagnes-sur-Mer (Alpes-Maritimes)
TEL 04 93 20 73 21 **FAX** 04 93 22 06 39
E-MAIL cagnard@relaischateaux.com **WEBSITE** www.le-cagnard.com

A READER'S REPORT RAISED some doubts about this lovely hotel, perched along the ramparts of an old hill village – specifically about standards of service in the Michelin-starred restaurant. It is far from the most expensive hotel in the Relais et Châteaux group, but it is pricey enough for expectations in this department to be high. We have inspected twice since then: happily all was well on both occasions.

Le Cagnard has been sensitively converted from a series of medieval houses, most with separate street entrances. In the main house there is a stunning, vaulted dining room where you eat by candlelight. But the real knock-out is the upper dining room, leading out on to the terrace: its elaborate painted ceiling slides away at the touch of a button, opening the room to the sky.

Bedrooms vary widely: most retain a medieval feel, thanks to the preservation of features such as stone floors, and are furnished with style, but incongruous exceptions remain. Three rooms in one house have a lovely flowery garden. Access in anything other than a small car is tricky, and getting to some rooms involves a bit of awkward suitcase-lugging.

~

NEARBY Château Grimaldi; Nice (15 km); Grasse (30 km).
LOCATION in middle of hill village, 2 km above main town of Cagnes; car parking 300 m away at entrance to village
FOOD breakfast, lunch, dinner; room service **PRICE** €€€€ **ROOMS** 25; 15 double and twin, 10 apartments, all with bath; all rooms have phone, TV, minibar, hairdrier; most have air conditioning **FACILITIES** dining room, bar, terrace
CREDIT CARDS AE, DC, MC, V **CHILDREN** accepted **DISABLED** no special facilities
PETS accepted
CLOSED never; restaurant closed Thurs lunch and Nov to mid-Dec
PROPRIETORS Barel Laroche family

THE SOUTH

LAGNES

LE MAS DES GRES
~ COUNTRY HOTEL ~

la route d'Apt, 84800 Lagnes (Vaucluse)
TEL 04 90 20 32 85 **FAX** 04 90 20 21 45
E-MAIL info@masdesgres.com **WEBSITE** www.masdesgres.com

NINA AND THIERRY CROVARA run their hotel in a restored farmhouse with such a friendly, relaxed attitude that parents bring their children here from far and wide on family holidays. For the very young, high chairs are provided in the dining room and cots in the bedrooms; and for older children, there's a video machine in one of the sitting rooms, table tennis and a pool outside. Bedrooms are functional – plainly decorated with rough plaster walls and Provençal fabrics – and hard to damage. There are two sets of connecting rooms, where Nina has thoughtfully added black-out blinds to prevent an interior dawn chorus.

Before dinner, guests sit outside on the vine-covered terrace and sip the delicious iced 'orange wine' made according to Thierry's own recipe. He is the chef, and though French, trained in Nina's native Switzerland. He takes his cooking seriously and, after consultations about allergies, likes and dislikes, produces a mainly regional no-choice menu six nights a week (the Crovaras take off one night to fit in with their guests). Menu planning also takes children into account. In between courses, Thierry emerges from his kitchen to introduce himself to new guests and chat to old ones.

There is some noise from the RN100 road but plans to declassify it should lighten the traffic considerably.

~

NEARBY L'Isle-sur-la-Sorgue (6 km); Avignon (28 km); golf.
LOCATION on RN100 outside village; car parking
FOOD breakfast, dinner; light lunch (in July and Aug)
PRICE €€-€€€€
ROOMS 14 double, twin, triple and family, all with bath; all rooms have phone, CD; TV on request
FACILITIES sitting rooms, TV room, dining room, terrace, garden, swimming pool, table tennis **CREDIT CARDS** MC, V **CHILDREN** welcome
DISABLED 2 ground-floor rooms **PETS** not accepted **CLOSED** Dec to Mar
PROPRIETORS Nina and Thierry Crovara

THE SOUTH

LLO

✳ AUBERGE ATALAYA ✳
~ VILLAGE INN ~

66800 Llo (Pyrénées-Orientales)
TEL 04 68 04 70 04 **FAX** 04 68 04 01 29
E-MAIL atalaya@francimel.com

THIS CHARMING SMALL HOTEL in superb unspoiled mountain country had our inspector in raptures: 'Magic'. The little village of Llo straggles up the mountainside, its stone buildings imperceptibly blending into the rock. The Catalan-speaking Cerdagne is half in Spain and half in France and the border seems to be quite indistinct. The Atalaya itself appears to be growing out of the crag on either side of a mountain road and is easily missed. Ingeniously sculpted, it is enchanting, built out of the materials of a ruined *mas* to be entirely in harmony with its natural surroundings. The distinguished cultured atmosphere inside emanates from the personality and taste of Mme Toussaint (who has been running the hotel on her own since the death of her husband). She is charming but speaks little English.

Among the favourable comments made by our readers, we have, however, had one criticism: 'There was a distinct tension and coldness about the senior staff almost amounting to rudeness. We were not the only people to notice this.' More reports please.

Antique furniture and tasteful fabrics give the natural feel of a home rather than a showroom. The terrace has private corners, and everywhere there are expansive, uplifting views. Superb food adds to the exhilarating sense of being on top of the world.

~

NEARBY Odeillo (10 km); Ront-Romeu (15 km).
LOCATION in the middle of the village, 2 km E of Saillagouse; car parking
MEALS breakfast, lunch, dinner **PRICE** €€€ **ROOMS** 13; 12 double, 1 suite, 10 with bath, 3 with shower; all rooms have TV, phone, minibar, safe **FACILITIES** sitting room, dining room, bar, terrace, garden, swimming pool **CREDIT CARDS** MC, V
CHILDREN accepted
DISABLED no special facilities
PETS accepted **CLOSED** early Nov to late Dec, mid-Jan to Easter
PROPRIETOR Mme Toussaint

THE SOUTH

MADIERES

CHATEAU DE MADIERES
～ CHATEAU HOTEL ～

Madières, 34190 Ganges (Hérault)
TEL 04 67 73 84 03 **FAX** 04 67 73 55 71
E-MAIL madieres@wanadoo.fr **WEBSITE** www.hotelvision.com/madieres-chateau

'EXCEPTIONAL,' ENTHUSED OUR INSPECTOR, after visiting this 14thC fortress, perched above the Vis river gorge and rescued from decay in the mid-1980s by the previous owner, Mme Brucy. After a career in fashion design in Paris, she transferred her artistic talent and expertise to more durable materials and, with her husband, created a remarkably successful and exciting blend of ancient and modern beauty. Since her death last year, the hotel has been taken over by M. Guyrat, and we would welcome new reports.

Comfortable rooms have been made within the existing framework of medieval walls and arches, with no loss to the historic feel of the place. No two bedrooms are alike; there's luxury and light and colour in abundance. All have modern bathrooms. The best are spacious and delightfully furnished, with bold colourful fabrics against white walls and oriental rugs on tiled floors. The public rooms are superb. The galleried sitting room has a vast Renaissance fireplace. The vaulted dining room, jutting out of the main building and with a terrace above, has spectacular views across the gorge through arched windows. A courtyard leads to a swimming pool with fitness room and terraces go down to the river below. The food is excellent and the welcome, warm. An ideal place to relax both mind and body.

NEARBY Cirque de Navacalles; Grottes des Demoiselles; Ganges.
LOCATION on hillside overlooking village, on crossroads of D48 and D25; car parking
MEALS breakfast, lunch, dinner
PRICE €€€€
ROOMS 12; 8 double, 4 apartments, all with bath or shower; all rooms have TV, phone, minibar, hairdrier
FACILITIES 3 sitting rooms, 2 dining rooms, 3 terraces, garden, swimming pool, fitness room, table tennis **CREDIT CARDS** AE, DC, MC, V **CHILDREN** accepted
DISABLED no special facilities **PETS** accepted **CLOSED** Nov to late Mar
PROPRIETOR M. Guyrat

THE SOUTH

MALATAVERNE

✳ LA DOMAINE DU COLOMBIER ✳
∼ OLD COACHING INN ∼

route de Donzère, 26780 Malataverne (Drôme)
TEL 04 75 90 86 86 **FAX** 04 75 90 79 40
E-MAIL domainecolombier@voila.fr **WEBSITE** www.domaine-colombier.com

METICULOUSLY RESTORED and full of flowers and colour, this pleasing 14thC stone building, once a stopover for pilgrims on the road to Santiago de Compostela, remains an ideal base for travellers (largely due to its position near the *autoroute* yet in the countryside). With its vine-clad façade, stone staircases, tiled roof, wrought-iron railings and penchant for flowers, this hotel really feels it is on the road to the South.

Wild flowers, gathered in the grounds, brighten every table and service is efficient and professional. When the weather is favourable (and the infamous mistral is not blowing) guests dine on the terrace, which is, again, packed with flowers and absolutely enchanting in the evening glow of lamplight. There is a large restaurant with a vaulted ceiling. Flowers appear everywhere, on the tablecloths, on curtains and bedspreads and wallpaper (floral fabrics and cane furniture are on sale in the hotel shop).

There has been a change of ownership since our last visit. M. and Mme Chochois are now in charge, and we would welcome reports.

∼

NEARBY Montélimar (20 km); Valence (50 km).
LOCATION on private estate, off D144a from A7 to Donzère; car parking
FOOD breakfast, lunch, dinner
PRICE €€€
ROOMS 25; 22 double and twin, 3 suites, 24 with bath, 1 with shower; all rooms have phone, TV, minibar; some rooms have hairdrier
FACILITIES sitting room, restaurant, terrace, garden, swimming pool, pétanque
CREDIT CARDS AE, DC, MC, V
CHILDREN welcome

DISABLED no special facilities
PETS accepted
CLOSED never
PROPRIETORS M. and Mme Chochois

THE SOUTH

MÉNERBES

LA BASTIDE DE MARIE
~ COUNTRY HOTEL ~

route de Bonnieux, Quartier de la Verrerie, 84560 Ménerbes (Vaucluse)
TEL 04 90 72 30 20 **FAX** 04 90 72 54 20
E-MAIL Bastide@c-h-m.com **WEBSITE** www.c-h-m.com

IT WAS TRICKY TO FIND (just one discreet sign, easy to miss, announces the hotel), and even trickier leaving (the automatic gates failed to respond). Once inside, we felt at first, perhaps unreasonably, irritated by the mannered, très *Côte Sud* style of the place, complete with whole walls of purpose-built bookshelves filled with purpose-bought old books, and young men with ponytails and people with pet dogs lounging about. Next we looked round the bedrooms of the old *mas*, now photo-shoot perfect in shades of grey and cream: very smart and comfortable, with excellent bathrooms. But we remained sceptical. Then we sat down to lunch ... which turned out to be quite possibly the best food we had eaten in a long list of recent gourmet experiences, served by a courteous and friendly staff. We began to soften; we began to think about the all-inclusive price, for which you get the room, breakfast, aperitif, lunch or dinner, afernoon tea, and as much of the *domaine* wine (the hotel owns the accompanying vineyard) as you wish. And we decided that, *Côte Sud* notwithstanding, the hotel was not unfairly priced – and really rather seductive.

Opened in June 2000, La Bastide de Marie is a sister to the Coin du Feu in Megève (see page 164); your comments would be appreciated.
~

NEARBY Bonnieux (10 km); Avignon (40 km).
LOCATION in vineyards, 2 km E of Ménerbes, discreetly signposted; car parking
FOOD breakfast, lunch, dinner; room service
PRICE €€€€
ROOMS 14; 8 double and twin, 6 suites, all with bath; all rooms have phone, TV, air conditioning, minibar, safe, hairdrier
FACILITIES sitting room, breakfast room, dining room, conservatory, boutique, wine shop, courtyard, terrace, garden, 2 swimming pools
CREDIT CARDS AE, DC, MC, V
CHILDREN accepted
DISABLED not suitable **PETS** accepted
CLOSED mid-Nov to mid-Mar
PROPRIETORS Jocelyne and Jean-Louis Sibuet

THE SOUTH

MINERVE

RELAIS CHANTOVENT
∼ VILLAGE HOTEL ∼

17 Grande Rue, 34210 Minerve (Hérault)
TEL 04 68 91 14 18 **FAX** 04 68 91 81 99

MINERVE, AN OLD CATHAR REFUGE, is that rare thing – a 14thC fortified hilltop town unspoiled, as yet, by the tourist business. Tourists there are, but the industry has not yet taken over and the small town continues to have an ongoing organic life which is very appealing. With only two narrow streets up and down, cars have to be left below. It is no effort (except for the handicapped) and well worth the inconvenience.

The hotel is really in three parts, each equally attractive. There is a restaurant and stunning terrace looking across a deep gorge to a layered limestone cliff populated by birds and with vineyards on the top level. Then there's a separate building with bedrooms and, around the corner in the next street, an old village house, restored with care and charm, with sitting room and fireplace, furnished in period harmony.

All the decoration is done with attention to detail, but no fuss – light walls, uncluttered, attractive etchings and paintings. The Evenous – he is a Breton and an expert in preparing abundant local produce for the table – are a totally dedicated couple, with taste and finesse and a real love for their home.

∼

NEARBY Carcassonne (45 km); Narbonne (32 km); St-Pons (29 km).
LOCATION in small historic town NW of Carcassonne with no access by car; car parking outside town
FOOD breakfast, lunch, dinner
PRICE (€)
ROOMS 10 double, 1 with bath, 9 with shower
FACILITIES sitting room, dining room, terrace
CREDIT CARDS MC, V
CHILDREN accepted
DISABLED not suitable
PETS accepted
CLOSED mid-Dec to mid-Jan
PROPRIETORS M. and Mme Evenou

THE SOUTH

MOUGINS

MANOIR DE L'ETANG
~ COUNTRY MANOR HOUSE ~

66 allée du Manoir, 06250 Mougins (Alpes-Maritimes)
TEL 04 93 90 01 07 **FAX** 04 92 92 20 70

'THE OVERALL FEEL to this place', writes our latest inspector, 'is expensive and discreet'. A quiet, orderly, elegant retreat from the bustle of fashionable Mougins, its imposing entrance is found in a residential suburb; thereafter a winding drive leads to the extremely pretty 19thC manor house. Pale stone, white shutters, a thick covering of virginia creeper. Inside, the reception area doubles as sitting room, with an open fireplace, strong colours and country furniture. The adjoining restaurant with its intense yellow walls overlooks the swimming pool, and there is a tiled dining terrace for summer eating. Views are low-key: gentle, green, rolling Southern countryside. The colourful garden is filled with different Mediterranean plants and trees.

Our inspector was only able to see one bedroom, which did not particularly impress her, but it was one of the least good. We know from past visits that the better rooms are individually decorated and pretty, with fresh fabrics, white walls and country furniture, some large with private terraces.

The restaurant serves 'Provençale' and 'Gastronomique' menus: monkfish, duck, lamb, *noix de veau poelée au jus de poivrons doux*, and so on.
~

NEARBY Cannes; Grasse; Picasso Museum at Vallauris (10 km).
LOCATION in extensive grounds, on Antibes road, 2 km from town centre; car parking
FOOD breakfast, lunch, dinner
PRICE €€€
ROOMS 21; 17 double and twin, 4 suites, all with bath; all rooms have phone, TV, minibar, safe; 2 have air conditioning
FACILITIES sitting area, restaurant, terrace, garden, swimming pool
CREDIT CARDS AE, DC, MC, V
CHILDREN accepted
DISABLED 2 specially adapted rooms
PETS not accepted
CLOSED Nov to Mar
PROPRIETOR Vincent Labro

THE SOUTH

MOUSTIERS-STE-MARIE

LA BASTIDE DE MOUSTIERS
∽ COUNTRY HOUSE HOTEL ∽

La Grisolière, 04360 Moustiers-Ste-Marie (Alpes-de-Haute-Provence)
TEL 04 92 70 47 47 **FAX** 04 92 70 47 48
E-MAIL bastide@i2m.fr **WEBSITE** www.bastide-moustiers.i2m.fr

THIS IS THE MADELEINE of chef and hotelier supremo Alain Ducasse. In a pale pink restored 17thC *bastide* overlooking green meadows on the edge of a village near the dramatic Verdon gorge, he has created his own rememberance of times past. His country house for lovers of Provence is a resounding triumph; delicious smells of cooking come from the kitchen all day. Chefs, in their whites, can be seen collecting salad and fresh herbs from a vegetable garden which is a work of art in itself. The *bastide* and the discreet swimming pool are surrounded by beds of lavender and each of the 12 romantically decorated bedrooms evokes a colour or an image of Provence. To sit on the terrace in the morning air with a bowl of *café au lait*, fresh bread from the village bakery and home-made rhubarb jam among green glazed pots overflowing with white petunias is a moment to be treasured. Dinner is just as memorable; traditional dishes with plenty of olive oil and garden vegetables. You might find *millefeuille de blettes braisées au parfum de sauge* or *agneau de Beauregard piqué de sarriette et rôti à la broche*. Upstairs, the sheets are being turned down as you eat.

∽

NEARBY Moustiers ceramics; Lac de Ste-Croix; gorges.
LOCATION within walking distance of Moustiers; car and garage parking
FOOD breakfast, lunch, dinner; room service
PRICE €€€€
ROOMS 12; 11 double and twin, 1 suite, all with bath; all rooms have phone, TV, air conditioning, minibar, hairdrier
FACILITIES sitting room, dining room, bar, terrace, garden, swimming pool, riding
CREDIT CARDS AE, DC, MC, V
CHILDREN welcome
DISABLED access possible
PETS not accepted
CLOSED never
PROPRIETOR Alain Ducasse

THE SOUTH

LE GRIMALDI
~ TOWN HOTEL ~

15 rue Grimaud, 06000 Nice (Alpes-Maritimes)
TEL 04 93 16 00 24 **FAX** 04 93 87 00 24
E-MAIL zedde@le-grimaldi.com **WEBSITE** www.le-grimaldi.com

NOT TO BE CONFUSED with the rather dreary-looking Nice Grimaldi just down the road, this upmarket and stylish little hotel was opened only in 1999. Englishwoman Joanna Zedde and her French husband gutted the fairly basic hotel that already occupied the elegant 1920s town house with its white shutters and wrought-iron balconies, aiming for something altogether smarter. The location – a lively area of stylish shops, bars and restaurants – is ideal, and the beach is only a ten-minute walk.

The ground floor is occupied by a large reception area decorated in bright reds and yellows which doubles as breakfast room, bar and sitting room; it is full of fresh flowers and leafy plants. The comfortable bedrooms are all tastefully (and not too fussily) decorated with co-ordinating Soleido fabrics and wallpapers set against cool white. Some are done out in vibrant sun colours, others are more restrained in shades of blue and green and the delicate wrought-iron furniture fits in well. There are two types of room; the 'Superiors' have sufficient space for an invitingly squashy sofa. Bright yellow towels make a splash in the immaculate all-white bathrooms. A classy B&B.

~

NEARBY Vieux Nice; Opéra; beach.
LOCATION on street just W of Vieux Nice; public car parking nearby (50 m)
FOOD breakfast
PRICE €€€
ROOMS 23 double and twin, all with bath; all rooms have phone, TV, air conditioning, minibar, safe, hairdrier
FACILITIES bar/breakfast room/sitting room, lift
CREDIT CARDS AE, DC, MC, V
CHILDREN accepted
DISABLED no special facilities
PETS accepted
CLOSED 3 weeks Jan
PROPRIETOR Joanna Zedde

THE SOUTH

NICE

LA PÉROUSE
~ TOWN HOTEL ~

11 quai Rauba-Capeu, 06300 Nice (Alpes-Maritimes)
TEL 04 93 62 34 63 **FAX** 04 93 62 59 41
E-MAIL lp@hroy.com **WEBSITE** www.hotel-la-perouse.com/lp

YOU WILL FIND LA PÉROUSE at the eastern end of the seafront, right beneath Nice's Château. Only the reception is on the street; all the rest is out back.

The reception area sets the tone; a welcoming little space done out in country fabrics and rustic furniture. The rest of the hotel – it was fully refurbished a couple of years ago – follows suit, with a mix of Provençal and country fabrics, pale floor tiles, bleached wood and wrought-iron furniture, warm sunny colours, country prints. Rustic terracotta tiles in the bathrooms, stone colours, fluffy white tiles. All rooms have a balcony or terrace of some kind; some are huge, especially those on the top floor; some have fabulous views over the sea.

The communal terrace lies right under the overhanging cliff and has a small heated pool. There is also a roof terrace with an outdoor Jacuzzi, small fitness suite, sauna and solarium. The breakfast room is pretty, with sofas and tables laden with the day's papers. You can eat meals under the lemon trees in summer.

The hotel is immaculately maintained with a very friendly staff and management.

~

NEARBY Château; port; Vieux Nice; Marché aux Fleurs; beach.
LOCATION on seafront; valet car parking in public car park
FOOD breakfast; lunch and dinner mid-May to mid-Sep
PRICE €€€€
ROOMS 63; 60 double and twin, 3 suites, all with bath or shower; all rooms have phone, TV, air conditioning, minibar, safe, hairdrier
FACILITIES dining room, breakfast room, bar, fitness room, lift, terraces, swimming pool **CREDIT CARDS** AE, DC, MC, V
CHILDREN accepted
DISABLED access difficult
PETS accepted
CLOSED never
MANAGER Laure Giometti

THE SOUTH

NICE

WINDSOR
~ TOWN HOTEL ~

11 rue Dalpozzo, 06000 Nice (Alpes-Maritimes)
TEL 04 93 88 59 35 **FAX** 04 93 88 94 57
E-MAIL contact@hotelwindsornice.com **WEBSITE** www.hotelwindsornice.com

THE HOTEL WINDSOR OCCUPIES an unassuming, turn-of-the-century building in a residential area of Nice not far from shops and the station. Once in the reception hall, however, a Thai shrine takes centre stage, Indonesian hangings adorn the walls and a delicate suspended sculpture occupies one corner. The soundtrack of a space ship launch livens up the lift ride to the fifth floor which has been turned into a fitness room (eastern style) and Moroccan hammam. This place is definitely different and very *à la mode*.

Twenty of the bedrooms have been decorated by contemporary artists, mostly along clean, simple lines. Some feature white on white, others bold colours, one has a wall covered in graffiti; each is unique. One room is decorated in sand colours by an artist who imagined himself in the chamber of a pyramid. Gold stars shine out of a midnight-blue night sky and music from Lawrence of Arabia starts up when you go into the bathroom. The remaining bedrooms are more uniform with modern frescoes of Italy or oriental scenes, natural fabrics and stylish white bathrooms; some have terraces. In summer, breakfast is served in the delightful garden full of exotic trees, shrubs and flowers, in winter in the bistro-style restaurant.

~

NEARBY Musée Massenat; Contemporary Art Museum; Vieux Nice.
LOCATION in centre of the new town, between train station and sea; car parking
FOOD breakfast, lunch in summer, dinner
PRICE ©©
ROOMS 58; 56 double and twin, 2 suites, all with bath or shower; all rooms have phone, TV, air conditioning, minibar, safe
FACILITIES restaurant, bar, fitness room, hammam, lift, terrace, garden, swimming pool
CREDIT CARDS AE, DC, MC, V
DISABLED no special facilities
PETS accepted
CLOSED never
PROPRIETOR Bernard Rédolfi

THE SOUTH

OLARGUES

DOMAINE DE RIEUMEGE
~ COUNTRY HOTEL ~

route de St-Pons, 34390 Olargues (Hérault)
TEL 04 67 97 73 99 **FAX** 04 67 97 78 52
E-MAIL rieumege@wanadoo.fr

IN A LOVELY, NATURAL SETTING of hills, rock, water, trees, shrubs and soft green grass, this sensitively restored 17thC stone house is in the middle of the Haut Languedoc national park and close to Olargues, one of the villages classed as the most beautiful in France. It is a perfect place for a stroll after dinner or before breakfast. There are few hotels in this area and although there is a road nearby, little traffic noise filters through. Deep, restful calm prevails. The attractive high-ceilinged beamed restaurant retains, even after restoration, its country barn origins. (The food our inspector had was excellent; the 'pleasant, not-too-professional service' was also much appreciated.)

Bedrooms are simply furnished with respectable antique pieces – and comfortable. The beamed sitting room, with open fire in cooler weather and oil lamps, is cosy, with some handsome antique furniture. A smaller separate building has been adapted to provide a luxury room and suite, complete with its own garden and private swimming pool. There is a wide range of accommodation here; three categories offer 'comfort', 'superior' and 'prestige', so there is something for all pockets. M. Henrotte took over from the Sylvas two years ago. Reports please.

~

NEARBY St-Pons (17 km); Castres (70 km); Béziers (50 km).
LOCATION in countryside 3 km outside Olargues; car parking
FOOD breakfast, lunch, dinner
PRICE ⓔⓔ
ROOMS 14; 10 double, 3 family, 1 suite, all with bath or shower; all rooms have phone; TV on request
FACILITIES sitting room, dining room, garden, swimming pool, tennis
CREDIT CARDS AE, MC, V **CHILDREN** accepted
DISABLED no special facilities
PETS accepted
CLOSED Jan to Mar
PROPRIETOR M. Henrotte

THE SOUTH

LE RELAIS DU VAL D'ORBIEU
~ CONVERTED MILL ~

11200 Ornaisons (Aude)
TEL 04 68 27 10 27 **FAX** 04 68 27 52 44 **E-MAIL** Relais.Du.Val.Dorbieu@wanadoo.fr
WEBSITE www.perso.wanadoo.fr/relais.du.val.dorbieu/

THIS HOTEL HAS BEEN cleverly designed to provide everything which the overnight traveller or long-stay holidaymaker could wish for – made to measure. Extensions with red-tiled roofs have been added to the original old mill to form an integrated complex of rooms and suites, four sides of which enclose a lush, secluded cloister. Rooms are bright, modern and newly decorated – 15 have their own terrace. The choice of accommodation is particularly flexible for families with children. Although parts of the hotel are old, there's no feeling of a museum but rather a highly efficient and comfortable hostelry. There is ample room for everyone in the spacious grounds. The swimming pool is equally serious and professional and is flanked by impressive stands of oleander. The excellent cooking – fish dishes are recommended – and wine cellar reflect the personal passion of the owner, M. Gonzalvez, the son of a *vigneron*. Quite a number of English wine merchants make this hotel their base to sample the wines of the Corbières. Another regular booking is by American cyclists who tour the region on two wheels. There's a full-time gardener and home-grown vegetables and herbs feature prominently on the menus.

~

NEARBY Narbonne (14 km); Carcassonne (44 km).
LOCATION in countryside outside Ornaisons; car parking
FOOD breakfast, lunch, dinner
PRICE €€€-€€€€
ROOMS 20; 14 double, 6 family suites, all with bath; all rooms have phone, TV, minibar, hairdrier
FACILITIES sitting room, dining room, meeting room, solarium, terraces, garden, swimming pool, tennis, practice golf, table tennis, *pétanque*
CREDIT CARDS AE, DC, MC, V
CHILDREN accepted
DISABLED 1 specially adapted room **PETS** accepted
CLOSED Dec; restaurant lunch Nov to Feb
PROPRIETORS M. and Mme Gonzalvez

THE SOUTH

PEILLON

AUBERGE DE LA MADONE
~ VILLAGE INN ~

06440 Peillon (Alpes-Maritimes)
TEL 04 93 79 91 17 **FAX** 04 93 79 99 36
E-MAIL madone@chateauxhotels.com **WEBSITE** www.chateauxhotels.com/madone

'**H**OW STUNNING', commented a recent visitor on seeing the setting for the first time. 'Delightful' was the one-word verdict offered by another on the top-of-the-range family-run *logis*, which happily combines a sense of special hospitality with affordable (though not low) prices. The Millos have now opened an annexe in the old part of the village – Auberge du Pourtail. Rooms here are less expensive and you eat at the Madone.

You may think that you have taken a wrong turning as you first spy Peillon, perched impossibly above, with little sign of any road leading up. Time stands still here. The medieval village consists of a few dark cobbled alleys leading up to the church, and tall stone houses looking out over rocky crests and distant forests.

The *auberge* is set just outside the walled village itself. Behind, paths lead off into the hills, past the grazing sheep with their tinkling bells; in front is the village car park and *boules* area. Within, the rather small bedrooms (with equally small balconies) are attractive and comfortable with stylish all-white bathrooms. Meals are served on the sunny terrace, under a large awning, or in the welcoming Provençal-style dining room. Cooking is above average, using organic local ingredients. An all-weather tennis court is another of the hotel's attractions.

~

NEARBY Monaco – palace, museums, exotic gardens; Nice (19 km).
LOCATION on edge of perched village, 19 km NE of Nice; ample car parking
FOOD breakfast, lunch, dinner
PRICE €€€
ROOMS 19; 16 double and twin, 8 with bath, 8 with shower, 3 suites with bath; all rooms have phone, TV; 9 have hairdrier
FACILITIES sitting room, bar, TV room, 2 dining rooms, terrace, tennis
CREDIT CARDS MC, V **CHILDREN** welcome
DISABLED access difficult **PETS** not accepted
CLOSED mid-Oct to mid-Dec, 2 weeks Jan; restaurant closed Wed
PROPRIETORS Millo family

THE SOUTH

PIOLENC

AUBERGE DE L'ORANGERIE
~ TOWN INN ~

4 rue de l'Ormeau, 84420 Piolenc (Vaucluse)
TEL 04 90 29 59 88 **FAX** 04 90 29 67 74
E-MAIL orangerie@orangerie.net **WEBSITE** www.orangerie.net

THIS CURIOUS LITTLE *auberge*, almost submerged by a jungle of greenery, is just off the main street of a small town that prides itself on its garlic festival. Owners Gérard and Micky Delarocque have given an original and imaginative 'retro' feeling to an 18thC house in a gated courtyard. The lively restaurant draws in local business people at lunchtime with dishes like *filets de rascasse à la provençale* and *noisettes de gigot d'agneau au basilic frais*. In the dining room, a collection of striking Georges de La Tour pictures are, in fact, painted by M. Delarocque, a talented copyist (and single-malt connoisseur). But the real fun starts upstairs, with Madame's evocative decoration and her charming written 'thoughts' on the theme of each room, which hang framed on the walls. The George Sand room has a portrait of the writer by Delacroix – or could it be a copy by M. Delarocque? The room named after Mme Récamier has a chaise-longue like the ones she made so fashionable. Behind the bohemianism, though, is a professional management, with orthodox ideas on things such as rules: no washing of clothes in bedrooms, for example.

Guests (minus children and pets) can also stay in 'La Mandarine' nearby, a Provençal farmhouse in its own grounds, with six rooms, and a pool.

~

NEARBY Orange (5 km); Avignon (35 km).
LOCATION in a side street off the main street; car parking
FOOD breakfast, lunch, dinner
PRICE (€); half-board obligatory in high season
ROOMS 5 double, 2 with bath, 3 with shower; all rooms have TV
FACILITIES dining room, terrace, garden
CREDIT CARDS MC, V
CHILDREN accepted
DISABLED no special facilities
PETS accepted
CLOSED never
PROPRIETORS M. and Mme Delarocque

HET ZUIDEN

LE POËT-LAVAL

LES HOSPITALIERS
~ VERBOUWD KASTEEL ~

Le Poët-Laval, 26160 La Bégude-de-Mazenc (Drôme)
TEL 04 75 46 22 32 **FAX** 04 75 46 49 99
E-MAIL hotel.hospitaliers@wanadoo.fr

LEZERS BLIJVEN ONDER DE INDRUK van dit aparte hotel. Wij ook trouwens. Het bevindt zich binnen de muren van een 13de-eeuws kasteel, op een toonaangevende plek boven het middeleeuwse dorp Le Poët-Laval (400 m).

De mooie oude, stenen gebouwen maakten vroeger deel uit van een bastion van de Ridders van Malta (het Maltezer kruis is het symbool van dit hotel). Spectaculair uitzicht over het beboste platteland en de heuvels vanaf het zwembad en het terras – waar tevens maaltijden worden geserveerd. De zeer comfortabele zitkamer bevindt zich – zeer ongewoon – op de bovenverdieping en deelt dit uitzicht. De vader van eigenaar Bernard Morin was een kunsthandelaar. Er zijn dan ook veel originele schilderijen te vinden in de slaapkamers, alsmede antieke, handbewerkte hardhouten meubels. Het restaurant heeft ook een interessante verzameling schilderijen. De tafels worden gedekt met mooi porselein, witte linnen tafelkleden en kaarsen. De bediening is vlekkeloos en het eten voortreffelijk. Het menu verandert dagelijks. De ontvangst van de charmante familie Morin is hartelijk en oprecht. De oudste zoon, Bernard, nam onlangs het hotel over van zijn vader en hij kookt graag met verse producten. Zijn jongere broer is de sommelier - er is een uitgebreide wijnkelder. Een verrukkelijk hotel dat een blijvende indruk zal maken op alle gasten.

~

OMGEVING Montélimar (20 km); Viviers (30 km).
LOCATIE in oud dorp, 5 km ten westen van Dieulefit; parkeerterrein vlakbij
ETEN ontbijt, lunch, diner **PRIJS** €€
KAMERS 24; 21 tweepersoons, 20 met bad, 1 met douche, 3 familiekamers met bad; alle kamers telefoon
FACILITEITEN 2 zitkamers, 2 eetkamers, bar, terras, zwembad
CREDITCARDS AE, DC, MC, V **KINDEREN** toegestaan
GEHANDICAPTEN geen speciale voorzieningen **HUISDIEREN** toegestaan
GESLOTEN half nov. tot feb.
EIGENAAR Bernard Morin

HET ZUIDEN

LE PONTET-AVIGNON

✳ AUBERGE DE CASSAGNE ✳
❧ HOTEL IN BUITENWIJK ❧

450 allée de Cassagne, 84130 Le Pontet-Avignon (Vaucluse)
TEL 04 90 31 04 18 **FAX** 04 90 32 25 09
E-MAIL cassagne@wanadoo.fr **WEBSITE** www.valruges.cassagne.com

LE PONTET IS EEN BUITENWIJK van Avignon met brede, drukke wegen en nieuwe woningbouwprojecten, wat nou niet direct de plek is voor een interessant hotel. Maar achter een hoge muur staat een voormalige cottage van het nabijgelegen château dat met veel moeite is omgebouwd tot een opmerkelijk comfortabel en aangenaam hotel. De keuken, met één Michelin-ster, wordt gerund door een leerling van Bocuse, en heeft een uitgebreide wijnkelder. Tijdens diner telden wij maar liefst 20 verschillende kaassoorten en 45 Côtes du Rhône-wijnen. Op het enigszins krappe terrein slaagt het hotel erin om ruimte te creëren door slim om te gaan met gazons, paden en landschapsarchitectuur. Alles wordt onberispelijk onderhouden; de cipressen zien eruit alsof iemand ze elke avond borstelt en kamt. De slaapkamers zijn groot en mooi, met frisse Provençaalse prenten. Ze hebben ook een eigen terras met tafel en stoelen, waar de gasten kunnen ontbijten – en dat doen ze ook. Kamers 16 en 17 bevinden zich zowat in het zwembad en zijn 's avonds zalig afgezonderd en rustig, vooral wanneer het in het restaurant een drukte van jewelste is door de mensen uit de buurt en de hotelgasten.

❧

OMGEVING Avignon (4 km); Aix-en-Provence (82 km); Arles (36 km).
LOCATIE in a rustige buitenwijk; parkeerterrein
ETEN ontbijt, lunch, diner   **PRIJS** €€€ - €€€€
KAMERS 30 tweepersoons, 28 met bad, 2 met douche; alle kamers hebben telefoon, TV, haardroger, minibar, kluis, airconditioning
FACILITEITEN 2 zitkamers, eetkamer, bar, fitness, sauna, tuin, zwembad, tennis, tafeltennis, boules   **CREDITCARDS** AE, DC, MC, V   **KINDEREN** welkom

GEHANDICAPTEN 3 aangepaste kamers
HUISDIEREN toegestaan
GESLOTEN nooit
EIGENAARS M. Gallon, M. Trestour en M. Boucher

HET ZUIDEN

PORQUEROLLES (ILE DE)

AUBERGE DES GLYCINES
~ HOTEL OP EILAND ~

place d'Armes, 83400 Ile de Porquerolles (Var)
TEL 04 94 58 30 36 **FAX** 04 9458 35 22
E-MAIL auberge.glycines@wanadoo.fr

ER ZIJN GEEN AUTO'S TE VINDEN op het eiland Porquerolles en als de dagjes-mensen eenmaal weg zijn is het er stil. Dit verrukkelijke hotel is een leuk, nonchalant en stralende gelegenheid in de kleine haven van Porquerolles. Het ligt het vlakbij rotsachtige beekjes om in te zwemmen en bij schitterende duikplaatsen.

Het hotel heeft lichtgele en blauwe luiken en is gebouwd rondom een binnenplaats vol citroenbomen, blauwe regen en een vijgenboom. Hier wordt het diner geserveerd op tafels met rode Provençaalse tafelkleedjes, beschut door de witte parasols. Het hele hotel is ingericht in stralende, frisse kleuren en is charmant en stijlvol. Beneden sieren droogbloemen en rieten hoeden de muren. Er liggen terracottategels op de vloeren. De slaapkamers hebben verschillende thema's en de moderne badkamers zijn smetteloos en hebben lichte tegels. De slaapkamers hebben Provençaalse prenten, spreien en gordijnen. De kamers zijn in het bezit van balkonnet-jes of terrassen met uitzicht op de binnenplaats of over de pijn- en eucalyptusbomen. Het diner bestaat uit veel verse vis en is van uitstekende kwaliteit. Wij genoten van loup de mer flambée met venkel, gegrild in een zoute korst, die werd opgebroken vóór het serveren. Jong, vriendelijk personeel; ongedwongen sfeer.

~

OMGEVING stranden; duiken; fietsen en wandelen; nationaal park
LOCATIE in Porquerolles op autovrij eiland, 5 minuten van strand; 20 minuten met boot vanaf La Tour Fondue (Hyères) of per watertaxi
ETEN ontbijt, lunch, diner **PRIJS** €€
KAMERS 13; 12 tweepersoons, 1 driepersoons, 10 met bad, 3 met douche; alle kamers hebben telefoon, TV, airconditioning
FACILITEITEN eetkamer, binnenhof, terras
CREDITCARDS DC, MC, V **KINDEREN** welkom
GEHANDICAPTEN geen speciale voorzieningen
HUISDIEREN toegestaan **GESLOTEN** half tot eind jan.
EIGENAAR Florence Venture

HET ZUIDEN

PORT-CROS (ILE DE)

LE MANOIR
~ HOTEL AAN DE KUST ~

Ile de Port-Cros, 83400 Hyères (Var)
TEL 04 94 05 90 52 **FAX** 04 94 05 90 89

PORT-CROS, HET EILAND dat in het midden ligt van de drie Iles d'Hyères, is een natuurreservaat waar geen voertuigen worden toegelaten, zelfs geen fietsen. Er wonen niet meer dan een handjevol mensen, dus het is er heel rustig. Het grote, 19de-eeuwse landhuis met groene luiken past perfect bij de groene en serene omgeving. De huidige eigenaar, Pierre Buffet, runt het hotel sinds de jaren zestig. Temidden van het weelderige, subtropische gebied vlakbij zee, lijkt het veel verder weg dan de 20 minuten die de pont erover doet om bij de drukke kust te komen. Er zijn verschillende zitkamers om in te relaxen, te lezen of te kaarten. En de ruime, comfortabele witte slaapkamers zijn eenvoudig maar elegant gemeubileerd met 19de-eeuwse meubels. Sommige kamers hebben een eigen terras.

Het omliggende terrein is weids en aantrekkelijk, vol met palm-, eucalyptus- en oleanderbomen. Er is ook een schitterend zwembad waaraan u kunt lunchen. U kunt gaan picknicken of een ontspannend tochtje maken in de motorboot van het hotel naar één van de nabijgelegen baaien. U moet lopen naar het dichtstbijzijnde zandstrand – ongeveer 25 minuten. De Provençaalse kookkunst wordt geprezen.

~

OMGEVING nationale park; Hyères; Toulon; Porquerolles.
LOCATIE op eigen terrein bij zee, op autovrij eiland
ETEN ontbijt, lunch, diner
PRIJS €€; half pension verplicht
KAMERS 22; 17 tweepersoons, 5 familiekamers, 15 met bad, 7 met douche; alle kamers hebben telefoon sommige met airconditioning
CREDITCARDS MC, V
KINDEREN toegestaan
GEHANDICAPTEN kamers op begane grond
HUISDIEREN niet toegestaan
GESLOTEN okt. tot april
EIGENAAR Pierre Buffet

HET ZUIDEN

RAMATUELLE

LA FERME D'HERMES
~ CHATEAU-HOTEL ~

route de l'Escalet, 83350 Ramatuelle (Var)
TEL 04 94 79 27 80 **FAX** 04 94 79 26 86

M ME VERRIER HEEFT DIT CHARMANTE HOTEL vernoemd naar haar geliefde, overleden Welsh-terriër. Inmiddels heeft een jonge versie zijn plaats ingenomen. Het verslag van onze inspecteur was absoluut lovend. 'Dit is een betoverende plek – voortreffelijk.'

Het hotel werd niet zo lang geleden gebouwd, maar is al helemaal ingeburgerd door de klimplanten en de grote hoeveelheid bomen, struiken, en groen. De wijnranken reiken bijna tot in het zwembad. Binnen is er veel aandacht besteed aan de details. De kamers zijn helemaal wit, met terracottategels – gepoetst met bijenwas – en bijpassende Provençaalse stoffen. De meubels zijn oud en van blank grenenhout. De slaapkamers hebben een eigen terras, een betegeld keukentje met een gas- en elektrisch fornuis, een oven, een gootsteen en een koelkast. Theedoeken worden elke dag vervangen en elke zaterdagochtend keert Madame terug van de markt met veel verse bloemen. Ontbijt bestaat uit vers brood en bolletjes en zelfgemaakte jam – dit is de enige maaltijd die hier wordt geserveerd – en kan op elk terras worden gegeten. De gasten worden als vrienden behandeld. Mme Verrier heeft aan alles gedacht: wekker, elektrisch muggenafweermiddel, strijkijzer en plank, een föhn, en zelfs een tandenborstel voor 'het geval dat'.

~

OMGEVING Ramatuelle (2 km); St-Tropez (10 km).
LOCATIE op eigen terrein in smalle laan 2 km van de stranden; parkeerterrein
ETEN ontbijt
PRIJS €€€
KAMERS 10 tweepersoons, alle met bad, telefoon, TV, kitchenette, terras
FACILITEITEN zitkamer, tuin, zwembad
CREDITCARDS DC, MC, V
KINDEREN wordt niet aangemoedigd
GEHANDICAPTEN geen speciale voorzieningen **HUISDIEREN** toegestaan
GESLOTEN nov. tot april
EIGENAAR Mme Verrier

Het Zuiden

La Figuiere
~≫ Hotel aan het strand ≪~

route de Tahiti, 83350 Ramatuelle (Var)
Tel 04 94 97 18 21 **Fax** 04 94 97 68 48

Er ontstaan in het hoogseizoen grote verkeersopstoppingen langs deze weg naar La Figuière. Het is echter ook de enige weg naar het bekende Tahiti-strand dat maar 500 meter verder ligt. Klinkt vreselijk? Het hotel zelf is verrassend vredig. U treft hier een oude boerenhoeve met meerdere aangebouwde vleugels en bijgebouwen. Het hotel ligt van de weg af in een grote tuin die grenst aan een wijngaard. In de tuin staan overal vijgen- en oleanderbomen. Het heeft een groot uitnodigend zwembad met veel luie stoelen. De kamers bevinden zich in enigszins onaantrekkelijke bijgebouwen, ze zijn eenvoudig en onberispelijk met witte muren, bijpassende Provençaalse stoffen, zware witte katoenen spreien en antiek. Veel slaapkamers hebben een eigen terras en zijn zeer rustig. De geur van bijenwas is door het hele huis te ruiken. De badkamers zijn ruim en de maisonnettes met twee bedden op een hoger niveau zijn zeer geschikt voor gezinnen.

Het restaurant, onder ander management, bevindt zich in een gebouw bij het zwembad. Er worden traditionele Provençaalse gerechten geserveerd en in de zomer kunt u op het terras eten.

~

Omgeving Tahiti strand (500 m); St-Tropez (2.5 km).
Locatie 2.5 km ten zuiden van St-Tropez op Rue L'Escalet; parkeerterrein
Eten ontbijt, lunch, diner
Prijs €€ - €€€
Kamers 40; 33 tweepersoons, 4 driepersoons, 3 familiekamers, 37 met bad, 3 met douche; alle kamers hebben telefoon, TV, airconditioning, minibar, kluis
Faciliteiten zitkamers, terras, tuin, zwembad, tennisbaan
Creditcards AE, DC, MC, V
Kinderen toegestaan
Gehandicapten 2 aangepaste kamers
Huisdieren toegestaan
Gesloten half okt. tot april
Eigenaar Mme Chaix

HET ZUIDEN

ROQUEBRUNE

LES DEUX FRERES
~ DORPSRESTAURANT-MET-KAMERS ~

06190 Roquebrune-Village Cap Martin (Alpes-Maritimes)
TEL 04 93 28 99 00 **FAX** 04 93 28 99 10
E-MAIL 2freres@webstore.fr **WEBSITE** www.lesdeuxfreres.com

DE 'TWEE BROERS' ZIJN DE TWEE ROTSEN die achter dit kleine hotel-restaurant opdoemen. Het hotel ligt op het plein van het onbedorven dorp Roquebrune. Het heeft een terras dat uitkijkt over een wirwar van villa's en exotische tuinen, de zee en, in de verte, de (onaangename) contouren van Monte Carlo.

Willem Bonestroo heeft een passie voor grote motorfietsen, maar dat weerhoudt hem er niet van Les Deux Frères met aanstekelijk enthousiasme te runnen. Het witgekalkte gebouw was vroeger een schoolgebouw (tot 1965) en hij heeft alles verfrissend eenvoudig gehouden. De benedenverdieping bestaat uit een bar/restaurant, een rustieke kamer gevuld met lange planten, prachtige verse bloemen en interessante, moderne kunst. Wij waren vooral onder de indruk van het eten: Provençaalse kookkunst met eigen inbreng – gemarineerde gamba's in gember en geserveerd met sinaasappelschil. De grappige slaapkamers zijn eenvoudig maar ingericht met een knipoog; de één is in nautische stijl met patrijspoorten als spiegels en roeiriemen als gordijnrails, een ander ('De 1001 Nachten') met goud en donkerblauw en zijden gordijnen terwijl de kleine witte bruidskamer is voorzien van een bed met baldakijn en een romantisch uitzicht.

~

OMGEVING Monte Carlo (5 km); stranden (5 km); Nice (22 km).
LOCATIE in dorpscentrum; openbare parkeerterrein in de buurt
ETEN ontbijt, lunch, diner
PRIJS €€
KAMERS 10; 8 tweepersoons, 2 eenpersoons, 9 met bad; alle kamers hebben telefoon, TV, video, haardroger
FACILITEITEN eetkamer, bar, terras
CREDITCARDS AE, DC, MC, V
GEHANDICAPTEN 1 kamer op begane grond **HUISDIEREN** toegestaan
GESLOTEN nooit; restaurant gesloten half nov. tot half dec. en zo. en ma. avond in winter
EIGENAAR Willem Bonestroo

HET ZUIDEN

ROQUEFORT-LES-PINS

❋ AUBERGE DU COLOMBIER ❋
～ CHATEAU HOTEL ～

06330 Roquefort-les-Pins (Alpes-Maritimes)
TEL 04 92 60 33 00 **FAX** 04 93 77 07 03
E-MAIL info@auberge-du-colombier.com

WE HOUDEN DIT EENVOUDIGE HOTEL toch in de gids ondanks een negatieve ervaring van een recente bezoeker. Hij vertelde: 'mijn eerste indruk was niet bijzonder goed, maar ik kon niet zo goed rondkijken omdat er een feest aan de gang was.' De prijzen van dit hotel zijn laag ondanks de grote tuin met terrassen en een aangenaam zwembad. De eenvoudige, Provençaalse, slaapkamers zijn keurig en comfortabel. De tuinen en het zwembad zijn gewoonweg prachtig.

Het gebouw is oud, laag en wit. De grote aantrekkingskracht is de omgeving –het hotel wordt omringd door lage, schaduwrijke bomen, met uitzicht over de beboste heuvels en de zee. Er is een aantrekkelijk terras om te eten in de zomer, een tennisbaan en meer dan genoeg ruimte rondom het zwembad om te luieren. Met slecht weer eet u in de aangename eetkamer met rustieke meubels. Het diner is hun trots en het ontbijt bestaat o.a. uit de 'lekkerste taartjes ooit'. Wij zijn benieuwd naar uw ervaringen.

OMGEVING St-Paul (10 km); Grasse (15 km).
LOCATIE op platteland bij de D2085, 15 km ten oosten van Grasse, 18 km ten noorden van Cannes; parkeerterrein
ETEN ontbijt, lunch, diner
PRIJS € - €€€
KAMERS tweepersoons, 2 appartementen, alle met bad, telefoon, TV
FACILITEITEN 2 eetkamers, zitkamer, bar, terras, tuin, zwembad, tennis, privé nachtclub
CREDITCARDS AE, DC, MC, V   **KINDEREN** toegestaan   **GEHANDICAPTEN** geen speciale voorzieningen
HUISDIEREN toegestaan
GESLOTEN jan
EIGENAAR Jacques Wolff

HET ZUIDEN

ROUSSILLON

MAS DE GARRIGON
~ VILLA OP HET PLATTELAND ~

route de St-Saturnin d'Apt, Roussillon, 84220 Gordes (Vaucluse)
TEL 04 90 05 63 22 **FAX** 04 90 05 70 01 **E-MAIL** mas-de-garrigon@wanadoo.fr
WEBSITE www.avignon-et-provence.com/mas-garrigon

'WE ARRIVEERDEN ZONDER RESERVERING en kregen heel vriendelijk een kamer aangeboden. De kamer was in Provençaalse stijl en zeer comfortabel, de badkamer groot en goed uitgerust. Het zwembad is een genot, vooral na een lange autorit, en de omgeving is een aangenaam wandelgebied. Het diner was gewoonweg heerlijk.'

Mas de Garrigon is een oude favoriet die ons veel plezier blijft bezorgen. De gezellige en stijlvolle sfeer wordt zeer gewaardeerd. Dit hotel, dat speciaal werd gebouwd door Christiane Druart in 1979, heeft iets van een traditionele Provençaalse boerenhoeve met een warrig dak waarvan de pannen kriskras door elkaar heen zijn gelegd. Het hotel staat geïsoleerd temidden van pijnbomen en planten, met uitzicht op de Luberon-heuvels. Aan de voorkant ligt een overdekt zwembad dat een landelijk uitzicht deelt met de zonnige terrassen van de slaapkamers. Het gebouw heeft meer van een woonhuis dan een conventioneel hotel. De gasten worden aangemoedigd om te neuzen in de goed aangevulde bibliotheek of om te luisteren naar klassieke muziek in de salon bij de openhaard. Het diner is vaak een levendig gebeuren waar gasten gezellig met elkaar kletsen in de intieme eetkamer die uitkijkt op het zwembad. Het eten, bereid door de hoog geprezen chef-kok Jean-Paul Minery, is heerlijk, met het accent op plaatselijke ingrediënten (truffels in de winter).

~

OMGEVING Roussillon (3 km) Gordes (7 km); Village des Bories (5 km).
LOCATIE op platteland bij de D2, 3 km ten noorden van Roussillon, 7 km ten oosten van de Gordes; parkeerterrein
ETEN ontbijt, lunch, diner **PRIJS** €€€; halfpension verplicht van mei tot okt.
KAMERS 9; 7 tweepersoons, 2 familiekamers, alle met bad, telefoon, TV, minibar en terras **FACILITEITEN** zitkamer, 3 eetkamers, bar, bibliotheek, terras, zwembad
CREDITCARDS AE, DC, MC, V **KINDEREN** toegestaan boven 12 jaar
GEHANDICAPTEN kamers op begane grond
HUISDIEREN toegestaan **GESLOTEN** half nov. tot maart; restaurant ma.
EIGENAAR Christiane Druart

HET ZUIDEN

AUBERGE DU PRESBYTERE
~ HOTEL IN DORP ~

place de la Fontaine, 84400 Saignon (Vaucluse)
TEL 04 90 74 11 50 **FAX** 04 90 04 68 51 **E-MAIL** auberge.presbytere@provence-luberon.com **WEBSITE** www.provence-luberon.com

OP DE DREMPEL VAN HET NATIONALE PARK van Luberon – een relatief onbekende regio - ligt het dorp Saignon op een heuvel. Het dorp heeft een veelbewogen geschiedenis, daterend vanaf de 11de eeuw. Dit pension bestaat uit drie huizen in het centrum, met uitzicht op het plein waar de dorpsfontein staat. Eén huis wordt bijna helemaal bedolven door een weerbarstige klimplant. De huizen zijn met elkaar verbonden, waarbij de kamers op de benedenverdieping allemaal achter elkaar liggen. De kamers op de bovenste verdieping liggen op verschillende niveaus met aparte gangen en trappen. Ze zijn allemaal charmant met glanzende terracotta- of houtenvloeren, laag gewelfd en met balken voorziene plafonds en een combinatie van rieten meubels met antiek. De hoffelijke, charmante Amerikaans-Franse eigenaar heeft zich in de afgelopen 14 jaar beziggehouden met de perfectie van de Provençaalse stijl.

Het restaurant is gesplitst in een knusse kamer met houten panelen voor de niet rokers, en een ander, ruimer gedeelte dat via openslaande deuren naar een grindterras leidt. Traditionele Provençaalse gerechten zijn duidelijk aanwezig op de dagelijks veranderende menukaart en er is altijd wel een visgerecht en een vegetarische schotel. Geen à la carte. Na het diner kunt u bijkomen op één van de crèmekleurige sofa's naast de openhaard in de beschaafde zitkamer of een glaasje drinken in de kleine, sfeervolle bar. Ook een populair trefpunt voor de dorpelingen.

~

OMGEVING Apt (4 km); Bonnieux (12 km); Aix (56 km).
LOCATIE in centrum van dorp; parkeerterrein in de buurt
ETEN ontbijt, lunch, diner **PRIJS** €€
KAMERS 10; 9 tweepersoons, 1 eenpersoons, alle met bad, telefoon, haardroger
FACILITEITEN zitkamer, eetkamer, bar **CREDITCARDS** MC, V **KINDEREN** toegestaan
GEHANDICAPTEN geen speciale voorzieningen **HUISDIEREN** toegestaan
GESLOTEN begin nov. tot eind feb.; restaurant woe., lunch do.
EIGENAAR Jean Pierre de Lutz

HET ZUIDEN

LA COLOMBE D'OR
~ HOTEL IN DORP ~

06570 St-Paul-de-Vence (Alpes-Maritimes)
TEL 04 93 32 80 02 **FAX** 04 93 32 77 78
WEBSITE www.la-colombe-dor.com

TOEN PAUL ROUX (grootvader van de huidige eigenaar) dit bescheiden pension opende in de jaren dertig, had hij nooit kunnen dromen dat La Colombe d'Or zou uitgroeien tot het bekende en chique hotel dat het vandaag is. Veel van zijn klanten waren kunstenaars die in St-Paul woonden. In ruil voor een kamer kreeg hij van hen een kunstwerk. Het werd een bekend trefpunt voor een kunstzinnig, Bohémien kliekje, en de opkomende jetset van de Rivièra. Tegenwoordig logeren hier veel rijke Amerikanen. Toch heeft de huidige eigenaar de sfeer van een ontspannen pension op het platteland enigszins weten te bewaren.

De kunst die op de muren prijkt en het beeldhouwwerk in de tuin zijn uitzonderlijk. De eetkamers met houten panelen hangen vol met Picasso, Miro en Chagall, genoeg om uw aandacht af te leiden van het nogal middelmatige eten. De stijl is zowel rustiek, chic als nonchalant - oude betegelde vloeren, natuurlijke kleuren en stoffen, mooi antiek, spectaculair keramiek, veel planten en overal kunst. In de zomer wordt het diner geserveerd op het zalige terras in de schaduw van de oude bomen. Het zwembad wordt het hele jaar door verwarmd. De killere dagen kunt u doorbrengen in een gezellige zitkamer met leren sofa's rondom de openhaard.

~

OMGEVING Fondation Maeght; Nice (15km); Grasse (25km).
LOCATIE aan rand van dorp, parkeerterrein
ETEN ontbijt, lunch, diner
PRIJS €€€€
KAMERS 26; 15 tweepersoons, 11 suites alle met bad of Spabad, telefoon, TV, airconditioning, haardroger
FACILITEITEN eetkamers, bar, zitkamers, terras, tuin, zwembad
CREDITCARDS AE, DC, MC, V
KINDEREN toegestaan **GEHANDICAPTEN** moeilijk toegankelijk **HUISDIEREN** toegestaan
GESLOTEN nov., 2 weken in jan.
EIGENAARS M. en Mme Roux

HET ZUIDEN

ST-PAUL-DE-VENCE

LE HAMEAU
~ VILLA OP HET PLATTELAND ~

528 route de la Colle, 06570 St-Paul-de-Vence (Alpes-Maritimes)
TEL 04 93 32 80 24 **FAX** 04 93 32 55 75
WEBSITE www.le-hameau.com

LE HAMEAU IS EEN VERZAMELING van 18de- en 19de-eeuwse Provençaalse villa's met rode daken. Ze zijn prachtig en bevinden zich buiten Vence. Er is een mooie tuin met sinaasappel- en mandarijnbomen die heerlijke geuren en voor de marmelade zorgen bij het ontbijt. De stijlvolle slaapkamers zijn elegant met een aantal adembenemende stukken antiek en voortreffelijke stoffen. Ook de badkamers zijn goed. Sommige zijn groot, anderen klein en knus. Een betoverende plek en je krijgt waar voor je geld.

De slaapkamers zijn voorzien van balken, donkerhouten meubels en tapijt op de rood betegelde vloeren; ze variëren behoorlijk in prijs en grootte. Velen hebben een eigen terras of balkon. Er is een koele, nette ontbijtkamer, maar het is veel leuker om buiten in de grote terrastuin te eten die ook een klein (maar fijn) zwembad heeft.

In 1999 heeft een jong Italiaans echtpaar Le Hameau overgenomen.

~

OMGEVING Fondation Maeght; Cagnes-sur-Mer (5 km); Nice (15 km); Grasse (25 km).
LOCATIE 1 km buiten dorp, 15 km ten noordwesten van Nice; parkeerterrein
ETEN ontbijt
PRIJS €€ - €€€
KAMERS 17; 14 tweepersoons, 3 appartementen, 15 met bad, 2 met douche, alle kamers hebben telefoon, TV, airconditioning, minibar, haardroger, kluis
FACILITEITEN ontbijtkamer, zitkamer, terras, tuin, zwembad
CREDITCARDS AE, MC, V
KINDEREN toegestaan
GEHANDICAPTEN kamers op begane grond
HUISDIEREN toegestaan
GESLOTEN half nov. tot half dec., half jan. tot half feb.
MANAGER Xavier Huvelin

HET ZUIDEN

St-Pons-de-Thomieres

LES BERGERIES DE PONDÉRACH
~ CHATEAU-HOTEL ~

route de Narbonne, 34220 St-Pons-de-Thomières (Hérault)
Tel 04 67 97 02 57 **Fax** 04 67 97 29 75

St-Pons-de-Thomieres is een aangenaam stadje dat ligt in de glooiende beboste heuvels van het Nationale Park van Haut Languedoc. Het restaurant-hotel is gebouwd in een 18de-eeuwse boerenhoeve en ligt net één kilometer buiten de stad. U vindt hier een groot terrein, een charmant binnenplaats en een rustige omgeving. Het hotel is van alle gemakken voorzien, maar het authentiek karakter heeft men weten te behouden. De slaapkamers met de houten balken zijn mooi en licht. Ze hebben allemaal een eigen terras met uitzicht op de boomgaard en de rivier.

De eigenaar, Monsieur Lentin, had vroeger een kunstgalerie, en dat is terug te vinden in de schilderijen die in de mooie zit- en eetkamer hangen. Misschien is het eten wel het hoogtepunt: er zijn vier menu's en bij de goedkoopste krijgt u zeker waar voor uw geld. De verse plaatselijke producten, vooral het varkensvlees zijn verrukkelijk, en de wijnkaart biedt een interessante selectie plaatselijke wijnen. Dit hotel is nieuw in deze gids: wij hopen dat uw verslagen ons oordeel zullen bevestigen wat betreft prijs en charme.

Omgeving Castres (52 km); Béziers (51 km).
Locatie 0.8 km buiten stad; parkeerterrein
Eten ontbijt, lunch, diner
Prijs €€
Kamers 7 tweepersoons met bad
Faciliteiten zitkamer, eetkamer, terras, tuin
Creditcards DC, MC, V
Kinderen toegestaan
Gehandicapten geen speciale voorzieningen
Huisdieren toegestaan
Gesloten begin nov. tot maart
Eigenaar M. Lentin

Het Zuiden

Mas des Carassins
~ Verbouwde boerderij ~

1 chemin Gaulois, 13210 St-Rémy-de-Provence (Bouches-du-Rhône)
Tel 04 90 92 15 48 **Fax** 04 90 92 63 47
E-MAIL carassin@pacwan.fr

Monsieur en Madame Ripert moesten na bijna 25 jaar met groot verdriet hun familiehotel Mas des Carassins verkopen in december 2000. Ze wisten pas dat ze het aan de juiste mensen verkopen toen ze Michel en Pierre tegenkwamen. Toen wij een bezoek brachten aan het hotel, waren de heer en mevrouw Ripert er ook om te kijken hoe het er uitzag na hun vertrek. Hoewel de laatste hand nog aan het huis werd gelegd, waren we allemaal even gecharmeerd.

Michel en Pierre weten wat ze willen en verwerken hun eigen stijl in het indrukwekkende hotel, ook in de zeven slaapkamers met zachte kleuren, terracottavloeren en chique stoffen. Ze hebben overal aan gedacht (een stukje tapijt ingewerkt in de tegels van de trappen om het geluid te dempen) en niets is te veel moeite: 'Het is een driesterrenhotel, maar we bieden graag een viersterren-service.' De zeven slaapkamers zijn onveranderd gebleven: dit wordt hun project voor volgend jaar. In de beschutte tuin hebben ze een adembenemende zwembad gebouwd. U kunt hier van een lichte lunch genieten. Vier avonden per week kunt u gebruik maken van een table d'hôte.

~

Omgeving Les Baux-de-Provence (7 km); Avignon (20 km).
Locatie in rustige laan, aan zuidrand van stad; parkeerterrein
Eten ontbijt, lichte lunch (half juni tot half sept.), avond snack (ma. woe. vrij. za.)
Prijs €€
Kamers 14 tweepersoons, driepersoons en familiekamers, alle met bad of douche; alle kamers hebben telefoon, TV, minibar; 9 kamers airconditioning; 7 kamers kluis
Faciliteiten zitkamer, eetkamer, terras, tuin, zwembad
Creditcards MC, V
Kinderen toegestaan   **Gehandicapten** 1 aangepaste kamer
Huisdieren toegestaan
Gesloten jan. tot apr.
Eigenaars Michel Dimeux en Pierre Ticot

HET ZUIDEN

ST-RÉMY-DE-PROVENCE

✳ DOMAINE DE VALMOURIANE ✳
⌒ CHATEAU-HOTEL ⌒

petite route des Baux, 13210 St-Rémy-de-Provence (Bouches-du-Rhône)
TEL 04 90 92 44 62 **FAX** 04 90 92 37 32
E-MAIL domdeval@wanadoo.fr **WEBSITE** www.valmouriane.com

ALS U GRAAG HERBES DE PROVENCE RUIKT, hoeft u alleen maar de ramen te openen in één van de kamers van het hotel Domaine de Valmourian van Philippe en Martina Capel. Verborgen in de rotsige heuvels van de Alpilles, ligt deze mooie verbouwde boerenhoeve omgeven door pijn-bomen, cipressen, rozemarijn, jeneverbes en lavendel – geuren en smaken die u weer tegenkomt in de eetkamer. Een beschut zwembad bevindt zich aan het einde van het brede gazon evenals de tennisbaan. En hebt u zin om het dorp in te duiken dan bent u binnen tien minuten in Les Baux. Aangezien auto's niet worden toegelaten kunt u hier misschien beter naar toe wandelen over een pad in een bosrijke omgeving.

Het huis heeft een betegelde vloer en is smaakvol ingericht met Provençaalse stoffen en mooie antieke meubels. De oude keuken, met grote openhaard, is een knusse winterkamer en in de zomer is er een overdekt terras voor eten in de openlucht: Het diner is Provençaals met veel traditionele kruiden en specerijen. U kunt ook kiezen uit een uitgebreide selectie van plaatselijke wijnen. Twee van de comfortabele slaapkamers hebben een eigen terras en de kamers op de beneden-verdieping hebben openslaande deuren die uitkomen op de tuin.

⌒

OMGEVING Les Baux-de-Provence (5 km); Avignon (24 km).
LOCATIE 4 km ten westen van de stad op weg naar Baux; parkeerterrein
ETEN ontbijt, lunch, diner **PRIJS** €€ - €€€
KAMERS 14; 12 tweepersoons, 1 familiekamer, 1 appartement, alle met bad, telefoon, TV, minibar, airconditioning **FACILITEITEN** zitkamer, bar, eetkamers, terras, tuin, zwembad, tennis **CREDITCARDS** AE, DC, MC, V **KINDEREN** welkom
GEHANDICAPTEN 1 aangepaste kamer
HUISDIEREN toegestaan
GESLOTEN nooit
EIGENAARS Philippe en Martina Capel

✳ **BOEK DIT HOTEL, BESPAAR GELD** ✳
TEL: 0044-(0)189 255 98 66
enquiries@chs-travelservice.com
ZIE PAGINA 7.

HET ZUIDEN

ST-TROPEZ

LA PONCHE
~ HOTEL IN DE STAD ~

3 rue des Remparts, 83990 St-Tropez (Var)
TEL 04 94 97 02 53 **FAX** 04 94 97 78 61
E-MAIL laponche@nova.fr **WEBSITE** www. nova.fr/ponche

ST-TROPEZ IS OP ZICH EEN DORP dat niet direkt in onze gids past maar hotel La Ponche wèl. Verscholen op een plein met uitzicht op de kleine vissershaven en piepkleine stranden van La Ponche, bieden deze groep 17de-eeuwse huizen een boeiende combinatie van verfijndheid en hartelijkheid. Wat ooit begon als een eenvoudige vissersbar in 1937, is door Simone Duckstein omgetoverd tot een smaakvol en artistiek viersterrenhotel met veel persoonlijke details. Schilderijen van Mme Duckstein voormalige echtgenoot sieren de muren.

U kunt op het terras eten met uitzicht op de zee of in één van de eetkamers binnen– onpretentieus maar chic. Het diner is gedenkwaardig, vooral de visgerechten. De slaapkamers zijn fascinerend en zeer comfortabel. Veel van hen zijn stijlvol opgeknapt met trendy kleuren en mooie badkamers.

OMGEVING stranden: Les Graniers (100 m); La Boullabaisse (1 km); Tahiti (4 km).
LOCATIE in hartje centrum, uitkijkend op Port des Pêcheurs; parkeerterrein en garage
ETEN ontbijt, lunch, diner
PRIJS €€€€
KAMERS 18; 11 tweepersoons, 2 familiekamers, 3 suites, 2 appartementen alle met bad, telefoon, TV, airconditioning, minibar, kluis
FACILITEITEN bar, eetkamer, zitkamer, lift
CREDITCARDS AE, MC, V
KINDEREN toegestaan
GEHANDICAPTEN toegang moeilijk
HUISDIEREN toegestaan
GESLOTEN half nov. tot half feb.
EIGENAAR Simone Duckstein

HET ZUIDEN

LE YACA
~ HOTEL AAN DE KUST ~

1 boulevard d'Aumale, 83994 St-Tropez (Var)
TEL 04 94 55 81 00 **FAX** 04 94 97 58 50
E-MAIL hotel-le-yaca@wanadoo.fr **WEBSITE** www.hotel-le-yaca.fr

MINDER DAN HONDERD METER van het schilderachtige Port des Pecheurs,
ligt hotel Le Yaca verspreid over een paar stadshuizen die tot één
geheel zijn gemaakt in het charmantste hoekje van het oude St-Tropez. De
indrukwekkende receptie is het centrale punt. Zodra u in de rest van het
huis komt, bevindt u zich in een wirwar van gangen en trappenhuizen. Pas
nu voelt u de geschiedenis van het oude gebouw.

Le Yaca is het tegenovergestelde van het flitsende St-Tropez (behalve
de prijzen natuurlijk). Discreet, nonchalant en chic. De enige glitter die u
hier zult aantreffen is in de mooi geweven Marokkaanse stoffen op de
bedden of in de oosterse lantarens die het eetterras verlichten. De
slaapkamers zijn individueel ingericht met smaak – het koele wit steekt af
tegen de oude terracottavloeren. Verder treft u hier antieke meubels,
schilderijen, hier en daar een tapijt of misschien wel een exotische
orchidee. De badkamers zijn smetteloos met badproducten van Hermès en
dikke witte badjassen. Er zijn twee verbluffend mooie suites en het
voortreffelijke Italiaanse eten wordt geserveerd in het ontspannende,
zonnige restaurant. Met warm weer kunt u buiten eten in de heerlijke,
vredige tuin naast het zwembad.

~

OMGEVING stranden: Les Graniers (100m); La Bouillabaisse (1 km); Tahiti (4 km).
LOCATIE in centrum van oude stad, 100 m van Port des Pecheurs; parkeerterrein
(openbare of privé)
ETEN ontbijt, lichte lunch op verzoek, diner
PRIJS €€€€€
KAMERS 27; 23 tweepersoons, 2 eenpersoons, 2 suites, alle met bad, telefoon, TV,
airconditioning, minibar, kluis, haardroger
FACILITEITEN eetkamer, bar, terras, tuin, zwembad
CREDITCARDS AE, DC, MC, V
GEHANDICAPTEN niet geschikt **HUISDIEREN** toegestaan
GESLOTEN half okt. tot april
EIGENAARS M en Mme Huret

HET ZUIDEN

LES STES-MARIES-DE-LA-MER

HOSTELLERIE DU MAS DE CACHAREL
～ CHATEAU HOTEL ～

route de Cacharel, 13460 Les Stes-Maries-de-la-Mer (Bouches-du-Rhône)
TEL 04 90 97 95 44 **FAX** 04 90 97 87 97
E-MAIL mail@hotel-cacharel.com **WEBSITE** www.hotel-cacharel.com

DIT KLEINE HOTEL IS GEBOUWD in de jaren zestig door filmregisseur en fotograaf Denys Colomb de Daunant. Het ligt een kilometer van de weg af op zo'n 70 hectare grond, grenzend aan een natuurreservaat. Onder het beheer van zoon Florian, een voormalige scheepsmakelaar, is het hotel eenvoudig en pretentieloos gebleven. Er is nergens een tv te bekennen en de kamers op de benedenverdieping zijn charmant met witte muren en hebben uitzicht op de binnenplaats en over de moerassen. In sommige kamers hangen grote foto's van paarden. U kunt hier ook paardrijden - de familie bezit zo'n zestig paarden.

Er is geen restaurant maar wel een bar met tafels in een grote schuur met stierenhoorns, veebellen en boerderijwerktuigen. Het pièce de milieu is een massieve 18de-eeuwse stenen openhaard. Een assiette campagnarde –met ham, geitenkaas en worst – wordt geserveerd met wijn tot acht uur 's avonds. De stallen kunnen op elke uur van de dag bezocht worden. De vogels hier zijn verbazingwekkend - er is een constante parade van flamingo's. Het drukke, toeristische Les Stes-Marie-de-la-Mer, 5 km verderop, lijkt een totaal andere wereld. Monsieur en Madame Colomb de Daunants zijn ontzettend prettige mensen.

～

OMGEVING Arles (39 km); Aigues-Mortes (31 km); Nîmes (54 km).
LOCATIE in de moerassen van de Camargue; parkeerterrein
ETEN ontbijt, lichte maaltijden (van 12.00 tot 20.00 uur)
PRIJS €€
KAMERS 15; 12 met bad, 3 met douche, alle met telefoon en verwarming
FACILITEITEN bar, schuur, tuin, zwembad, paardrijden
CREDITCARDS MC, V
KINDEREN welkom
GEHANDICAPTEN 1 geschikte kamer
HUISDIEREN toegestaan
GESLOTEN nooit
EIGENAARS familie Colomb de

HET ZUIDEN

LES STES-MARIES-DE-LA-MER

MAS DE LA FOUQUE
CHATEAU-HOTEL

route du Petit-Rhône, 13460 Les Stes-Marie-de-la-Mer (Bouches-du-Rhône)
TEL 04 90 97 81 02 **FAX** 04 90 97 94 84
E-MAIL masdelafouque@francemarket.com **WEBSITE** www.masdelafouque.com

TIJDENS EEN DINER BIJ KAARSLICHT vertelt een jonge vrouw haar geliefde hoeveel ze van hem houdt. Maar zijn blik is ergens anders op gericht: een grote grijze reiger wadend door de vijver. Door het venster geniet u 's avonds van een prachtig weids uitzicht: witte paarden en kleine zwarte stieren van de Camargue dwalen rond de rietstengels van de moerassen en hordes roze flamingo's vliegen over u heen. Dit Spaansachtige witgekalkte hotel, aan de rand van het water, lijkt een beetje op Southfork (de ranch uit de bekende tv-serie Dallas). Mas de la Fouque is echter een luxueuze viersterren hotel met een helikopter landplaats, exotische badkamers en jacuzzi's. Er wordt van u verwacht dat u zich kleedt voor het diner.

Veel van de mooie kamers – goed beschermd tegen muggen en voorzien van ventilators – hebben een eigen terras die over de lagune zijn gebouwd waar u goed kunt zonnebaden en naar vogels kunt kijken (neem een verrekijker mee). Witte rieten stoelen maken de salon licht en ruim. Er is een comfortabele bar, behangen met illustraties van werktuigen van rond de vorige eeuwwisseling. Het eten is voortreffelijk, met heerlijke regionale gerechten. Veel van de groenten en kruiden komen van eigen bodem. De Mas is kortgeleden van eigenaar gewisseld. Uw reacties zijn welkom.

OMGEVING Arles (35 km); Aigues-Mortes (26 km); Nîmes (50 km).
LOCATIE in de Camargue, 4 km ten noordwesten van de stad; parkeerterrein
ETEN ontbijt, lunch, diner
PRIJS €€€; halfpension in hoogseizoen verplicht
KAMERS 13; 10 tweepersoons, 1 familiekamer, 2 suites, alle met bad, telefoon, TV, airconditioning, minibar, haardroger; 4 kamers hebben whirlpool
FACILITEITEN 2 zitkamers, bar, eetkamer, terras, tuin, zwembad, vissen, putten
CREDITCARD AE, DC, MC, V **KINDEREN** toegestaan
GEHANDICAPTEN 1 aangepaste kamer **HUISDIEREN** toegestaan
GESLOTEN begin nov. tot eind maart; restaurant sept. tot half juli; ma. lunch en di.
EIGENAAR Didier Rivière

HET ZUIDEN

LE SAMBUC

MAS DE PEINT
~ CHATEAU-HOTEL ~

Le Sambuc, 13200 Arles (Bouches-du-Rhône)
TEL 04 90 97 20 62 **FAX** 04 90 97 22 20
E-MAIL hotel@masdepeint.net **WEBSITE** www.masdepeint.com

DIT HOTEL IS WAT WIJ 'CAMARGUE-CHIC' NOEMEN. De familie Bon, de eigenaren, hebben veel geld geïnvesteerd om dit bereiken. Het eigen familiewapen is zichtbaar op het witte linnen van dit exquise hotelletje. Madame Bon, een architect en interieurontwerpster, heeft veel aan het gebouw veranderd om het aantrekkelijk te maken. Zo vindt u hier ruime kamers met houten balken, zandstenen vloeren, gestoffeerd in een kleur die het best te omschrijven is als gesuikerde amandelen, en verder nog prachtig antiek. Het geheel doet eerder denken aan een privé-vleugel voor gasten dan een hotel, wat ook de bedoeling is. Iedereen eet, soms wat ongemakkelijk, in de ouderwetse keuken, waaruit uitnodigende geuren u tegemoet komen; de groenten en kruiden komen uit de tuin. Er hangt een werktuig in de gang, de kasten zijn gevuld met boeken, er is ook een rustig leeskamertje en u krijgt een krant aan de ontbijttafel. Jacques Bon, een stieren- en paardenfokker, is overal te vinden. Hij nodigt bezoekers uit om zijn vee en boerderij te komen bezichtigen. De slaapkamers zijn klassiek; met kleine houten trappen die naar de badkamer leiden. Er bevindt zich een discreet zwembad niet ver van het huis.

~

OMGEVING Arles (20 km); Avignon (36 km); Nîmes (31 km).
LOCATIE landelijke omgeving; parkeerterrein
ETEN ontbijt, lunch, diner
PRIJS €€€€
KAMERS 11; 8 tweepersoons, 3 suites, alle met bad, telefoon, TV, airconditioning, minibar, safe
FACILITEITEN zitkamers, eetkamer, tuin, zwembad, paardrijden
CREDITCARD AE, DC, MC, V
KINDEREN welkom
GEHANDICAPTEN geen speciale voorzieningen
HUISDIEREN toegestaan
GESLOTEN begin jan. tot half maart
EIGENAREN M. en Mme Bon

HET ZUIDEN

HOTEL DES DEUX ROCS
~ HOTEL IN DORP ~

place Font d'Amont, 83440 Seillans (Var)
TEL 04 94 76 87 32 **FAX** 04 94 76 88 68

DIT BETOVERENDE HOTEL met blauwe luiken in een charmant middeleeuws dorp op een heuvel, is al lang een van onze favoriete logeeradressen. Alles blijft hetzelfde bij Deux Rocs en dat is ook de aantrekkingskracht. U krijgt hier wat u verwacht van een klein onbedorven hotel in de Provence. Het begint al bij het ontbijt bij de fontein op het plein en de stralend ingetogen inrichting van Madame Hirsch. 'Ik kwam voor één nacht, maar bleef zes dagen,' aldus het commentaar van een bezoeker in het gastenboek. Werd deze gast, net zoals vele anderen, verliefd op het brede 18de-eeuwse trappenhuis? Of op de zo levendig, in rood en wit geblokte slaapkamer? Of op de kamer met Toile de Jouy op de muren? Of wellicht op de kleine salon met openhaard? Madame Hirsch en haar assistente Mme Francine kwamen hier jaren geleden aan en samen geven ze het hotel de flair die het zo aantrekkelijk maakt. Ouderwetse badkamers en traditioneel en voortreffelijk eten.

~

OMGEVING Lac de St-Cassien (15 km); Grasse (32 km); St-Raphael (33 km); Cannes (47 km); Gorges du Verdon (40 km).
LOCATIE op heuvel van klein dorp; enkele parkeerplaatsen, of op straat
ETEN ontbijt, lunch, diner
PRIJS €€
KAMERS 14 tweepersoons, 6 met bad, 8 met douche; alle kamers hebben telefoon
FACILITEITEN zitkamer, bar, eetkamer, terras
CREDITCARD MC, V
KINDEREN toegestaan
GEHANDICAPTEN moeilijk toegankelijk
HUISDIEREN toegestaan
GESLOTEN nov tot half maart
EIGENAAR Mme Hirsch

HET ZUIDEN

SÉRIGNAN-DU-COMTAT

HOSTELLERIE DU VIEUX CHATEAU
∼ HOTEL IN DORP ∼

route du Ste-Cécile-les-Vignes, 84830 Sérignan-du-Comtat (Vaucluse)
TEL 04 90 70 05 58 **FAX** 04 90 70 05 62

TOEN WE ONS EEN WEG BAANDEN door de rommelige receptie, vol stapels boeken en een luie kat, haalde Madame haar schouders op en zei: ' één dezer dagen word ik nog eens georganiseerd.' De 18de-eeuwse boeren-hoeve is omgebouwd tot een hotel en veroverde ons hart. Niet vanwege de ligging in het pittoreske dorp, niet vanwege het hoog aangeschreven restaurant of de ruime kamers en niet vanwege de redelijke prijzen maar vanwege het fantastische echtpaar Truchot. Zij namen dit hotel over in 1991 en ze houden van de zaak: Madame is in een hotelkeuken geboren, de oma van Monsieur is een cuisinière de maître geweest. Ze hebben ook altijd het restaurant gerund, Le Pré du Moulin, maar moesten dit opgeven toen Madame te veel last van jicht kreeg. Een jong echtpaar - Pascal Alonso, een begaafde chef-kok, en zijn Zwitserse vrouw Caroline - hebben daar nu de dagelijkse leiding overgenomen. Er is een half pension arrangement voor hotelgasten. Het restaurant dat zich in een schuurachtig gebouw bevindt is zowel populair bij de hotelgasten als bij de plaatselijke bewoners. Het hotel is traditioneel en innemend en heeft een ouderwetse bar, zit- en ontbijtkamers en een zonnig terras. De meeste slaapkamers zijn groot en comfortabel. Sommige hebben mooie nieuwe houten terrassen.

∼

OMGEVING Orange (8 km); Avignon (40 km); Mont Ventoux.
LOCATIE aan rand van dorp, achter de weg naar Ste-Cécile-les-Vignes; parkeerterrein
ETEN ontbijt, lunch, diner; halfpension verplicht van april tot okt.
PRIJS €€
KAMERS 8; 7 tweepersoons, 1 familiekamer, 7 met bad, 1 met douche, alle met bad, telefoon, TV, minibar, haardroger; sommige kamers hebben safe
FACILITEITEN zitkamer, bar, ontbijt room, restaurant, terras, tuin, zwembad
CREDITCARD AE, MC, V **KINDEREN** welkom
GEHANDICAPTEN 1 kamer op begane grond **HUISDIEREN** niet toegestaan
GESLOTEN 2 weken in feb. 1 week in nov., 2 weken in dec.
EIGENAREN M.en Mme Truchot

HET ZUIDEN

TOURRETTES-SUR-LOUP

AUBERGE DE TOURRETTES
~ DORPSRESTAURANT-MET-KAMERS ~

11 route de Grasse, 06140 Tourrettes-sur-Loup (Alpes-Maritimes)
TEL 04 93 59 30 05 **FAX** 04 93 59 28 66
E-MAIL info@aubergedetourrettes.fr **WEBSITE** www.aubergedetourrettes.fr

DE BEGAAFDE CHEF-KOK CHRISTOPHE DUFAU en zijn Deense vrouw Katrine, openden hun restaurant-met-kamers in een typisch dorpspension in juli 2000. Hoog in de Midi-heuvels ligt Tourrettes op slechts enkele kilometers van het toeristische St-Paul. Het is vredig en heeft weinig pretentie. Het hotel staat aan de rand van het dorp met uitzicht op de onbedorven, beboste heuvels en de kust.

Het centrale punt in het huis is het ruime, open restaurant zonder tussenmuren met een glazen serre en fabelachtig uitzicht. De inrichting is eenvoudig, stijlvol, schoon en hedendaags. Met warme betegelde vloeren, wittinten, linnen tafelkleedjes, veel hout en een olijfboom in een terracottapot. Er is ook een terras. Wij waren behoorlijk onder de indruk van het eten. Verse, plaatselijke ingrediënten (veel verse kruiden uit de tuin) worden bereid met gevoel en kundigheid: zeekreeft terrine op smaak gebracht met sinaasappel; asperges geserveerd met parmezaanse kaas en een zachte mousseline; gestoofde kip met ingemaakte citroenen. De slaapkamers hebben dezelfde eenvoudig maar stijlvolle achtergrond; ze weerspiegelen de kleuren van de Provence. Een hedendaagse uitvoering van een traditioneel thema.

~

OMGEVING Vence (6 km); St-Paul-de-Vence (11 km); Nice (25 km).
LOCATIE aan hoofdweg aan rand van dorp; parkeerterrein
ETEN ontbijt, lunch, diner
PRIJS €€
KAMERS 6 tweepersoons, alle met bad, telefoon, TV, minibar
FACILITEITEN eetkamer, bar, tuin, terras
CREDITCARD AE, DC, MC, V
KINDEREN toegestaan
GEHANDICAPTEN moeilijk toegankelijk
HUISDIEREN toegestaan
GESLOTEN 1 week eind nov, half jan tot half feb.
EIGENAREN Christophe en Katrine Dufau

HET ZUIDEN

TRIGANCE

✳ CHATEAU DE TRIGANCE ✳
~ VERBOUWD KASTEEL ~

83840 Trigance (Var)
TEL 04 94 76 91 18 **FAX** 04 94 85 68 99
E-MAIL trigance@relaischateaux.com **WEBSITE** www.relaischateaux.com/trigance

JEAN-CLAUDE THOMAS EN ZIJN VROUW zijn nu langer dan 30 jaar de eigenaren van dit karaktervolle en comfortabele hotel vlakbij de indrukwekkende Gorges du Verdon. Ook hun zoon William helpt mee. Trigance blijft een hartelijke trefpunt in een ruige regio met weinig dorpen. Bij aankomst bent u wellicht een beetje verbaasd. Is dit fort, hoog gelegen op een rotspunt, echt het hotel? (Ja) En als dat zo is, hoe komen we daar? (Via 100 treden – wees gerust, uw bagage wordt voor u gedragen.) Eenmaal binnen waant u zich in de Middeleeuwen. Monsieur Thomas heeft dit 11de-eeuwse kasteel met moeite opgebouwd, steen voor steen. Als u wilt kunt u de foto's van de verschillende fases van dit ongelooflijke project bekijken. De indrukwekkende gewelfde eetkamer is verlicht met kaarsen en er staat een ridder met wapenuitrusting bij de ingang. De raamloze maar zeer sfeervolle zitkamer, is gemeubileerd in middeleeuwse stijl. De meeste slaapkamers (gebouwd in de heuvel) hebben hemelbedden, antiek meubilair, wandkleden en vaandels en er is een verbluffend mooi uitzicht. Het eten is verrassend goed.

~

OMGEVING Gorges du Verdon (10 km); Castellane (20 km).
LOCATIE op 750 m. hoogte met uitzicht op klein dorp, 10 km ten noordwesten van Comps-sur-Artuby; parkeerterrein
ETEN ontbijt, lunch, diner; roomservice
PRIJS €€ - €€€
KAMERS 10 tweepersoons, alle met bad, telefoon, TV, haardroger
FACILITEITEN zitkamer, eetkamer, terras
CREDITCARD AE, DC, CMC, V

KINDEREN toegestaan
GEHANDICAPTEN niet geschikt
HUISDIEREN toegestaan
GESLOTEN nov. to half maart
EIGENAREN familie Thomas

✳ BOEK DIT HOTEL, BESPAAR GELD ✳
TEL: 0044-(0)189 255 98 66
enquiries@chs-travelservice.com
ZIE PAGINA 7.

HET ZUIDEN

VACQUERAS

DOMAINE DE LA PONCHE
~ CHATEAU-HOTEL ~

84190 Vacqueras (Vaucluse)
TEL 04 90 65 85 21 **FAX** 04 90 65 85 23
E-MAIL domaine.laponche@wanadoo.fr **WEBSITE** www.hotel-laponche.com

'WAT EEN VONDST', schreef een lezer ons over dit nieuwe hotel in het wijngebied vlakbij de grillige Dentelles de Montmirail. 'Weliswaar waren we moe, hongerig en zochten we dringend een bed toen we dit plekje vonden, maar we konden ons geluk niet op. Onze kamer was enorm met een indrukwekkende badkamer en het diner was voortreffelijk.'

Groots is hier het sleutelwoord: gebalkte plafonds en uitzonderlijk grote slaapkamers. Stijlvol ingericht met pastelkleuren op de muren en gietijzeren bedden. De duurdere kamers hebben een zitkamer en de badkamers zijn groot en voortreffelijk. Ook de openbare kamers zijn ruim; de eenvoudige zitkamer is knus met een grote openhaard.

Dit mooie, oude 17de-eeuwse gebouw met blauwe luiken, omgeven door wijnranken, olijfbomen en cipressen, is vier jaar geleden omgebouwd tot een hotel door een Zwitserse vrouw, haar Franse echtgenoot en haar zuster. De zussen kunnen beide goed koken en hun verse pasta past goed bij de Provençaalse gerechten. Lichte lunches worden geserveerd rondom het mooie zwembad omgeven door bloemen.

OMGEVING Côtes-du-Rhône wijngaarden; Vaison-la-Romaine (20 km).
LOCATIE bordjes op 2 km ten noorden van Vacqueras, op D8 naar Cairanne; parkeerterrein
ETEN ontbijt, lunch, diner
PRIJS €€€
KAMERS 6; 4 tweepersoons, 2 suites, alle met bad, telefoon, haardroger
FACILITEITEN zitkamer, eetkamer, terras, tuin, zwembad
CREDITCARD MC, V
KINDEREN toegestaan
GEHANDICAPTEN moeilijk toegankelijk
HUISDIEREN toegestaan
GESLOTEN nooit
EIGENAREN Ruth Spahn, Madeleine Frauenknecht, Jean-Pierre Onimus

HET ZUIDEN

VAISON-LA-ROMAINE

HOSTELLERIE LE BEFFROI
~ HOTEL IN DE STAD ~

rue de l'Évêché Haute Ville, 84110 Vaison-la-Romaine (Vaucluse)
TEL 04 90 36 04 71 **FAX** 04 90 36 24 78

HET HOTEL BESTAAT UIT TWEE MOOIE huizen in dezelfde straat in deze middeleeuwse stad op de heuvel. Eén huis is gebouwd door de Comte de Saint Véran in de 16e eeuw en het andere, 17de-eeuwse huis was ooit de woning van de Marquis de Taulignan. In beide huizen vindt u veel balken, oud steen en gepolijste rood betegelde vloeren. De terrassen kijken uit op de nieuwe stad die rondom twee Romeinse opgravingen is gebouwd. De Beffroi ligt op het hoogste punt waardoor u zelfs bij heet zomerweer verkoeling vindt.

De vriendelijke, jonge en drukke eigenaar, Yann Christiansen (het hotel is al drie generaties in de familie) en zijn vrouw, Christine, zijn altijd op zoek naar nieuwe manieren om het hotel nog comfortabeler en geschikter te maken voor hun gasten. Let op: niet alle kamers hebben badkamers. Rond lunchtijd worden er salades geserveerd op het terras – een daverend succes. Het diner is traditioneel Provençaals. Het zwembad heeft een mooi uitzicht over de daken. De vindingrijke midgetgolfbaan in de buurt is een extra attractie voor in de zomer.

OMGEVING Orange (25 km); Avignon (40 km).
LOCATIE in oude stad, tegen een steile heuvel; parkeerterrein
ETEN ontbijt, lunch, diner
PRIJS €€
KAMERS 22; 21 tweepersoons, 1 eenpersoons, 10 met bad, 12 met douche; alle kamers hebben telefoon, TV, minibar, haardroger
FACILITEITEN zitkamer, eetkamer, terras, tuin, zwembad, midget-golf (zomers)
CREDITCARD AE, D, V, MC
KINDEREN welkom
GEHANDICAPTEN niet geschikt
HUISDIEREN toegestaan
GESLOTEN feb tot eind maart; restaurant half nov. to april
EIGENAREN M. en Mme Christiansen

HET ZUIDEN

VALENCE

✳ MAISON PIC ✳
～ HOTEL IN DE STAD ～

285 avenue Victor Hugo, 26001 Valence (Drôme)
TEL 04 75 44 15 32 **FAX** 04 75 40 96 03
E-MAIL pic@relaischateaux.fr **WEBSITE** www.pic-valence.com

HET ETEN WORDT SERIEUS GENOMEN bij Maison Pic. Ondanks het overlijden van Jacques Pic in 1992 blijft dit (onder het toezicht van dochter Anne) één van de beste restaurants in het land met, twee Michelin-sterren. Toch is het nog steeds verfrissend eenvoudig. In Huize Pic draait het echter niet alleen om kaviaar en zeebaars. Het gaat ook om het hotelletje zelf dat door de grootvader van Anne vele jaren geleden is geopend. In 1997 werd het uitgebreid en omgebouwd tot Hôtel des Senteurs (de naam Pic blijft buiten te zien) en de Auberge du Pin.

De bestaande vijf slaapkamers zijn gerenoveerd in een mooie Provençaalse stijl. Tien grote, stijlvolle kamers zijn eraan toegevoegd met damast, antieke tapijten en marmeren badkamers. De kamers verschillen in maat en toch zijn zelfs de 'kleine' tweepersoonskamers ruim. Sommige kamers zijn uitzonderlijk mooi. De huidige generatie Pics besteedt veel aandacht aan het hotel en dat is te zien. Het uitnodigende terras, het zwembad en de tuin zijn niet veranderd. De kamers bij Pic zijn bijna nooit leeg.

OMGEVING bergen van Vercors; de Rhône.
LOCATIE in centrum; parkeerterrein
ETEN ontbijt, lunch, diner
PRIJS €€€€
KAMERS 15 tweepersoons, alle met bad, telefoon, TV, airconditioning, minibar, haardroger, safe
FACILITEITEN zitkamer, eetkamer, terras, zwembad, Frans biljard
CREDITCARD AE, DC, MC, V   **KINDEREN** toegestaan   **GEHANDICAPTEN** 1 aangepaste kamer
HUISDIEREN toegestaan
GESLOTEN nooit; restaurant zo. avond, ma., 3 weken jan.
EIGENAAR Anne Pic

HET ZUIDEN

LA ROSERAIE
~ VILLA IN DE STAD ~

avenue Henri Giraud, 06140 Vence (Alpes-Maritimes)
TEL 04 93 58 02 20 **FAX** 04 93 58 99 31

DEZE LICHTROZE VILLA uit de belle époque lijkt op eerste gezicht een druk familiehuis. Rieten hoeden en bosjes droogbloemen, oude foto's en prenten sieren de muren. Met de komst van de nieuwe eigenaar begonnen ook de renovaties: mooie, gietijzeren tuinmeubels en houten, koloniale zonnebedden hebben het witte plastic vervangen. De begroeide tuin staat vol met exotische planten en bomen: een bananenboom, een 100-jaar oude magnolia, wat sinasappelbomen en een oleander. De receptie/zitkamer is uitnodigend met lage balken, een kleine stenen openhaard en Provençaalse stoffen. De geur van lavendel is overal te ruiken.

De slaapkamers zijn grotendeels hetzelfde gebleven: stralend en zonnig. Een bijzonder mooie kamer ligt op zolder, met zware balken, ruwe bakstenen muren en een gewelfd raam onder het dak en een prachtig bewerkt gietijzeren bed. Een andere kamer heeft een bad met pootjes met handgemaakte keramiektegels uit Salernes. Alle kamers zijn vlekkeloos en comfortabel. Het hotel bevindt zich niet in het mooiste deel van Vence.

~

OMGEVING kapel van Matisse, Vence oude stad; Cannes (5 km).
LOCATIE in buitenwijk van stad; 10 km ten noorden van Cagnes-sur-Mer; parkeerterrein
ETEN ontbijt
PRIJS €€
KAMERS 13 tweepersoons, 11 met bad, 2 met douche; alle kamers hebben telefoon, TV, minibar, haardroger, sommige safe, 1 kamer airconditioning
FACILITEITEN zitkamer, ontbijtkamer, terras, tuin, zwembad
CREDITCARD AE, DC, MC, V
KINDEREN toegestaan
GEHANDICAPTEN 4 kamers op begane grond
HUISDIEREN toegestaan
GESLOTEN half nov tot half feb.
EIGENAAR M. Marteton

HET ZUIDEN

VENCE

AUBERGE DES SEIGNEURS ET DU LION D'OR
~ HOTEL IN DE STAD ~

place du Frêne, 06140 Vence (Alpes-Maritimes)
TEL 04 93 58 04 24 **FAX** 04 93 24 08 01

DEZE AUBERGE IS SINDS 1895 IN GEBRUIK als hotel en in de familie sinds 1936. Het enige dat hier verandert, zijn de gezichten van de gasten, waaronder ooit kunstenaars als Renoir en Modigliani. Eenmaal binnen vindt u een grote, nogal sombere receptie met oude betegelde vloeren, grove rustieke antieken meubels, een olijfpers, een spinnewiel en een grote harige hond. Naast het hotel is het restaurant, waar Madame Rodi lekkere gerechten met lam of kip klaarmaakt op het oude spit boven het vuur. U kunt hier ook heerlijke vissoep krijgen en le tourton des patres, een soort kwarktaart. Het ontbijt is eenvoudig maar bijzonder lekker met fruit, kwark, kaas, verschillende soorten brood en zelfgemaakte jam. De slaapkamers zijn een beetje Spartaans, maar wel charmant. Er staat mooi antiek en veel kamers hebben nog oorspronkelijke terracottategels op de vloer. Frisse Provençaalse stoffen en schalen verse fruit maken ook deel uit van de dagelijkse charme. De kamers variëren behoorlijk qua vorm en maat en de badkamers worden gerenoveerd. Eigenlijk vindt u hier dus niets modern. En pas op dat u niet begint over een tv, website of zelfs een brochure. Wellicht zal er in de loop der tijd wat moderniteit insluipen als Madame het hotel uiteindelijk overdoet aan haar dochter, maar hopelijk ook weer niet te veel.

~

OMGEVING kapel van Matisse; Vence oude stad; Cannes (5 km).
LOCATIE op plein dichtbij stadscentrum; openbaar parkeerterrein
ETEN ontbijt, lunch, diner
PRIJS €
KAMERS 10 tweepersoons, alle met douche
FACILITEITEN zitkamer, eetkamer, bar
CREDITCARD AE, DC, MC, V
KINDEREN toegestaan **GEHANDICAPTEN** moeilijk toegankelijk
HUISDIEREN toegestaan
GESLOTEN half nov. tot half maart; restaurant gesloten ma., di. lunch
EIGENAAR Daniele Rodi

HET ZUIDEN

VILLENEUVE-LEZ-AVIGNON

HOTEL DE L'ATELIER
~ HOTEL IN DE STAD ~

5 rue de la Foire, 30400 Villeneuve-lez-Avignon (Gard)
TEL 04 90 25 01 84 **FAX** 04 90 25 80 06
E-MAIL hotel-latelier@libertysurf.fr

DEZE BED & BREAKFAST IN EEN 16de-eeuws kardinaalshuis is al lang favoriet in onze Zuid-Frankrijk gids. Maar we kregen te horen dat het de laatste tijd een beetje in verval is geraakt en dat is precies hoe Agnès Berméjo en Gui Lainé, de charmante nieuwe eigenaren, het aantroffen toen ze het overnamen in augustus 2000. Agnès en Gui die uit de reclame- en filmwereld komen, gebruikten hun scherpzinnigheid om een hotel met groots karakter en stijl neer te zetten. Ze waren blij met de vele mooie elementen: het stenen trappenhuis, de grote, oude, houten deuren, plafonds met balken en oude openhaard. Daarnaast hebben ze voor een frisse inrichting gekozen met mooie stoffen, lampen en muurverlichting, een melange van houten en geverfde meubels, sisal op de vloer en schilderijen en kunstobjecten. Een aantal objecten uit hun eigen verzameling wordt om de zo veel tijd door Agnès tentoongesteld. Alle slaapkamers zijn verschillend en eenvoudig, doch elegant.

Achter in het huis is een uitnodigende binnenplaats, waar u kunt ontbijten onder de schaduw van een vijgenboom en wijnranken. Achter de stenen poort vindt u een prachtige begroeide 'geheime tuin', met een weelde aan oleanderbomen, geraniums en klimrozen. Het is moeilijk te geloven dat u binnen 10 minuten met de bus, over de Rhône, in Avignon bent.

~

OMGEVING Avignon; Fort St-André; Chartreuse du Val de Bénédiction.
LOCATIE in centrum; parkeerterrein
ETEN ontbijt
PRIJS €
KAMERS 23 tweepersoons, alle met bad of douche, telefoon, TV, haardroger
FACILITEITEN zitkamer, ontbijtkamer, tuin
CREDITCARD AE, DC, MC, V
KINDEREN toegestaan **GEHANDICAPTEN** niet geschikt **HUISDIEREN** toegestaan
GESLOTEN nov. tot half dec.
EIGENAREN Agnès Berméjo en Gui Lainés

HET ZUIDEN

ARGELES-SUR-MER

✳LE COTTAGE✳
HOTEL AAN DE KUST

21 rue Arthur-Rimbaud,
66703 Argèles-sur-Mer
(Pyrénées-Orientales)
TEL 04 68 81 07 33
FAX 04 68 81 59 69 **E-MAIL**
hotel.lecottage@wandoo.fr
WEBSITE www.hotellecottage.com
ETEN ontbijt, lunch, diner
PRIJS €€ **KAMERS** 34 **GESLOTEN**
half okt. Tot april; restaurant
maandag- en zaterdagmiddag

ARGELES-SUR-MER is praktisch de laatste stop in Frankrijk voor de Spaanse grens. Le Cottage is een vrolijk, modern vakantiehotel in een rustig woongebied met uitzicht op de bergen. Rieten en gietijzeren meubels zorgen voor een licht en vrolijk interieur maar het werkelijke geheim van deze plek is het restaurant L'Orangeraie. Het restaurant heeft een goede naam opgebouwd door zijn benadering van de regionale kookkunst en de goede wijnkaart. Het kaarslicht en de tafeltjes met roze tafelkleedjes onder de palmbomen, zijn een geweldige combinatie. Reserveren via ons reisbureau – zie pagina 7.

CASTILLON-DU-GARD

✳LE VIEUX CASTILLON✳
DORPSHOTEL OP HEUVELTOP

rue Turion Sabatier, 30210
Castillon-du-Gard (Gard)
TEL 04 66 37 61 61
FAX 04 66 37 28 17
E-MAIL vieux.castillon@ wandoo.fr
WEBSITE relaischateaux.fr/
vieuxcastillon
ETEN ontbijt , lunch, diner
PRIJS €€€€ **KAMERS** 35
GESLOTEN begin jan. tot eind feb.; restaurant maandag- en dinsdagmiddag

HET WAS EEN GOED PLAN om een paar mooie ruïnes te laten staan van deze verzameling middeleeuwse huizen, en de rest in een luxeus hotel te veranderen. Het hotel heeft een adembenemend uitzicht over de wijn-gaarden van de Ventoux-vallei. Door de beschermende buitenmuren heeft de mistral 's winters geen kans om binnen te dringen en blijft het koel in de zomer. De gebloemde kamers variëren wat in grootte en uitzicht. In het restaurant, aan de andere kant van de brug is de kwaliteit van het eten goed. De wijnkaart is prima; er is genoeg keuze uit het Côtes du Rhône-assortiment. Prachtige tuinen en leuk zwembad maken het geheel com-pleet. Reserveren via ons reisbureau – zie pagina 7.

HET ZUIDEN

CAZILHAC

LA FERME DE LA SAUZETTE

VERBOUWDE BOERDERIJ

route de Villefloure, 11570
Cazilhac (Aude)
TEL 04 68 79 81 32
FAX 04 68 79 65 99
ETEN ontbijt, diner
PRIJS €
KAMERS 5
GESLOTEN nov, Kerst tot feb.

IN DE OUDE STENEN BOERDERIJ van Chris en Diana Gibson wacht u een hartelijke ontvangst. De vijf goed ingerichte en comfortabele kamers en prachtige badkamers vindt u boven de oude wijnmakerij. Ontbijt en diner (allebei heerlijk) worden rond een grote ronde tafel genuttigd. In de winter is er een openhaard en in de zomer kunt u genieten van de veranda, het terras en de tuin.

LOURMARIN

AUBERGE LA FENIERE

RESTAURANT-MET-KAMERS

route de Cadenet, 84160
Lourmarin (Vaucluse)
TEL 04 90 68 11 79
FAX 04 90 68 18 60
E-MAIL Reine@wanadoo.fr
WEBSITE www.tabledereine.com
ETEN ontbijt, lunch, diner
PRIJS €€€ KAMERS 9
GESLOTEN half nov. tot feb.

ALS U EEN FIJNPROEVER BENT kunnen wij u dit restaurant aanraden. Reine Sammut is chef-kok; een getalenteerde en charmante vrouw. De 'vrouwelijke' invloeden zijn zeker te vinden in gerechten als foie gras gesauteerd in honing, een taartje van zeebaars met gecarameliseerde appels of pigonneau fermier met Camargue-rijst. De kamers, met klein terrasje uitkijkend op het uitnodigende zwembad, zijn modern, misschien zelfs een beetje te. In de tuin staan twee kitscherige caravans voor een romantisch uitje voor twee. Het ontbijt is om van te watertanden.

THE SOUTH

LE BOSQUET
COUNTRY HOTEL

74 chemin des Périssols, 06580
Pégomas (Alpes-Maritimes)
TEL 04 92 60 21 20
FAX 04 92 60 21 49
FOOD breakfast
PRICE €-€€
ROOMS 16
CLOSED Feb

'WHAT HAVE YOU GOT against Le Bosquet?' writes a puzzled aficionado of our guides who notes that it had disappeared from these pages in recent years. 'We love it, and standards are just the same as ever.' It's true that we did drop Le Bosquet because of some critical reports, but we are happy to reinstate it this year with the strong endorsement of this reader. Set between Cannes and Grasse in a plain 1960s building, with large shady grounds which include fruit trees, a pool and tennis court, it is the sort of unpretentious yet beguiling family-run hotel beloved of this guide. As well as the simple bedrooms, there are seven useful studios with kitchenettes and private terraces. A warm welcome and homemade jam for breakfast.

MAS DE BRUGASSIERES
COUNTRY GUESTHOUSE

Plan-de-la-Tour, 83120 Ste-
Maxime (Var)
TEL 04 94 55 50 55
FAX 04 94 55 50 51 **E-MAIL**
mas.brugassieres@free.fr **WEBSITE**
www.mas-des-brugassieres.com
FOOD breakfast **PRICE** €-€€
ROOMS 14 **CLOSED** mid-Oct to
mid-Mar

'VERY RELAXED – an excellent place to unwind,' is the verdict of one visitor to this modern 'farmhouse' set in lush gardens surrounded by vineyards. 'Yes, it's got a laid-back feel,' says our reporter. 'The tone is set by a huge wooden sofa from Sumatra piled with Indian cushions, with lots of pot plants dotted around, and a friendly, shaggy dog padding about.' Bedrooms are fairly basic but cheerful, with rustic tiled floors, functional furniture, Indian cotton bedspreads and Moroccan lamps; the Provençal tiled bathrooms are each in a different colour. Some lead directly on to the pretty, rambling garden and swimming pool. Breakfast is informal, served from 8 am until whenever you like, or you can rise late and have brunch by the pool.

THE SOUTH

ST-LAURENT-DU-VERDON

LE MOULIN DU CHATEAU

VILLAGE HOTEL

04500 St-Laurent-du-Verdon (Var) **TEL** 04 92 74 02 47 **FAX** 04 92 74 02 97 **E-MAIL** LMDCH@club-internet.fr **WEBSITE** www.provenceweb.fr/04/moulin-du-chateau **FOOD** breakfast, dinner **PRICE** €-€€ **ROOMS** 10 **CLOSED** mid-Nov to mid-Feb

A DEVOTEE OF OUR GUIDES wrote to us with such enthusiasm about this new hotel in a tiny village close to the Gorges du Verdon that we hurried to send our own inspector there, who warmly concurred. Swiss-French Nicolas Stämpfli and his Swiss-Italian wife Edith, both ex-teachers, took four years to convert their old mill into an utterly peaceful retreat with simple, colourful bedrooms and delicious 'Mediterranean' set-menu dinners, which are presented with the easy-going grace and good humour that imbues the whole hotel. The restaurant is only open to residents and there is no swimming pool – so that guests can enjoy total peace and quiet.

ST-PAUL-DE-VENCE

LE SAINT-PAUL

VILLAGE HOTEL

86 rue Grande, 06570 St-Paul-de-Vence (Alpes-Maritimes) **TEL** 04 93 32 65 25 **FAX** 04 93 32 52 94 **E-MAIL** stpaul@relaischateaux.fr **WEBSITE** www.relaischateaux.com./stpaul **FOOD** breakfast, lunch, dinner; room service **PRICE** €€€€ **ROOMS** 19 **CLOSED** 3 weeks Dec, 3 weeks Jan

IF YOU CAN AFFORD IT, here is another exceptionally captivating place to stay in pricey St-Paul-de-Vence, in a beautifully restored 16thC former private residence in the centre of the village. The interior has been done out with real panache; smallish bedrooms are beautifully decorated, many with *trompe l'oeil* murals of sea views framed by tropical plants. Some of the rooms have real views across hills and valley towards the sea, and these are the most desirable. The elegant restaurant is also decorated here and there with frescoes of flowers and fruit, and there is a little terrace for summer dining. The cooking of Frédéric Buzet is praised by Gault Millau and by recent guests alike. Solicitous, friendly service. A treat.

THE SOUTH

OSTALARIA CARDABELA

RESTAURANT-WITH-ROOMS

10 place Fontaine, 34725 St-Saturnin-de-Lucian (Hérault) **TEL** 04 67 88 62 62 **FAX** 04 67 88 62 82 **FOOD** breakfast; lunch and dinner (at Mimosa) **PRICE** €- €€ **ROOMS** 7 **CLOSED** late Oct to mid-Mar; restaurant Mon, Sep to Jun Sun dinner

THIS SMALL, ELEGANT HOTEL in a quiet village west of the Hérault has recently been added as another string to the bow of the Mimosa, a superb restaurant down the road at St-Guiraud (tel 04 67 96 67 96; fax 04 67 96 61 15) where Bridget Pugh, a former prima ballerina, pursues her present career as a top-flight *cuisinière*. Her husband David, oh lucky man, devotes much of his time to stocking his cellar with wine good enough to match her cooking. The bedrooms in this old stone house named after a thistle are a fair size and stylishly decorated; there is a kitchen for guests' use and free transport to the Mimosa and back.

LA TABLE DU COMTAT

VILLAGE HOTEL

Séguret, 84110 Vaison-la-Romaine (Vaucluse)
TEL 04 90 46 91 49
FAX 04 90 46 94 27
FOOD breakfast, lunch, dinner
PRICE €€
ROOMS 8 double and twin, all with bath; all rooms have phone, TV
CLOSED Feb

'SURELY THE MOST CHARMING small hotel in Provence', says one devotee of this eyrie at the top of one of the region's most captivating villages. It's certainly a business getting there by car, winding up round steep, narrow streets, but once tucked into a parking space at the top you are rewarded by magnificent views of the plain below, and by the delights of a much modernized, but essentially old-fashioned *auberge*. The food is not cheap, but it is good, if eclectic, the public rooms light and airy and the bedrooms simple and comfortable, with attractive fabrics and furnishings. The delightful terrace shares the view, and there is a swimming pool.

THE SOUTH

LE THOR

LA BASTIDE ROSE

COUNTRY GUESTHOUSE

99 chemin des Croupières, 84250
Le Thor (Vaucluse)
TEL 04 90 02 14 33
FAX 04 90 02 19 38
E-MAIL poppynicole@yahoo.com
WEBSITE www.bastiderose.com
FOOD breakfast; lunch and dinner
by arrangement **PRICE** €€€
ROOMS 7 **CLOSED** never

ON A BANK OF THE SORGUE, this lovely old former paper mill, now the home of Poppy and Pierre Salinger (famous as JFK's speech writer) is protected from the world by trees and lawns. Poppy used to be an antiques dealer and her professional eye shows in the style she has brought to the house. Guests have the run of the downstairs – including an open kitchen and an honesty bar – and upstairs the bedrooms are washed in striking colours with some beautiful antiques and little pieces of Limoges: the suites have wonderful views. There are fridges on the upstairs landings for guests to use. Cold lunches are on offer and dinner as well if you book a day ahead.

TORNAC

DEMEURES DU RANQUET

COUNTRY RESTAURANT-WITH-ROOMS

route St-Hippolyte-du-Fort,
Tornac, 30140 Anduze (Gard)
TEL 04 66 77 51 63 **FAX** 04 66 77
55 62 **E-MAIL** ranquet@mnet.fr
FOOD breakfast, lunch, dinner
PRICE €€ €€€ **ROOMS** 10
CLOSED Oct to Apr; restaurant mid-Sep to mid-Jun Tues dinner, Wed

SET AMONGST PINES and scrub oak in the peaceful foothills of the Cévennes, the Demeures du Ranquet is the kind of place that lingers in the memory for all the right reasons. The main building, a long, low well-restored farmhouse, is principally devoted to the restaurant and the comfortable bedrooms are in chalets scattered amongst the trees on the slope above the swimming pool – some are air conditioned. In summer the restaurant's tables sally forth on to the terrace and out under the trees where hammocks also lie in wait to help you through those long hours between lunch and dinner. The cuisine is a real treat: inventive, original and fresh, and supported by an excellent wine list.

THE SOUTH

VALLON-PONT-D'ARC

LE MANOIR DU RAVEYRON
VILLAGE INN

rue Henri Barbusse 07150 Vallon-Pont-d'Arc (Ardèche)
TEL 04 75 88 03 59
FAX 04 75 37 11 12
FOOD breakfast, lunch, dinner
PRICE €
ROOMS 15
CLOSED Nov to Mar

IT SOUNDS GRAND, but is nothing of the sort: this is the sort of rustic village inn that is the bedrock of French hotelkeeping – a two-fireplace *logis* offering simple but satisfactory accommodation, modest prices, a warm welcome and excellent wholesome food (visit the place on a Sunday and you'll find it bursting at the seams with lunching families). The hotel faces an ugly modern building; but the surroundings do not intrude, because the old stone building is set well back from the street, behind gates and a large and leafy courtyard garden. We get occasional reports confirming our recommendation of the Manoir, but there are new owners since our last visit, so we would welcome more.

CORSICA

HOTELS IN CORSICA

WE HAVE NEVER FOUND more than a handful of hotels in Corsica which fit our criteria and live up to our exacting standards; maybe we are missing some hidden gems – do let us know if there is a hotel, however simple, perhaps deep in the interior, or on a little cove, that you love, or at least that you would happily return to. We know of plenty of places which are 'perfectly okay', but only a few which stand out. It's a shame, because Corsica is a wonderful place. The rugged island, with a turbulent history to match, looks like a mountain thrust from the sea, pointing an accusatory and gnarled northern finger, Cap Corse, toward the Genoan Riviera. Its wild and often surprising scenery is its chief glory, ringed by a 960-km coastline of world-class sandy beaches, quiet coves, fishing villages, jagged headlands and tumbling rocks. The interior comprises an extraordinary variety of landscapes. There are snow-capped mountains, rocky peaks and clear pools and streams, forests of chestnut and *laricio* pine (used by the Romans for masts), vineyards, olive and orange groves, tropical palms, even a region of arid desert. Almost two-thirds is covered with the thick tangle of scented shrubs and wild flowers known as *maquis*.

As well as the recommendations which follow, we would like to give honourable mention to La Giraglia, at Barcaggio (tel 04 95 35 60 54), a simple, creeper-covered stone building in a superb position overlooking the sea in a lovely wild part of Corsica, well off the beaten track; and to Sole e Monti (tel 04 95 78 62 53), another simple. peaceful *auberge* at Quenza, a hill village in the centre of Corse-du-Sud near the beauty spot, Col de Bavella.

CORSICA

CALVI

LA SIGNORIA
COUNTRY HOTEL

*route de la Fôret de
Bonifato, 20260 Calvi (Corse)*
TEL 04 95 65 93 00
FAX 04 95 65 38 77
E-MAIL info@hotel-la-signoria.com
WEBSITE www.hotel-la-signoria.com
FOOD breakfast, dinner
PRICE €€€€ **ROOMS** 10
CLOSED Nov to Apr

L A SIGNORIA made its first appearance in the previous edition of our guide and since then we have had positive feedback from two readers, both extolling its virtues of peace and quiet, its calm atmosphere, stylish simplicity and its eclectic, rustic-chic Mediterranean decoration – paint effects on plaster walls and on doors, uncluttered rooms and so on. The hotel is a 17thC country house set in lush grounds which are filled with trees -- eucalyptus, olives, palms and pines. Inventive and delicious food is served in a beamed, ochre-washed dining room, or, in warmer weather, on the terrace at prettily painted wrought-iron tables and chairs overlooking the smart and inviting swimming pool. There is also tennis and a *hammam* (steam room).

ERBALUNGA

CASTEL' BRANDO
VILLAGE GUESTHOUSE

*Erbalunga, 202222 Brando
(Corse)*
TEL 04 95 30 10 30
FAX 04 95 33 98 18
E-MAIL castelbrando
@chateauxhotels.com **WEBSITE**
www.chateauxhotels.com
/castelbrando
FOOD breakfast
PRICE €€ **ROOMS** 15 **CLOSED**
mid-Nov to mid-Mar

W E'VE BEEN ALERTED to this 'absolutely delightful' hotel by a reader. 'It's just one of those things' he comments. 'The owners have an innate understanding of how to create an attractive, welcoming atmosphere.' Erbalunga is a postcard-pretty fishing village and artists' colony and the hotel is a 19thC mansion, restored with care and flair by local couple Joèlle and Jean-Paul Piéri. The grounds are full of magnificent palm trees, and there are shady places to sit and take breakfast or tea. The apartments, with kitchenettes, make an excellent base, and the charming hosts will tell guests about the best places to dine, and sights off the beaten track. More reports welcome.

CORSICA

MONTICELLO

A PASTURELLA
VILLAGE INN

Monticello, 20220 l'Ile-Rousse (Haute-Corse)
TEL 04 95 60 05 65
FAX 04 95 60 21 78
E-MAIL info@a-pasturella.com
WEBSITE www.a-pasturella.com
FOOD breakfast, lunch, dinner
PRICE €€ **ROOMS** 12 **CLOSED** early-Nov to mid-Dec

W E HAVE ALWAYS BEEN fond of this modest little 'gem', set in a peaceful hill village in the lovely Balagne region, with views which sweep down to L'Ile-Rousse and its bay, noted for its fine sandy beaches. The inn stands on the village square, its bar at the very heart of local life, and its restaurant much appreciated for wholesome and generous food, with specialities such as *fricassée de sardines à la Nepita, piatu casanu, terrine de cabri, soupe de poissons, tianu de calamars*. Bedrooms are simple and functional, with a dash of colour in the curtains and bedspreads. The four rooms in the annexe are the best bet, because they have balconies which, like the other rooms, have fine views over the valley.

PORTICCIO

LE MAQUIS
SEASIDE HOTEL

20166 Porticcio (Corse-du-Sud)
TEL 04 95 25 05 55
FAX 04 95 25 11 70 **E-MAIL** hotel.le.maquis@wanadoo.fr
FOOD breakfast, lunch, dinner; room service
PRICE €€€€€
ROOMS 25
CLOSED never

L E MAQUIS IS SET in a breathtakingly pretty spot, perhaps the prettiest of any hotel in Corsica, on a little inlet in the Gulf of Ajaccio, overlooking verdant gardens and a beautiful stretch of sandy beach. Proprietress Mme Salini is very much in charge, and her hotel, opened in 1972, is carefully decorated, with comfortable bedrooms. Ask for a room overlooking the sea, with a terrace. In L'Arbousier, the hotel's restaurant, excellent meals are served by the pool in warm weather – mostly seafood and traditional Corsican dishes. A quiet, sophisticated hotel on an otherwise crowded coast; for nature lovers the wild beauty of inland Corsica is close at hand. Reports please.

HOTEL NAMES

In this index, hotels are arranged in order of the most distinctive part of their name; very common prefixes such as 'Auberge', 'Hôtel', 'Hostellerie' and 'Le/La/Les' are omitted, but more significant elements such as 'Château' are retained.

HOTEL NAMES

HOTEL NAMES

HOTEL NAMES

HOTEL LOCATIONS

In this index, hotels are arranged by the name of the city, town or village they are in or near. Hotels located in a very small village may be indexed under the name of a larger place nearby.

Hotel Locations

HOTEL LOCATIONS

HOTEL LOCATIONS